THE COEN BROTHERS
ENCYCLOPEDIA

THE COEN BROTHERS
ENCYCLOPEDIA

Lynnea Chapman King

ROWMAN & LITTLEFIELD

Lanham • Boulder • New York • London

Published by Rowman & Littlefield
A wholly owned subsidiary of The Rowman & Littlefield Publishing Group, Inc.
4501 Forbes Boulevard, Suite 200, Lanham, Maryland 20706
www.rowman.com

16 Carlisle Street, London W1D 3BT, United Kingdom

British Library Cataloguing in Publication Information Available

Library of Congress Cataloging-in-Publication Data
King, Lynnea Chapman, 1967–
  The Coen Brothers encyclopedia / by Lynnea Chapman King.
    pages cm
  Includes bibliographical references and index.
  Includes filmography.
  ISBN 978-0-8108-8576-9 (cloth : alk. paper) — ISBN 978-0-8108-8577-6 (ebook) 1. Coen,
Joel—Encyclopedias. 2. Coen, Ethan—Encyclopedias. 3. Motion picture producers and directors—
United States—Biography—Encyclopedias. I. Title.
  PN1998.3.C6635K57 2014
  791.4302'330922—dc23
                                                                2014016462

Printed in the United States of America

For Kyle, who abides

CONTENTS

ACKNOWLEDGMENTS

I would like to thank my family—Kyle, Dev, Tiernan, Brent, Janet, and Loretta—who stepped in to fill the gap during this project. Special thanks as well to those colleagues and friends who read entries and entertained my questions and theories throughout this process. Thank you, Stephen Ryan, for persisting with this project and for your infinite patience in the face of Fibber McGee and all things Murphy, and much gratitude to the late James M. Welsh, who mentored and encouraged me to accept a challenge he knew I could complete.

INTRODUCTION

On a long flight from Florida to Texas, I passed the time by watching Joel and Ethan Coen's *O Brother, Where Art Thou?*, and as I did so, the man seated next to me leaned over and commented, "I like old movies . . . the actors could do so much more with their faces and their bodies, without all of the special effects." Rather than engage my row-mate in an extended discussion of Digital Intermediate and how *O Brother* was on the leading edge of a trend toward the digitization of cinema, I concurred and continued watching Everett, Pete, and Delmar dash and duck their way across the field and away from the chain gang. Reflecting on his comments, however, it seems that perhaps one of the dominant characteristics of Coen films is that they engender remarks like the one on the plane: they approximate a genre or style of cinema—noir, crime drama, screwball comedy—while simultaneously remaining "A Film by Joel and Ethan Coen." This juxtaposition of allusion and originality, of homage and "wackiness," to quote the filmmakers themselves, serves to define and identify the brothers' projects and is, I might assert, one of the reasons that viewers return to their pictures. There is a special delight in observing the attention to detail in the golden light of an evening in the sitting room, curtains blowing gently in the open window, as *The Ladykillers'* Professor G. H. Dorr reads from Poe's "To Helen," the composition of a shot and the masterful lighting thereof. And there is delight as well, as the strains of instrumental baroque shift to hip-hop as Dorr and company push bags of, well, bags . . . over the railing of the bridge and watch them drop onto the garbage barge below. The first scene and its beauty of composition would not lead us to anticipate the second, but there it is. Another example might be the intrusion of a bear riding a horse, or rather, a bearskin-clad travelling dentist riding a horse through the wintry, barren backwoods of the Indian Territories, an appearance that brings to a complete halt the gentle pace of Rooster Cogburn's recollections of his former lives, as he and Mattie Ross slowly traverse the wilderness in *True Grit*. But in that moment, when the bear-man appears, the viewer is reminded that this is a Coen film, and in Coen films, talking bears do indeed interrupt the conversational rhythm of a scene, just as Busby Berkeley-esque dance scenes, in which Maude Lebowski is dressed as a Valkyrie, interrupt the Dude's meditation on the sounds of the bowling league playoffs in *The Big Lebowski*. That's what the Coens do.

Joel and Ethan Coen assert that they create their films by devoting themselves to the details—those details in which we delight—and immersing themselves in the process of design and production, but when the project is finished, it's finished.

Coen fans and critics alike, however, seek to dissect and connect the films, finding tropes and themes and technical devices that, when combined, create significance, a meaning beyond the material, whether political or social or religious or philosophical. It must be true, we claim, that all Coen films are about U.S. foreign policy, or the afterlife, or . . . . The filmmakers, however, disagree. The films stand for themselves, even when we want them to be about something more.

After viewing *Inside Llewyn Davis* for the first time, I left the theatre with more questions than answers. Processing the experience, I turned to a couple who had also just seen the film, and I inquired, "What did you think?" They responded in unison "I don't know." I once again concurred. As we parted ways, though, the man remarked over his shoulder "Maybe it sucks to be him?" And I understood what he meant. We felt like Larry Gopnik in *A Serious Man*, asking a rabbi, "Why does he make us feel the questions, if he's not going to give us the answers?"

The films of the Coen brothers are filled with mysteries and ambiguities: is there a severed head in Barton's box? What happened to the cross-country cat in *Inside Llewyn Davis*? Were Chigurh and Ed Tom Bell in that hotel room at the same moment? Did Tom really love Verna, or were his actions prompted entirely by his loyalty to Leo? Perhaps those mysteries are the very reason why Coen fans return to the films again and again, though the dialogue, cinematography, and art direction alone might prompt repeated viewings. Perhaps the intrigue is in the not knowing, in the many, many possible readings that exist for each film. And better, perhaps everybody gets to be correct: *O Brother, Where Art Thou?* can be an old-timey film; *Burn After Reading* can be a treatise on U.S. foreign policy; and the mosquito in *Barton Fink* can represent film critics who feed on the films of the Coens. In such an impossible universe, one interpretation of *Miller's Crossing* is as valid as the next. Or so say the filmmakers. Certainly Joel and Ethan Coen themselves aren't giving anything away, refusing to resolve the ambiguities for us, or, alternately, further muddying the waters with their various and contradictory comments on their films.

This volume does not seek to answer the questions raised by the films, to serve as the answer or the definitive reading of the films of the Coen Brothers, though some entries, particularly those on the films themselves, pause for analysis and offer theories regarding the individual works. Instead, the entries present a variety of perspectives, perhaps even creating additional questions in the process, which is likely what Joel and Ethan Coen intend after all.

Note: The entries that follow make use of the Internet Movie Database for purposes of filmography; all other sources are listed with each entry.

ANDERSON, J. TODD

Raised in New Carlisle, Ohio, Anderson attended Wright State University. Following his graduation in 1984, he applied for the storyboarding position on the Coens' second film *Raising Arizona* (1987) and subsequently worked in the art department on *Miller's Crossing* (1990), *Barton Fink* (1991), *The Hudsucker Proxy* (1994), *Fargo* (1996), *The Big Lebowski* (1998), *O Brother, Where Art Thou?* (2000), *The Man Who Wasn't There* (2001), *Intolerable Cruelty* (2003), *The Ladykillers* (2004), *No Country for Old Men* (2007), *Burn After Reading* (2007), *A Serious Man* (2009), *True Grit* (2010), and *Inside Llewyn Davis* (2013). In addition to his work with the Coens, Anderson has served as storyboard artist for Jodie Foster's *Little Man Tate* (1991), Barry Sonnenfeld's *The Addams Family* (1991), George Clooney's *Confessions of a Dangerous Mind* (2002) and *Leatherheads* (2008), and Frank Oz's *The Stepford Wives* (2004).

With Ethan Coen, Anderson cowrote the screenplay for *The Naked Man* (1998), which Anderson then directed, starring Michael Rappaport. The film was produced by Coen regular Ben Barenholtz, but despite the contributions of Coen and Barenholtz, the film was not well-received. Anderson earned his first acting credit as "Victim in the field" in *Fargo*, though in the film's closing credits, Anderson's name was not listed. Instead, a symbol appeared in lieu of his name, resembling that used by the artist formerly known as Prince. Subsequent acting credits include appearances in *Confessions of a Dangerous Mind, Leatherheads*, and David Grovic's *The Bag Man* (2014), among others. In 2008, Anderson appeared in the horror spoof *My Mummy*, which he also directed and cowrote with George R. Willeman. Joel and Ethan Coen also referenced Anderson in their re-adaptation of Charles Portis's novel *True Grit*, as one of Tom Chaney's aliases was John Todd Anderson.

As the Coens' storyboard artist, Anderson works closely with the filmmakers as they develop the shot list into a series of images during the preproduction process. He describes his role in the process as that of "the extension cord from their brain to my little clipboard," further noting that that his function is to translate the language of the script into the visuals of the film. For his part, Joel Coen characterizes Anderson as a "catalyst," as the brothers rethink the film and use him as a sounding board while they prepare to shoot the project.

References

Clint O'Connor, "From *Raising Arizona* to *True Grit*: Coen Brothers' Storyboarder J. Todd Anderson at Cleveland Cinematheque," *Cleveland.com*, October 8, 2010; William Preston Robertson, *The Big Lebowski: The Making of a Coen Brothers Film* (New York: W.W. Norton & Company, 1998).

ARKIN, ADAM (1956–)

Born August 19, 1956, in Brooklyn, New York, Adam Arkin is the son of actor Alan Arkin. He attended the Professional Children's School in New York and the Herbert Berghof Studio, also in New York. He first appeared on-screen in a bit part in *The Monitors* (1969), which he followed with made-for-television movies in the early 1970s. He was cast in one-time roles on the television series *Happy Days* (1975), *Barney Miller* (1975), and *Hawaii 5-0* (1975), prior to his first recurring role in *Busting Loose* (1977). Arkin was cast in the short-lived series *Teachers Only* (1982), *Tough Cookies* (1986), and in the higher profile *Knots Landing* (1989–1990). In 1991, Arkin debuted on Broadway in Paul Rudnik's *I Hate Hamlet*, earning a Tony nomination for his performance, which he followed with *Fiorello!* off-Broadway in 1994. From 1990 to 1995, he had a periodically recurring role on *Northern Exposure*, and he is well known for his role as Dr. Aaron Shutt in *Chicago Hope* (1994–2000). He returned to the Broadway stage again in *Brooklyn Boy* (2005) and the same year appeared with Will Smith in *Hitch*. From 2007 to 2009, he played a more substantive role in the series *Life*, and in 2009 he appeared as Ethan Zobelle in the popular FX series *Sons of Anarchy*. He returned to FX in 2012 in the series *Justified* (2012–2014).

Arkin has appeared in one Coen film, *A Serious Man* (2009), in which he plays divorce lawyer to the film's main character, Larry Gopnik (Michael Stuhlbarg). Though a minor part, Arkin describes the character as "another cog in the wheel of the machinery that is slowly crushing Larry," reinforcing the collective misery that descends upon Larry. The film, which focuses on a Jewish family in the Minneapolis area in 1967, has been characterized by viewers as perhaps autobiographical, and while the filmmakers deny this claim, Arkin recognizes that it must be "a very personal film for [the Coens], because of some of the vulnerabilities of the characters."

References

"Adam Arkin," *FocusFeatures.com*, *A Serious Man*, Cast & Crew; "Adam Arkin," *New York Times*, Movies & TV; Naomi Pfefferman, "Get Serious: The Coen Brothers," *JewishJournal.com*, September 2, 2009. See also *A SERIOUS MAN*.

B

BADALUCCO, MICHAEL (1954–)

Badalucco was born in Brooklyn, New York, on December 20, 1954, the son of a movie set carpenter. He appeared at the age of ten as an uncredited extra in Sidney Lumet's *Fail Safe* (1964), a set his father was working on at the time. He studied theatre at the State University of New York at New Palz, where he appeared in several University productions and where he met Coen regular, John Turturro. Together, Turturro and Badalucco appeared in an off-Broadway production of Sam Shepard's *Tooth of Crime*, where they were seen by Robert De Niro, who then assisted both of them in getting small roles in *Raging Bull* (1980). Badalucco continued in bit parts and as a character actor in such films as *Desperately Seeking Susan* (1985), *Jungle Fever* (1991), and *Miller's Crossing* (1990), prior to being cast in Turturro's directorial debut, *Mac* (1992). He then returned to smaller roles in *Sleepless in Seattle* (1993), *Clockers* (1995), and *One Fine Day* (1996), which starred Michelle Pfeiffer, who later recommended him for a small part in the ABC television legal drama *The Practice*. Instead of the small role, Pfeiffer's husband, series creator David E. Kelley, wrote the part of Jimmy Berluti for Badalucco, which he played from 1997 to 2004 and for which he won the Emmy Award for Outstanding Supporting Actor in a Drama Series in 1999. Also in 1999, he appeared as David Berkowitz, Son

of Sam, in Spike Lee's *Summer of Sam*. He has appeared in numerous television series, including *Law & Order* (1993), *Ally McBeal* (1999), *Boston Public* (2001), *Monk* (2008), and, with Steve Buscemi, in *Boardwalk Empire* (2010). In 2010 he held a recurring role in *The Young and the Restless*, and in 2013, he appeared in Turturro's film *Fading Gigolo*, which featured Woody Allen as a pimp. In addition to his brief role as Johnny Caspar's driver in *Miller's Crossing*, Badalucco has appeared as George "Babyface" Nelson in the Coens' *O Brother, Where Art Thou?* (2000) and as Frank the barber in *The Man Who Wasn't There* (2001).

Although the historical bank robber George Nelson died in 1934, the fictional Nelson, as portrayed by Badalucco in *O Brother, Where Art Thou?*, holds up banks throughout rural Mississippi in 1937, leaving in his wake dead cows and astonished bystanders. Seeking the notoriety achieved by other Depression-era bank robbers, Badalucco's Nelson hits several banks in one day, only to have his ego crushed when one bank patron recognizes him as "Babyface" Nelson, a moniker that devastates him and prompts his morose departure from the film's action. He returns, however, near the film's conclusion, en route to the electric chair. Nelson jubilantly celebrates his capture, convinced that his execution will overcome his nickname and cement his place in history as a notable criminal.

The following year, in the Coens' *The Man Who Wasn't There* (2001), Badalucco was cast in the role of Frank, brother-in-law to Ed Crane (Billy Bob Thornton), brother to Doris Crane (Frances McDormand). Ed and Frank are both barbers in Frank's shop, and Frank's defining characteristic is his ability to talk nonstop, about trapping beaver for their pelts, tying flies, or the latest in fashion. His character appears in contrast to that of Ed, who simply cuts the hair and doesn't say much, but near the end of the film, Frank is rendered speechless and inconsolable by the misfortune that befalls his sister Doris.

References

"Michael Badalucco," *New York Times*, Movies & TV; "Michael Badalucco Biography," *Starpulse.com*. See also *THE MAN WHO WASN'T THERE, O BROTHER, WHERE ART THOU?*

BARDEM, JAVIER (1969–)

Born in Spain, March 1, 1969, to a family of actors, Javier Bardem is the son of actress Pilar Bardem, brother to actor Carlos Bardem and actress Monica Bardem, and grandson to actor Rafael Bardem. His earliest on-screen appearance was in 1974, in a brief, uncredited role in the Spanish television show *El picaro* (*The Scoundrel*). He was cast in a recurring role in the series *Segunda ensenanza* (1986) and his film debut was in *Las edades de Lulu* (*The Ages of Lulu*) (1990), which he followed with Pedro Almodovar's *Tacones lejanos* (*High Heels*) (1991), *Huevos de oro* (*Golden Balls*) (1992), and *Boca a boca* (*Mouth to Mouth*) (1995), among others, quickly becoming a rising star in Spanish cinema. He worked again with Almodovar in *Carne tremula* (*Live Flesh*) (1997), and also in 1997 appeared in his first English-language film *Perdita Durango*, with Rosie Perez.

Bardem's performance in Julian Schnabel's *Before Night Falls* (2000) earned him an Oscar nomination for Best Actor, the first Spanish actor to receive an Academy Award nomination. He was then cast in the lead role in John Malkovich's directorial debut *The Dancer Upstairs* (2002) and appeared in Michael Mann's *Collat-*

Javier Bardem in *No Country for Old Men* (2007)

eral (2004), which starred Tom Cruise. He starred in Alejandro Amenabar's *Mar adentro* (*The Sea Inside*) (2004), which won the Oscar for Best Foreign Language Film of the Year, and he received both the Oscar and the Golden Globe for Best Supporting Actor for his portrayal of serial killer Anton Chigurh in Joel and Ethan Coen's *No Country for Old Men* (2007). He appeared in Woody Allen's *Vicky Cristina Barcelona* (2008), with Scarlett Johansson and Penelope Cruz, for which he received a nomination for the Best Actor Golden Globe, and he earned the Academy Award nomination for Best Actor in *Biutiful* (2010). Bardem played Bond villain Silva in Sam Mendes's *Skyfall* (2012) and appeared in Ridley Scott's *The Counselor* (2013), which was written by Cormac McCarthy.

As Anton Chigurh in *No Country for Old Men*, Bardem sported a haircut and wardrobe inspired by a photograph located by Coen costume designer Mary Zophres. Taken around 1979 in West Texas, the picture captured the look the filmmakers sought, and the resultant haircut inspired an onslaught of comments by reviewers: the *Daily Mail* described the coiffure as "a scary, Prince Valiant haircut," and *Empire*'s Ian Nathan in turn characterized it as "the domed haircut of a psychopathic Monkee." The cosmetic details only served to accentuate a performance that was widely praised by film critics and the Academy as well. *Rolling Stone*'s Peter Travers deemed Bardem's performance "stupendous," having created "a monster for the ages." His Chigurh was "lumpen, expressionless, and as unstoppable as an Old Testament curse," claims *Slate*'s Dana Stevens, a role that he "eloquently underplayed," concludes the *Daily Mail*. In addition to the Oscar for Best Supporting Actor, Bardem's performance earned awards from the Screen Actors Guild, the New York Film Critics Circle, and the Toronto Film Critics Association, among many others.

References

"Javier Bardem," *Biography.com*; "Coen Brothers Give Us Another Fine Mess with *No Country for Old Men*," *Daily Mail*; Ian Nathan, "*No Country for Old Men*: Heaven Be Praised, the Brothers Go Grim Again," *EmpireOnline.com*; Dana Stevens, "*No Country for Old Men*: Why the New Coen Brothers' Masterpiece Disappoints," *Slate.com*, November 8, 2007; Peter Travers, "*No Country for Old Men*," *Rolling Stone*, November 1, 2007. See also *NO COUNTRY FOR OLD MEN*.

BARTON FINK (1991)

DIRECTOR: Joel Coen and Ethan Coen (uncredited). SCREENPLAY: Joel Coen and Ethan Coen. PRODUCER: Ethan Coen and Joel Coen (uncredited); Graham Place (Co-producer). EXECUTIVE PRODUCERS: Ben Barenholtz, Bill Durkin, Jim Pedas, and Ted Pedas. PHOTOGRAPHY: Roger Deakins. EDITING: Roderick Jaynes. ORIGINAL MUSIC: Carter Burwell. PRODUCTION DESIGN: Dennis Gassner. SET DECORATION: Nancy Haigh. COSTUME DESIGN: Richard Hornung.

CAST: John Turturro (Barton Fink), John Goodman (Charlie Meadows), Judy Davis (Audrey Taylor), Michael Lerner (Jack Lipnick), John Mahoney (W. P. Mayhew), Tony Shalhoub (Ben Geisler), Jon Polito (Lou Breeze), Steve Buscemi (Chet), Frances McDormand (Stage Actress voice, uncredited), Barry Sonnenfeld (Page, uncredited).

RUNNING TIME: 116 minutes. Color.

RELEASED THROUGH: Twentieth Century Fox Film Corporation. PREMIERE: May 1991 (Cannes International Film Festival).

ACADEMY AWARDS: Best Actor in a Supporting Role (nominated: Michael Lerner), Best Art Direction–Set Decoration (nominated: Dennis Gassner and Nancy Haigh), Best Costume Design (nominated: Richard Hornung).

DVD: 20th Century Fox Home Entertainment.

John Turturro in *Barton Fink* (1991)

Barton Fink (John Turturro), Broad-way playwright and toast of the town, has received fabulous reviews on his first play and is subsequently offered a job in Holly-wood, writing for Capitol Pictures. Initially reluctant to abandon his dream of writ-ing for the theatre of the common man in exchange for the superficiality of the mov-ies, Barton nevertheless accepts the offer and arrives in Los Angeles to begin writing for the pictures. He is to be housed at the Hotel Earle in a small, dank room, com-plete with stained, peeling paint on the ceiling, patterned, sagging wallpaper, and, by way of decor, a lone picture of a sun-bathing beauty who languidly gazes out to the ocean. Barton has been commis-sioned to write a Wallace Beery wrestling picture with that "Barton Fink feeling," a genre about which he knows nothing, and studio head Jack Lipnick (Michael Lerner) informs Barton that everyone is expecting great things. Beset by writer's block and a lack of understanding about the inner workings of Hollywood, Barton

sits before his vintage Underwood type-writer, uncertain how to begin the project. He seeks counsel from Ben Geisler (Tony Shalhoub), the slick, fast-talking producer of the picture, who bombards Barton with clichés and platitudes, advising him to visit with other writers if he needs assistance. Encountering screenwriter W.P. Mayhew (John Mahoney) in the men's room of an upscale restaurant, Barton hopes Mayhew can offer him inspiration and instruction, but the "finest novelist of our time" instead drinks to excess and is reduced to a wailing, pitiful drunk who is of no help to Barton.

The directionless Barton makes the acquaintance of his neighbor at the hotel, salesman Charlie Meadows (John Good-man), who sells insurance and peace of mind. As they talk over whiskey poured into hotel glasses, Barton explains his desire to create a "theatre for the masses," filled with "the stuff of life," borne of "the life of the mind." Charlie, who valiantly attempts to share his own stories, tales of a real com-mon man, is repeatedly interrupted by the idealistic musings of Barton, who little realizes his opportunity to learn from an "average working stiff." As the relationship between Charlie and Barton develops, so does the magnitude of Barton's writer's block, his deadline for a script treatment creeping closer as the wallpaper sags and the heat becomes oppressive. In an act of desperation, he telephones Audrey Taylor (Judy Davis), Mayhew's secretary and lover, begging her to come to his room and help him with the script treatment for Lipnick, which eludes him though it need only be ideas, painted in broad strokes. Audrey arrives, whereupon Barton discovers that her many duties include writing Mayhew's scripts, and she claims to have penned his last two novels. Barton is devastated by this news, but this does not prevent him from being seduced by Audrey; he wakes the next morning to find she has been murdered in his bed, and panicked, he seeks the assistance of Charlie, who disposes of the body and disappears on business to the head office in New York City. Before Charlie departs, however, he places in Barton's care a mysterious package, wrapped in brown paper and tied with a string.

Shortly thereafter, Barton is visited by two Los Angeles Police Department detectives, looking for Mad Man Karl Mundt, whom Barton knows as Charlie Meadows. Mundt/Meadows, it seems, is a serial killer who beheads his victims, including a recently-discovered woman who Barton realizes must be Audrey. Returning to his room, Barton suspects that the appropriately sized package could indeed be a human head, and somehow drawing inspiration from that fact, he composes his script for the Beery wrestling picture, a work he claims is something big, something important. Before he can turn the script in to Lipnick, however, the detectives return, discovering Barton's bloodstained mattress and accusing him of Audrey's

murder. It appears that Barton is done for. He is rescued by Charlie, who returns in a fiery rage and shoots down the detectives in the blazing hall of the hotel. "You don't listen!" he thunders at Barton, calling him a tourist with a typewriter who has come into Charlie's home and behaved rudely. Charlie, the serial killer Mundt, claiming only to "help people out," retreats into his room, hallway ablaze, leaving Barton, his singed script, and the box. Barton delivers his masterpiece to Lipnick, who is not pleased and deems the story junk; he tells Barton that he's not to leave town, as he's under contract, and everything he writes from this time forward belongs to Capitol Pictures. Barton is no longer "a writer, but a write-off." Taking Charlie's box, Barton retreats to the seashore where he finds a sunbathing beauty gazing out into the waves, striking the pose of the woman in the picture from his room. Barton Fink, having escaped his hotel, is trapped in this place, Hollywood.

The impetus for this film, say the Coens, was the idea of a "huge neglected old hotel," in which John Turturro and John Goodman interact. Initially, the hotel was to also contain a group of eccentric inhabitants, but as the project developed, the tenants narrowed to only the two men. The Hotel Earle itself acts as a character in the film, characterized by the *Washington Post*'s Rita Kempley as "an organic being," akin to The Flying Dutchman, "a gurgling, heaving, purgatory," and the Coen brothers acknowledge this is by design. Joel states that Ethan often conceptualized the hotel as "a ghost ship floating adrift, where you notice signs of the presence of other passengers, without every laying eyes on any" and notes that they "wanted the whole thing to feel organic and decayed," using the colors green and yellow "to suggest a feeling of putrefaction" as Charlie reverts to the serial killer Karl Mundt.

Written in just three weeks while on hiatus from composing the screenplay for *Miller's Crossing* (1990), Joel and Ethan Coen have indicated that *Barton Fink* was created with several of its actors in mind: Barton himself was created to be played by John Turturro, Charlie Meadows was written for John Goodman, and the part of W.P. Mayhew was intended for John Mahoney. Beyond these connections between actors and the parts written for them, some of the film's characters were inspired by historical figures as well. Barton Fink is loosely patterned on Clifford Odets, an American playwright and screenwriter of the 1930s and 1940s. Fink and Odets share some of the same background, both working on Broadway prior to moving to Hollywood to write for the pictures, and Odets was involved with the Group Theatre in New York in the early 1930s, a group devoted to creating works of social significance rather than focusing on the entertainment and economic value of theatre. Fink, ostensibly, is likewise dedicated to a theatre of, about, and for the common man, and he frequently discusses his desire to create "a theatre for the masses," to make a difference, though he cannot bring himself to listen to Charlie Meadows, the one common man with whom he is acquainted. Prior to his departure for Los Angeles, Barton is concerned about the integrity of his work and Hollywood's potential distraction from his purported mission as a writer, and upon meeting W.P. Mayhew and observing his fall from greatness, it becomes clear to Barton that Hollywood can indeed destroy an author. Odets himself noted that "Hollywood, like Midas, kills everything it touches," though Odets wrote successfully for both stage and film for many years. Barton, by contrast, struggles with his first Hollywood assignment, the wrestling picture.

W. P. "Bill" Mayhew, as well, is inspired by a historical figure, Southern author William Faulkner. Like Mayhew, the alcoholic Faulkner wrote for the movies, and the project on which Mayhew is rather unsuccessfully working, *Slave Ship* (1937), was actually written by Faulkner for Twentieth Century Fox. Mayhew's drinking incapacitates the author, while Faulkner, by contrast, continued both drinking and writing in Hollywood for some time. The film's Faulknerian allusions are not limited to Mayhew, however. Like Barton Fink, Faulkner's first studio writing job was to draft a remake of a Wallace Beery wrestling picture, and also like Barton, Faulkner worked for years as a scriptwriter, bound by clever studio contracts such that Jack Warner could "boast about employing America's best writer for peanuts."

John Mahoney, who plays W.P. Mayhew, physically resembles William Faulkner, who had an affair with Howard Hawks's secretary, but the Coens are careful to note that both of the authors in the film, Odets and Faulkner, only superficially resemble the *Barton Fink* characters that were loosely based on them. The final historical allusion in the film is that of the character Jack Lipnick, played by Michael Lerner. While Lerner somewhat resembles Louis B. Mayer and many critics saw the Lipnick character as inspired by Mayer, the Coens note that Lipnick is a composite character, a combination of Mayer, Jack Warner, whom Lerner played in the made-for-television movie *This Year's Blonde* (1980), and Harry Cohn, whom he depicted in the CBS movie *Rita Hayworth: The Love Goddess* (1983). The scene in *Barton Fink* in which Lipnick dons a military uniform is taken from the life of Jack Warner, who joined the army and ordered a uniform from his wardrobe department following the advent of World War II.

Ethan Coen has commented on the irony of that scene, which he describes as "one of the most surreal elements in the movie," as it is "one of the few to have been drawn directly from Hollywood lore."

John Goodman, who plays Meadows, had previously worked with the Coens in *Raising Arizona* (1987) and was cast in *Barton Fink* because of his established on-screen persona, that of the good-natured, easy-going, likable man. The Coens sought to capitalize on the innately positive reaction of the audience to Goodman, as they reveal later in the film that the "common man" Meadows is a front for the serial killer Karl Mundt. The audience discovers, as does Barton, that Charlie is not what he seems, and as Goodman's character devolves into a raging, homicidal killer, he berates Barton for his failure to listen and for his complaint to the front desk about the noise in Charlie's room, which the viewer now realizes may have been murder in progress. The Coens note the connection between the hotel and Goodman's Charlie, as the hotel was "the externalization of the character played by John Goodman. Sweat falls from his brow like wallpaper falls from the walls," and near the film's conclusion, as the hallway blazes with fire and Charlie's anger, "when Goodman says he's prisoner of his own mental state, that it's like a hell, the hotel has already taken on that infernal appearance."

While the film earned only just over $6 million at the box office, domestically, with a production budget of $9 million, *Barton Fink*'s critical reception was largely positive. Reviewers praised the lighting and cinematography of Roger Deakins and the production design of Dennis Gassner, as well as the performances, particularly of Turturro, Goodman, and Lerner; Eddie Robson's *Coen Brothers* cites Shaun Usher of the *Daily Mail*, who deemed it the "film of the decade, never mind the year." The substance of the film, however, was more problematic for critics. Because of its setting and subject matter, *Barton Fink* is often viewed as an indictment of Hollywood, specifically because of its treatment of writers and filmmakers. The Coens claim, however, that Barton's experience in the industry is not one that they share. Allied with Circle Films, their production company for *Blood Simple* (1984), *Raising Arizona* (1987), *Miller's Crossing* (1990), and *Barton Fink*, and with distributor Twentieth Century Fox, which released their second, third, and fourth films, the brothers negotiated deals that allowed them to maintain complete control over their pictures, giving Fox the right of refusal but no additional input regarding the final products. If not a comment on the industry, then, critics alternately see *Barton Fink* as representative of the rise of Nazism and the subsequent Holocaust; a metaphor for hell, prompted perhaps by the film's tagline "Between heaven and hell, there's always Hollywood!"; an "allegorical horror film"; and a nightmare from which Barton should awake at the conclusion of the film, one in which Charlie does not actually exist but is a symbol of Barton's severe writer's block. As might be expected, Joel and Ethan Coen characterize the film in quite a different manner. Ethan refers to it as "a buddy movie for the '90s," although a careful reader might question the tenor of that statement, and Joel deems it "sort of like a black comedy," but both decline to speak to any larger meaning or message in the film. They continue to assert that "there's no larger purpose outside of the story itself," and that "what isn't crystal clear isn't intended to become crystal clear, and it's fine to leave it at that." They do elaborate somewhat by speaking to the genre of the film, indicating that *Barton Fink* is "kind of a Polanski movie," falling into the "'Person Alone in the Room' genre." Unlike many of their films, *Barton Fink* is not modeled on a predetermined genre such as noir, gangster, or western, but instead "doesn't belong to any genre," states Joel, as "the movie's neither really a comedy nor a drama," though playwright Arthur Miller notes that "artistically, it belongs to a genre of mere chaos." Joel goes on to state that despite the lack of generic affiliation, "if it has a lineage, it's obviously one that begins with [Roman] Polanski," which would certainly include the Polanski films *The Tenant* (1976) and *Repulsion* (1965).

The Coens would not have known, while making the film, that Polanski would be head of the jury at the Cannes Film Festival, where *Barton Fink* was winner of the prestigious Palme d'Or and also received awards for Best Actor, John Turturro, and Best Director, Joel Coen. Following the Festival, the rules were revised so that no film could win three awards in one year.

References

"*Barton Fink*," *Variety*; Michel Ciment and Hubert Niogret, "A Rock on the Beach," in *The Coen Brothers: Interviews*, ed. William Rodney Allen (Jackson: University Press of Mississippi, 2006); Jim Emerson, "That Barton Fink Feeling: An Interview with the Brothers Coen," in *The Coen Brothers: Interviews*, ed. William Rodney Allen (Jackson: University Press of Mississippi, 2006); Rita Kempley, "*Barton Fink*," *Washington Post*, August 21, 1991; Marie-Jose Lavie, "Barton Fink and William Faulkner," in *Joel & Ethan Coen: Blood Siblings*, ed. Paul A. Woods (London: Plexus Publishing, 2003); R. Barton Palmer, *Joel and Ethan Coen* (Urbana: University of Illinois Press, 2004); Eddie Robson, *Coen Brothers* (London: Virgin Books, 2003). See also CARTER BURWELL, STEVE BUSCEMI, JUDY DAVIS, ROGER DEAKINS, DENNIS GASSNER, JOHN GOODMAN, NANCY HAIGH, MICHAEL LERNER, JOHN MAHONEY, JON POLITO, TONY SHALHOUB, JOHN TURTURRO.

THE BIG LEBOWSKI (1998)

DIRECTOR: Joel Coen and Ethan Coen (uncredited). SCREENPLAY: Ethan Coen and Joel Coen. EXECUTIVE PRODUCERS: Tim Bevan and Eric Fellner. PRODUCERS: Ethan Coen and Joel Coen (uncredited); John Cameron (Co-producer). PHOTOGRAPHY: Roger Deakins. EDITING: Ethan Coen and Joel Coen (as Roderick Jaynes) and Tricia Cooke. MUSIC: Carter Burwell. MUSICAL ARCHIVIST: T Bone Burnett. PRODUCTION DESIGNER: Rick Heinrichs. SET DECORATION: Chris L. Spellman. COSTUME DESIGN: Mary Zophres.

CAST: Jeff Bridges (Jeffrey Lebowski/The Dude), John Goodman (Walter Sobchak), Julianne Moore (Maude Lebowski), Steve Buscemi (Donny Kerabatsos), David Huddleston (Jeffrey Lebowski/The Big Lebowski), Philip Seymour Hoffman (Brandt), Tara Reid (Bunny Lebowski), Peter Stormare (Nihilist #1), Flea (Nihilist #2), Torsten Voges (Nihilist #3), John Turturro (Jesus Quintana), Peter Siragusa (Gary the Bartender), Sam Elliott (The Stranger), Harry Bugin (Arthur Digby Sellers), Ben Gazzara (Jackie Treehorn), Jon Polito (Da Fino).

RUNNING TIME: 117 minutes. Color.

RELEASED THROUGH: Gramercy Pictures.

PREMIERE: February 15, 1998 (Berlin Film Festival).

DVD: Universal Studios Home Entertainment.

The seventh feature film by Joel and Ethan Coen, *The Big Lebowski* opens with the Sons of the Pioneers' "Tumbling Tumbleweeds" and voice-over narration by The Stranger (Sam Elliott), as the camera follows a tumbleweed cartwheeling through the desert and scrub brush, into the streets and sidewalks of Los Angeles. The Stranger begins a tale set in the early 1990s, "way out West," the story of a man—not a hero—

From left: Jeff Bridges, John Goodman, and Steve Buscemi in *The Big Lebowski* (1998)

but a man for his time and place. This man is Jeffrey Lebowski, the Dude (Jeff Bridges), his Dudeness, El Duderino, an unemployed former member of the Seattle Seven, author of the Port Huron Statement—the first draft, not the compromised second draft—and one-time roadie for Metallica. The Dude fills his days with bowling and smoking pot, until two thugs break into his house, demanding that he give them the money that his wife, Bunny (Tara Reid), owes to Jackie Treehorn (Ben Gazarra).

The Dude, however, is not married, nor is he the Jeff Lebowski they seek, and realizing that his is not the home of a millionaire, with its spare furnishings and filthy toilet, they depart, but not before one of the men urinates on the living room rug. Less concerned about the break-in or the physical abuse suffered at the hands of the intruders, the Dude is very disturbed about the rug, as it really tied the room together. This offense against his home décor sets the narrative into motion, and he and his league bowling buddies, Walter Sobchak

(John Goodman) and Donny Kerabatsos (Steve Buscemi), determine that the proper course of action would be for the Dude to visit Jeff Lebowski (David Huddleston), the Big Lebowski, who is indeed a millionaire and should therefore be well-equipped to pay for the damage to the rug. Lebowski, however, deems the Dude an unemployed slob looking for a handout and demands that he leave without delay, which the Dude does, but not before helping himself to one of Lebowski's fine Oriental rugs.

The Dude is summoned back to the Lebowski home, where he finds the wheelchair-bound millionaire in seclusion, distraught at the kidnapping of his beloved wife Bunny. He commissions the Dude to serve as the courier when the kidnappers make their demands, though in the interim, the Dude is free to do as he chooses. In one of the film's many bowling scenes, the Dude develops and explains to Walter and Donny his theory in which Bunny has arranged her own kidnapping to elicit money from the Big Lebowski, as her spending habits do not meet with his approval. In addition to the forthcoming call from the kidnappers, the Dude is preparing for the all-important league play-off games, where his team will face Jesus Quintana (John Turturro), a convicted pedophile who bowls for the opposing team in a hairnet and purple leisure suit with matching shoes.

Intruders once more enter the Dude's home, knocking him out and stealing back the Lebowski rug. He awakens to the sound of the beeper going off; the kidnappers have demanded that one million dollars be delivered by a lone courier, and Lebowski and his assistant Brandt (Philip Seymour Hoffman) stress to the Dude the importance of the task, as Bunny's life is in his hands. The uninvited Walter accompanies him on the delivery, having prepared a satchel of unwashed underwear as a ringer for the briefcase full of money. The substitute bag is dropped, the kidnappers take the bait, and the Dude fails to retrieve Bunny. The men retire to the bowling alley to ponder the situation, and while there, the Dude's ancient, beat-up car is stolen, along with the briefcase full of cash, a tape deck, and some Creedence Clearwater Revival tapes.

The Dude receives a summons from Maude Lebowski (Julianne Moore), daughter of Jeffrey Lebowski and a Fluxus artist, whose associates retrieved the valuable Oriental rug from the Dude's apartment. Maude, like the Dude, believes that Bunny has not been kidnapped and offers him $100,000 to recover the missing million dollars. He then must face the very angry Lebowski, who presents the Dude with a severed toe, presumably Bunny's, as proof of the kidnappers intent to harm the captive woman. The Dude returns home, where his apartment is invaded once again, this time by the Nihilist Uli Kunkel, who is also a porn star and one of the kidnappers. Kunkel and his henchmen demand the

money within twenty-four hours, or the Dude will meet with serious and painful consequences. In a stroke of good luck, the Dude's car has been located, tape deck and Creedence intact, but the briefcase and the million dollars are missing. There is, however, a clue in the vehicle, a history paper written by a high school student, Larry Sellers, son of Arthur Digby Sellers (Harry Bugin), author of 156 episodes of the long-running television western series *Branded*.

The Dude and Walter visit the Sellers home, hoping to intimidate young Larry into giving up the briefcase, but they leave empty-handed. At home, the Dude is visited by men representing the adult movie mogul Jackie Treehorn, who still wants the money Bunny owes him. At the Treehorn estate in Malibu, the Dude explains that Larry Sellers has Lebowski's money, and as thanks for this information, Treehorn drugs the Dude. While unconscious, he experiences a hallucination that takes the form of a highly choreographed and costumed Busby Berkeley–like production, in which Maude, dressed like a Valkyrie, and the Dude, in cable-repairman attire, bowl, surrounded by dancing bowling pins. The dream sequence concludes with the Nihilists, in red spandex bodysuits, chasing the Dude with enormous scissors. At home again, the Dude finds Maude awaiting him, and after sex, the Dude has an epiphany regarding the case. He and Walter drive to the Lebowski home, realizing en route that there was no kidnapping at all. The briefcase was empty, as Lebowski stole the money for himself and gave the Dude a ringer for the ransom. There was no cash, and the Dude is therefore not responsible for it.

They confront the Big Lebowski, accusing him of embezzling funds from his foundation and using the kidnapping as a cover-up. The case has been solved. The Nihilists, however, have not reached this same conclusion and still want their ransom money. They set fire to the Dude's car at the bowling alley, and in the subsequent scuffle, Donny has a heart attack and dies. Walter and the Dude scatter his ashes at the seashore and adjourn to the bowling alley, where the Dude encounters the Stranger, who concludes his story by informing the viewer that a Little Lebowski is on the way. And "the human comedy keeps perpetuating itself, down through generations, westward the wagons, across the sands of time."

Following their Oscar-winning *Fargo* (1996), the Coens released *The Big Lebowski,* though they would note that the *Lebowski* script was completed prior to that of *Fargo* and the delay in production was due to the schedules of Jeff Bridges and John Goodman, without whom they did not want to make the film. The genesis of the project was in the characters and the actors who would play them, Goodman's Walter and Bridges' Dude, and the writers placed these two men in Los Angeles in the early 1990s and added bowling and a case of mistaken identity. The characters themselves were inspired by people whom the Coens had met in Los Angeles while filming *Barton Fink* (1991) and included Pete Exline, "Uncle Pete," a Vietnam veteran who was obsessed with and defined by the war, and who, with a friend, once confronted a teenage carjacker with a baggie containing a piece of homework he had left in the car when he abandoned it. When the Coens visited Exline at his Los Angeles home, which they characterize as a "dump," he commented to them that his "rug really tied the room together." Though the line is spoken by the Dude in the film, Exline served somewhat as an inspiration for Walter, along with John Milius, director of *Conan the Barbarian* (1981) and *Red Dawn* (1984), whom the Coens describe as a great storyteller, gun enthusiast, survivalist-type, and "a macho show-off," says Ethan Coen.

Walter, "whose instincts are always wrong," notes Ethan, is an observant Jew, an element inspired by neither Exline nor Milius but which the brothers added as "a peg to hang a few gags on him."

The character of the Dude was inspired by Jeff Dowd, who refers to himself as the "Pope of Dope" and whom others call the Dude, a pacifist and former member of the Seattle Seven. Roger Ebert, who knew Dowd, describes him as "tall, as shaggy and sometimes as mood-altered as Jeff Lebowski, although much more motivated." The idea of combining the militant veteran Milius/Exline character with that of the pacifist Dude amused the Coens, and they added bowling as a way to have the characters interact with one another. The role of the Dude was not written for Bridges, but once the Coens thought of him, he was the only actor they considered for the part. Described by one writer as a man from whom "you get a secondhand high just looking at him," the Dude is thrust into a world of kidnapping, embezzlement, and million-dollar ransoms, an unlikely detective in an increasingly bizarre mystery.

The plot itself derives from Raymond Chandler: set in Los Angeles, with what Joel Coen characterizes as a "hopelessly complex plot," *Lebowski* is influenced to some degree by Chandler's novel *The Big Sleep,* published in 1939 and adapted into the 1946 Howard Hawks film of the same name, starring Humphrey Bogart. Bogart plays detective Philip Marlowe, hired by a wealthy, wheelchair-bound man to protect his irresponsible and flighty younger daughter. The similarities to *Lebowski* are clear, though Ethan Coen asserts that Robert Altman's adaptation of Chandler's *The Long Goodbye* (1973) is "the most important antecedent to the movie." He specifically references Elliott Gould's Marlowe who functions, like the Dude, as a sort of "anti-Marlowe," a man of his time, "and yet not, wandering around L.A. in a suit." The Dude similarly ambles around L.A. in a bathrobe and jellies, an improbable detective who ultimately solves the case, though not before he endures the endless plot twists and complications. Joel Coen asserts, however, "the plot is sort of secondary to the other things. . . . If people get a little bit confused, I don't think it's necessarily going to get in the way of them enjoying the story," calling the complexity of the plot "ultimately unimportant." The characters, and the interaction between them, are the focus of the film; Joel Coen describes the relationship as a sort of marriage, an "odd couple formed by Jeff and John, their fluctuating relationship."

Having conceived of these two main characters, a setting, and the Chandler-like plot, the filmmakers inserted the supporting cast: Steve Buscemi as Donny, who has very few lines, the brothers say, because his character in *Fargo* talked non-stop; John Turturro as the bowling pederast Jesus Quintana, his character inspired by a role he played in *Ma Puta Vita*, a play from the 1980s; Sam Elliott as the Stranger, a part that was written specifically for him; Peter Stormare, with whom they had worked in *Fargo*, as a nihilist/porn star/kidnapper; and Red Hot Chili Peppers' bassist Flea. Julianne Moore, Philip Seymour Hoffman, David Huddleston, and Tara Reid rounded out the cast, and as Jackie Treehorn, they cast Ben Gazzara, whom, Ethan Coen notes, looks like Norris the Butler in *The Big Sleep*, combined with echoes of Hugh Hefner.

Of the eclectic group of characters, the brothers note that they are "always looking to make characters geographically or sociologically or ethnically as specific as we possibly can. The more specific they are, the easier it is to develop them and make them more interesting for ourselves and for the audience." The Stranger, then,

is very Western in appearance and voice; Jesus is Hispanic, though Turturro himself is of Italian descent; Walter is Polish; the Nihilists are intended to appear German, though Stormare is Swedish; and Moore's Maude uses an accent that Ethan characterizes as a "vague, non-specific geographically, swell finishing school for girls in Switzerland accent," which Moore created for the part. As an ensemble, the characters are reminiscent of the 1960s, though the action of the film takes place at the beginning of the 1990s, says Joel Coen. "It's a contemporary movie about what's become of people who were formed and defined by that period," and how those people now function thirty years later.

The film was shot on location throughout Los Angeles as well as on a soundstage in West Hollywood, and upon its release, *The Big Lebowski* was not initially well received. Reviews focused on the overly complex plot, which Kenneth Turan of the *Los Angeles Times* deemed "disjointed, incoherent and even irritating." As a result of the Chandleresque narrative, says *Slate's* Alex Ross, "we lose track not only of plot devices but of whole characters, who come and go without finding a reason to be." In a common complaint about the Coens' self-conscious approach to film, Todd McCarthy of *Variety*, as cited in Robson's *Coen Brothers*, concluded that the film "adds up to considerably less than the sum of its often scintillating parts, simply because the film doesn't seem to be about anything other than its own cleverness." The *Dallas Observer* similarly characterized the Coens as "arty schlockmeisters," and in a sideways compliment, *Rolling Stone* proclaimed *Lebowski* "the best movie ever set mostly in a bowling alley." What praise the film received was largely directed toward the casting—which the *Washington Post* found "perfect"—and the cinematography of Roger Deakins, whom Turan calls a "master." Roger Ebert, however, observed that "*The Big Lebowski* is about an attitude, not a story," an assessment Jeff Bridges echoes in his appraisal of the picture: "I think it's a film about grace, how amazing it is that we're all allowed to stay alive on this speck hurled out into space, being as screwed up as we all are."

The film earned only $28 million domestically, and the box office plus the reviews indicate that the picture should have been written off as inferior. *Lebowski* gained momentum as time passed, however, reaching cult-film status and spawning events, festivals, and a religion. In 2002, Will Russell and Scott Shuffitt instituted the Lebowski Fest, a two-day event that features a movie party and a bowling party. On the tenth anniversary of the film's release, the Lebowski Fest included a cast reunion that included Jeff Bridges, John Goodman, John Turturro, Steve Buscemi, and Julianne Moore. In 2005, Oliver Benjamin founded the Church of the Latter-Day Dude, "Dudeism, the slowest growing religion in the world." At the church's website, one can become ordained as a "Dudeist priest," an order that boasts 200,000 members worldwide, and read the Dudespaper and the "Take It Easy Manifesto." Benjamin coauthored *The Abide Guide: Living Like Lebowski* (2011) with the "Arch Dudeship" Dwayne Eutsey. Also on the film's tenth anniversary, a Tumblr site initiated The Big Lebowski Challenge, in which a viewer watches the film and emulates the Dude's behavior, smoking when he smokes and drinking when he drinks. One writer characterized the growth of the film's popularity as no longer cult-film, but rather cultish in nature.

While the film garnered no high-profile honors at the Academy Awards or Golden Globes, it was granted the Golden Aries by the Russian Guild of Film Critics. Additionally, the published screenplay for *Lebowski* notes that the script won the 1998 Bar Kochba Award, "honoring achievement in the arts that defy racial and religious stereotyping and promote appreciation for the multiplicity of man." The honor was awarded by Rabbi Emmanuel Lev-Tov, whose memoir is entitled *You with the Schnozz*.

References

Jason Bailey, "'*The Big Lebowski* Feels Thrown Together': Cult Films Critics Got Wrong," TheAtlantic.com, April 18, 2013; David Bennun, "The Coen Brothers," in *The Coen Brothers: Interviews*, ed. William Rodney Allen (Jackson: University Press of Mississippi, 2006); Michel Ciment and Hubert Niogret, "The Logic of Soft Drugs," in *The Coen Brothers: Interviews*, ed. William Rodney Allen (Jackson: University Press of Mississippi, 2006); *Dudeism.com*; Roger Ebert, "*The Big Lebowski*," RogerEbert.com, March 10, 2010; Ashley Fetters, "Still Abiding after 15 Years: The Laid-back World of *Lebowski* Worship," *TheAtlantic.com*, March 6, 2013; Desson Howe, "*Big Lebowski*: Rollin' a Strike," *Washington Post*, March 6, 1998; "The Lebowski Challenge," *TheFiveSecondRule.tumblr.com*; *LebowskiFest.com*; Andy Lowe, "The Brothers Grim," in *The Coen Brothers: Interviews*, ed. William Rodney Allen (Jackson: University Press of Mississippi, 2006); Ian Nathan, *Ethan and Joel Coen* (Paris: Cahiers du cinema Sarl, 2012); Ray Pride, "Coen Job," in *The Coen Brothers: Interviews*, ed. William Rodney Allen (Jackson: University Press of Mississippi, 2006); William Preston Robertson, *The Big Lebowski: The Making of a Coen Brothers Film* (New York: W.W. Norton & Co., 1998); Eddie Robson, *Coen Brothers* (London: Virgin Books, 2003); Alex Ross, "Bogus Nights: The Immorality of Indie Film," *Slate.com*, March 8, 1998; Michael Sragow, "All Duded Up," *Dallas Observer*, March 5, 1998; Gary Susman, "Making It Clear: The Coen Brothers," in *The Coen Brothers: Interviews*, ed. William Rodney Allen (Jackson: University Press of Mississippi, 2006); Peter Travers, "*The Big Lebowski*," *Rolling Stone*, March 6,

1998; Kenneth Turan, "Nutcase Noir and Gee-zer Noir," *Los Angeles Times*, March 6, 1998. See also JEFF BRIDGES, HARRY BUGIN, T BONE BURNETT, CARTER BURWELL, STEVE BUS-CEMI, ROGER DEAKINS, SAM ELLIOTT, BEN GAZZARA, JOHN GOODMAN, RICK HEINRICHS, PHILIP SEYMOUR HOFFMAN, DAVID HUDDLESTON, JULIANNE MOORE, JON POLITO, TARA REID, PETER SIRAGUSA, PETER STORMARE, JOHN TURTURRO, MARY ZOPHRES.

BLOOD SIMPLE (1984)

DIRECTOR: Joel Coen and Ethan Coen (uncredited). SCREENPLAY: Joel Coen and Ethan Coen. EXECUTIVE PRODUCER: Daniel F. Bacaner. PRODUCERS: Ethan Coen and Joel Coen (uncredited); Mark Silverman (Associate Producer). PHOTOGRAPHY: Barry Sonnenfeld. EDITING: Roderick Jaynes and Don Wiegmann. MUSIC: Carter Burwell. PRODUCTION DESIGN: Jane Musky. SET DECORATION: Nancy Griffith. COSTUME DESIGN: Sara Medina-Pape.

CAST: John Getz (Ray), Frances McDormand (Abby), Dan Hedaya (Julian Marty), M. Emmet Walsh (P.I. Loren Visser), Samm-Art Williams (Meurice), Holly Hunter (Helene Trend—voice, uncredited), Barry Sonnenfeld (Marty vomiting—voice, uncredited).

RUNNING TIME: 96 minutes. Color.

RELEASED THROUGH: Circle Films. Premiere: September, 1984 (Deauville Film Festival, France).

DVD: MGM Home Entertainment.

Joel and Ethan Coen's first feature film, *Blood Simple*, was filmed on location in Texas and centers on a lover's triangle comprised of Julian Marty (Dan Hedaya), his wife Abby (Frances McDormand), and her lover Ray (John Getz). The film begins with the voice of private detective Loren Visser (M. Emmet Walsh), explain-ing to the viewer that in Texas, it's best not to count on other people, as "down here, you're on your own." As Loren speaks, the camera moves through a series of images that exemplify the Texas landscape: the open road, pump jacks, and oil refineries, silhouetted against broad Texas horizons.

The narrative then begins, following Ray and Abby as they drive through the night toward Houston accompanied by heavy rain and the rhythmic beat of the windshield wipers. Behind them in a Volkswagen Beetle is Loren, and when Ray and Abby stop for the night in a motel, the private investigator snaps photos of them through the room's window. Loren returns the photos to Marty at his bar, a neon-laden, wooden-floored drinking establishment and sometime strip club, where Marty glowers about his wife's infidelity and phones his wife and her lover first at the hotel and then at Ray's apartment. Abby and Ray return to her home just long enough for her to locate the pearl-handled .38 revolver that Marty gave her for their first anniversary, and Ray, who tends bar at Marty's place, returns to work long enough to turn in his resignation and request his back pay: two weeks' salary. Aware that Ray is Abby's lover, Marty refuses to pay him and threatens to shoot Ray should he ever return to the bar.

Having considered his options, Marty meets Loren on a point overlooking the river and offers the P.I. $10,000 to kill both Abby and Ray, a job that Loren accepts. To provide an alibi, Marty takes a fishing trip to Corpus Christi while Loren plans and executes the hit, providing Marty with pictures when he returns from the coast. Marty, shaken by the sight of his dead wife in bed with Ray, is satisfied with the evidence and pays for the murders, only to be shot in the chest by Loren, who has stolen Abby's gun and used it on her husband. Loren departs with the money and the

Dan Hedaya (left) and M. Emmet Walsh in *Blood Simple* (1984)

photos, leaving behind Marty, still sitting in his chair, blood dripping onto the wooden floor. Arriving home, Loren discovers that he has left his lighter at the bar and that Marty has kept one of the photos of the dead couple, placing it in the bar's safe as insurance against a double cross by Loren.

Ray and Abby are not, however, dead. Loren doctored the photos to trick Marty into paying, and when Ray arrives at the bar after hours, hoping to take his two weeks' salary from the safe, he finds Marty dead and Abby's gun at the scene. Assuming that Abby killed her husband, Ray cleans up the blood, places Marty in the back seat of his car, and transports him out into the Texas countryside. As he drives through the night, Ray hears a noise from the back seat, and pulling over, he discovers that Marty is not, after all, deceased. Wounded and trying to escape, Marty crawls along the deserted highway,

but Ray recaptures him and buries him alive in the middle of a field. Returning to Abby's new apartment, Ray assures her that he has taken care of it all, though Abby has no knowledge of Marty's death.

Needing to secure both his lighter and the missing photo, Loren breaks into the bar and begins beating the safe with a hammer but is interrupted when Abby arrives. Abby sees the break-in, the damaged safe, and the general state of disarray in the office, and concludes that Ray returned to claim his wages and attempted to break into the safe. Abby confronts Ray at his home, where he confesses that he buried Marty alive; frightened, Abby first confides in Meurice (Samm-Art Williams) and then returns home, where Ray awaits her in the dark. When Abby turns on the lights, Loren shoots Ray through the window from an apartment across the street, but before he can kill Abby as well, she extinguishes the lights. Loren enters the apartment, intending to finish the job, but Abby crawls through a window to the next apartment, thinking that it is Marty who is trying to kill her, and pins Loren's hand to the windowsill with a knife when he attempts to follow her. Loren frees himself but is shot by Abby through the bathroom door. Her final words in the film are "I'm not afraid of you, Marty," at which Loren laughs, telling her that he'll be sure tell Marty if he sees him.

Following his time in the undergraduate film program at NYU, Joel Coen lived in New York City, where he worked as assistant editor on the low-budget horror films *Fear No Evil* (1981) and *The Evil Dead* (1981). Ethan Coen had moved in with his brother following his own graduation from Princeton in 1979, and while they worked some on scripts for others, the brothers began considering writing and directing a film of their own. Inspired by the fundraising strategy of Sam Raimi, with whom Joel had worked on *The Evil Dead*, the Coens made a two-minute trailer for the project they wanted to film, which included a revolver being loaded, Marty's burial scene, and light streaming through bullet holes in a wall, and they used this teaser to raise the money for *Blood Simple*. Returning to the area where they grew up, Joel lived near Minneapolis for a year, raising $750,000 from wealthy donors in St. Louis Park and $550,000 from smaller donors, including their parents, Ed and Rena Coen. With the funds, Joel and Ethan filmed the project free of Hollywood input, financial or otherwise, and therefore had complete control of the entire process. Joel recalls, "the main consideration from the start was that we wanted to be left alone, without anyone telling us what to do. The way we financed the movie gave us that right." To make a film on their $1.5 million budget, they needed to select material that would

be inherently economical, and they decided on a thriller, adding elements of horror for good measure.

The brothers composed a crime story influenced by the novels of James M. Cain, whose stories are about "a small group of people doing very non-special effects-type of stuff to each other," says Ethan, factors that fit well with the budget for their film. Cain's hardboiled detective novels have long been fodder for the film industry, providing source material for Billy Wilder's *Double Indemnity* (1944), Michael Curtiz's *Mildred Pierce* (1945), and Tay Garrett's *The Postman Always Rings Twice* (1946), and the Coens often reference Cain as an inspiration for their films. The plot of *Blood Simple* acts in the inverse of *The Postman Always Rings Twice* and *Double Indemnity*, as the Coen version of the story features a man who commissions the murder of his wife and her lover, whereas Cain's tales involved the murder of the husband by the wife and her lover. As they would in *The Man Who Wasn't There* (2001), the Coens sought to emulate the literature that produced noir films, rather than the films themselves, but reviewers labeled the Coen brothers' first picture as noir, despite the filmmakers' intentions otherwise. Ethan Coen concedes that *Blood Simple* is "plain, mean, ordinary people doing bad things to each other in the dark, so I guess that qualifies it as film noir," but they purposefully set the film in Texas, an atypical locale for the genre, which traditionally takes place in urban areas. In addition to the unique setting for the film, Joel was familiar with the area, as he had briefly attended graduate school at the University of Texas in Austin, and during that time he met individuals from the local film industry. The brothers found that they could make a low-budget, independent film there, and the mythical quality of Texas, the Wild West, seemed appropriate to the plot and characters of their project, as Joel Coen characterized the subject matter of the film to be "deadly passion."

Blood Simple takes its name from a term in Dashiell Hammett's novel, *Red Harvest*. The protagonist, a detective, states, "If I don't get away soon I'll be going blood-simple like the natives," referring to the psychological effects that manifest themselves in a murderer after the crime is committed. Both Ray and Loren ultimately go "blood simple" over the course of the film. Convinced that his lover killed her husband, Ray resorts to burying Marty alive in the middle of a West Texas crop field and assures Abby that he's taken care of everything if they can just keep their heads. Ray, however, is clearly not keeping his head. He cannot recall the location of his windbreaker, which he threw into the incinerator after he used it to clean up copious amounts of blood at the murder scene. He is packing his belongings, planning to flee the city in his car, which continues to seep blood through the towels he places in the back seat. He cannot sleep, and he (correctly) sees danger around every corner, standing in Abby's darkened apartment, looking out into the night, trying to see what is coming for him. Loren, too, goes blood simple. He initially does not kill Ray and Abby, electing instead to murder Marty, who is a much more likely candidate for death: a cruel, abrasive, controlling man with an unpredictable temper. However, when Loren discovers that Marty kept a picture of the supposed murder scene and that his lighter has been left behind at Marty's bar, his carefully constructed crime begins to unravel and he needs to tie up the loose ends. He beats at the safe with a hammer, hiding in the bathroom when Abby appears at the bar. He breaks into Ray's apartment, the bar, and Abby's new apartment, making mysterious phone calls to Abby. He ultimately breaks through the wall of one apartment into another and shoots holes from one room to the next. Both men become blood simple, and both men die as a result.

While the Coens note that the film's concept began with the situation, rather than the characters, as in *Raising Arizona* (1987) or *Barton Fink* (1991), they did write the part of Loren Visser with M. Emmet Walsh in mind, as the Coens had seen him in Ulu Grosbard's *Straight Time* (1978). Walsh accepted the part because he liked the character, not because he thought the film had any potential for success. The rest of the cast was located through auditions, and while the Coens initially approached Holly Hunter for the part of Abby, she was currently committed to another project and recommended that her roommate, Frances McDormand, audition for the part. They rounded out the cast with John Getz and Dan Hedaya, and the film was shot over eight weeks, with Joel directing, Ethan producing, and Barry Sonnenfeld serving as cinematographer.

Prior to filming *Blood Simple*, Joel, Ethan, and Barry Sonnenfeld saw Bernardo Bertolucci's *The Conformist* (1970) and Carol Reed's *The Third Man* (1949), to help determine the visual style and lighting of their own film. Because they had no distributor for the film, the filmmakers dismissed the idea of making *Blood Simple* in black and white, which could yield the film unmarketable. Instead, they shot in color and made the movie dark, using colored neon signs, for example, to emphasize the darkness around the lights. Regular viewers of Coen films will recognize in *Blood Simple* elements that would become Coen trademarks, even at this early stage: the picture's unusual camera angles, shots, and movement, creative use of the film's soundtrack, a multitude of cinematic and literary references, stylized dialogue, dark humor, and eccentric characters who are doomed from the outset, often due to circumstances of their own making. The camerawork in particular garnered much comment from reviewers, who remarked on the creative shots of the ceiling fans, the under-the-sink shot from Loren's point of view, and the tracking shot that runs down the bar at Marty's place, essentially running over an inebriated bar patron, among other inventive uses of the camera. In one particularly celebrated scene, the camera rushes toward Abby and Ray on his front lawn, using the shaky-cam technique the brothers borrowed from Sam Raimi in *The Evil Dead*. This method of filming involved a camera mounted in the middle of a twelve-foot wooden plank, with a handle placed at each end. Two grips ran across the set, carrying the plank, and the camera moves quickly through the scene, without bouncing over the ground at that speed. Hal Hinson, describing the resultant footage, states "The camera swoops and pirouettes as if in a Vincente Minnelli musical; at times it scuttles just inches above the ground, at shoe-top level, crawls under tables, or bounces down hallways." In its write-up on the film, the Sundance Film Festival writes that "The pace of *Blood Simple* is so deliberate, and the camera angles so disorienting, that at first you think they must be kidding," and perhaps kidding would be an accurate way to characterize the Coens' approach to film overall, but this little film would soon demonstrate that it was no joke.

With the film completed, the Coens then needed a distributor for the picture. For a time, they lived in Los Angeles with Sam Raimi, shopping the picture to studios who were not interested. Ultimately, it was Ben Berenholtz of Circle Films who agreed to distribute the film, and following the film's success, Berenholtz signed the filmmakers to an additional three-picture deal. *Blood Simple* premiered at the Deauville Film Festival in France and was shown at the Toronto International Film Festival, the New York Film Festival, and the Sundance Film Festival, where it was designated as Best Dramatic Feature. During its initial run, the film earned a 150 percent return for its investors and was lauded by many critics as an extraordinary first effort by the new filmmakers. Hinson commented that the Coens "don't make movies like beginners," deeming the film an amalgam of Hitchcock, Bertolucci, Fritz Lang, and Orson Welles.

Not all writers were as enthusiastic about the film, however. Stephane Braunschweig, in "Blood Simple," initiated the discussion of style versus substance in Coen films, a criticism that would become commonplace in future Coen film reviews, and Braunschweig felt that the filmmakers privileged the look of the film over an interesting plot. The *New York Times'* Janet Maslin commented early in her review, "a lot of dying is done in *Blood Simple*, and almost none of it is done right," though by the conclusion of her piece, Maslin predicted that Joel Coen was "headed for bigger, even better, things." Collectively, the critics were pleased. *Variety* described the film as "a finely crafted and intriguingly written picture," a "colorful, moody piece with a texture that's very true-to-life," and Roger Ebert deemed the film "one of the best of the modern films noir, a grimy story of sleazy people trapped in a net of betrayal and double-cross." In a re-screening of the film in 2013, Christopher Sailor of the Atlanta Film Festival declared it "nothing less than one of the most remarkable debut films of all time."

In July of 2000, the Coens re-released *Blood Simple* as a director's cut, having revisited the film and determining that it warranted some additional attention. Ethan Coen explains this unusual decision, as no other Coen film has been recut: "Because it's our only movie that wasn't released by a studio, the elements for it weren't archived anywhere," he says. "We had to go back and find the print and sound elements. It was impossible to find a good print of the movie, and we were afraid that if any more time passed, we wouldn't be able to find the original elements to make new prints." Joel adds that as long as they were working with the sound, they "figured we might as well cheat a little bit and fix up the picture." They had no outtakes, trims, or alternative takes with which to work, so the alterations were limited to making cuts to the existing scenes and rearranging shots. When it was released in its new form, however, it featured an introduction by Mortimer Young, of Forever Young Film Preservation, who sits at his dark-wood desk, pipe in hand, reading a gilt-edged tome. Young introduces the new *Blood Simple*, reminding the viewer that upon its release, the film shattered box office records and "ushered in the era of the independent cinema." Young is played by George Ives, who also appeared in *The Man Who Wasn't There* and as Mortimer Young in a similar introduction to *The Big Lebowski* (1998), and in this introduction/spoof, he goes on to remind readers that because "filmographic techniques were in their infancy" fifteen years ago when the film was made, it warranted preservation, including removing the boring parts and adding "other things," by way of new "ultra-ultra sound" technology. In reality the changes, explained by Ethan Coen in the *New Yorker*, amounted to shortening the film by five minutes and "editorial smoothing" so that "scenes that were once inept are now merely awkward." The director's cut was released on July 7, 2000 and played for sixteen weeks, earning almost $1.7 million. The screenplay was remade by Chinese director Zhang Yimou in 2009, with the Coens' permission, and released in China as *A Woman, A Gun and a Noodle Shop*. The remake cost $12 million and earned $38 million in China. It was set in Gansu province in the seventeenth century and was well received internationally.

References

Stephanie Braunschweig, "Blood Simple," in *Joel & Ethan Coen: Blood Siblings*, ed. Paul A. Woods (London: Plexus, 2003); Eric Breitbart, "Joel and Ethan Coen," in *Joel & Ethan Coen: Blood Siblings*, ed. Paul A. Woods (London: Plexus Publishing, 2003); "Blood Simple," *History.Sundance. org*, "Blood Simple: Review from *Variety*," in *Joel & Ethan Coen: Blood Siblings*, ed. Paul A. Woods (London: Plexus Publishing, 2003); Michel Ciment and Hubert Niogret, "Interview with Joel and Ethan Coen," in *The Coen Brothers: Interviews*, ed. William Rodney Allen (Jackson: University Press of Mississippi, 2006); Ethan Coen, "Slashing *Blood Simple*," *New Yorker*, July 3, 2000; Roger Ebert, "*Blood Simple*," *RogerEbert.com*, July 14, 2000; Hal Hinson, "Bloodlines," in *The Coen Brothers: Interviews*, ed. William Rodney Allen (Jackson: University Press of Mississippi, 2006); Chris Lee, "Zhang Yimou Remakes the Coen Brothers' *Blood Simple*," *Los Angeles Times*, August 29, 2010; Janet Maslin, "*Blood Simple*, A Black-Comic Romp," *New York Times*, October 12, 1984; Patricia McConnico, "Joel Coen," *Texas Monthly*, October 1998; Ian Nathan, *Ethan and Joel Coen* (Paris: Cahiers du cinema Sarl, 2012); Kim Newman, "Goose Bumps," in *Joel & Ethan Coen: Blood Siblings*, ed. Paul A. Woods (London: Plexus Publishing, 2003); Eddie Robson, *Coen Brothers* (London: Virgin Books, 2003); Christopher Sailor, "*Blood Simple*—Death and Texas," *AtlantaFilmFestival.com*. See also CARTER BURWELL, JOHN GETZ, DAN HEDAYA, FRANCES MCDORMAND, BARRY SONNENFELD, M. EMMET WALSH.

BOROWITZ, KATHERINE (1954–)

Born July 5, 1954, in Chicago, Illinois, Borowitz attended Yale Drama School, where she met her husband and frequent Coen collaborator, John Turturro; they were married in 1985. Her first on-screen appearance was in *The World According to*

Garp (1981), and in 1982, she debuted off-Broadway in *Lennon*. She was then cast in *Harry & Son* (1984), directed by Paul Newman and starring Newman and Robby Benson. She worked in television as well, with small parts on the series *Miami Vice* (1984) and *Hothouse* (1988), and in the made-for-television movie *Growing Pains* (1984) and the mini-series *Evergreen* (1985). In 1990, she appeared in the Mike Figgis film *Internal Affairs*, starring Richard Gere, which she followed with a return to the stage, in the off-Broadway production of *The Resistible Rise of Arturo Ui* (1992). In 1992, she appeared in her husband John Turturro's directorial debut in the film *Mac*. She frequently works with Turturro, with roles in *Illuminata* (1998), *Romance & Cigarettes* (2005), and *Fading Gigolo* (2013), all of which he directed, and they appeared together in Michael Di Jiacomo's *Somewhere Tonight* (2011). They worked on Broadway together, in *Relatively Speaking* (2011), three one-act plays directed by John Turturro, one of which was written by Ethan Coen.

Borowitz has appeared in two films by Joel and Ethan Coen: *The Man Who Wasn't There* and *A Serious Man* (2009). As Ann Nirdlinger Brewster in *The Man Who Wasn't There* (2001), Borowitz plays the heiress to the Nirdlinger department store fortune and the wife of Big Dave Brewster (James Gandolfini). Though a small role, Borowitz shares a memorable scene with Billy Bob Thornton's Ed Crane in which she discusses the other-worldly experiences of her husband. Her appearance in *A Serious Man* was momentary, as a friend at a picnic.

References

"Katherine Borowitz," *BroadwayWorld.com*. See also *THE MAN WHO WASN'T THERE*.

BRIDGES, JEFF (1949–)

The son of actors Lloyd and Dorothy Bridges, Jeff Bridges began his film career with an uncredited appearance as an infant in the 1951 film *The Company She Keeps*, in which his mother and brother Beau appeared as well. Born December 4, 1949, in Los Angeles, California, Bridges continued his on-screen appearances as a child on his father's television series *Sea Hunt* (1958–1960) and *The Lloyd Bridges Show* (1962–1963). Jeff Bridges was sent to a military academy in high school, his parents' attempt to encourage discipline in the teen, but he returned to and graduated from public high school. Following graduation, he enlisted in the Coast Guard Reserves and then relocated to New York, where he studied acting at the Herbert Berghof Studio. His television work continued with *The Loner* (1965) and *Lassie* (1969), and he returned to film in *Halls of Anger* (1970) and Peter Bogdanovich's adaptation of Larry McMurtry's *The Last Picture Show* (1971), for which Bridges earned the Academy Award nomination for Best Actor in a Supporting Role. He was Oscar nominated for the second time, again as Best Actor in a Supporting Role, for *Thunderbolt and Lightfoot* (1974), a heist film starring Clint Eastwood. He appeared in Michael Cimino's *Heaven's Gate* (1980) and in *TRON* (1982), as Kevin Flynn/Clu, a role he would reprise in 2010's *TRON: Legacy*. In 1984 he earned his third Oscar nomination for his role in *Starman*. He worked with Robin Williams in *The Fisher King* (1991) and Barbra Streisand in *The Mirror Has Two Faces* (1996), and in 2000, he played President Jackson Evans in the political drama *The Contender*, for which he was nominated for both a Golden Globe and also an Oscar as Best Actor in a Supporting Role. He appeared in the Oscar-nominated *Seabiscuit* (2003) and as a mentor-turned villain in the 2008 comic-book adaptation *Iron Man*, in the George Clooney–produced *The Men Who Stare at Goats* (2009), and in 2013's *R.I.P.D.* with Ryan Reynolds and Kevin Bacon. Bridges has appeared in two films by Joel and Ethan Coen: as the Dude in *The Big Lebowski* (1998) and as Rooster Cogburn in the 2010 adaptation of Charles Portis's novel *True Grit*.

Musically inclined from a young age, Bridges took piano lessons at the encouragement of his mother but subsequently quit. He then took up the guitar, forming a band with classmate John Goodwin, a friendship he has maintained into his adult life. At age sixteen, he composed a song that appeared in the 1969 film *John and Mary*, and also as a teen, he sold two songs to music producer Quincy Jones. Music continued to be a part of his acting career as well, as "*The Fabulous Baker Boys* (1989) was all about getting steeped in jazz," he states, and on the *Heaven's Gate* set, "Kris Kristofferson brought along many of his musician friends, like Ronnie Hawkins, Stephen Bruton, and T Bone, and our down time was all spent making music." T Bone Burnett, who worked with Bridges on the film *Crazy Heart* (2009), selected the soundtrack for *The Big Lebowski*, and worked as well with the Coens on *O Brother, Where Art Thou?* (2000), *The Ladykillers* (2004), and *Inside Llewyn Davis* (2013). Portraying musician Bad Blake in *Crazy Heart* (2009), Bridges was nominated for and won the Oscar for Best Performance by an Actor in a Leading Role. In 2000, he released his first album, *Be Here Soon*, and following his role in *Crazy Heart*, he released the eponymous album, *Jeff Bridges* (2011), produced by T Bone Burnett with contributions by Roseanne Cash, Sam Phillips, and Ryan Bingham, who received an Oscar for "The Weary Kind," from the *Crazy Heart* soundtrack.

The part of the Dude in *The Big Lebowski* was not written for Bridges, but the screenplay describes him as "a man in whom casualness runs deep." When casting the part, then, it seems inevitable that the Coens would turn to the actor described by film critic Pauline Kael, in Devin Freedman's "The *GQ* Cover Story," as "the most natural and least self-conscious screen actor that has ever lived." Ethan Coen explains the choice of Bridges: "Jeff can do those sorts of slow-metabolism characters without being boring," and reviewers widely praised Bridges's performance. Janet Maslin of the *New York Times* deemed the Dude "a role so right for him that he seems never to have been anywhere else," and *Rolling Stone*'s Peter Travers described Bridges's work in the film as "a performance of laid-back comic perfection." Sam Elliott, who played the Stranger in *Lebowski*, commented, "it's never going to get better than working opposite an actor like Jeff Bridges. That's as good as it gets."

As Reuben "Rooster" Cogburn in the Coen re-adaptation of Charles Portis's 1968 novel *True Grit* (2010), Bridges assumed the role for which John Wayne won his only Oscar, in Henry Hathaway's 1969 adaptation of the novel. The 2010 Coen adaptation, however, is not a remake of Hathaway's earlier film, and Bridges's Cogburn is not a reenactment of Wayne's performance, though some critics viewed Bridges's Cogburn as precisely that. David Carr of the *New York Times* characterized Bridges's performance as "the Dude playing the Duke with a dash of Bad Blake," referring to his previous characters, Jeff "the Dude" Lebowski and Bad Blake, the country musician from *Crazy Heart*. Comparisons to Wayne were unavoidable, though Bridges did, at times, fare well in those comparisons. Roger Ebert comments that "Bridges doesn't have the archetypal stature of the Duke. Few ever have. But he has here, I believe, an equal screen presence," concluding that when the audience watched Wayne, they were aware of the presence of the Duke, but when viewers watch Bridges, they see Rooster Cogburn.

Graham Fuller, of *Sight and Sound*, however, asserts that "the Coens do not elicit actorly shtick from Bridges, as they did in *The Big Lebowski* (1998), or reference his own sizeable iconography—growl, bark and lumber though his Cogburn does." Critics spent much time discussing Bridges's line delivery as Cogburn, as some reviewers were unable to understand his growls and found his dialogue undecipherable. David Edelstein of *New York Magazine* described Bridges's approach as one in which he "has lowered his voice, dropped it down into a pool of tobacco juice and phlegm, and the words that come out are only semi-recognizable." Others deemed his lack of articulation as appropriate to the character: "Bridges sounds as if he's talking through his collar, in a vocal performance that's entertaining no matter what he's saying, whether or not we understand it," states Nicholas Rapold of *Film Comment*. Bridges was nominated for the Academy Award for Best Actor for his turn at Cogburn.

References

David Bennun, "The Coen Brothers," in *The Coen Brothers: Interviews*, ed. William Rodney Allen (Jackson: University Press of Mississippi, 2006); "Jeff Bridges," *Biography.com*; "Jeff Bridges," *New York Times*, Movies & TV; David Carr, "The Coen Brothers, Shooting Straight," *New York Times*, December 10, 2010; Roger Ebert, "*True Grit*," *RogerEbert.com*, December 21, 2010; David Edelstein, "Punch, Drunk, Love," *New York*, December 12, 2010; Angie Errigo, "*True Grit*: The Dude Bests the Duke in a New Coens Masterpiece," *Empire.com*; Devin Friedman, "The *GQ* Cover Story: Jeff Bridges," *GQ*, October 2013; Graham Fuller, "No Country for Young Girls," *Sight and Sound*, 21.2 (2011); Will Harris, "Sam Elliott on George Clooney's Eyes, Jeff Bridges' Dudeness, and Working with Ron Swanson," *A.V.Club.com*, October 10, 2013; Desson Howe, "*Big Lebowski*: Rollin'

a Strike," *Washington Post*, March 6, 1998; *JeffBridgesMusic.com*; Janet Maslin, "*The Big Lebowski*: Film Review: A Bowling Ball's-Eye View of Reality," *New York Times*, March 6, 1998; Nicholas Rapold, "*True Grit*," *Film Comment*, 47.1 (2011); Peter Travers, "*The Big Lebowski*," *Rolling Stone*, March 6, 1998. See also *THE BIG LEBOWSKI*, *TRUE GRIT*.

BROLIN, JOSH (1968–)

Born February 12, 1968, in Los Angeles, California, the son of actor James Brolin and wildlife activist Jane Cameron Agee, Josh Brolin was raised on a horse ranch and studied acting as a teen in Los Angeles with Stella Adler prior to his first on-screen appearance in *The Goonies* (1985). He then spent almost a decade on television series such as *Highway to Heaven* (1986), a starring role in *Private Eye* (1987–1988), and a recurring role in *The Young Riders* (1989–1992), which was codirected by his father. He returned to film with appearances that included *Bed of Roses* (1996), *The Mod Squad* (1999), and *Milwaukee, Minnesota* (2003). Brolin starred in the 2003 television series *Mister Sterling* and was cast as Jedediah Smith in the mini-series *Into the West* (2005).

Brolin experienced a career breakthrough in a series of films in 2007, first with a role in Robert Rodriguez's *Planet Terror* (2007); then in the Coen brothers' *No Country for Old Men*, with Tommy Lee Jones and Javier Bardem; in *The Valley of Elah*, also with Jones; and in *American Gangster*, with Denzel Washington. He also appeared in the Coen-directed segment *World Cinema*, a part of *To Each His Own Cinema* (2007). In 2008, Brolin played President George W. Bush in Oliver Stone's *W* and was nominated by the Academy for Best Performance by an Actor in a Supporting Role for his appearance in Gus Van Sant's *Milk* (2008). He worked with the Coens again in 2010 in the re-adaptation of the Charles Portis novel, *True Grit*. With Matt Damon, among others, he produced the documentaries *The People Speak* (2009), based on Howard Zinn's *A People's History of the United States* (1980), and *The People Speak UK* (2010).

As Llewelyn Moss in *No Country for Old Men*, Brolin played one of three lead roles, with Tommy Lee Jones and Javier Bardem. Brolin's Moss stumbles upon a satchel of cash, the unclaimed profits of a drug deal gone wrong on the plains of West Texas. The film's narrative follows Moss as he seeks to evade Bardem's Anton Chigurh, a serial killer hired by drug lords to retrieve their missing millions. The *Guardian*'s Peter Bradshaw proclaimed Brolin "absolutely superb in the plum role of Llewelyn Moss," and Peter Travers of *Rolling Stone* writes that Brolin "rips into the role like a man possessed, giving Moss the human touch the part needs."

In the Coens' *True Grit*, Brolin's role is smaller, that of Tom Chaney, a murdering horse thief whose actions set in motion the film's plot, in which Mattie Ross (Hailee Steinfeld) and Rooster Cogburn (Jeff Bridges) follow Chaney through the Indian Territory. Roger Ebert characterizes Brolin's Chaney as "a complete and unadulterated villain, a rattlesnake who would as soon shoot Mattie as Rooster," and *Time*'s Richard Corliss further describes the fugitive as "a creature as small and pitiable as his crime was grand and mean." Though Brolin's reviews were largely positive, David Edelstein, writing for *New York*, deemed Brolin's Chaney a "bewildered troglodyte."

References

Peter Bradshaw, "*No Country for Old Men*," *Guardian*, January 17, 2008; Richard Corliss, "*True Grit*: Trading the Dude for the Duke," *Time*, December 25, 2010; Roger Ebert, "*No Country for Old Men*," *RogerEbert.com*, December 21, 2010; David Edelstein, "Punch, Drunk, Love," *New York*, December 12, 2010; "Josh Brolin," *Biography.com*; "Josh Brolin," *New York Times*, Movies & TV; Peter Travers, "*No Country for Old Men*," *Rolling Stone*, November 1, 2007. See also *NO COUNTRY FOR OLD MEN, TRUE GRIT*.

BUGIN, HARRY (1929–2005)

Born March 10, 1929, in New York City, Bugin attended the American Academy of Dramatic Arts following high school. He played string bass and guitar with bands, including Glenn Miller. His film debut was a small part in *The Man Who Saw Tomorrow* (1981), which he followed with *The Last American Virgin* (1982) and television appearances in the made-for-television movie *The Last Day* (1983) and on the series *America's Most Wanted: America Fights Back* (1989). He was cast in John Turturro's directorial debut, *Mac* (1992), and worked with Al Pacino in *City Hall* (1996) and Stanley Tucci in *Joe Gould's Secret* (2000). His final film was *Game 6* (2005), which starred Michael Keaton and Robert Downey Jr. He died in 2005 at the age of 76.

Bugin appeared in three Coen films: as Pete, the elevator man in *Barton Fink* (1991), as Aloysius, the sinister assistant of Sidney J. Mussburger (Paul Newman) and agent of evil in *The Hudsucker Proxy* (1994), and as Arthur Digby Sellers, writer for the television series *Branded*, in *The Big Lebowski* (1998). See also *THE BIG LEBOWSKI, THE HUDSUCKER PROXY*.

BURN AFTER READING (2008)

DIRECTOR: Ethan Coen and Joel Coen. SCREENPLAY: Joel Coen and Ethan Coen. EXECUTIVE PRODUCER: Tim Bevan, Eric Fellner, and Robert Graf. PRODUCER: Ethan Coen and Joel Coen; David Diliberto (Associate Producer). PHOTOGRAPHY: Emmanuel Lubezki. EDITING: Roderick Jaynes. MUSIC: Carter Burwell. PRODUCTION DESIGN: Jess Gonchor. ART

DIRECTION: David Swayze. SET DECORATION: Nancy Haigh. COSTUME DESIGN: Mary Zophres.
CAST: George Clooney (Harry Pfarrer), Frances McDormand (Linda Litzke), Brad Pitt (Chad Feldheimer), John Malkovich (Osborne Cox), Tilda Swinton (Katie Cox), Richard Jenkins (Ted), J. K. Simmons (CIA Superior), Elizabeth Marvel (Sandy Pfarrer).
RUNNING TIME: 96 minutes. Color.
RELEASED THROUGH: Focus Features. PREMIERE: August 27, 2008 (Venice Film Festival).
DVD: Universal Studios Home Entertainment.

Burn After Reading (2008) was Joel and Ethan Coen's follow-up to the Academy Award–winning Best Picture *No Country for Old Men* (2007), though the brothers note that it would be inaccurate to consider the films as sequential, as *Burn After Reading* was completed prior to *No Country*. Set in the Washington, D.C., area, the film opens on CIA analyst Osborne "Ozzy" Cox (John Malkovich), who has been demoted from his position on the Balkans desk to a job at the State Department. Apparently, Ozzy has a drinking problem. Rather than submit himself to the humiliation of a lower security clearance, Ozzy quits his job, electing to operate as a consultant and write his memoirs. Ozzy's wife, Katie (Tilda Swinton), is a pediatrician and is having an affair with Harry Pfarrer (George Clooney), formerly with the Treasury and now with the federal marshals, and Harry's wife, Sandy (Elizabeth Marvel) writes the popular children's book series, Oliver the Cat. Learning of Ozzy's resignation and his plan to write for a living, Katie is counseled by her attorney to first obtain his financial records and then initiate divorce proceedings against him, which she does.

In the process, however, the computer disk with the Coxes' financials and Ozzy's partially written memoirs mysteriously appears in the women's locker room at Hardbodies Fitness Center, at which Linda Litzke (Frances McDormand), Chad Feldheimer (Brad Pitt), and Ted (Richard Jenkins), the manager are employed. Discovering that the disk contains "sensitive CIA shit," Chad and Linda attempt to return it to Osborne Cox, hoping for a Good Samaritan reward for their efforts. Linda has discovered that her medical insurance will not cover elective plastic surgeries—liposuction, rhinoplasty, facelift, and breast augmentation—and she desperately needs quick cash so that she can reinvent herself and become competitive in the DC online dating pool. Osborne, however, refuses to "play ball," informs Chad that demanding cash in return for his disk is a felony, punches Chad in the face, and commissions

From left: Richard Jenkins, Brad Pitt, and Frances McDormand in *Burn After Reading* (2008)

a fellow "spook" to follow Chad and Linda. Undeterred by Osborne's unwillingness to participate in their blackmail scheme, Linda determines they should deliver his secrets to the Russian Embassy, where they attempt to sell them, promising the bewildered attaché that they can obtain even more sensitive material if the price is right.

Having signed up on an Internet dating site, Linda periodically goes out with different men over the course of the film, and one of those men is Harry, who in addition to his marriage to Sandy and his affair with Katie, frequents the same online dating service as Linda. While juggling her personal life and her battles with the ever-resistant insurance agency, Linda pushes on in her bid to cash in on the opportunity which has presented itself to her and Chad. Katie now resides alone, as she changed the locks and set out Ozzy's belongings on the steps, and in an attempt to obtain additional state secrets, Chad stakes out the Cox home, where he observes Katie and Harry enter the house for a midday tryst. Upon their exit, he breaks in to retrieve more saleable information, but Harry returns from his post-coital run to shower and dress, spooking Chad into hiding. Harry, discovering Chad in the closet, shoots him in the head and disposes of the body.

Midway through the film, Ozzy's former supervisor, Palmer Smith (David Rasche) visits the office of his CIA superior (J. K. Simmons) to explain the situation: who is sleeping with whom, who is being tailed and by whom, the contents and location of the computer disk, and the murder of Chad and the subsequent dumping of his body in the Chesapeake Bay. Harry discovers that his wife's lawyer has assigned a private investigator to follow him and therefore knows about his affair; Linda is forcibly removed from the Russian Embassy after learning that the disk is worthless; and Ozzy, at this point, is drinking himself into a stupor daily while working himself into a rage over the events that have transpired. When he discovers that his wife has cleaned out their bank account, he determines to break into his former house and reclaim his possessions. While at the house, he discovers Ted, the manager at Hardbodies, who has been commissioned by Linda to steal additional classified information from Cox in order to trade those secrets for the safe return of Chad, who of course is already dead. Ozzy first shoots and then assaults Ted. Linda meets Harry once more, and while initially it appears that the two might be an excellent match, Harry's paranoia overcomes him and he attempts to flee the country.

In the final review of this very odd case file, the two CIA men assess the events and individuals involved: Harry is to be allowed to escape to Venezuela, where he cannot be extradited to the United States and therefore will remain; Ozzy was observed attacking Ted with an axe in the street, was subsequently shot by another CIA agent, and remains in a coma; Chad's body has been recovered from the Bay and burned; and Ted's body has been disposed of as well. The remaining detail is Linda Litzke, who will agree to keep quiet if her plastic surgeries are paid for by the CIA, which agrees to do exactly that.

The Coens have indicated that the genesis for *Burn after Reading* was not the story or even the characters, but rather the actors with whom the brothers were interested in working. "We started with the cast, thinking about parts," Joel states. "We thought about what would be fun to see from these various actors, some of whom we worked with before, some of whom we hadn't. What would be fun to see them play?" The idea of the film grew from there. Set in Washington, D.C., where some exteriors were filmed on location, the film was shot primarily in New York, where both

Coens reside and where George Clooney was working on another project at the time.

The film was made on a budget of $37 million and grossed over $163 million worldwide and $60 million domestically, and there were reviewers who praised the film, including Chris Tookey of the U.K.'s *Daily Mail*, who deemed *Burn After Reading* "Cleverly plotted and brilliantly acted, this is up there with *Fargo* and *Raising Arizona* as the Coens' finest comedic work." The critical consensus, however, was that this film was a misfire and certainly didn't live up to the Oscar-winning reputation established by the filmmakers mere months prior. A brief skimming of just the titles of reviews provides a snapshot of its reception: "Burned Out" (*Nation*), "Baffled after Seeing" (*Time*), and "Burn before Watching" (*National Review*), among others. Of particular concern to critics was the plot of the film, which is complicated, at best. Peter Travers of *Rolling Stone* writes "The film is blissfully free of speechmaking. That also goes for coherence," and *Nation*'s Stuart Klawans describes the film as "full of clowns and foolery, signifying nothing, *BAR* is as deliberately self-canceling a story as you would expect from its title." The ensemble cast and multiple plot lines contributed to the reviewers' confusion, as "In their world, everything intersects, but it does not connect," claims Sukhdev Sandhu of the *Telegraph*, and *Empire*'s Ian Nathan similarly concludes that "each stage of the ever-increasing anarchy is entirely logical, but the net result is insanity." Beyond the plot, the technical aspects of the film drew fire as well. *Time*'s Richard Corliss took issue with Emmanuel Lebezki's photography, which Corliss described as "all shiny surfaces and slick camera choreography, it looks so smart it can fool you into thinking something clever is going on or will start in just a minute. Instead, the movie devolves until it practically dissolves, and the only

laughter you might hear is from the guys behind the camera."

A more common criticism was in regard to the characters of the film, described by one writer as "a confederacy of dunces, a bestiary of repellent creatures," though some reviewers considered them merely stupid rather than repellent. Commentary regarding their intelligence ranged from Ross Douthat of *National Review*, who deemed the characters "too stupid to live," to *Time*'s Corliss, who states "They're not falling-down stupid; they radiate the subtler variety of idiocy that can be mistaken for charm, decency or even brilliance." Malkovich's Osborne Cox might disagree with the terms "charm" and "decency," however, as he broadly characterizes humanity as a "league of morons," and even George Clooney concurs with Cox, calling this film the third installment of his Coen "idiot trilogy." In the film's publicity materials, the Coens state that they see these characters as "knuckleheads, but not unloveable ones. We asked the actors to embrace their inner knucklehead." Regardless of the description applied to the characters of *Burn after Reading*, their simplicity allows the plot to proceed unchecked, much in the way that *Fargo*'s (1996) downward spiral is set into action by the poorly conceived kidnapping plot of Jerry Lundegaard, a character not known for his intellectual prowess.

Ethan Coen characterizes the project as a film "about the covert world of the CIA and internet dating," adding that *Burn After Reading* is "our version of a Tony Scott/Jason Bourne type of movie— without the explosions." The filmmakers maintain, however, that while they began writing about espionage in the nation's capitol, "It's not really a spy story. It became something else," says Joel Coen. What that "something else" is, however, is not entirely clear. Richard Corliss asks bluntly "What the heck kind of film is this?" Some viewers read the film as a political statement, one in which the Coens provided a commentary on the agencies tasked with keeping classified intelligence just that: classified. Others saw the film as a direct criticism of George W. Bush and his administration, though Ethan Coen addresses this point specifically, stating, "It's certainly not about George Bush," and adding that "it's not really meant to be a comment on Washington."

The characters, however, have clearly seen numerous spy films, and their actions are guided by an awareness of what should happen next, were they living in such a film. Ozzy's tortured attempts to compose his "mem-wah" are based on his concept of what the career of a CIA analyst looks like, ignoring the fact that his position involved no thrilling adventures and crisis-averting discoveries. The very presence of the disk, containing the memoirs and columns of "raw data," prompts Chad and Linda to assume that they are in possession of state secrets, and when Ozzy refuses to pay, they take the disk to the Russians, as that's what one does with valuable classified information in spy films. Harry Pfarrer's career, in which he served as a bodyguard to state officials, has been so uneventful that he has never discharged his weapon in twenty-five years of service, and yet he boasts frequently about his "important" position and frequently references his gun, as that would be appropriate in the celluloid world of personal protection. Even Katie, who emasculates Ozzy by accurately observing that no one would be interested in his life's story, believes that she and Harry are creating a new life together, as lovers do on the screen, when in reality, Harry is simultaneously unfaithful to and emotionally dependent on his absent and equally unfaithful wife. The technical aspects of the film reinforce the delusion of the characters, specifically in regard to the score. "We wanted something big and bombastic, something

important sounding but absolutely meaningless," says Joel Coen, to which Ethan adds "since the characters thought they were all in a spy movie, for whatever reason [Carter Burwell] thought the composer should be similarly deluded." This juxtaposition of the ominous score and the pseudo-espionage unfolding before the viewer was described by *Newsweek*'s David Ansen as "wittily counterintuitive: it never signals that we're watching a comedy." The camerawork, as well, approximates the spy genre, with its satellite-view opening sequence, ankle-level tracking shots, and mysterious surveillance shots.

While there is much to laugh at in *Burn After Reading*, there is a bleakness to the film that belies the ridiculousness of its characters. Philip French of the *Guardian* describes the film's tone as bordering on the nihilistic, and *Salon*'s Andrew O'Hehir deems the film a "bleaker portrait of human life than the brooding, smoldering *No Country for Old Men* or any other Coen film," and for his part, Ethan Coen admits that the film is "pretty bleak," though a characterization of that sort would not be unusual for a film by Joel and Ethan Coen. *Burn After Reading* takes its place in the category of "lesser" Coen films, and for their next project, the brothers turned to adaptation once again, a formula which had worked with *No Country* and which they would apply to Charles Portis' *True Grit*.

References

David Ansen, "The Coens' Funny Bones," *Newsweek*, September 15, 2008; Richard Corliss, "Baffled by *Burn After Reading*," *Time*, August 31, 2008; Ross Douthat, "Burn before Watching," *National Review*, October 20, 2008; Philip French, "*Burn After Reading*," *Guardian*, October 18, 2008; Stuart Klawans, "Reviews: *Burn After Reading, Moving Midway*," *Nation*, September 17, 2008; Tim Kroenert, "Coens' Cynical Spy Spoof," *EurekaStreet.com*, October 23, 2008;

Emanuel Levy, "*Burn After Reading*: Shooting a Joel and Ethan Coen Wild Comedy," *Emanuel-Levy.com*, August 24, 2008; Ian Nathan, "*Burn After Reading*: Concoctions of Two Dangerous Minds," *EmpireOnline.com*; Andrew O'Hehir, "No Country for Human Beings," *Salon.com*, September 12, 2008; Nicolas Rapold, "*Burn after Reading*," *Sight & Sound*, 18.11 (2008); Sheila Roberts, "Brad Pitt & Cast Interview: *Burn After Reading*," *MoviesOnline.ca*; Sukhdev Sandhu, "Brad Pitt and George Clooney star in *Burn After Reading*: Review," *Telegraph*, October 17, 2008; Chris Tookey, "*Burn After Reading*: Pitt the Halfwit Steals the Show with the Greatest Ever Portrayal of Stupidity," *Daily Mail*, October 17, 2008; Peter Travers, "*Burn After Reading*," *Rolling Stone*, September 12, 2008; J. M. Tyree and Ben Walters, "League of Morons," *Sight & Sound*, 18.11 (2008); Susan Wloszczyna, "Feel the 'Burn' with the Coen Brothers," *USA Today*, September 12, 2008. See also CARTER BURWELL, GEORGE CLOONEY, JESS GONCHOR, NANCY HAIGH, RICHARD JENKINS, JOHN MALKOVICH, ELIZABETH MARVEL, FRANCES MCDORMAND, BRAD PITT, J. K. SIMMONS, TILDA SWINTON, MARY ZOPHRES.

BURNETT, T BONE (1948–)

Born Joseph Henry Burnett on January 14, 1948, in St. Louis Missouri, Burnett was raised in Fort Worth, Texas, where he spent his teen years in a juke joint where B.B. King and Junior Parker played the blues. At seventeen, he bought his own recording studio, and in 1965, he began making records. In 1975, Bob Dylan invited him to play guitar on his Rolling Thunder Revue tour, following which he, David Mansfield, and Steven Soles formed the Alpha Band. The group released three albums, at which point Burnett went solo, releasing *Truth Decay* (1980), *Trap Door EP* (1982), *Proof Through the Night* (1983), and *Behind the Trap Door EP* (1984). In 1986, he released an acoustic album, *T Bone Burnett*, and he

began producing albums, including Elvis Costello's *King of America* (1986), among others. In 1992, he released his album *The Criminal Under My Own Hat*, which would be his last album until 2006, when he released *The True False Identity*, which featured new, original songs from Burnett, and *Twenty-Twenty—The Essential T Bone Burnett*, a compilation of forty of his own songs from 1965 to 2006. In 2008, he released *Tooth of Crime*, an album inspired by his collaboration with playwright Sam Shepard.

Burnett worked with the Coen brothers on *O Brother, Where Art Thou?* (2001), *The Big Lebowski* (1998), *The Ladykillers* (2004), and *Inside Llewyn Davis* (2013), as well as on *Down from the Mountain* (2000), a documentary that featured the *O Brother* soundtrack and artists. Burnett also produced the documentary *Another Day, Another Time: Celebrating the Music of Inside Llewyn Davis* (2013), which included performances by Jack White, Joan Baez, Oscar Isaac, Patti Smith, and Marcus Mumford, among others. His television work includes the HBO series *True Detective* (2014), for which he served as executive music producer and composer, and the ABC series *Nashville* (2012), as executive music producer and co-composer for the first season. In 2012, he collaborated with John Mellencamp and Stephen King on the theatrical production *Ghost Brothers of Darkland County*. He was nominated for an Academy Award for Best Music, Original Song, with Elvis Costello, for the song "Scarlet Tide," from *Cold Mountain* (2004), and he won the Oscar for Best Achievement in Music Written for Motion Pictures, Original Song, for *Crazy Heart* (2009), which starred Jeff Bridges. He has won thirteen Grammy Awards, including Producer of the Year in 2002 and five Grammies for his work on *O Brother, Where Art Thou?*.

References

James Mottram, "T Bone Burnett: *Inside Llewyn Davis*? It's the Story of My Life," *Independent*, January 19, 2014; *TBoneBurnett.com*; "T Bone Burnett," *Biography.com*. See also *THE BIG LEBOWSKI, DOWN FROM THE MOUNTAIN, INSIDE LLEWYN DAVIS, THE LADYKILLERS, O BROTHER, WHERE ART THOU?*

BURWELL, CARTER (1955–)

Born November 18, 1955, Burwell took piano lessons as a child, though he did not enjoy them and abandoned the piano for a time. In high school, a friend introduced Burwell to improvised blues on the piano, an approach to music that suited him much better. He has stated that the creative aspect of music appeals to him, while playing music written by others does not. Burwell attended Harvard University, where he studied animation and electronic music while also studying at the MIT Media Lab. Following his graduation in 1977, he became a teaching assistant at the Harvard Electronic Music Studio. His 1979 animated film *Help, I'm Being Crushed to Death by a Black Rectangle* won first place at the Jacksonville Film Festival, and in the 1980s, Burwell played in a number of bands, including The Same, Thick Pigeon, and Radiante.

Burwell has taught film scoring at the Sundance Composer's Lab, the School of Sound (UK), Columbia University, and NYU, among others. He began working with the Coen brothers when a mutual acquaintance, Skip Lievsay, sound editor for *Blood Simple*, asked him if he had any interest in working on a film, and served as composer on all of their films through 2010: *Blood Simple* (1984), *Raising Arizona* (1987), *Miller's Crossing* (1990), *Barton Fink* (1991), *The Hudsucker Proxy* (1994), *Fargo* (1996), *The Big Lebowski* (1998), *O Brother, Where Art Thou?* (2000), *The Man Who Wasn't There* (2001), *Intolerable Cruelty* (2003), *The Ladykillers* (2004), *No Country for Old Men* (2007), *Burn After Reading* (2008), *A Serious Man* (2009), and *True Grit* (2010). Burwell, in characterizing his working relationship with the Coens, states that "We have an informal, maybe even slightly formal agreement, that we're going to work with each other until we die. . . . I'd be happy to do their films the rest of my life." Burwell did not, however, work with the Coens on *Inside Llewyn Davis* (2013).

References

CarterBurwell.com; Eddie Robson, *Coen Brothers* (London: Virgin Books, 2003). See also *BARTON FINK, THE BIG LEBOWSKI, BLOOD SIMPLE, BURN AFTER READING, FARGO, THE HUDSUCKER PROXY, INTOLERABLE CRUELTY, THE LADYKILLERS, THE MAN WHO WASN'T THERE, MILLER'S CROSSING, NO COUNTRY FOR OLD MEN, O BROTHER, WHERE ART THOU?, RAISING ARIZONA, A SERIOUS MAN, TRUE GRIT.*

BUSCEMI, STEVE (1957–)

Born December 13, 1957, in Brooklyn, New York, and raised in Long Island, Buscemi began his acting career in high school, when he auditioned for plays during his senior year. His first role was that of Baby John, the youngest member of the Jets, in *West Side Story*. He moved on to Nassau Community College, where he studied Liberal Arts but dropped out after one term and worked various jobs including at a gas station, in a restaurant, and driving an ice cream van. Having passed the civil service exam, Buscemi waited for his name to rise to the top of the list for a fire service position and in the interim, he returned to acting, attending the Lee Strasberg Institute. He took classes with John Strasberg and moved to the East Village, working odd jobs and going to casting calls and auditions. He began work with the New York Fire Department in Little Italy and did stand-up comedy at night, and in 1982, he formed a comedy partnership with Mark Boone Junior, who appeared in the television show *Sons of Anarchy* (2008–2013). In 1986, Buscemi starred in Bill Sherwood's *Parting Glances*, a film about AIDS, and in 1988, he worked with Jim Jarmusch on *Mystery Train*, shot in Memphis, an experience which influenced his own work as a director. In 1992, Quentin Tarantino cast Buscemi as Mr. Pink in *Reservoir Dogs*, his first high-profile role. His television work includes *L.A. Law* (1991), the television mini-series *Lonesome Dove* (1989), *30 Rock* (2007–2013), and the lead role in HBO's *Boardwalk Empire* (2010–2013). His first Coen film was *Miller's Crossing* (1990), which was followed by *Barton Fink* (1991), *The Hudsucker Proxy* (1994), *Fargo* (1996), and *The Big Lebowski* (1998). He also appeared in "Tuileries," the Coens' short that was part of the collection *Paris, je t'aime* (2006). He played Angelo in John Turturro's musical comedy, *Romance & Cigarettes* (2005). Best known for his work in independent film, Buscemi has also appeared in mainstream Hollywood films such as *Con Air* (1997), *Armageddon* (1998), *Mr. Deeds* (2002), and *Spy Kids 2* (2002) and *Spy Kids 3D* (2003).

Behind the camera, Buscemi first directed *Trees Lounge* (1996), and his work as director on the third season episode of *The Sopranos*, "Pine Barrens," earned him an Emmy nomination. He directed four episodes of the HBO series and appeared as Tony Soprano's cousin, Tony Blundetto, in the fifth season of the show. He has also directed episodes of *30 Rock*, *Nurse Jackie*, *Oz*, and *Homicide: Life on the Street*. In 2000, he directed *Animal Factory*, a prison drama with Willem Dafoe, and in 2005, he

directed Liv Tyler, Casey Affleck, and Kevin Corrigan in *Lonesome Jim*.

As the fast-talking Mink in *Miller's Crossing*, Buscemi appeared opposite Gabriel Byrne's Tom Reagan in only one scene, but his character plays an integral part in the complicated plot. Like Tom, Mink is playing all the angles, simultaneously allying himself with Caspar's henchman Eddie Dane and with Bernie Bernbaum (John Turturro), and these diverging associations culminate in the discovery of Mink's disfigured corpse in the woods of Miller's Crossing. The role, given to Buscemi because he could deliver the lines most quickly, was followed by another small part in *Barton Fink*, as the hotel clerk and shoe shine man, Chet. One reviewer has characterized Buscemi's technique as acting in italics.

In *The Hudsucker Proxy*, Buscemi appears briefly as the beatnik bartender at Ann's 440, the happening carrot juice bar in Greenwich Village where Amy Archer (Jennifer Jason Leigh) and Norville Barnes (Tim Robbins) celebrate New Year's Eve. Buscemi was cast in a more substantial role in the Coens' sixth film, *Fargo* (1996), as the chatty, turtleneck-clad kidnapper Carl Showalter. With his partner, Gaear Grimsrud (Peter Stormare), Carl is commissioned to kidnap the daughter of a wealthy businessman, Wade Gustafson (Harve Presnell); when the getaway turns violent and the body count climbs, Carl meets his end in one of the most iconic scenes in the Coen repertoire: at the hands of his co-conspirator, in a wood chipper. Joel and Ethan Coen state that they wrote the part of Carl specifically for Buscemi, with whom they had worked briefly on three previous occasions. *Fargo* earned praise from film critics, as did Buscemi, whose combined performance with Stormare was characterized as akin to Laurel and Hardy.

References

"Steve Buscemi," *Biography.com*; Barbara Cramer, "*Fargo*," *Films in Review*, 47.56 (1996); Nick Laird, "Steve Buscemi: 'I Hope People Remember the Shutdown in the Next Elections,'" *Guardian*, October 20, 2013; "Steve Buscemi," *New York Times*, Movies & TV; Eddie Robson, *Coen Brothers* (London: Virgin Books, 2003); Adrian Wootton, "Steve Buscemi: *The Guardian*/NFT Interview," *Guardian*, July 12, 2001. See also *BARTON FINK, THE BIG LEBOWSKI, FARGO, THE HUDSUCKER PROXY, MILLER'S CROSSING, PARIS, JE T'AIME*: "TUILERIES."

BYRNE, GABRIEL (1950–)

Born May 12, 1950, in Dublin, Ireland, Byrne trained for a period at seminary in England, prior to studying archeology at University College in Dublin. He expected exotic adventures in which he would discover lost cities; instead, he found "rain, mud and scraping things with little brushes and being shouted at and bumping into people in confined spaces and not finding the lost city." Abandoning his archeological aspirations, he taught Gaelic and Spanish for a time and then turned his attentions to acting. In his late twenties, Byrne appeared first on stage at the Abbey Theatre, followed by soap opera roles on Irish television, and then on film in John Boorman's *Excalibur* (1981). He relocated to England, where he worked with The Royal Court and National Theaters, and in the late 1980s, Byrne moved to the United States, where he appeared in such films as *Hello Again* (1987) and *Siesta* (1987). While he has worked steadily since the late 1980s, including the role of Tom Reagan in the Coen brothers' 1990 film, *Miller's Crossing*, Byrne is not typically characterized as a leading man in Hollywood. His best-known works include *The Usual Suspects* (1995), *The Man in the Iron Mask* (1998), and the

HBO television series *In Treatment* (2008–2011), for which he was twice nominated for the Emmy for Outstanding Lead Actor in a Drama series and won a Golden Globe award. In 2000, Byrne played the lead in the Broadway production of *Moon for the Misbegotten*, receiving a Tony nomination for his role. His additional television appearances include *Madigan Men* (2000), *Secret State* (2012), and *Vikings* (2013).

While Marcia Gay Harden used 1930s gangster films like *The Public Enemy* (1931) to create her character of Verna Bernbaum, Byrne found that Humphrey Bogart, James Cagney, and Paul Muni had little to offer him by way of inspiration for the character of Tom, "the man who walks behind the man, and whispers in his ear." Instead, he watched chess players at a cafe in SoHo and contemplated the man who accompanies the pope, about whom "you know nothing . . . and yet he's the one who knows to the last cent what the Vatican is worth." He did not study gangsters and tough men but rather men who silently manipulate situations. While Leo and his associates were intended to have Irish heritage, the Irish accent was not part of the Coens' plan for *Miller's Crossing*. When Byrne read the script, however, he suggested that the dialogue's rhythm and style were Irish and asked to read his lines with his own accent. The accent met the approval of the Coens, and Albert Finney then took on the accent as well.

The *Guardian* describes Byrne's Tom Reagan as "a surprisingly subtle portrait of a man who wants to be king," and Byrne describes Tom, the calculating "smart guy" mob lieutenant, as a loner, a manipulator whose downfall occurs because "he naively believes that he can control everything around him, when in fact, that is not possible on any level." Undeterred by this lack of control, however, Tom manages the people and events of the film, playing rival organizations against each other, doing what he has to do to protect mob boss Leo. What he has to do, specifically, is to betray his friend and employer Leo by sleeping with his girlfriend, Verna, join forces with the enemy, Johnny Caspar, and ultimately kill Bernie Bernbaum, the only violent act Tom performs in the film. While the gangsters around him do not hesitate to shed blood at a moment's notice, often with relish, Tom maintains his position as the man of reason, the man behind the man, ultimately, though sometimes secretly, loyal to Leo. John Turturro, who plays Bernie in the film, comments that *Miller's Crossing* is about one man's journey, "a person who loses his soul," and in addition to his soul, Tom loses his friend, his job, and the girl in the process, in a performance that *Rolling Stone* characterized as "a tough, sorrowful performance of rare distinction."

References

Nancy Bilyeau, "The Quiet Fire of Gabriel Byrne," *Rolling Stone*, November 1, 1990; "Gabriel Byrne," *Biography.com*; Jean-Pierre Coursodon, "A Hat Blown by the Wind," in *Joel & Ethan Coen: Blood Siblings*, ed. Paul A. Woods (London: Plexus Publishing, 2003); Derek Malcolm, "*Miller's Crossing*," *Guardian*, February 14, 1991; DVD Special Features, *Miller's Crossing*, 20th Century Fox Home Entertainment, 2003; Alex Simon, "Gabriel Byrne: Talk to Me," *TheHollywoodInterview.com*, December 28, 2012; Peter Travers, "*Miller's Crossing*," *Rolling Stone*, September 22, 1990. See also *MILLER'S CROSSING*.

CAGE, NICOLAS (1964–)

Cage was born Nicolas Coppola on January 7, 1964, in Long Beach, California, the son of choreographer Joy Fogelsang and literature professor August Coppola, and nephew of director Francis Ford Coppola. He became inspired to act when he saw James Dean in *Rebel Without a Cause* (1955) and *East of Eden* (1955), and following a summer class at the American Conservatory Theatre in San Francisco, he dropped out of high school at age 15 to pursue an acting career. He changed his name to Nicolas Cage to distance himself from his director uncle, selecting "Cage" from the comic book character Luke Cage.

Cage first appeared on-screen in the television movie *Best of Times* (1981) and his film debut was in Amy Heckerling's *Fast Times at Ridgemont High* (1982). In the mid-1980s, he appeared in such films as *Valley Girl* (1983), Coppola's *Rumble Fish* (1983) and *The Cotton Club* (1984), and *Peggy Sue Got Married* (1986). He worked with Cher in *Moonstruck* (1987), for which he received a Golden Globe nomination; with Laura Dern in David Lynch's *Wild at Heart* (1990); and with James Caan and Sarah Jessica Parker in *Honeymoon in Vegas* (1992), again earning a Golden Globe nomination for his performance. In 1995, Cage costarred with Elizabeth Shue in Mike Figgis's *Leaving Las Vegas*, for which he won the Oscar for Best Actor in a Leading Role

and the Golden Globe for Best Performance by an Actor in a Motion Picture—Drama.

Following his Academy Award, Cage appeared in a series of action films, which included *The Rock* (1996), *Con Air* (1997), *Face/Off* (1997), as well as the crime thriller *Snake Eyes* (1998) and Martin Scorsese's *Bringing Out the Dead* (1999). Cage worked with Spike Jonze in *Adaptation* (2002), with Ridley Scott in *Matchstick Men* (2003), with Oliver Stone in *World Trade Center* (2006), and with Werner Herzog in *The Bad Lieutenant: Port of Call—New Orleans* (2009). He has lent his voice to the animated films *Christmas Carol: The Movie* (2001), *The Ant Bully* (2006), *G-Force* (2009), *Astro Boy* (2009), and *The Croods* (2013).

Cage turned to producing in 2000, with *Shadow of the Vampire*, followed by *The Life of David Gale* (2003), *The Wicker Man* (2006), and *The Sorcerer's Apprentice* (2010), among others. In 2002, Cage both produced and directed his first film, *Sonny*, starring James Franco, and in 2007–2008, he served as executive producer for the NBC mini-series *The Dresden Files*.

Cage appeared in one film by Joel and Ethan Coen, *Raising Arizona* (1987). Upon reading the film's script, Cage enthused "the script was incredible, one of the best I'd ever read," adding, "I loved Hi, he has a rhythm all his own." The Coens, however, were initially reluctant to cast Cage, as his films to that point had been urban, and *Raising Arizona* was clearly a rural film. Cage persisted, was allowed to test for the part, and was cast. When filming began, Cage's enthusiasm manifested itself in a desire to make suggestions regarding the project and his character, but the Coen brothers, having fully conceptualized the film prior to production, preferred to shoot Cage's scenes as planned. The result was some tension on the set, though all parties remained civil. For the role, Cage adopted a Woody Woodpecker hairdo and sported a "Hudsucker Industries" patch on his work uniform at the sheet metal factory. Cage's performance was well received for the most part, and reviews often focused on the intentionally cartoonish aspects of his character. Rita Kempley of the *Washington Post* wrote, "He's got that blank look that Wile E. Coyote gets after he's been hit between the eyes with an anvil," and the *New Yorker*'s Pauline Kael commented that "Cage has sometimes been expected to carry roles that he wasn't ready for, but his youth works for him here. He's a lowlife caricature of a romantic hero, trying to do the right thing by everybody."

References

"Nicolas Cage," *Biography.com*; Ben Child, "Nicolas Cage at SXSW 2014: 'It Really Sucks Being Famous Right Now,'" *Guardian*, March 11, 2014; Pauline Kael, "Manypeeplia Upsidownia," *New Yorker*, April 20, 1987; Rita Kempley, "*Raising Arizona*," *Washington Post*, March 20, 1987; Eddie Robson, *Coen Brothers* (London: Virgin Books, 2003). See also *RAISING ARIZONA*.

CAMPBELL, BRUCE (1958–)

Born June 22, 1958, in Royal Oak, Michigan, Campbell, along with friends Sam Raimi and Rob Tapert, raised $350,000 to fund the film *The Evil Dead* (1981), directed by Raimi and starring Campbell. He appeared in the sequels *Evil Dead II* (1987) and *Army of Darkness* (1992), as well

as *Crimewave* (1985), which Joel and Ethan Coen cowrote with Raimi, and all three of Raimi's *Spider-Man* films (2002, 2004, 2007). He played the title role in the television series *The Adventures of Brisco County, Jr.* (1993–1994) and had recurring roles in the series *Lois & Clark: The New Adventures of Superman* (1995), *Ellen* (1996–1997), and *Xena: Warrior Princess* (1996–1999) and *Hercules: The Legendary Journeys* (1995–1999), both of which were executive produced by Sam Raimi. He played Sam Axe in the USA Network television series *Burn Notice* (2007–2013) and lent his voice to such animated projects as *The Ant Bully* (2006), *The Replacements* (2006–2009), *Cloudy with a Chance of Meatballs* (2009), and *Cars 2* (2011).

Campbell's production credits include all three Raimi *Evil Dead* films, the 2013 remake of *The Evil Dead*, directed by Fede Alvarez and produced as well by Sam Raimi, and *Crimewave*. He co-executive produced and starred in the television series *Jack of All Trades* (2000). His directorial credits include episodes of *Hercules* and *Xena* and the film *My Name is Bruce* (2007), in which B-Movie star Bruce Campbell is mistaken for his character, Ash, from *The Evil Dead*.

Campbell appeared as Smitty in *The Hudsucker Proxy* (1994) and in uncredited roles in *Intolerable Cruelty* (2003) and *The Ladykillers* (2004).

References

"Bruce Campbell," *Filmbug.com*. See also *THE HUDSUCKER PROXY*, SAM RAIMI.

CASELLA, MAX (1967–)

Born June 6, 1967, in Washington, D.C., as Max Deitch, Casella was raised in Massachusetts and developed an interest in acting when he was cast as Tiny Tim in a community theatre production of *A Christmas Carol*. His first professional acting role was in a Boston-area production of *Cyrano de Bergerac* in 1981, and following high school, he moved to New York, where he attended the American Academy of Dramatic Arts. At age twenty, he participated in a summer theatre workshop at the London Academy, and upon return to the United States, his initial on-screen appearances were television roles, including the series *The Equalizer* (1988) and *Kate and Allie* (1989) and the television movie *Maverick Square* (1990). His early film roles include *Newsies* (1992), *Ed Wood* (1994), and *Sgt. Bilko* (1996), and his Broadway debut was playing the warthog Timon in the original Broadway production of *The Lion King* (1997). He would appear again on Broadway in *The Music Man* (2000) and off-Broadway in *Svejk* (2004), *Souls of Naples* (2005), and *Timon of Athens* (2011).

Casella is best known for his depictions of Vinnie Delpino on the television series *Doogie Howser, MD* (1989–1993) and Benny Fazio on HBO's *The Sopranos* (2001–2007), with James Gandolfini. He worked with Coen collaborator George Clooney in *Leatherheads* (2008), with Steve Buscemi in HBO's *Boardwalk Empire* (2010), and with Sam Mendes in *Revolutionary Road* (2008). He appeared in Woody Allen's *Blue Jasmine* (2013) and with Allen in *Fading Gigolo* (2013), directed by Coen regular John Turturro. Casella has lent his voice to a number of animated works, including television's *Hey Arnold!* (1996) and *The Legend of Tarzan* (2001), the film *The Little Mermaid 2: Return to the Sea* (2000), and the video game *Jak and Daxter: The Precursor Legacy* (2001).

Casella was cast as Pappi Corsicato, proprietor of the Gaslight Café in the Coens' folk music film *Inside Llewyn Davis* (2013). Casella's character was based on Sam Hood, who owned the Gaslight Café in Greenwich Village in the early 1960s, and Mike Porco, who owned Gerde's Folk City, where a *New York Times* reporter discovered Bob Dylan in October of 1961. Pappi allows folk musicians to play for tips at the coffee house/bar on the weekends, as did Hood and Porco, though Corsicato boasts of exchanging sex with female performers, such as Jean Berkey, played by Carey Mulligan, for the opportunity to take the stage.

References

"Max Casella," *BroadwayWorld.com*; "Max Casella," *TCM.com*; "Babita Persaud, "A Few Moments with Max Casella," *Orlando Sentinel*, June 28 1992. See also *INSIDE LLEWYN DAVIS*.

CEDRIC THE ENTERTAINER

Born Cedric Antonio Kyles on April 24, 1964, in Jefferson City, Missouri, Cedric attended Southeast Missouri State University, earning a degree in communications. Following graduation, he worked in the insurance business while appearing in comedy competitions in St. Louis. In addition to his comedy routine, Cedric recited poetry and sang onstage, and when he encouraged a comedy show host to introduce him as an entertainer rather than a comedian, his stage name, Cedric the Entertainer, was coined. In 1992, he appeared on the television comedy program *It's Showtime at the Apollo* and the BET's *Comicview*, which he followed with *Def Comedy Jam* in 1995. In 1994, he received BET's Richard Pryor Comic of the Year Award, and in 1998, he appeared in the film *Ride*. He was a regular on *The Steve Harvey Show* (1996–2002), and his subsequent films include *Big Momma's House* (2000), *Barbershop* (2002) and *Barbershop 2: Back in Business* (2004), *Lemony Snicket's A Series of Unfortunate Events* (2004), and *Cadillac Records* (2008). He appeared in the Spike Lee documentary *The Original Kings of Comedy* (2000), with Steve Harvey, D. L. Hughley, and Bernie Mac.

Cedric has lent his voice to such animated features as *Ice Age* (2002), *Madagascar* (2005), *Madagascar: Escape 2 Africa* (2008), *Madagascar 3: Europe's Most Wanted* (2012), *Planes* (2013), and to the television series *The Proud Family* (2001–2005) and *The Boondocks* (2007). He worked with Don Cheadle and Chiwetel Ejiofor in *Talk to Me* (2007), with Forest Whitaker and Keanu Reeves in *Street Kings* (2008), and with Tom Hanks and Julia Roberts in *Larry Crowne* (2011). His producing credits include, among others, the television series *Cedric the Entertainer Presents* (2002–2003), *The Honeymooners* (2005), based on the 1950s television series and in which he starred as Ralph Kramden, *Dance Fu* (2011), his directorial debut, in which he also appeared, and the TV Land series *Soul Man* (2012–2014), which he created and in which he played the lead role of Reverend Boyce "The Voice" Ballentine.

Cedric the Entertainer appeared in the Coen brothers' *Intolerable Cruelty* (2003), with Catherine Zeta-Jones and George Clooney. He played Gus Petch, a private detective and videographer who specializes in surprising unfaithful spouses in compromising positions. A free agent, Petch alternately works for Marilyn Rexroth (Zeta-Jones), who seeks to entrap her philandering husband, and Miles Massey (Clooney), who seeks evidence with which to incriminate Marilyn. The *New York Times* characterized Cedric's performance as one in which he "delivers the crassest lines with what can only be called hammy understatement; his years of stand-up have taught him that less is all."

References

"Cedric the Entertainer," *Biography.com*; Elvis Mitchell, "Film Review: A Lawyer's Good Teeth Help in Court and Love," *New York Times*, October 10, 2003. See also *INTOLERABLE CRUELTY*.

CHENOWITH, ELLEN

Ellen Chenowith's career had its genesis at New York's Actors Studio, where she worked as an office manager in the 1970s. There she observed Lee Strasberg and Elia Kazan and the actors with whom they worked, her initial exposure to the behind-the-scenes work that contributes to a production. She first worked in casting when she assisted Mike Fenton, casting director for the made-for-television film *City in Fear* (1980); she recommended then-unknown Mickey Rourke, whom she had met at the Actors Studio. Chenowith set up an office in Los Angeles and subsequently cast Barry Levinson's *Diner* (1982) and went on to work again with Levinson on *The Natural* (1984), *Avalon* (1990), *Bugsy* (1991), and *Toys* (1992), among others. Chenowith used her knowledge of the New York theatre scene to assist her as she worked, casting theatre actors such as Kevin Bacon, Annette Benning, Bill Pullman, and Ellen Barkin in their break-through Hollywood roles. She has worked on several projects with George Clooney, including his directorial debut *Confessions of a Dangerous Mind* (2002) and his follow-up films *Good Night and Good Luck* (2005), *Leatherheads* (2008), *The Ides of March* (2011), and *The Monuments Men* (2014). In addition to her frequent work with Barry Levinson and Joel and Ethan Coen, she has regularly cast the films of directors Clint Eastwood and Tony Gilroy.

Chenowith began casting Coen films with *O Brother, Where Art Thou?* (2000), following which she also cast *The Man Who Wasn't There* (2001), *Intolerable Cruelty* (2003), *The Ladykillers* (2004), *No Country for Old Men* (2007), *Burn After Reading* (2008), *A Serious Man* (2009), *True Grit* (2010), and *Inside Llewyn Davis* (2013).

References

Scott Macaulay, "How to Cast a Coen Brothers' Film," *FocusFeatures.com*, *A Serious Man*,

October 23, 2009; Robert Simonson, "The Other Chenoweth: Casting Director Gives Stage Actors Their Film Careers," *Playbill.com*, September 21, 2009.

CLOONEY, GEORGE (1961–)

Clooney was born May 6, 1961, in Lexington, Kentucky, to a family of entertainers which includes his father, Nick Clooney, newsman and talk show host, and his aunt Rosemary Clooney, singer and actor. As a child, George Clooney appeared on his father's local talk show, and he later followed his father into broadcast journalism, which he studied at Northern Kentucky University. Dropping out of college, Clooney worked as a shoe salesman and a farmhand until his cousin Miguel Ferrer and his uncle, Oscar winner Jose Ferrer, offered him work as an extra in a film in Kentucky. The film was never released, but the experience prompted Clooney to move to Los Angeles to pursue an acting career, where he worked as a chauffeur for his aunt while looking for acting jobs. His first recurring role was on the television show *Facts of Life* (1985–1987), which he followed with *Roseanne* (1988–1991) and *Bodies of Evidence* (1992). He appeared in the film *Return of the Killer Tomatoes* (1988), and in 1994, Clooney was cast in the television hospital drama *ER*, the role that launched him into the public eye and a movie career. While still with *ER*, he appeared in Robert Rodriguez's *From Dusk to Dawn* (1996), played Batman in *Batman & Robin* (1997), and starred with Jennifer Lopez in Steven Soderbergh's *Out of Sight* (1998). Clooney left *ER* in 1999 and subsequently appeared in *Three Kings* (1999) and the Coens' *O Brother, Where Art Thou?* (2000).

Clooney played the title role of Danny Ocean in the *Ocean's Twelve* franchise that began in 2001, Soderbergh's remake of the 1960 Frank Sinatra, Dean Martin, Sammy Davis Jr. film. Clooney also appeared in both *Ocean* sequels; all three films featured an ensemble cast including Brad Pitt, Julia Roberts, Don Cheadle, and Matt Damon, among others. In 2004, Clooney produced and starred in *Syriana*, for which he received the Oscar for Best Supporting Actor. He cowrote, directed, and appeared in *Good Night and Good Luck* (2005), earning Academy Award nominations for director and screenplay, and in 2013, he produced *Argo*, which won the Oscar for Best Picture. He received Golden Globe awards for his roles in *O Brother, Syriana,* and *The Descendants* (2011). Simultaneous to these successes, Clooney became politically active in a visible way, opposing the Iraq War and raising funds after the September 11, 2001, attacks and Hurricane Katrina. Clooney travelled to Sudan in 2006 with his father to document the Darfur crisis, and upon his return to the United States, Clooney spoke in Washington, D.C., and at the UN regarding genocide in Darfur and coordinated fundraisers to support the cause. He shared a Peace Summit Award with Don Cheadle in 2007 and in 2008 was appointed a UN peace envoy.

In 1999, Clooney and Steven Soderbergh formed the production company Section Eight, which would produce Clooney's directorial debut, *Confessions of a Dangerous Mind* (2002) and such Clooney vehicles as *Ocean's Eleven, Twelve,* and *Thirteen, Good Night and Good Luck, Syriana,* and *Michael Clayton* (2007); the partnership dissolved in 2006. That same year, Clooney formed the production company Smoke House, with partner Grant Heslov; their debut film was *Leatherheads* (2008), followed by *The Men Who Stare at Goats* (2009), *The American* (2010), and *The Ides of March* (2011), all of which starred Clooney. Smoke House produced the Oscar-winning *Argo* (2012), *August: Osage County* (2013), and *The Monuments Men* (2014). Clooney's directorial credits also include *Good Night and Good*

Luck, Leatherheads, The Ides of March, and *The Monuments Men.*

Clooney's first Coen film was *O Brother, Where Art Thou?* (2000). According to Clooney, the Coens wrote the part of Everett McGill in *O Brother*, with him in mind, and when they offered it to him, they described Everett as "one of the dumbest guys you'll ever meet, and we thought you'd be perfect." He said yes "without even reading the first page." His performance as the smooth-talking con man was often compared to that of studio-era star Clark Gable, an "elusive, highly mannered performance that appears to belong . . . to a vanished era," notes the *New York Times'* A. O. Scott, who concludes that "We never forget that, whatever else the script may demand, we're watching a movie star." For his part, Clooney deems Everett the first role of his "idiot trilogy."

In his second Coen film, *Intolerable Cruelty* (2003), Clooney plays Miles Massey, divorce attorney extraordinaire who matches wits with Catherine Zeta-Jones as Marilyn Rexroth. Initially representing Marilyn's first husband, Rex, in their divorce, he subsequently crafts the "Massey prenup" for Marilyn's second marriage and becomes the groom in her third. As the self-absorbed, fast-talking Massey, Clooney preens before any available reflective surface, compulsively checks his teeth, and, writes *Rolling Stone*'s Peter Travers, "isn't afraid to look goofy." While Clooney often elicits comparisons to classic Hollywood leading men, including Gary Cooper and Cary Grant, reviewers compared his Massey to the Coens' Freddy Riedenschneider in *The Man Who Wasn't There* (2001) and Billy Flynn in *Chicago* (2002). Ethan Coen, however, claims that Clooney considered Massey a descendant of Ulysses Everett McGill, Clooney's character in *O Brother, Where Art Thou?*.

Rounding out Clooney's trilogy of Coen films is his performance as Harry Pfarrer, U.S. marshal, retired, in *Burn After Reading* (2008). Once again, his character was compared to that of Everett McGill, from *O Brother*, though the *New York Times* characterized Pfarrer as "a much more dangerous and darker character." Pfarrer romances his way through the film, with Tilda Swinton's Katie, Frances McDormand's Linda, and, incidentally, with his wife Sandy (Elizabeth Marvel). Unlike most of the characters in the film, Clooney's Pfarrer survives, though he flees to Venezuela, pursued by his guilty conscience and paranoia.

References

"George Clooney," *Biography.com;* Peter Bradshaw, "*Intolerable Cruelty*," *Guardian*, October 24, 2003; Roderick Conway Morris, "Film Reviews: *Burn After Reading* and *Jerichow*," *New York Times*, August 28, 2008; A. O. Scott, "*O Brother, Where Art Thou?* Film Review: Hail, Ulysses, Escaped Convict," *New York Times*, December 22, 2000; Gary Susman, "*O Brother* Is Classic Coen Brothers," *Boston Phoenix*, December 28, 2000; Peter Travers, "*Intolerable Cruelty*," *Rolling Stone*, October 9, 2003; Ben Walters, "Bringing Up Alimony," *Sight & Sound*, BFI.org. See also *BURN AFTER READING, INTOLERABLE CRUELTY, O BROTHER, WHERE ART THOU?*

COBB, RANDALL "TEX" (1950–)

Born May 7, 1950, in Bridge City, Texas, Cobb attended Abilene Christian College, where he played football. Cobb became a heavyweight boxer, with a record of forty-three wins, seven losses, and one draw; his most famous bout was against heavyweight champion Larry Holmes in 1982, a brutally uneven fight, which he lost in fifteen rounds, and following which Howard Cosell vowed to never call another fight, a vow he kept. In 1993, *Sports Illustrated* published an article stating that Cobb, with opponent Sonny Barch, arranged to fix a fight in which Cobb beat Barch, following which they took cocaine together. In 1999, a jury ordered Time, Inc. to pay Cobb $10.7 million for libel; the decision was reversed on appeal in 2002.

In addition to his time as a boxer, Cobb has been a songwriter and an actor, appearing first in *The Champ* (1979), which he followed with a small role in *Uncommon Valor* (1983) and a number of made-for-television movies and television series. His subsequent film roles include *The Golden Child* (1986), with Eddie Murphy, *Fletch Lives* (1989), with Chevy Chase, and *Ace Ventura: Pet Detective* (1994) and *Liar Liar* (1997), with Jim Carrey. He had a recurring role in the series *In the Heat of the Night* (1990–1991) and appeared in the series finale of *Walker, Texas Ranger* (1998–2001). In 2008, at the age of 54, Cobb graduated with honors from Temple University with a degree in Sport and Recreation Management, a degree he earned while working construction.

Cobb additionally appeared in Joel and Ethan Coen's second film, *Raising Arizona* (1987), as Leonard Smalls/The Lone Biker of the Apocalypse, a leather-clad disheveled giant of a man who rides a motorcycle through the dreams of H.I. McDunnough (Nicolas Cage), a harbinger of doom. Of the role, Cobb states that playing the biker who threw grenades at rabbits was "a real stretch," adding, "I don't think I was anybody's hero for picking up a tiny baby and setting him on a full road." In its review of the film, *Variety* deemed Smalls "a weak and unfocused creation with Cobb's performance lacking the teeth to make the character stick." In their own comments on Cobb, the Coens have noted that he was difficult to work with and that they had no plans to cast Cobb again anytime soon.

References

"Randall 'Tex' Cobb," *BoxRec.com*; "Jury Awards 'Tex' Cobb $10.7M," *CBS.com*, June 11, 1999; Richard Hoffer, "Concussions and Songs: Tex Cobb Lives in Nashville and Dabbles in Music Arena," *Los Angeles Times*, March 12, 1989; Phil Sheridan, "Pugilist, Thespian—Now a Scholar Boxer Tex Cobb Was Schooled in the KO. Temple Trained Him to Get His B.S.," *Philly.com*, January 26, 2008; John Spong, "Randall 'Tex' Cobb: His Life after Boxing Hasn't Been Easy, But Don't Count Him Out Yet," *Texas Monthly*, September, 2001; "*Raising Arizona*: Review from *Variety*," in *Joel & Ethan Coen: Blood Siblings*, ed. Paul A. Woods (London: Plexus Publishing, 2003). See also *RAISING ARIZONA*.

COEN, JOEL (1954–) AND ETHAN (1957–)

Joel Daniel Coen was born November 29, 1954, in St. Louis Park, a suburb of Minneapolis, Minnesota, to Edward and Rena Coen. Raised in England, Ed attended the London School of Economics and later became a professor of economics at the University of Minnesota; Rena was a professor of fine arts at St. Cloud State University. Ethan Jesse Coen was born September 21, 1957; their older sister, Deborah, became a doctor. Of their upbringing, the brothers have stated that while both of their parents were orthodox Jews, their mother was the strict one. "She toed the line in terms of party dogma," recalls Joel. "My father, Ed, just went along for the ride. We were shocked to learn he ate Welsh rarebit at the Campus Club. I thought, 'Welsh rarebit—that's made with bacon, isn't it?'" The brothers have commented that their parents "were very polite about our movies," says Joel. "They were pleased that we did well in the movie business," adds Ethan. "That's very nice. Good job," says Joel.

Joel Coen (left) and Ethan Coen on the set of *Blood Simple* (1984)

The brothers were raised on Dean Jones Disney movies, Tarzan movies, Jerry Lewis, Doris Day, Tony Curtis, and Bob Hope comedies, influences that would manifest themselves in Coen films in decades to come. Ethan began writing in elementary school, where he composed a play about King Arthur, and jointly, the brothers published a newspaper, the *Flag Street Sentinel*, which sold for two cents a copy and lasted only two issues. In the mid-1960s, a friend, Ron Neter, suggested they mow lawns to raise money, with which they could buy a camera. They did so, purchasing a Vivitar Super 8 and proceeding to make their first films. Another friend, Mark Zimering, "Ziemers" acted in the films, with Ethan playing the female roles, in his sister's tutu. These early projects included *Zeimers in Zambezi* (c. 1970), inspired by Cornel Wilde's *The Naked Prey* (1966), *Ed . . . A Dog*, their version of *Lassie Come Home* (1943), and *The Banana Film* in which Zeimers plays a vagrant who excels in sniffing out bananas. Of these films, Joel recalls,

"we didn't really understand the most basic concepts of filmmaking—we didn't know that you could physically edit film—so we'd run around with the camera, editing it all in the camera. We'd actually have parallel editing for chase scenes. We'd shoot in one place, then run over to the other and shoot that, then run back and shoot at the first spot again." The brothers wrote scripts for the films, including one titled *Coast to Coast*, which Joel maintains they never filmed. Ethan describes the film as having "twenty-eight Einsteins in it," as "the Red Chinese were cloning Albert Einstein."

In high school, they joined the Eight and a Half Club, a film society led by teacher Pete Peterson, where they viewed for the first time Francois Truffaut's *The 400 Blows* (1959). Both brothers attended Simon's Rock of Bard College in Great Barrington, Massachusetts, following which Joel went on to study film at New York University, which he claims he chose "because it had a late application deadline—I missed all the others." He adds, "I was a cipher there; I sat in the back of the room with an insane grin on my face." His college thesis, a thirty-minute film titled *Soundings*, was about a woman who has sex with her deaf boyfriend while fantasizing aloud about his neighbor. In 1979, Joel briefly attended graduate school, studying film at the University of Texas at Austin, as he had married a woman who was in the graduate program in Linguistics there. However, the marriage ended and Joel quit school after one semester, returning to New York.

Following Bard College, Ethan attended Princeton where he majored in Philosophy, because, he claims, he was uncertain what to do with his life. At one point, he dropped out of school, only to reapply to the University. He missed the application deadline, however, and his subsequent excuse for the tardiness was a doctor's note from a surgeon at "Our Lady of the Eye, Ear, Nose, and Throat," which stated that his arm had been blown off in a hunting accident; he was readmitted, but not until he had seen the college psychiatrist. During this time, Ethan married, though briefly, and wrote his senior thesis, "Two Views of Wittgenstein's Later Philosophy." Having graduated from Princeton in 1979, he moved to Manhattan, where he lived with Joel and the two began writing scripts.

Returning from Texas to New York, Joel began working in the film industry, first as assistant editor on Frank LaLoggia's *Fear No Evil* (1981), and around this time as well, he was fired from his editing position on the film *Nightmare* (1981). He then worked as assistant film editor on Sam Raimi's *The Evil Dead* (1981). The Coens were inspired by Raimi's approach to funding the film, in which he, Bruce Campbell, and Robert Tappert approached professionals in the Detroit area, previewing twenty minutes of film footage and asking each potential donor for a $5,000 invest-ment in their first film. They raised almost $400,000, and Joel and Ethan determined to fund their own film in such a manner. The film, *Blood Simple*, was written by the brothers, taking its title from a line in Dashiell Hammett's novel *Red Harvest*. The novel's protagonist, a detective, states "If I don't get away soon I'll be going blood-simple like the natives," referring to the psychological effects that manifest themselves in a murderer after the crime is committed. The brothers filmed a two-minute trailer and shopped it to Minneapolis professionals to raise money for production. Joel recalls that they screened the clip "at the Suburban World . . . a great name for a beautiful theatre with constellation lights, all really old-school." They raised $750,000 from wealthy donors in St. Louis Park and $550,000 from smaller donors, including their parents, Ed and Rena Coen, which they then used to shoot the picture in and around Austin, Texas. Joel explains their choice of location: "during the nine months or a year that I spent in Austin, I met a number of people who were connected with the film industry, and that led to the shooting of *Blood Simple*."

Following the filming of *Blood Simple*, Joel Coen married Frances McDormand, who played Abby in the film, and in 1987, the brothers would release their second film, *Raising Arizona*. The Coens passed on the opportunity to direct *Batman* for Warner Brothers, opting instead to write *Miller's Crossing* and *Barton Fink* (1991). Following the 1990 release of *Miller's Crossing*, Ethan Coen married Tricia Cooke, who worked in the editing department on Coen films from *Miller's Crossing* to *The Man Who Wasn't There*. They have two children, a daughter, Dusty, and a son, Buster. In 1996, Joel Coen and Frances McDormand adopted their son Pedro from Paraguay.

Barry Sonnenfeld referred to the brothers as "a two-man ecosystem," and reviewers often call them the "two-headed director," comments that indicate the means by which the two men create their films. The entire process is collaborative, beginning with the conceptualization and writing of the script, which they close themselves in their New York office and hash out, pacing and smoking as they talk. On set, the filmmakers communicate almost telepathically, with just a word or two in lieu of an entire conversation. When they talk in interviews, they complete each other's sentences, and their vision for their films is as unified as their communication. J. Todd Anderson, storyboard artist for the Coens, has stated that when he approaches the directors separately with the same question, more often than not he'll receive the same answer from each man. Joel and Ethan developed these habits in writing, directing, and editing early in their career, and their process remains quite similar three decades later.

As their list of completed pictures has grown, the brothers have gathered around them a cadre of crew and actors who continue to work with them from film to film: Roger Deakins, cinematographer; Mary Zophres, costume designer; Dennis Gassner, production designer; and Ellen Chenowith, casting director, among others, appear in the credits of many Coen films. Deakins has appeared so often that *Empire* christened him "a third Coen brother." The continuity and effectiveness of the group effort has not escaped the attention of the awards circuit, as the crew often amass nominations at a rate nearly equaling that of the actors and the filmmakers themselves. Regarding these individuals who return to work with the Coens time and again, Joel Coen has stated "These are people who are so good at what they do. They're up for anything on our movies. We've been lucky enough to assemble a team of the best people working in these areas."

In front of the camera, Frances McDormand, John Goodman, John Turturro, Steve Buscemi, George Clooney, Jon Polito, and Harry Bugin, among others, have appeared in parts ranging from cameos to lead roles, and while the filmmakers will cast newcomers such as Michael Stuhlbarg, Hailey Steinfeld, and Oscar Isaac in their projects, regular viewers of Coen films will not be surprised to see the return of Holly Hunter or J. K. Simmons to another picture by Joel and Ethan. Both new and returning actors praise the filmmakers, from their abilities as writers to the way in which they conduct their shoots. Marcia Gay Harden, who played Verna in *Miller's Crossing* (1990), comments, "They're not dictated to by studios about needing to hire this actor because they're going to bring in this much money and put this many butts in the seats," a practice which allows the brothers to not only make casting decisions free from studio pressure but also to write characters with specific actors in mind, an approach they often utilize.

The Coens fully conceptualize their films prior to filming, including a finished, polished script and detailed storyboards for each shot, which results in shorter shooting days, celebrated by Brad Pitt and Carey Mulligan, as well as a pleasant working environment, described by John Malkovich as a "very calm set, a fun set." John Turturro characterizes the process as "very low stress," adding, "If I could make a movie with them every couple of years I would, just because of the pleasure of it." Holly Hunter attributes the atmosphere on set to the fact that "Joel and Ethan function without their egos. . . . Or maybe their egos are so big they're completely secure with anybody who disagrees with them." Examples of this statement might be Nicolas Cage, Woody Harrelson, and Javier Bardem, who all attempted to contribute to the development of their characters and the script while filming with Joel and Ethan Coen, only to be politely declined. The brothers are so certain about their scripts prior to production that the lines require no rewriting during shooting, which can be unusual in the film industry. Tilda Swinton declared the script for *Burn After Reading* (2008) to be "so rock solid, mean machine," and of the same film, Malkovich describes the script as being so clear that it's "almost like it's scored." Richard Jenkins, who appeared in *Burn After Reading* and *The Man Who Wasn't There* (2001), characterized the process as one in which the filmmakers "give an actor responsibility; they know what they want, but they also want you to bring something to the role," and *A Serious Man*'s (2009) Fred Melamed concurs, as "Very often, your ideas about a character are your own inventions, and they may not necessarily derive from the intention of the writer. But the Coens write very fully realized characters, while also giving you room for invention."

The characters created by Joel and Ethan Coen invite comment from viewers and critics alike, who vacillate between the cult adoration afforded *The Big Lebowski*'s Dude, Walter, and Jesus and indignation at the ways in which the writer/filmmakers depict and subsequently treat their characters such as Larry Gopnik, Llewyn Davis, Jerry Lundegaard, and Barton Fink, among others. Ella Taylor of the *Village Voice* suggests that "just about every character the Coens create is meant to affirm their own superiority," an assessment seconded by Kent Jones, who quips, "Do they like the people they create? . . . Yes, in the same way that a hunter likes his trophies." The filmmakers address this oft-repeated charge, stating, "it's a fundamental misperception, the charge of condescension. Because the only people who can really answer this is us, and we feel very affectionate toward all of these characters." Regardless of their

affection toward their creations, the brothers do admit that they deliberately "dream up horrible situations to put the characters through" claims Joel Coen, to which Ethan adds that they then "make it worse." In an interview about *Inside Llewyn Davis* (2013), Joel Coen states "there's no drama that's interesting to us in triumph over adversity, or emerging success—unless, of course, it's followed by horrible failure," a comment that applies not only to Llewyn Davis, but to the panoply of Coen characters from *Blood Simple* on.

A companion claim regarding Coen characters is that they are cartoonish, a charge leveled by *Newsweek*'s David Ansen, who characterizes them as having "the bold outlines of cartoon figures that might have been devised by a combination of Tex Avery and George Grosz," and while the filmmakers deliberately created the characters of *Raising Arizona* as comic exaggerations whose actions mimic those of a ball bouncing through a pinball machine, reviewers have extended that assessment to include the ensemble of *The Ladykillers* (2003), *Burn After Reading*, and *O Brother, Where Art Thou?* (2000) as well. Roger Ebert deemed Professor G. H. Dorr and company as comic strip creations, and writers often described Osborne Cox and Ulysses Everett McGill as buffoons. This character-as-cartoon discussion often becomes an accusation of stereotyping, as occurred with *Raising Arizona*. A Tempe newspaper, upon obtaining a leaked copy of the script, found the characters unflattering and insulting to the residents of the region, a reaction similar to that of some critics who viewed the depictions of Fargo residents or the Jewish community as offensive in *Fargo* (2006) and *A Serious Man*. This reaction is the direct opposite of the intended effect, asserts Joel Coen: "If you have a character that's specific ethnically, or regionally—let's say this character is from Minnesota, or this character is Jewish, or this character is a Unitarian from Omaha—that character is supposed to stand in and represent all Jews, or all Unitarians from Omaha, or all Minnesotans, and of course that's ridiculous." He continues, explaining that the writers "make the character as specific as possible, so that it's a specific individual that you're talking about, not that whole class of people."

This attempt at a deliberate departure from realism has garnered criticism as well, to which Joel Coen responds, "We don't do realism, and if that's what you go to the movies for, you're not necessarily going to like our stuff." Ethan continues, "Who goes to the movies for that?" noting that much of Hollywood film isn't the real world either, and citing *Pretty Woman*, which he describes as "about a businessman that comes to L.A. and hires a prostitute to accompany him to all his business meetings, functions, that he has. It's a huge mainstream success. My God, that's realistic? People say we're weird?" When challenged about the unrealistic aspects of *O Brother*, Joel summed up the brothers' approach thusly: "It's not about reality. It's supposed to be a make believe place."

Rather than realism, the filmmakers seek instead, to entertain. Joel Coen cites Raymond Chandler, whom the brothers have acknowledged as a major influence upon their body of work, along with James M. Cain and Dashiell Hammett; Chandler claimed that "All good art is entertainment and anyone who says differently is a stuffed shirt and juvenile at the art of living," and the Coens appear to have embraced this philosophy completely. As early as *Blood Simple*, Coen collaborator and cinematographer Barry Sonnenfeld claimed, "it wasn't our intention to make an art film, but to make an entertaining B movie," to which Joel adds, "We're not making movies to

enlighten the audience. We're making them to make them scream."

Both audiences and reviewers, however, are often dissatisfied with the idea that Coen films are merely entertainment, as they want to unravel them, create meaning from them, and assign themes and morals which are largely not intended by the filmmakers. The brothers resist the concept that there is a "right" way to read their films; Ethan states, "we don't give cues about how you're supposed to react. That's just boring Hollywood filmmaking, where you give clear cues for what everyone's supposed to be feeling and how everything's supposed to be taken." Their reluctance to impose meaning extends to their work with actors as well. Oscar Isaac, star of *Inside Llewyn Davis*, notes, "They don't go for the big ideas or 'meaning.' They are practical and pragmatic. It's to do with an adjustment of pace or inflection here. Make the line mean this or that. Joel distilled directing down to 'tone management.'" Gabriel Byrne echoes Isaac's assessment, as he asked the directors about the meaning of the hat in *Miller's Crossing*, a question repeated with frequency by interviewers. Ethan asserts that the hat "doesn't 'represent' anything, it's just a hat blown by the wind," to which Joel adds, "It's an image that came to us, that we liked, and it just implanted itself. It's kind of a practical guiding thread, but there's no need to look for deep meanings," advice which the filmmakers apply to all of their pictures.

Of their process, Ethan states, "We don't operate very intellectually," says Ethan. "You just figure, does this feel right or not? It's always a kind of feeling, a taste thing." "Making movies is mostly just answering questions," says Joel. "And the questions are usually very specific about what this should look like, should the character be wearing this, saying this instead of that? And the only way to answer that, as Ethan was saying, is a nonintellectual, intuitive sort of feeling in your head." The decisions that comprise their films, then, rather than culminating in some larger thematic statement, are made because they work with the vision the directors had for the film. Sonnenfeld explains, "Topics and themes are incredibly unimportant to the Coens. It's about movie storytelling in the abstract—i.e., fooling around with fodder." To the Coens, this "fooling around" is the fun of the process, the portion they find interesting, creating stylized pieces that build upon genres well-established during the early days of Hollywood, absorbed through the myriad movies ingested by the siblings during their childhood in Minnesota.

Their approach, however, results in the familiar refrain of "style over substance" leveled at the filmmakers on a regular basis. *Rolling Stone* asserts that the Coens turn their films into an "academic exercise. It's as if the brothers admired the Swiss-watch precision of the original and wanted to take it apart to see how the pieces would work in a new setting. As an experiment, it's fascinating. But damn if the fiddling doesn't suck the life out of the laughs." While these comments are specific to *The Ladykillers*, others have applied similar critiques. Nicolas Rapold, writing for *Sight & Sound*, maintains "all films by the Coen brothers feel like period pieces suspended in time, even those set in the present day. In their clockwork concoctions—shot, designed, and plotted to precise specifications—every last heightened bit is accounted for," and his colleague Ben Walters characterizes *Burn After Reading* in much the same way: "It's another Coen film that resembles a genre picture only long enough to break the glass, another assassination attempt on Hollywood. In this regard, they resemble

Billy Wilder, that sceptical inhabitant of Hollywood genres."

Heavily laden with allusion and even homage and often anchored in cinematic traditions, their films are often read by reviewers as meta-cinema. The *Guardian*'s Peter Bradshaw, writing of *Intolerable Cruelty* (2003), states, "It's as if the stylized gestures, decor and relationships constitute a brilliantly creative commentary on the comedy genre, rather than an actual example of comedy," an effect characterized by Roger Ebert as the Coens "standing to one side of their work: It's the puppet and they're the ventriloquists. The puppet is sincere, but the puppetmaster is wagging his eyebrows at the audience and asking, can you believe this stuff?" Sheila Benson of the *Los Angeles Times* more broadly states, "Self-conscious formalism has been the Coens' signature." While the stylization and the allusions are deliberate, the filmmakers are mystified by "the perception that our movies are parodies, which I have never understood. People will say 'This movie is a parody of a gangster movie,' when it was never our intention to parody the genre." Joel concludes, "You know, we're pretty oblivious to the expectations honestly. We don't trouble ourselves too much with what people might be expecting from this or that," and this freedom from expectations has enabled the brothers to continue developing the projects that interest them, without concern for box office or critical reception.

The Academy has amply rewarded Joel and Ethan Coen for their body of work: each brother has received four Oscars, and their films have been nominated for over thirty Academy Awards, in addition to the various other honors bestowed upon them. In typical Coen fashion, the brothers approach their accolades wryly: Ethan comments, "the physical award is so iconic. It's a shape that everyone knows. You stick 'em there in the office," and Joel adds, "We could *bowl* with these things! Just line 'em up."

While Joel Coen has limited his work to collaborative projects with his brother, Ethan Coen has through the years written works in addition to their combined efforts, including poetry, drama, and fiction, endeavors he considers recreational, calling himself a "gentleman playwright." In 1998, Ethan released a collection of short stories titled *Gates of Eden*, fourteen tales that reviewers noted shared similarities to the films of the Coens. *Empire*'s Ian Nathan writes of the collection, "It is a frenetic mix of noir parody and whimsical homages to his Minnesotan upbringing that read like microcosms of the films," and Nicholas Patterson of the *Boston Phoenix* identifies those Coen "hallmarks" present in the collection as "close attention to diction, a fine eye for ethnic conflict, and a taste for grotesque violence and deadpan humor." The *Gates of Eden* audiobook includes voice work by Coen regulars Steve Buscemi, John Goodman, William H. Macy, and John Turturro, as well as Matt Dillon and Ben Stiller. Ethan credits Dashiell Hammett as an influence on his fiction, just as it is in the films he creates with Joel Coen.

Also in 1998, Ethan collaborated on a script with J. Todd Anderson, storyboard artist for many Coen films, and the resultant film was entitled *The Naked Man*. The film struggled to find a distributor, and upon its release, it did not do well, prompting Ethan to state, "On its own terms it is a very funny movie. But that's all it has to offer, which, sadly, isn't enough."

Ethan's 2001 collection of poetry, *The Drunken Driver Has the Right of Way*, similarly prompted reviewers to draw connections to the Coen films. Shawn Badgley of the *Austin Chronicle* likens the range and

propensity to allusion of their cinematic projects to the way in which Ethan's poems bounce from "Edward Lear nonsense and rollicking sea chanteys to Byronic outcast verse and bombastic balladry, all the while staging a mock battle with some kind of anxiety of influence that borders on the self-indulgent," a comment not dissimilar to those about the characters that populate the films of Joel and Ethan Coen.

With his brother Joel, Ethan also composed a radio sound play entitled *Sawbones* (2005), which they directed and which stars Steve Buscemi, Philip Seymour Hoffman, Brooke Smith, John Slattery, Marcia Gay Harden, and John Goodman.

In addition to the poetry and short stories, Ethan Coen has penned a number of one-act plays, each debuting at the Atlantic Theatre Company. *Almost an Evening* (2008), directed by Neil Pepe, is comprised of three one-act plays: "Waiting," which tries the patience of a soul bound for hell; "Four Benches," about a British secret service agent who meets an unfortunate end; and "Debate," in which two versions of God engage in a heated exchange. Coen collaborator Carter Burwell commented on the production, stating that "Ethan loves a philosophical paradox, which he usually inflicts on a character ill-prepared intellectually to deal with it," a comment that could apply to any number of characters from the Coen film canon. Ben Brantley of the *New York Times* further suggests that much like their films, Ethan's drama "is touched by the premise that hell lurks right under the surface of, or just around the corner from, everyday life."

Offices (2009), also directed by Neil Pepe, is comprised of "Peer Review," about the shortcomings of corporate culture as told by a disillusioned, whiny worker; "Homeland Security," which addresses the difficulties inherent in working in the government agency; and "Struggle Session," wherein a manager is fired, rehired, and promoted in the span of one day. The *Guardian* describes Coen's offices as "sites of grotesque posturing, pitiful self-delusion and occasional bouts of absurd violence," and Brantley concludes that *Offices* "mostly sustains the illusion that it's meatier than it is."

In *Happy Hour* (2012), characterized by the *New York Times* writer Charles Isherwood as a "wearying evening," the production's three one-act plays are "End Days," featuring a bar patron who laments the state of the world; "City Lights," set in the 1970s, about a guitar player who misplaces his demo tape; and "Wayfarer's Inn," about a travelling businessman who shares a hotel room, and his existential musings, with a coworker. The trio of plays was once again directed by Neil Pepe, and though the *Huffington Post* deemed the collection "bleak," reviewer Mark Kennedy ultimately concluded that Ethan Coen "is masterful at left-of-center monologues and uses dialogue to show that people are destined to just get confused when expressing themselves and will ultimately misunderstand each other."

On Broadway, Ethan contributed a one-act play to the 2011 production *Relatively Speaking*, an evening of three short plays; his was titled "Talking Cure." The collection was panned by the *Village Voice*'s Michael Feingold, who described Coen's portion as "unfunny and unfinished scribble."

In 2013, David Cromer directed Ethan's first full-length play, *Women or Nothing*, about a lesbian couple who want a child. Cromer describes the script as "the most interesting conversation I'd ever read and the most interesting sort of love scene I'd ever read. It was just something really original in the form of something that's

not original," and the *Village Voice* praised one of the characters as "a fast-talking, flat-affected society doyenne whose every line is an impeccably timed half-paragraph gush of condescension, passive-aggression, and occasional wisdom."

Ethan Coen returned to poetry in 2012, with his collection *The Day the World Ends*, released, as readers and critics alike noted, the very year the Mayan calendar predicted the end of the world. Of writing poetry, Ethan notes that writing verse is like solving crosswords: "Having it all work out so that it feels natural but falls into the meter and rhymes—it's all a very artificial, but again, satisfying mental exercise."

References

Kaleem Aftab, "There's Nowt as Queer as Folk: Inside the Coen Brothers," *Independent*, January 8, 2014; William Rodney Allen, ed., *The Coen Brothers: Interviews* (Jackson: University Press of Mississippi, 2006); David Ansen, "The Coens' Funny Bones," *Newsweek*, September 15, 2008; Shawn Badgley, *The Drunken Driver Has the Right of Way*: Poems," *Austin Chronicle*, November 2, 2001; Sheila Benson, "*Miller's Crossing*: Stylish but Remote," *Los Angeles Times*, October 5, 1990; Peter Bradshaw, "*Intolerable Cruelty*," *Guardian*, October 24, 2003; Ben Brantley, "A World Right Around the Corner from Hell," *New York Times*, January 23, 2008; "Ethan Coen's One-Act Plays to Make UK Debut?" *BroadwayWorld.com*, October 14, 2013; "Theatre of the Ear," *CarterBurwell.com*; Cassie Carpenter, "Character Studies: Marcia Gay Harden," *Backstage.com*, December 17, 2003; Donald Clarke, "Inside Llewyn Davis Star Oscar Isaac on Folk, Film and Working with Cats," *Irish Times*, January 24, 2014; Edward Douglas, "John Malkovich on the Coens' *Burn After Reading*," *ComingSoon.net*, September 10, 2008; Roger Ebert, "*Intolerable Cruelty*," *RogerEbert.com*, October 10, 2003; David Edelstein, "Thieves Like Us," *Slate.com*; Michael Feingold,

"*Relatively Speaking* Is Relatively Lame," *Village Voice*, October 26, 2011; Peter Freed, "Raising *Ladykillers*: Coens Hit Remake Trail with Black Comedy Update," *USA Today*, March 23, 2004; "Ethan Coen Assumes Office of American Work-Ethic Satirist," *TheGuardian.com*, Film Blog; Horatia Harrod, "Hollywood's Mischief-Makers: An Interview with the Coen Brothers," *Telegraph*, January 18, 2014; Charles Isherwood, "Life Is Grim, and Then Things Tend to Get a Lot Worse," *New York Times*, December 5, 2011; Mark Kennedy, "Ethan Coen's *Happy Hour* Is a Bitter, Bleak Two Hours," *HuffingtonPost.com*, December 5, 2011; Mark Kennedy, "Playwright Ethan Coen Fears He's Selling Out," *HuffingtonPost.com*, September 13, 2013; Stuart Klawans, "Burned Out," *Nation*, October 6, 2008; Emanuel Levy, "*Burn After Reading*: Shooting a Joel and Ethan Coen Wild Comedy," *EmanuelLevy.com*, August 24, 2008; Franz Lidz, "Biblical Adversity in a 60's Suburb," *New York Times*, September 23, 2009; Patricia McConnico, "Joel Coen," *Texas Monthly*, October, 1998; Celia McGee, "A Coen Brother Scales Down to the Stage," *New York Times*, January 6, 2008; "Fred Melamed," *FocusFeatures.com*, *A Serious Man*, Cast & Crew; James Mottram, *The Coen Brothers: The Life of the Mind* (Dulles, Virginia: Brassey's, 2000); Smitri Mundhra, "Interview with Joel Coen," *Ign.com*, November 2, 2001; "Ethan Coen's 'Recreational' Writing Projects," *NPR.org*, April 16, 2009; Ian Nathan, *Ethan and Joel Coen* (Paris: Cahiers du cinema Sarl, 2012); Sean O'Neal, "John Turturro," *AVClub*.com, June 28, 2011; Nicholas Patterson, "Gates of Ethan," *Boston Phoenix*, BostonPhoenix.com, November 1998; Nicolas Rapold, "*Burn After Reading*," *Sight & Sound*, 18.11 (2008); Sheila Roberts, "Brad Pitt and Cast Interview, *Burn After Reading*," *MoviesOnline.ca*; Alan Scherstuhl, "Ethan Coen's *Women or Nothing* Is Imperfect Human Comedy," *Village Voice*, September 18, 2013; Ella Taylor, "For *A Serious Man*, Coen Brothers Aim Trademark Contempt at Themselves," *Village Voice*, September 29, 2009; J. M. Tyree and Ben Walters, "League of Morons," *Sight & Sound*, 18.11 (2008); Damon Wise, "Uncut Interview: Joel and Ethan Coen," *Uncut.co.uk*; Paul A. Woods, ed., *Joel & Ethan Coen: Blood Siblings* (London: Plexus Publishing, 2003).

CRIMEWAVE (1985)

Written collaboratively by Ethan Coen, Joel Coen, and Sam Raimi prior to the Coens' *Blood Simple* (1984) and following Raimi's *The Evil Dead* (1981), *Crimewave*'s narrative is told by way of an extended flashback that begins when Vic Ajax (Reed Birney) is placed in an electric chair to be executed for the murder of Donald Odegard (Hamid Dana), co-owner of a security system company. The crime was committed by thugs hired by Odegard's partner, Ernest Trend (Edward R. Pressman), who kill Trend in the process, and though Vic claims he is innocent, only Nancy (Sheree J. Wilson) can corroborate this fact. She has, however, sought refuge in a convent, and Vic's exoneration appears unlikely. At the film's conclusion, Nancy appears to testify of his innocence, Vic is freed, and the two are married.

Alternately titled *The XYZ Murders* and *Broken Hearts and Noses*, the film was directed by Raimi and includes among its cast members Joel and Ethan Coen in cameo appearances as reporters at the execution. Steve Jenkins characterizes the film as "the frenetic, comic-strip energy of *The Evil Dead*, combined with *Blood Simple*'s rather more knowing and darker brand of humorous excess," a mixture that he declares "unsatisfactory." In a slightly more charitable review, *Variety* deemed the film "boisterous, goofy, cartoonish comedy in the *Airplane* mold," noting that the "production looks pretty cheap and its impact evaporates immediately upon final fadeout," concluding that "laughs are abundant enough to make this a passably funny entertainment."

Though the film was written collaboratively and directed by Raimi, the three filmmakers have for all purposes disowned the film, as it was not only recast one week before production but also heavily reedited prior to its release, a development with which Raimi was not happy and that negatively affected the resultant product and prompted the Coens to insist on final cut for their own films, beginning with *Blood Simple.*

References

"*Crimewave:* Review from *Variety,*" in *Joel & Ethan Coen: Blood Siblings*, ed. Paul A. Woods (London: Plexus Publishing, 2003); Steve Jenkins, "*Crimewave,*" in *Joel & Ethan Coen: Blood Siblings*, ed. Paul A. Woods (London: Plexus Publishing, 2003); Eddie Robson, *Coen Brothers* (London: Virgin Books, 2003). See also SAM RAIMI.

D

DAMON, MATT (1970–)

Born October 8, 1970, in Boston, Massachusetts, Damon made the acquaintance of his lifelong friend and collaborator Ben Affleck at the age of ten. Both attended the Rindge & Latin preparatory school, following which Damon attended Harvard for a time. He left the University to pursue a career in acting and first appeared on screen in a small part in *Mystic Pizza* (1988), which he followed with a larger role in *School Ties* (1992), with Brendan Fraser. In 1997, he and Affleck cowrote and appeared in *Good Will Hunting*, with Robin Williams; the film was nominated for nine Academy Awards and fully launched the careers of Affleck and Damon. The two shared the Oscar for Best Screenplay, and Williams was awarded the Oscar for Best Supporting Actor. Following this success, Damon appeared in Steven Spielberg's *Saving Private Ryan* (1998), in Anthony Minghella's *The Talented Mr. Ripley* (1999), and has starred in *Ocean's Eleven* (2001) and its sequels *Ocean's Twelve* (2004) and *Ocean's Thirteen* (2007), all with George Clooney and Brad Pitt, among others. He played the title role in *The Bourne Identity* (2002) and the follow-ups *The Bourne Supremacy* (2004) and *The Bourne Ultimatum* (2007). Damon was nominated for a Best Supporting Actor Oscar for his role in *Invictus* (2009) and received two Golden Globe nominations

in 2009, Best Supporting Actor for *Invictus* and Best Performance by an Actor in a Motion Picture—Musical or Comedy for *The Informant!* (2009). His television appearances include roles in *Entourage* (2009), *Cubed* (2009), and *30 Rock* (2010–2011), and his production credits include *Project Greenlight* (2001–2005) and the documentaries *The People Speak* (2009) and *The People Speak UK* (2010).

Matt Damon appeared in the Coens' 2010 re-adaptation of *True Grit* (2010), as Texas Ranger LaBoeuf, who accompanies Mattie Ross (Hailee Steinfeld) and U.S. Marshall Reuben "Rooster" Cogburn (Jeff Bridges) as they pursue the murderer Tom Chaney, who killed Mattie's father. Mattie does not welcome LaBoeuf's presence, calling him a "rodeo clown," while Cogburn tolerates him only because of the sizeable reward they will split upon their return with Chaney. Even so, Cogburn refers to LaBoeuf as a "brush popper" and insults him—and his position as Texas Ranger—at every opportunity. Described by Manohla Dargis of the *New York Times* as having "a luxurious mustache that sits on his lip like a spoiled Persian cat," and by Christopher Kelly of *Texas Monthly* as "an endearing buffoon," Damon himself describes LaBoeuf as "a true nincompoop." Damon and the Coens envisioned the character as a Cliff Clavin of the Old West, "a Tommy Lee [Jones] who didn't know what he was talking about—and never stopped talking," a comparison that references the fact that Tommy Lee Jones is himself a Harvard graduate.

Damon's performance met with mixed reviews. Rex Reed of the *New York Observer* characterizes Damon as "hopelessly miscast," though most critics viewed both the film and Damon's performance positively. *Empire*'s Angie Errigo says that "Damon fits gracefully into the Coen company as the cocky galoot," and Peter Travers of *Rolling Stone* praises Damon, who "puts everything into the role and rides it to glory."

References

Geoff Boucher, "Matt Damon Enjoys Being 'a True Nincompoop' in *True Grit*," *Los Angeles Times*, December 26, 2010; Manohla Dargis, "Wearing Braids, Seeking Revenge," *New York Times*, December 21, 2010; Angie Errigo, "*True Grit*: The Dude Bests the Duke in a New Coens Masterpiece," *EmpireOnline.com*; Christopher Kelly, "Best Western," *Texas Monthly*, 39.1 (2011); "Matt Damon," *New York Times*, Movies & TV; Rex Reed, "*True Grit*," *New York Observer*, December 15, 2010; Peter Travers, "*True Grit*," *Rolling Stone*, December 21, 2010; Kenneth Turan, "Movie Review: *True Grit*," *Los Angeles Times*, December 22, 2010. See also *TRUE GRIT*.

DAVIS, JUDY (1955–)

Born in Perth, Western Australia, on April 23, 1955, Davis left convent school at the age of seventeen to tour Asia with a rock band. Following the six-month tour, she attended the Western Australia Institute of Technology and then the National Institute of Dramatic Art, where she starred opposite Mel Gibson in *Romeo and Juliet*. She appeared briefly in the film *High Rolling in a Hot Corvette* (1977) before receiving the role of Sybylla Melvyn in *My Brilliant Career* (1979), which established her screen career and garnered her the award for Best Actress from the British Film Academy and the Australian Film Institute. Davis was then cast in such films as *Winter of Our Dreams* (1981) and *Heatwave* (1982), prior to winning an Emmy for her role as Golda Meir in the television mini-series *A Woman Called Golda* (1982) and receiving her first Academy Award nomination for her work in *A Passage to India* (1984). Subsequent films included *Naked Lunch* (1991); Woody Allen's *Alice* (1990) and *Husbands and Wives* (1992), for which she received her second Oscar nomination; *Deconstructing Harry* (1997); and *Celebrity* (1998), also Woody Allen films. Her television roles were initially in made-for-television movies, including such roles as Lillian Hellman in *Dash and Lilly* (1999), Judy Garland in *Life with Judy Garland: Me and My Shadows* (2001), and Nancy Reagan in *The Reagans* (2003). She later appeared in the television mini-series *The Starter Wife* (2007), which became the series of the same name in 2008. Davis again worked with Woody Allen in 2012's *To Rome with Love* and appeared in a series of eight short films by Baz Luhrmann, which feature conversations between fashion icons Elsa Sciaparelli, played by Davis, and Muiccia Prada (2012). She has been nominated for six Golden Globe Awards, winning the 1992 Best Performance by an Actress in a Motion Picture Made for Television for *One Against the Wind* and again in 2002 for her portrayal of Judy Garland.

Davis has appeared in one film by Joel and Ethan Coen, *Barton Fink* (1991), as Audrey Taylor, lover, muse, and ghostwriter to novelist W. P. Mayhew (John Mahoney). When Barton Fink (John Turturro) turns to Audrey for assistance with his screenplay, she ends up murdered in his bed and ultimately beheaded by Madman Karl Mundt (John Goodman), events which mark a turning point in the film's narrative. *Rolling Stone* deemed Davis's Audrey as "beautifully acted," and for her performance, she received the New York Film Critics Circle Award for Best Supporting Actress.

References

"Judy Davis," *TCM.com*, Turner Classic Movies; Peter Travers, "*Barton Fink,*" *Rolling Stone*, August 21, 1991. See also *BARTON FINK*.

DEAKINS, ROGER (1949–)

Born May 24, 1949, and raised in Torquay in Devon, England, Deakins initially attended Bath Academy of Art, where he developed an interest in photography, which in turn led him to the National Film School. His earliest film work was on documentaries, shooting in Ethiopia, India, Sudan, and Rhodesia, following which he worked with such directors as Michael Radford and Mike Figgis. In 1994, he served as cinematographer for Frank Darabont's *The Shawshank Redemption* starring Tim Robbins, for which Deakins received his first Oscar nomination. He went on to work with Robbins in *Dead Man Walking* (1995) and with Martin Scorsese in *Kundun* (1997), Ron Howard in *A Beautiful Mind* (2001), and Sam Mendes in *Jarhead* (2005) and *Revolutionary Road* (2008). His role as cinematographer for *Barton Fink* (1991) marked the onset of his work with Joel and Ethan Coen, a collaboration that continued through *The Hudsucker Proxy* (1994), *Fargo* (1996), *The Big Lebowski* (1998), *O Brother, Where Art Thou?* (2000), *The Man Who Wasn't There* (2001), *Intolerable Cruelty* (2003), *The Ladykillers* (2004), *No Country for Old Men* (2007), *A Serious Man* (2009), and *True Grit* (2010). Deakins has received eleven Oscar nominations for Best Achievement in Cinematography, including *Fargo, O Brother, Where Art Thou?, The Man Who Wasn't There*, two nominations in 2007 for *No Country for Old Men* and Andrew Dominik's *The Assassination of Jessie James by the Coward Robert Ford*, and

a nomination for *True Grit*. He became a member of the American Society of Cinematographers in 1994, and in 2011, the ASC honored Deakins with the Society's Lifetime Achievement Award. In 2013, he was named a Commander of the British Empire (CBE) by Queen Elizabeth II, the first cinematographer to receive the award.

On working with Deakins, Joel and Ethan Coen state that they selected him when their cinematographer Barry Sonnenfeld moved on to directing his own films; they were familiar with Deakins's work in such films as *Sid and Nancy* (1986), *Stormy Monday* (1988), and *Pascali's Island* (1988). The brothers were putting together their team for *Barton Fink* and contacted Deakins through his agent, who discouraged him from working on the project, noting that the film "was very strange, and that it seemed to be two different movies." Undeterred, he met with the Coens in London and signed on to work with the pair. Deakins has since credited his work on *Barton Fink* as a turning point in his career, as he had recently completed *Air America* (1990), a project with which he was not pleased, and had decided he wanted to work with smaller projects rather than larger ones. The brothers approached him at precisely the right time, then, resulting in a collaboration that has spanned over two decades.

The Coens are enthusiastic about the knowledge and insight Deakins brings to their films: "From shot design, to lighting, to how and when you move the camera, Roger is brilliant at bringing some extra dimension that changes the entire feeling of what you're doing," says Joel Coen, continuing, "We've worked with a lot of operators, and Roger is by far the best." For each picture, Deakins is included early in the process, at the storyboarding stage. The first draft of the storyboards is created with artist J. Todd Anderson, following which the filmmakers bring in Deakins, using the cinematographer as "a sounding board for the movie in its entirety" states Joel Coen, who has characterized Deakins as "the third collaborator" on their films. They incorporate Deakins's ideas into the second draft of storyboards, which are then used for shooting. Of this process, Deakins says, "I've never worked with anybody else who storyboards like they do," adding that with other directors, storyboards are used as a reference rather than a guide for the shooting process. He explains, "On a Coen brothers movie, it's much more of a template for what you actually shoot. . . . You could look at the images on file, and there's not much variation."

As a result of this process and the many films they have worked on together, the directors and cinematographer do not require extensive discussion on-set: "Their sets are very quiet," says Deakins. "They know what they want, and they know when they've got it. They work very economically." From their perspective, the filmmakers recall that during filming for *Barton Fink*, "we constantly looked in the viewfinder," but on subsequent films *The Hudsucker Proxy* and *Fargo*, they looked at the shots less and less, a process which they describe as reflecting "the growing affinity with our cinematographer. He understood our intentions more and more and we trusted him more and more. When we work regularly with a collaborator, a kind of telepathic language is established."

Their fifth project together, *O Brother, Where Art Thou?*, quickly gained fame for being the first U.S. studio feature to be digitally color-corrected in its entirety, and Deakins spent almost two months on the process, digitally removing every trace of green from the footage of the lush Mississippi landscape. For *The Man Who Wasn't There*, the goal was luminescent black-and-white imagery, but the filmmakers were contractually obligated to create a color master for foreign markets. In a novel solution, Deakins shot on color stock and printed on Kodak 5269, a black-and-white stock designed for film titles. He won his second ASC Award for *The Man Who Wasn't There*.

The introduction of the Digital Intermediate (DI) process into filmmaking caused a furor in the industry, as many cinematographers deemed it "cheating," a process that devalued the films that employed the technique. Deakins, however, embraced DI as one of the many tools that he could utilize in creating pictures. Recalling the controversy, Deakins states "I thought that was a pretty stupid argument, really, because it's the final product that matters. The look of the film, however it's done, is still the cinematographer's vision in my mind. People said the same when color film came in, didn't they? The world evolves, and image-making evolves." Ethan Coen has further noted that *True Grit* was the last film that Deakins shot on film, following which he shifted to shooting digitally. For Deakins, the emphasis is not on the process but rather on the script. In choosing his projects, he asks himself, "Is this something I want to go and see in the cinema myself? Is it something that moves me? Are the characters interesting, do they have something to say to me? Do they change? Do they develop during the film?" adding, "I read a script and I'll say, 'Yeah, that affects me in some way.' But I will never read a script and think, 'Oh, that will be visually interesting.'"

While Deakins was unavailable to shoot *Inside Llewyn Davis*, the Coens' 2013 film based on the Greenwich Village folk scene of the early 1960s, he did serve as cinematographer on *Unbroken* (2014), based on the true story of Louis Zamperini (Jack O'Connell), an Olympic runner who was taken captive by the Japanese during World War II. The screenplay was written by Joel and Ethan Coen, Richard LaGravenese, and William Nicholson, and was adapted from the book by Laura Hillenbrand. The film is directed by Angelina Jolie.

References

Kyle Buchanan, "From *Shawshank* to *Skyfall*, How Master Cinematographer Roger Deakins Got These Ten Shots," *Vulture.com*, February 21, 2013; Michel Ciment and Hubert Niogret, "A Rock on the Beach," in *The Coen Brothers: Interviews*, ed. William Rodney Allen (Jackson: University Press of Mississippi, 2006); Manohla Dargis and A. O. Scott, "'We Are the Establishment Now': The Coen Brothers Look Wryly at Their Films," *New York Times*, September 4, 2013; Jim Emerson, "That Barton Fink Feeling: An Interview with the Brothers Coen," in *The Coen Brothers: Interviews*, ed. William Rodney Allen (Jackson: University Press of Mississippi, 2006); "Roger Deakins: Sticking to the Script," *FocusFeatures.com*, *A Serious Man*, In Depth, January 7, 2010; Roger Deakins, "The DI, Luddites, and Other Musings," *RogerDeakinsOnline.com*; Patricia Thompson, "A League of His Own," *American Cinematographer*, January, 2011. See also *BARTON FINK, THE BIG LEBOWSKI, DIGITAL INTERMEDIATE, FARGO, THE HUDSUCKER PROXY, INTOLERABLE CRUELTY, THE LADYKILLERS, THE MAN WHO WASN'T THERE, NO COUNTRY FOR OLD MEN, O BROTHER, WHERE ART THOU?, A SERIOUS MAN, TRUE GRIT.*

DELBONNEL, BRUNO (1957–)

Born in 1957 in Nancy, Meurthe-et-Moselle, France, cinematographer Bruno Delbonnel attended the Université Paris-Sorbonne and the École supérieure libre d'études cinématographiques, also in Paris. He graduated in 1978 and directed the short film *Realites rares*, prior to moving to New York. Following a brief stay, he returned to France, where he filmed commercials, working with director Jean-Pierre Jeunet, with whom he would also work on his first films, the short *Le bunker de la derniere rafale* (1981) and *Pas de repos pour Billy Brakko* (1984). He served as cinematographer for Francis Renaud, among others, and again with Jeunet on *Le fabuleux destin d'Amélie Poulin (Amélie)* (2001), for which he received his first Oscar nomination. He was again nominated for *Un long dimanche de fiançailles* (2004), for *Harry Potter and the Half Blood Prince* (2009), and for his work with the Coen brothers on *Inside Llewyn Davis* (2013). He directed *Le grand cirque* in 1989 and *Paso doble* in 2006, and in 2005, Delbonnel served as cinematographer on the Coen segment "Tuileries" in *Paris, je t'aime.*

For his work on *Inside Llewyn Davis*, Glenn Kenny of *RogerEbert.com* commended Delbonnel for his lighting and camerawork, suggesting that his cinematography "doesn't just cast a mood, it conjures a mode of existence," and the New York created by the entire design team garnered much praise along these same lines. The *New Yorker* concurred, stating "the whole movie is so beautifully shot, by Bruno Delbonnel, that, if anything, the beauty hazes over the shabby desperation that, by custom, should plague the struggling artist."

References

"Bruno Delbonnel," *Internet Encyclopedia of Cinematographers*; Glenn Kenny, "*Inside Llewyn Davis,*" *RogerEbert.com*; Anthony Lane, "It's Cold Outside," *New Yorker*, December 9, 2013. See also *INSIDE LLEWYN DAVIS, PARIS JE T'AIME.*

DIGITAL INTERMEDIATE

The process by which film is digitized, altered, and, in the early era of DI, returned to film for distribution, allowing filmmakers to manipulate color, formatting, editing, and special effects. The Coens' *O Brother, Where Art Thou?* (2000) was the first film to undergo the DI process in its entirety, a technique deemed necessary by the Coens and cinematographer Roger Deakins, as the film was shot in the green countryside of the Mississippi summer, and the filmmakers envisioned ochre-colored scenes for the picture. Cinematographer Roger Deakins scanned, digitized, and color-corrected the film to achieve *O Brother*'s yellow-brown, Depression-era landscapes.

DOWN FROM THE MOUNTAIN (2001)

DIRECTOR: Nick Doob, Chris Hegedus, D. A. Pennebaker. EXECUTIVE PRODUCERS: T Bone Burnett, Ethan Coen, and Joel Coen. PRODUCERS: Bob Neuwirth and Frazer Pennebaker; Rebecca Marshall (Associate Producer). PHOTOGRAPHY: Joan Churchill, Nick Doog, Chris Hegedus, Bob Neuwirth, Jehane Noujaim, D. A. Pennebaker, and Jojo Pennebaker. EDITING: Nick Doob, D. A. Pennebaker. MUSIC DIRECTOR: T Bone Burnett. RUNNING TIME: 98 minutes. RELEASED THROUGH: Cowboy Booking International, June 6, 2001.

Directed by veteran documentarian D. A. Pennebaker (*Don't Look Back*, 1967, and *Moon over Broadway*, 1997), with frequent collaborator Chris Hegedus (*The War Room*, 1993), and cinematographer/director Nick Doob. Recorded live at a May 24, 2000, Nashville Ryman Auditorium concert to benefit the Country Music Hall of Fame, this documentary includes numbers by Alison Krauss, Chris Thomas King, The Cox Family, the Fairfield Four, Emmylou Harris, Gillian Welch, and Ralph Stanley, among others who appeared on the soundtrack for *O Brother Where Art Thou?* (2000). John Hartford served as master of ceremonies for the concert; included are several songs that did not appear on the *O Brother* soundtrack, including an original song by Chris Thomas King. The documentary includes commentary by the artists as well as rehearsals for the concert and the final performances.

References

A. O. Scott, "*Down from the Mountain* (2001) Film Review," *New York Times*, June 15, 2001; Matt Zoller Seitz, "*Down from the Mountain*, Pennebaker's *O Brother* Doc," *New York Press*, June 28, 2001. See also *O BROTHER WHERE ART THOU?*, T BONE BURNETT.

DRIVER, ADAM (1983–)

Born November 19, 1983, in San Diego, California, Driver was raised in Indiana after his parents divorced. He joined the Marines at age eighteen, shortly after the attacks of September 11. Following two years of service, he left the Marines due to an injury and attended the University of Indianapolis for a year. He was then accepted to Juilliard, where he studied drama, graduating in 2009. He cofounded the nonprofit Arts in the Armed Forces, whose mission is to bring performing arts to members of the military.

His first on-screen appearances included the television series *The Unusuals* (2009) and *Law and Order* (2010). He also appeared in the made-for-television movies *You Don't Know Jack* (2010) with Al Pacino, and HBO's *The Wonderful Maladays* (2009). His Broadway debut was in *Mrs. Warren's Profession* (2010) and he appeared off-Broadway in *Angels in America: Perestroika* (2010) and *Angels in America: Millennium Approaches* (2010). He returned to Broadway in *Man and Boy* (2011) and played Cliff in the off-Broadway Roundabout Theatre Company Production of *Look Back in Anger* (2012). Driver had a small part in Clint Eastwood's *J. Edgar* (2011) and a more substantial role in Noah Baumbach's *Frances Ha* (2012) and played Samuel Beckwith in Steven Spielberg's Oscar-winning *Lincoln* (2012). He had a recurring role as Adam Sackler in the HBO series *Girls* (2012–2014), for which he received an Emmy nomination for Outstanding Supporting Actor in a Comedy Series (2012). Driver appeared as Al Cody in the Coens' *Inside Llewyn Davis* (2013).

As a member of the John Glenn Singers, a pop-folk trio in *Inside Llewyn Davis*, Al Cody records the song "Please, Mr. Kennedy" with Llewyn Davis (Oscar Isaac) and Jim Berkey (Justin Timberlake). Cody, a fellow struggling folk musician, is in the process of changing his name from Arthur Milgram to Al Cody and allows Llewyn to stay on Cody's couch for a few days. Llewyn discovers that Cody, too, has recorded a folk album, and Cody puts Llewyn in touch with blues musician Roland Turner (John Goodman) and beat poet Johnny Five (Garrett Hedlund), with whom Llewyn rides to Chicago.

References

"Adam Driver," *BroadwayWorld.com*; "Adam Driver," *InsideLlewynDavis.com*, Cast; Erik Peipenberg, "No Combat Duty but Plenty of Curtain Calls," *New York Times*, February 21, 2011. See also *INSIDE LLEWYN DAVIS*.

DURNING, CHARLES (1923–2012)

Born February 28, 1923, in Highland Falls, New York, Charles Durning was raised in a large Irish family, one of ten children; he lost five siblings to disease and his father died when Charles was a child. He left home at sixteen and worked odd jobs to support himself, one of which was as an usher in a vaudeville theatre. His first onstage appearance occurred when a comic was unable to perform because of intoxication, and Durning took the stage instead, an opportunity that began a lifelong love for the stage. He joined the U.S. Army, serving during World War II and was among the first wave of soldiers to land at Omaha Beach in the invasion of Normandy on D-Day, 1944. The only member of his unit to survive the landing, he was then captured in the Battle of the Bulge and later escaped; he was decorated with a Silver Star and three Purple Hearts.

Having returned from the war, Durning was inspired by James Cagney and pursued a career in acting. He attended the American Academy of Dramatic Arts in New York City, and despite being discouraged from acting by his instructors, he continued his dream of performing. During this time, he worked as a taxi driver, night watchman, and a dance instructor and began appearing in television roles in 1953. His first film role was in *Harvey Middleman, Fireman* (1965), and in his nearly fifty-year career, he appeared in such films as *The Sting* (1973), *Dog Day Afternoon* (1975), *The Muppet Movie* (1979), *Tootsie* (1982), and *Dick Tracy* (1990), primarily in supporting roles. He was twice nominated for the Academy Award for Best Actor in a Supporting Role, for *The Best Little Whorehouse in Texas* (1982) and *To Be or Not to Be* (1983), and in 1991, he won the Golden Globe for Best Supporting Actor in a Television Mini-Series for his role as John "Honey Fitz" Fitzgerald in *The Kennedys of Massachusetts* (1990).

On stage, he often worked with Joseph Papp, who established the Public Theater and the New York Shakespeare Festival, and Durning appeared in stage versions of *On Golden Pond*, *That Championship Season*, and *Inherit the Wind*. He won the Tony Award for his role as Big Daddy in the Tennessee Williams play *Cat on a Hot Tin Roof* (1990). His television career was equally long and impressive, with appearances in *All in the Family* (1973), *Baretta* (1975), *Hawaii Five-O* (1975), *Evening Shade* (1990–1994), *Homicide: Life on the Street* (1998), *The Practice* (1998–2000), *Everybody Loves Raymond* (1998–2002),

Monk (2007), and *Family Guy* (1999–2009). He was nominated for nine Emmy Awards for his work on television, and the Screen Actors Guild awarded him a Lifetime Achievement Award in 2008.

In the title role of Waring Hudsucker in the Coens' 1994 *The Hudsucker Proxy*, Durning's role is ostensibly limited to the first ten minutes of the film. He presides over the annual financial report at the Hudsucker Industries Board of Directors meeting, at the conclusion of which he leaps from the window to his death. "We cast Durning on the idea that a fat person falling 40 floors is a lot funnier than a thin person falling 40 floors," said Joel Coen. "Charles actually used to be a dancer and all that stuff he does at the beginning where he gets up and digs his heel and shakes the tension out of his body was all Charles. He choreographed all his movements." While his screen time in *Hudsucker* is brief, Waring Hudsucker's legacy as the Founder and President of Hudsucker Industries dominates the corporate climate of the film, as do jokes at the former executive's expense. In a surprise encore appearance, his final scene in the film finds him in an angel's robe, complete with wings and a hula-hoop of a halo and strumming a child's guitar, having learned his lessons in the next life, if not in the last.

Durning then appeared as Menelaeus "Pass the Biscuits" Pappy O'Daniel in *O Brother Where Art Thou?* (2000), a role that is some combination of Texas governor/U.S. senator/flour magnate W. Lee "Pappy" O'Daniel and Jimmie Davis, governor of Louisiana, reported author of "You Are My Sunshine." The film's politically savvy Governor O'Daniel mass communicates, presses the flesh, and hoe-downs his way across rural Mississippi in his bid for reelection, crossing paths with the Soggy Bottom Boys and ultimately absolving them of their crimes, prior to establishing them as his "brain trust" for his second term.

His final film was *Captured Hearts* (2013), in which he played Santa Claus, a role he had played several times throughout his distinguished career. Durning died of natural causes on Christmas Eve, 2012. He was 89.

References

Robert Berkvist, "Charles Durning, Prolific Character Actor, Dies at 89," *New York Times*, December 25, 2012; "Charles Durning," *Biography.com*; Erica Rowell, *The Brothers Grim: The Films of Ethan and Joel Coen* (Lanham, MD: Scarecrow Press, 2007); Chris Weigand, "Charles Durning Obituary," *Guardian*, December 25, 2012. See also *THE HUDSUCKER PROXY, O BROTHER, WHERE ART THOU?*

ELLIOTT, SAM (1944–)

Elliott was born August 9, 1944, in Sacramento, California, and raised in Oregon, where at the age of nine he determined that he wanted to be an actor. He attended the University of Oregon, majoring in English and psychology, following which he became a contract player for 20th Century Fox. His first on-screen appearances were a series of bit parts in the television crime drama *Felony Squad* (1968–1969), and in 1969 he appeared in his first film, *Butch Cassidy and the Sundance Kid*, with Robert Redford and Paul Newman. While he did not interact with the film's leading lady, Katharine Ross, they would appear together in the 1978 film *The Legacy* and would marry in 1984. In the 1970s and early 1980s, he worked extensively in television, playing the lead in several made-for-television movies, including Evel Knievel in *Evel Knievel* (1974), and appeared in the television series *Mission Impossible* (1970–1971) and *Hawaii 5-0* (1974), among others, and in the television mini-series *Once an Eagle* (1976–1977), *Wild Times* (1980), and *A Death in California* (1985).

Elliott is primarily known for his work in the western genre, which he began in *Butch Cassidy and the Sundance Kid*; continued with his television roles as Tell Sackett in *The Sacketts* (1979) and Sam Houston in *Houston: The Legend of Texas* (1986), and in *The Shadow Riders* (1982), with Tom Selleck; and cemented with his appearances as Virgil Earp in *Tombstone* (1993) and the Stranger in the Coen brothers' *The Big Lebowski* (1998). In 1991, he and wife Katharine Ross adapted the Louis L'Amour novel *Conagher* for a TNT television movie, in which they both appeared. In addition to his work in westerns, Elliott has appeared in a number of war films, including *Gettysburg* (1993), the made-for-television movie *Rough Riders* (1997), and *We Were Soldiers* (2002), with Mel Gibson, and in films as diverse as the film adaptation of Marvel Comic's *Hulk* (2003) and the fantasy *The Golden Compass* (2007). He also provided voice work for the animated films *Barnyard* (2006) and *Marmaduke* (2010).

Elliott's status as iconic westerner contributed to being cast as the Stranger in *The Big Lebowski*. The Coens sent him the script while he was working in Texas on *Rough Riders* with John Milius, and their approach to convince him to take the part was to write him into the script itself, with lines that stated, according to Elliott, "There's this Western voiceover, and 'Tumblin' Tumbleweeds' is playing in the background, and the voiceover sounds not unlike Sam Elliott," and "And here's The Stranger, looking not unlike Sam Elliott." Elliott was convinced and accepted the part. He recognized, however, how incongruous his character was in the film; Ethan Coen recalls that Elliott asked the filmmakers "What am I doing in this movie?" to which they responded "we don't know either."

References

"Sam Elliott," *Biography.com*; Will Harris, "Sam Elliott on George Clooney's Eyes, Jeff Bridges' Dudeness, and Working with Ron Swanson," *Avclub.com*, October 13, 2013; "Sam Elliott," *New York Times*, Movies & TV; Eddie Robson, *Coen Brothers* (London: Virgin Books, 2003). See also *THE BIG LEBOWSKI*.

FARGO (1996)

DIRECTOR: Joel Coen and Ethan Coen (uncredited). SCREENPLAY: Ethan Coen and Joel Coen. EXECUTIVE PRODUCERS: Tim Bevan and Eric Fellner. PRODUCERS: Ethan Coen and Joel Coen (uncredited); John Cameron (Line Producer). PHOTOGRAPHY: Roger Deakins. EDITING: Ethan Coen and Joel Coen (as Roderick Jaynes). MUSIC: Carter Burwell. PRODUCTION DESIGN: Rick Heinrichs. ART DIRECTION: Thomas P. Wilkins. SET DECORATION: Lauri Gaffin. COSTUME DESIGN: Mary Zophres.

CAST: William H. Macy (Jerry Lundegaard), Steve Buscemi (Carl Showalter), Peter Stormare (Gaear Grimsrud), Kristin Rudrüd (Jean Lundegaard), Harve Presnell (Wade Gustafson), Tony Denman (Scotty Lundegaard), Frances McDormand (Marge Gunderson), John Carroll Lynch (Norm Gunderson), Jose Feliciano (Himself), J. Todd Anderson (Victim in field), Bruce Campbell (Soap Opera Actor).

RUNNING TIME: 98 minutes. Color.

RELEASED THROUGH: Gramercy Pictures. PREMIERE: March 8, 1996.

DVD: MGM Home Entertainment.

ACADEMY AWARDS: Best Actress in a Leading Role: Frances McDormand; Best Writing, Screenplay Written Directly for the Screen: Ethan Coen and Joel Coen; Best Picture (nominated: Ethan Coen); Best Actor in a Supporting Role (nominated: William H. Macy); Best Director (nominated: Joel Coen); Best Cinematography (nominated: Roger Deakins); Best Film Editing (nominated: Ethan Coen and Joel Coen, as Roderick Jaynes).

Joel and Ethan Coen's sixth feature film, *Fargo*, begins on the snow-swept plains of the upper-Midwest, accompanied by Carter Burwell's dramatic score, which suggests to the viewer that something momentous is about to occur. What the viewer sees, however, in addition to a lone bird fighting the howling winds sweeping the snowscape, is the ponderously slow progress of a car, approaching the camera and towing a trailer. The viewer cannot be certain why this car and its slow trek through drifting snow might be important, but both the music and the steady, lingering camerawork tell us that it is indeed significant.

The driver of that car is Jerry Lundegaard (William H. Macy), who has arranged to have his wife kidnapped in order to secure the million-dollar ransom for himself, as he is deeply in debt. Jerry, who lives with his family in Minneapolis, has falsified documents at his place of employ and illegally obtained $320,000. He needs the ransom funds to cover up his embezzlement; additionally, he has discovered a promising business deal, a parking lot in Wayzata, and he needs $750,000 to bring his dreams of prosperity to fruition. Jerry has married well; his wife, Jean (Kris-

Frances McDormand in *Fargo* (1996)

tin Rudrüd), is the daughter of Wade Gustafson (Harve Presnell), and Wade is quite
wealthy. Gustafson, however, has made it
clear that he considers Jerry incompetent
at best, and while Jean and their son Scotty
(Tony Denman) will be well cared for, Jerry
has no claim to the Gustafson fortune. Jerry
turns instead to the kidnapping scheme,
and to achieve his ends, Jerry has hired
Carl Showalter (Steve Buscemi) and Gaear
Grimsrud (Peter Stormare) to kidnap—
but not harm—Jean in return for $40,000
in cash, to be paid when Jerry receives
the ransom. Prior to the abduction, Jerry
meets with the kidnappers in Fargo, North
Dakota, arranging details and delivering
to them a new Cutlass Ciera, which he has
stolen from the Gustafson car dealership
where he works. The abduction transpires
without problem, though Jean initially
shows great resourcefulness in resisting and
eluding her attackers; however, en route to
their hideout, Carl and Gaear are stopped
by a state trooper, whom Gaear shoots and
kills, along with two passersby who happen

upon them while the crime is in progress.
Leaving behind this carnage, the kidnappers and their captive retreat to a cabin in
the woods where Carl and Gaear await their
portion of the ransom money.

The film then follows the efforts of
Marge Gunderson (Frances McDormand),
chief of police in Brainerd, Minnesota, as
she investigates the triple homicide, a journey which takes her to the Twin Cities and
back again. Seven months pregnant, Chief
Gunderson accurately pieces together the
series of events that resulted in the three
murders, though she cannot yet account
for the players or the motive in the crime.
The film then begins to move between the
three narratives: Jerry, as he informs his
father-in-law of the kidnapping and antici-
pates a ransom call; Carl, Gaear, and Jean,
as they shiver in the lakeside house, watching soap operas on a television with poor
reception; and Marge, who eats much and
often, all the while nearing a solution to the
crimes. The plot lines converge, as Marge
traces the kidnappers' phone call to the car

dealership where Jerry works and Wade Gustafson attempts to deliver the ransom money and is shot and killed by Carl in the process. Carl, discovering that the ransom is a million dollars, rather than $80,000 as Jerry had led the kidnappers to believe, buries most of the money in the snow next to a fence line on a long, deserted stretch of Minnesota highway and returns to Gaear and the cabin with only $80,000. Marge locates the kidnappers' cabin on the lake and discovers Gaear, who has killed Jean and is disposing of the recently deceased Carl in the wood chipper. Jerry, realizing that his carefully orchestrated plan is collapsing around him, hides Gustafson's body in the trunk of a car and takes to the road, only to be apprehended by the law in a roadside motel in North Dakota.

Marge, who has sleuthed her way to a closed case, returns to her home and husband, and the film closes with her reassurance, to herself as well as to Norm (John Carroll Lynch), that "we're doin' pretty good."

In addition to its seven Oscar nominations, which resulted in two wins, *Fargo* was nominated for the Palme d'Or and won Best Director for Joel Coen, at the Cannes Film Festival. Additionally, the film was nominated for four Golden Globes: Best Motion Picture—Comedy/Musical; Best Director—Motion Picture; Best Performance by an Actress in a Motion Picture—Comedy or Musical; and Best Screenplay—Motion Picture.

The picture's budget was $7 million, the worldwide box office receipts totaled over $60 million, and critics and reviewers responded positively to the film, for the most part. Roger Ebert deemed it "one of the best films I've ever seen," and Arnold Wayne Jones of the *Dallas Observer* wrote that "*Fargo* is a concert performance—an illuminating amalgam of emotion and thought,"

concluding "It's *Seven* filtered through the sunny perspective of *Forrest Gump*."

The film's opening was especially fascinating for the press. *Fargo* begins with the caption "This is a true story. The events depicted in this film took place in Minnesota in 1987. At the request of the survivors, the names have been changed. Out of respect for the dead, the rest has been told exactly as it occurred," and initially, reviewers accepted this statement at face value. Film critics from the *Washington Post*, the *National Review*, *New York*, and the *New York Times*, among others, embraced the fact that *Fargo* was based on real events, and Joel and Ethan Coen encouraged that belief, stating in interviews that the crimes had indeed occurred. The film's credits, however, assured viewers that the characters and events of the picture were intended to bear no resemblance to actual persons or events. This contradiction led the *New York Post* to investigate the supposed Minnesota crime and announce that they were unable to locate any record of such a crime or series of crimes in the state in the last thirty years, and certainly not in 1987. Faced with evidence of their duplicity, the Coens admitted that the film's events were fiction rather than fact.

In their discussions prior to and following the revelation of the film's fictional status, Joel and Ethan Coen explained their choice of material and their decision to claim that the events of the film were real. Their theory was that if viewers are told that a story is true, the audience "gives you permission to do things that they might not if they're essentially coming in expecting to watch a fictive thriller." That permission included the audience's willingness to observe Marge and Norm in their home, participating in mundane tasks such as eating breakfast together and watching television in bed. Joel Coen explains that "the impulse here was to de-dramatize things rather than to dramatize things," and this approach applied to the murders and the subsequent investigations as well as to the home life of Marge and Norm. As a result, the style of *Fargo* is based far more in realism than their recent films had been, as *The Hudsucker Proxy* (1994) contained elements of the fantastic, as did *Barton Fink* (1991). *Fargo* focuses on characters who are very ordinary, and while the events which bring them together are violent and at times bizarre, the characters themselves are inherently banal, says Joel Coen. Compounding the banality of the everyday routines depicted by the film are the flat effect of the Midwestern accent and the polite nature of "Minnesota nice," says Ethan Coen, a concept that would be familiar to both Coens, as they were raised in Minnesota; Ethan further notes that "my whole association with Minnesota, where we grew up, was very dull." The goal, claim the brothers, was "an attempt to bring both the villains and the hero down to a recognizable, ordinary scale," and for the villains specifically, the intent was "to go against the Hollywood cliché of the bad guy as the super-professional who controls everything he does." Because most criminals are closer to the ordinary person than to cinematic super-villains, says Ethan, *Fargo* is then "closer to life than the conventions of cinema and genre movies."

This "real-life" approach to film was ultimately just another stylization, like those employed in their earlier, overtly-stylized films, Joel Coen notes, though not the style one might expect from a crime film. The filmmakers wanted "the camera to tell the story as an observer," and the approach was successful, as reviewer Leonard Klady characterizes the film as "direct, documentary-style filmmaking." The palette of the film is decidedly white, *film blanc*

rather than film noir, though the Coens shot the film on cloudy days to emphasize the "bleak aspect of living in that area in the wintertime—what the light and this sort of landscape does, psychologically," says Joel. The opening sequence of the car and the trailer pushing through the blowing snow was built on the idea of blurring the line between the land and the sky, obscuring the horizon in a haze of blowing snow; one writer characterized Roger Deakins' cinematography as "a huge blanket of snow, the image turning fuzzy at the edges to suggest recession into infinity." Only the telephone lines define the landscape initially, and as the car mounts a small rise only then does the situation reveal itself: "the whole idea of the car emerging ghostlike out of the snow—that whiteness and weirdness—was important to us," the Coens state. Enhancing this weirdness is the score of the film, which seems much grander than the events that transpire on the screen. The ominous music warns the viewer that peril looms on this flat, windswept plain, while the nondescript sedan that fills the center of the screen seems anything but menacing. Carter Burwell, who composed the score, intended for the viewer to sense this contradiction: "I wanted the movie to be bombastic enough that you might just believe it was a real police story and yet, also through bombast, maybe make you just laugh a little bit," he states. The film ends as it began, focusing on the everyday events that comprise this "crime story," demonstrating that drama exists in small ways and places and that crime is borne of petty desires that become personal tragedies.

Joel and Ethan Coen have stated that they selected the title of the film because they liked the sound of the word, instead of calling the film "Brainerd," for example. They assure viewers that there is no hidden meaning to the title, and that may be so.

However, that statement, like the brothers' assurances that the film is based on actual events, may also be inaccurate, as *Fargo* is a film of misdirection from beginning to end. The film's title might lead the viewer to assume that the action takes place in Fargo, North Dakota. However, the film is largely set in Minnesota, specifically Brainerd and the Twin Cities, with the exception of one early scene in the Blue Ox bar in Fargo where Jerry commissions the kidnapping of his wife and the penultimate scene at a roadside motel outside of Bismarck, North Dakota, in which Jerry is apprehended by authorities. Jerry's plan is itself inherently misleading, for a number of reasons: he has planned the kidnapping of his own wife and hired the men to execute the crime, making it appear that he has no knowledge of the plan; he further tells the kidnappers that the ransom is $80,000 and they will receive $40,000, but the amount he requests from Wade is a million dollars. The necessity for the arranged kidnapping is also based in misdirection, as Jerry has received $320,000 from General Motors, using a fax with illegible vehicle identification numbers to obtain the funds. When questioned about the documentation, he assures GM that he has mailed the list of VINs, and of course, that is not the case. When Jerry meets with Wade and Stan Grossman, he leads them to believe that he wants a loan for the parking lot deal, which may be true to some degree, but his more pressing financial need is to clear up his debt with GMAC.

Misdirection is not limited to Jerry Lundegaard, however, as the kidnapper Carl engages in similarly deceptive activities. His attempt to divert the state trooper from his legal duties by bribing him with a fifty-dollar bill leads to the shooting death of the trooper and two others. Later in the film, Carl hides the better part of a million dollars in the Minnesota snow, returning to Gaear with only the $80,000 they had

anticipated. The police, too, are victims of misdirection. When the Brainerd police arrive at the scene and begin investigating the crimes, Lou initially believes that the first three letters in the criminals' license plate are DLR, but Marge sets him straight, explaining that the letters more likely stand for Dealer. Perceptive though she may be, Marge is susceptible to being misled herself, as she is taken in by Mike Yanagita's story of having been married to Linda Cooksey, who died after a heroic battle with leukemia. It is Marge who has the final word, however. Near the film's conclusion, as she drives Gaear toward Brainerd and the punishment that awaits him, Marge discusses with him the ways in which he has been deceived as well. Dismayed at the violence that resulted from greed, she tells him "There's more to life than a little money, ya know?" Her comments, and the final scene which shows Marge and Norm together in bed, quietly anticipating the birth of their child in the spring, shift the focus from the many misdirections of the film to the ordinary, even banal moments that comprise a person's life.

In 2003, Kathy Bates directed a television pilot based on the film *Fargo*, written by Bruce Paltrow and Robert Palm and starring Edie Falco as Marge and Paltrow as Deputy Sheriff Lou. The Coens were not involved with the project, it did not develop into a series, and Joel Coen has stated that "I can't say that we weren't happy that it died." However, in the spring of 2014, FX aired a ten-part series based on the film, starring Billy Bob Thornton as a drifter who arrives in a small, upper-Midwestern town and Martin Freeman as the insurance agent whose life is thrown into chaos by the arrival of the drifter. The character of Marge does not appear in the series, and Joel and Ethan Coen gave their blessing to the project, serving as executive directors for the show.

References

David Bennun, "This Is a True Story," in *The Coen Brothers: Interviews*, ed. William Rodney Allen (Jackson: University Press of Mississippi, 2006); Peter Biskind, "Joel and Ethan Coen," in *Joel & Ethan Coen: Blood Siblings*, ed. Paul A. Woods (London: Plexus Publishing, 2003); Greg Braxton, "TCA: FX's *Fargo*: Like the Movie, but Different," *LATimes.com*; Michel Ciment and Hubert Niogret, "Closer to Life Than the Conventions of Cinema," in *The Coen Brothers: Interviews*, ed. William Rodney Allen (Jackson: University Press of Mississippi, 2006); Thomas Doherty, "*Fargo*," *Cineaste* 22.2 (1996); Roger Ebert, "*Fargo*," *RogerEbert.com*, March 8, 1996; Graham Fuller, "Do Not Miss *Fargo*," in *Joel & Ethan Coen: Blood Siblings*, ed. Paul A. Woods (London: Plexus Publishing, 2003); Desson Howe, "In Cold Blood in Cold Climes," *Washington Post*, March 8, 1996; Arnold Wayne Jones, "The Perfect Crime," *Dallas Observer*, March 7, 1996; Leonard Klady, "Review: *Fargo*," *Variety*, February 11, 1996; Eddie Robson, *Coen Brothers* (London: Virgin Books, 2003); Erica Rowell, *The Brothers Grim: The Films of Ethan and Joel Coen* (Lanham, MD: Scarecrow Press, 2007). See also J. TODD ANDERSON, CARTER BURWELL, STEVE BUSCEMI, BRUCE CAMPBELL, ROGER DEAKINS, RICK HEINRICHS, WILLIAM H. MACY, FRANCES MCDORMAND, HARVE PRESNELL, KRISTIN RUDRÜD, PETER STORMARE, MARY ZOPHRES.

FINNEY, ALBERT (1936–)

Born May 9, 1936, in Manchester, England, the son of a bookmaker, Finney attended the Royal Academy of Dramatic Arts at age seventeen and subsequently became a member of the Royal Shakespeare Company. His film career began in 1960 with *The Entertainer* and was followed by *Saturday Night and Sunday Morning* (1960). He was offered the title role in *Lawrence of Arabia* (1962), which he declined, appearing instead in *Tom Jones* (1963), for which he received an Academy Award nomination. In 1965, with actor Michael Medwin, Finney began Memorial Enterprises, a production company that produced films from 1967 to 1981, including his first film as director, *Charlie Bubbles* (1967). A five-time Academy nominee, he has never won an Oscar, though he did receive BAFTA, Golden Globe, and Emmy Awards for his portrayal of Winston Churchill in the TV movie *The Gathering Storm* (2002). Best known for his roles in *Two for the Road* (1967, with Audrey Hepburn), *Annie* (1982), *Erin Brockovich* (2000), *Big Fish* (2003), and *The Bourne Ultimatum* (2007), Finney battled kidney cancer between 2007 and 2012 and consequently worked very little in film or on stage during this time. Following his successful treatment, he appeared in *The Bourne Legacy* (2012) and *Skyfall* (2012). Finney has appeared in one Coen brothers film, *Miller's Crossing* (1990).

The part of Leo, the Irish mob boss challenged by upstart Italian gangsters in *Miller's Crossing*, was originally written for Trey Wilson, who played Nathan Arizona in *Raising Arizona* (1987), but when Wilson died suddenly just before shooting began, Finney agreed to take the part. While in New Orleans for filming, Finney immersed himself in the city and its culture, leading the St. Patrick's Day parade and participating in the nightlife of Bourbon Street. Gabriel Byrne, who played Tom Reagan in the film, suggests that had there been a mayoral election in New Orleans that year, Finney certainly would have won it, hands down. According to Barry Sonnenfeld, cinematographer for the film, Finney so enjoyed the filming process that he remained in New Orleans after Leo's scenes were completed, making a cameo appearance as the matron in the ladies' room scene with Byrne and Marcia Gay Harden.

The *New Yorker* deemed Finney "the most entertaining performer in the movie," the *Los Angeles Times*, "breathtaking," and the *Guardian* called his performance "a seemingly effortless diversion into territory that once belonged to Edward G. Robinson." While the film itself was met with criticism both laudatory and scathing, reviews across the spectrum acknowledge Finney as one of the most successful aspects of the film. Though the part was not originally written for him, Ethan Coen has stated that after the fact, "it's impossible for us to imagine any other actor than Finney in the Leo role." Adopting an Irish accent for the part, Finney's Leo acts as one corner of the lover's triangle in the film, appearing opposite Byrne's Tom and Harden's Verna. While the film presents Leo as a mob boss propped up by his right-hand man, Tom, what Leo lacks in smarts, he makes up for in heart—the Coen brothers call him "lionhearted." He is propelled through the plot by his love for Verna, his jealousy at Tom's relationship with Verna, and his desire for revenge against the Italian gangsters who challenge his authority and disrupt his organization.

Finney's most memorable scene in the film certainly garnered much attention, the scene in which Leo escapes an assassination attempt by rolling off the roof of his burning house, Tommy gun in hand. Critics often mentioned and primarily praised the night-time scene, which is accompanied by Frank Patterson's performance of "Danny Boy." The scene serves to offset the abundance of snappy dialogue that pervades the film and acts as a nod to the obligatory gun battles in gangster films of the 1930s. Joel Coen states that this scene is Leo "in his element . . . Leo as the boss, Leo as the guy in control of the situation," and though

this is true, Leo goes into hiding following the shootout, as his organization attempts to fend off Johnny Caspar's challenge for control of the city. The filmmakers deemed this midpoint of the film as "about time at that point to shed a little blood," following which the body count steadily rises and the film moves toward its conclusion. Leo appears very little in the second half of the film, but he remains the motivating factor to Tom's actions. Out of loyalty to and affection for Leo, Tom orchestrates a series of events that will reinstate him as a governing force, and Leo ultimately succeeds because Tom ensures he succeeds. This return to power comes at a cost, however, as at the film's conclusion, Leo has won the girl and the gang wars, but must govern the city without any further help from Tom.

References

"Albert Finney," *Biography.com*; Steven Levy, "Shot by Shot," in *The Coen Brothers: Interviews*, ed. William Rodney Allen (Jackson: University Press of Mississippi, 2006); Derek Malcolm, "*Miller's Crossing*," *Guardian*, February 14, 1991; DVD Special Features, *Miller's Crossing*, 20th Century Fox Home Entertainment, 2003; Terrence Rafferty, "*Miller's Crossing*," *New Yorker*, November 5, 1990; John H. Richardson, "The Joel and Ethan Story," in *Joel & Ethan Coen: Blood Siblings*, ed. Paul A. Woods (London: Plexus Publishing, 2003); Alex Simon, "Gabriel Byrne: Talk to Me," *TheHollywoodInterview. com*, December 28, 2012; Paul Taylor, "Actor Albert Finney—Son of Salford—Loves to Come Home," *Manchester Evening News*, November 30, 2012. See also *MILLER'S CROSSING*.

GANDOLFINI, JAMES
(1961–2013)

Born September 18, 1961, in Westwood, New Jersey, the son of a bricklayer/custodian and a school cafeteria chef, Gandolfini attended Rutgers University, where he received a degree in communications. He then worked odd jobs, including driving a truck and tending bar prior to enrolling in acting classes at age twenty-five. His first on-screen appearance was in the film in *Shock! Shock! Shock!* (1987), and from this obscure start, he appeared on Broadway in a revival of *A Streetcar Named Desire* (1992). He was cast in Sidney Lumet's *A Stranger among Us* (1992), Tony Scott's *True Romance* (1993) and *Crimson Tide* (1995), and Barry Sonnenfeld's *Get Shorty* (1995). He worked again with Lumet on *Night Falls on Manhattan* (1996), with Clint Eastwood in *Midnight in the Garden of Good and Evil* (1997), and with Joel Schumacher in *8MM* (1999). In 1995, Gandolfini returned to Broadway, appearing in *On the Waterfront*. In many of his film roles, he played a gangster, and in 1999 he was cast in the role that would define him, as mob boss Tony Soprano in HBO's *The Sopranos*. The series ran for six seasons, during which time he received the Golden Globe for Best Performance by an Actor in a TV Series—Drama (1999) and three Primetime Emmy Awards for Outstanding Lead Actor in a Drama Series (2000, 2001, 2003). He appeared in the film *Romance & Cigarettes* (2005), directed by Coen collaborator John Turturro, and following the conclusion of *The Sopranos*, he returned to work with Tony Scott in *The Taking of Pelham 1 2 3* (2009) and appeared in the Oscar-winning *Zero Dark Thirty* (2012). Gandolfini was nominated for a Tony for his performance in Broadway's *God of Carnage* (2009).

Gandolfini served as executive producer for three television movies: *Alive Day Memories: Home from Iraq* (2007), *Wartorn:1861–2010* (2010), and *Hemingway and Gellhorn* (2012), all for HBO, and was executive producing and starring in the HBO mini-series *Criminal Justice* (2013) when he died at the age of fifty-one of a heart attack. Robert De Niro stepped in to play Gandolfini's part and conclude the series, and Gandolfini continued to be credited as executive producer, posthumously.

Gandolfini appeared in one Coen film, *The Man Who Wasn't There* (2001), as Big Dave Brewster; he was not initially interested in the role, as he wanted a break between seasons of *The Sopranos*. Having committed, however, his performance was characterized as "a force of nature" by *Rolling Stone*'s Peter Travers. Big Dave is having an affair with Doris Crane (Frances McDormand), wife of Ed Crane (Billy Bob Thornton), an arrangement that results in Ed's attempted blackmail of Big Dave. Ed discovers, as Andrew O'Hehir notes, that "any character [Gandolfini] plays is the last person in the world one should try to blackmail."

References

"James Gandolfini," *Biography.com*; Dave Itzkoff, "James Gandolfini Is Dead at 51: A Complex Mob Boss in *The Sopranos*," *New York Times*, June 19, 2013; Andrew O'Hehir, "*The Man Who Wasn't There*," *Salon.com*, October 31, 2001; David Remnick, "Postscript: James Gandolfini, 1961–2013," *New Yorker*, June 19, 2013; Peter Travers, "*The Man Who Wasn't There*," *Rolling Stone*, November 2, 2001. See also THE MAN WHO WASN'T THERE.

GASSNER, DENNIS (1948–)

Born in 1948 in Vancouver, British Columbia, Canada, Gassner played football in college but turned down an offer to try out with the Los Angeles Rams to continue his studies in graphic design. He designed record album covers prior to beginning his work in the film industry. Gassner served as production assistant on Francis Ford Coppola's *Apocalypse Now* (1979), which he followed with the Coppola films *One from the Heart* (1982) and *Rumble Fish* (1983), as a graphic designer on both projects. He stepped up to production designer with *The Hitcher* (1986) and subsequently worked on *Field of Dreams* (1989), Barry Levinson's *Bugsy* (1991), Kevin Costner's *Waterworld* (1995), and Peter Weir's *The Truman Show* (1998).

Gassner won the Oscar for Best Art Direction-Set Decoration, with Nancy Haigh, for their work on *Bugsy*, and he and Haigh were nominated for art direction and set decoration for Sam Mendes's *Road to Perdition* (2002). He worked with Tim Burton on *Big Fish* (2003), with Mendes again on *Jarhead* (2005), and with Marc Forster on *Quantum of Solace* (2008). With Anna Pinnock, Gassner was Oscar nominated for art direction for *The Golden Compass* (2007), for which he won the Art Directors'

Guild Award for Excellence in Production Design. His second Art Directors' Guild Award was for his work on *Skyfall* (2012).

Gassner served as production designer for six Coen brothers' films: *Miller's Crossing* (1990), *Barton Fink* (1991), *The Hudsucker Proxy* (1994), *O Brother, Where Art Thou?* (2000), *The Man Who Wasn't There* (2001), and *The Ladykillers* (2004). He was Oscar nominated for Best Art Direction-Set Decoration for his work on *Barton Fink*.

References

"Dennis Gassner," *TCM.com*; "Dennis Gassner," *TV.com*. See also BARTON FINK, THE HUDSUCKER PROXY, THE LADYKILLERS, THE MAN WHO WASN'T THERE, MILLER'S CROSSING, O BROTHER, WHERE ART THOU?

GAZZARA, BEN (1930–2012)

Born August 28, 1930, in New York City, Gazzara was the son of Italian immigrants. He became interested in acting at the Madison Square Boys' Club, where he took the stage for the first time at the age of twelve. After studying engineering at the City College of New York, Gazzara turned to acting after he dropped out of school. He studied at the Actor's Studio with Lee Strasberg and debuted off-Broadway in *End as a Man* (1953), which he followed with *Cat on a Hot Tin Roof* (1955), and *A Hat Full of Rain* (1956), for which he received a Tony Award nomination for Best Actor. Gazzara began his on-screen career in the television series *Treasury Men in Action* (1952–1953), *Danger* (1952–1954), and *Justice* (1954), and his first film appearance was a lead role in *The Strange One* (1957). He starred in the series *Arrest and Trial* (1963–1964) and *Run for Your Life* (1965–1968), earning three Golden Globe nominations for Best TV Star—Male (1966, 1967, 1968).

In the 1970s he appeared in a number of made-for-television movies, including *When Michael Calls* (1972) with Michael

Douglas, Michael Crichton's *Pursuit* (1972), and *The Trial of Lee Harvey Oswald* (1977) with Lorne Greene. He continued to appear on Broadway during the 1970s as well, earning Tony nominations for his work in Eugene O'Neill's *Hughie* (1975), in David Scott Milton's *Duet* (1975), and in Edward Albee's *Who's Afraid of Virginia Woolf?* (1976). Over his long and productive career, he worked with such directors as Otto Preminger in *Anatomy of a Murder* (1959), with John Cassavetes in *Husbands* (1970), *The Killing of a Chinese Bookie* (1976), and *Opening Night* (1977), and with Peter Bogdanovich in *They All Laughed* (1981), among others.

Gazzara lived in Italy during the 1980s, where he appeared in films as well, and he periodically returned to the Hollywood screen in such films as David Mamet's *The Spanish Prisoner* (1997), Vincent Gallo's *Buffalo '66* (1998), and Spike Lee's *Summer of Sam* (1999). He won the Emmy Award for Outstanding Supporting Actor in a Miniseries or a Movie for *Hysterical Blindness* (2002) and toured in a one-man play about Yogi Berra from 2003 to 2005. In addition to his career as an actor, Gazzara directed episodes of *Run for Your Life* (1967–1968), *The Name of the Game* (1971), and *Columbo* (1974–1975), as well as the Italian film *Oltre l'oceano* (*Beyond the Ocean*) (1990). In 2004, Gazzara published his memoir, entitled *In the Moment: My Life as an Actor*. Speaking of Gazzara, actor and director Sean Penn has said "There's something so energized and unapologetically male about Ben—he's a throwback to an American archetype associated with Hemingway." Gazzara died in New York City in 2012, of pancreatic cancer.

Gazzara appeared in one film by Joel and Ethan Coen, *The Big Lebowski* (1998), as porn star mogul Jackie Treehorn. Though Gazzara's role is limited to one scene in the film, Treehorn is the catalyst for the film's plot, as his thugs mistake the Dude (Jeff Bridges) for the "Big" Lebowski (David Huddleston), and the action ensues from a subsequent unfortunate incident with the Dude's rug.

References

Dennis McLellan, "Ben Gazzara, 1930–2012," *Los Angeles Times*, February 4, 2012; "Ben Gazzara," *Biography.com*; "Ben Gazzara," *New York Times*, Movies & TV; Matt Schudel, "Ben Gazzara, Stage, Film, and TV Actor Dies at 81," *Washington Post*, February 4, 2012. See also *THE BIG LEBOWSKI*.

GETZ, JOHN (1946–)

Born October 15, 1946, in Davenport, Iowa, and raised in Mississippi, Getz attended the University of Iowa and then the American Conservatory Theater in San Francisco. He worked with the Napa Valley Theater Company, following which he relocated to New York where he was cast in a recurring role in *Another World* (1964). He appeared off-Broadway in *Macbeth* and *Measure for Measure* with the New York Shakespeare Festival, *Tartuffe* at the LaJolla Playhouse, and *The Seagull* at the Old Globe San Diego, making his Broadway debut in *They're Playing Our Song* (1979). In 1974, he was cast in the made-for-television movie *Killer Bees*, which he followed with his first film appearance in *The Happy Hooker* (1975). In the late 1970s, he had a recurring role in the television series *Rafferty* (1977), and he made one-time appearances in such series as *Wonder Woman* (1977), *Barnaby Jones* (1978), *Three's Company* (1980), and twice appeared on *Ryan's Hope* (1978–1981). Following his 1984 role in *Blood Simple*, Getz played the lead in the series *MacGruder and Loud* (1985) and appeared in the films *The Fly* (1986) and *The Fly II* (1989). He worked with Oliver Stone in *Born on the Fourth of July* (1989) and with Martin Sheen in *Fortunes of War*

(1994), while appearing in numerous television movies during the 1990s. He made frequent appearances on the series *Ned and Stacy* (1995–1996), *Maggie* (1998–1999), and *Joan of Arcadia* (2003), as well as *The West Wing* (2006), *King of Queens* (2004–2006), and *Day Break* (2006–2007).

Getz's film career continued periodically, with roles in David Fincher films *Zodiac* (2007) and *The Social Network* (2010), and he played Paul Jobs in the biopic *Jobs* (2013), about the life of Steve Jobs. His primary on-screen appearances on television include *NCIS* (2010), *Law and Order: Special Victims Unit* (2013), and *Bones* (2014).

As Ray in *Blood Simple*, Getz plays the employee of Julian Marty (Dan Hedaya) and the lover of Marty's wife, Abby (Frances McDormand), caught in a complicated narrative of violence and desire that brings him to murder and mental instability. Though Hal Hinson's review of the film deemed both Ray and Abby as "bland and uninteresting" and their relationship as lacking fireworks, Getz's performance in the film propelled his career to a new level, as he has worked steadily since his appearance in the film, becoming a well-known face, if not a household name.

References

Hal Hinson, "Bloodlines," in *The Coen Brothers: Interviews*, ed. William Rodney Allen (Jackson: University Press of Mississippi, 2006); "John Getz," *BroadwayWorld.com*; "John Getz," *NYTW.org*, Company Biographies; Eddie Robson, *Coen Brothers* (London: Virgin Books, 2003). See also *BLOOD SIMPLE*.

GONCHOR, JESS (1962–)

Born July 15, 1962, in New York City, Gonchor attended Mammaroneck High School, where he became involved in theatre. He received his bachelor's degree in Technical Theater from the State University of New York, Brockport, and began his career working on theatre productions off-Broadway. In 1993, Gonchor served as assistant art director for *Teenage Mutant Ninja Turtles III* and as art director for the vampire comedy *Love Bites* (1993). He worked as construction foreman on Clint Eastwood's *A Perfect World* (1993), Rob Reiner's *The American President* (1995), the 1996 adaptation of Arthur Miller's *The Crucible*, and *City of Angels* (1998), starring Nicolas Cage and Meg Ryan. As art director, he worked on *The Story of Us* (1999), *Identity* (2003), and *The Last Samurai* (2003), prior to serving as production designer for *Capote* (2005) and *The Devil Wears Prada* (2006), among others.

Gonchor began working with Joel and Ethan Coen on *No Country for Old Men* (2007) and continued as production designer for *Burn After Reading* (2008), *A Serious Man* (2009), *True Grit* (2010), and *Inside Llewyn Davis* (2013). With Nancy Haigh, Gonchor was Oscar nominated for Best Achievement in Art Direction for their work on *True Grit*. As Gonchor prepared for *True Grit*, Joel and Ethan Coen advised him not to view the 1969 film, starring John Wayne, but instead to focus on the novel by Charles Portis, as the filmmakers considered their project to be a re-adaptation of the book rather than a remake of the earlier Wayne film.

Characterizing his work with the Coens, Gonchor has commented "It's a true collaboration and like working with two other production designers—they just get it." He further notes, "There's something not exactly real about the look of their movies," adding "they're not hung up on replicating things," an observation echoed by reviewers of Coen films, often as a criticism of their projects.

References

Peter Caranicas, "Nitty-Gritty of Designing for the Coens," *HollywoodHappenings.org*; "Jess Gonchor," *FocusFeatures.com*, *A Serious*

Man, Cast & Crew; "Jess Gonchor, Production Designer," *HamiltonWatch.com*; "Wares of the Worlds," *Variety.com*, February 4, 2011. See also *BURN AFTER READING, INSIDE LLEWYN DAVIS, NO COUNTRY FOR OLD MEN, A SERIOUS MAN, TRUE GRIT.*

GOODMAN, JOHN (1952–)

A native of Affton, Missouri, Goodman was born June 20, 1952, and was raised by his mother, Virginia, after his father died of a heart attack. He attended Southwest Missouri State University on a football scholarship, but following an injury, he quit the sport and studied drama with classmates Kathleen Turner and Tess Harper. Upon graduation, he moved to New York and worked as a bouncer and appeared in children's theatre while pursuing his acting career. His off-Broadway debut was in *A Midsummer Night's Dream* and he appeared on Broadway in 1978 with Dennis Quaid, Bruce Willis, and Kevin Kline in *Loose Ends*, but the play was not considered a success. Goodman's film debut was in *Jailbait Babysitter* (1977), which was followed by the television movie *The Face of Rage* (1983) and various small roles on television and film through the mid-1980s. In 1985 he played Pap Finn in Roger Miller's *Big River*, and that same year he was cast in a prominent role in David Byrne's *True Stories*. He worked with Richard Dreyfus and Holly Hunter in Steven Spielberg's *Always* (1989) and with Nicholas Cage in Martin Scorsese's *Bringing Out the Dead* (1999). From 1988–1997, Goodman played Dan Conner in Roseanne Barr's long-running television series *Roseanne*, for which he received three Golden Globe nominations for Best Actor, with one win (1993), and seven Emmy nominations for Outstanding Lead Actor in a Comedy Series. Beyond *Roseanne*, his television work is extensive and includes multiple appearances on *Saturday Night Live* (1998–2000) and recurring roles in *The West Wing* (2003–2004), *Treme* (2010–2011), and *Community* (2011–2012). Goodman has also done voice work for a number of animated films and television shows, among which are *The Simpsons* (1999), *The Emperor's New Groove* (2000), *Monster's Inc.* (2001) and *Monster's University* (2013), and *The Princess and the Frog* (2009). As his public profile continued to grow, Goodman commented in a *Vanity Fair* interview that his fame has "just always been embarrassing to me," describing his ardent fans and the persistent paparazzi as "more interested in fame than they are in me, certainly." He concludes that his fame "doesn't necessarily have anything even to do with me. There's just too much celebrity culture. It's worthless coin." Some of Goodman's popularity can be attributed to his roles in films by Joel and Ethan Coen, as he has appeared in six Coen pictures: *Raising Arizona* (1987), *Barton Fink* (1991), *The Hudsucker Proxy* (1994), *The Big Lebowski* (1998), *O Brother, Where Art Thou?* (2000), and *Inside Llewyn Davis* (2013).

In Goodman's debut Coen role as Gale Snoats in *Raising Arizona*, Gale and his brother Evelle (William Forsythe) emerge from the earth covered in mud, having tunneled their way out of prison. The brothers elude the law by hiding out at the home of Ed and H.I. McDunnough (Holly Hunter and Nicolas Cage), but when they discover that the missing Nathan Arizona Jr. has been kidnapped by the McDunnoughs, the Snoats brothers abduct the toddler themselves, hoping to secure the ransom money for the return of the child. In its review, *Variety* characterized Goodman as "an actor who can communicate friendliness and goodwill in spite of his foolishness," deeming the Snoats brothers' scenes as "the most animated and entertaining in the picture."

As Barton Fink's fellow hotel resident at the Hotel Earle in *Barton Fink*, Goodman appears as Charlie Meadows, a traveling salesman who sells insurance and peace of mind. A common man, he discusses the challenges of a working life and shows Barton some basic wrestling moves, but as the narrative progresses, he becomes Barton's accessory in disposing of Audrey Taylor's (Judy Davis) corpse. Shortly thereafter, his character becomes that of his alias, "Mad Man" Karl Mundt, a serial killer wanted for murdering and beheading his victims across the country. Desson Howe of the *Washington Post* characterizes Goodman's Charlie as a man whose "pumpkin-shaped body and booming voice create an engaging, head-scratching working man—with ominous undertones," and it was precisely that tension between the affable, chatty Charlie and the underlying danger of the serial killer Mundt which interested the Coen brothers. The film relies on the shift toward the macabre midway through the film, and that movement is facilitated by a corresponding shift in Goodman's character(s).

Goodman appeared in voice only in the Coens' 1994 *The Hudsucker Proxy*, as newsreel announcer Karl Mundt but had a more substantive role as Walter Sobchak in *The Big Lebowski*. As sidekick to Jeff Bridges's "Dude," Goodman's Walter delivers frequent tirades about bowling, the Vietnam War, and the entitled attitudes of the wealthy Bunny Lebowski (Tara Reid). Ray Pride, in his *Newcity* review, describes Walter as "a bullet-headed, barely contained titan of rage, running on the fumes of cracked belief," and Janet Maslin of the *New York Times* praises Goodman's performance, in which he rants "with a furious irrelevance that contrasts perfectly with the Dude's cavalier mode." The *Washington Post*'s Desson Howe further deems Goodman the "breakout star of the show."

As Big Dan Teague, the one-eyed Bible salesman and chanting Klansman in *O Brother*, Goodman played a man of large appetite, who first preys upon the gener-osity and then the pocketbooks of escaped convicts Everett and Delmar. He makes his second appearance in the film at the fiery, musical KKK rally, narrowly escaping the loss of his good eye only to be crushed beneath a burning cross.

It would be over a decade before Goodman would work with Joel and Ethan Coen again. Their next collaboration was *Inside Llewyn Davis*, in which Goodman plays Roland Turner, a polio-stricken drug addict and blues man with whom Llewyn (Oliver Isaac) catches a ride to Chicago. Roland is accompanied by Johnny Five, his valet and chauffer, played by Garrett Hedlund. Joe Morgenstern of the *Wall Street Journal* characterizes Goodman's Turner as "a pool hustler cum hipster musician who seems to be a drugged-out amalgam of Dr. John and the singer-songwriter Doc Pomus," musicians who lived and played during the early 1960s of the film, and the *Guardian*'s Tom Shone notes that "Goodman is a terrific gasbag, as rolling and unstoppable as lava."

References

Desson Howe, "*Barton Fink*," WashingtonPost.com, August 23, 1991; "John Goodman," *Biography.com*; "John Goodman," *New York Times*, Movies and TV; John Heilpern, "Out to Lunch with John Goodman," *Vanity Fair*, January, 2014; Janet Maslin "*The Big Lebowski* (1998): Film Review: A Bowling Ball's-Eye View of Reality," *New York Times*, March 6, 1998; Joe Morgenstern, "*Davis*: Exquisitely Played, Haunting Harmonics," *Wall Street Journal*, December 5, 2013; Ray Pride, "Coen Job," in *The Coen Brothers: Interviews*, ed. William Rodney Allen (Jackson: University Press of Mississippi, 2006); Tom Shone, "*Inside Llewyn Davis*: A Masterpiece 'Antimusical' from the Coen Brothers," *Guardian*, December 5, 2013. See also BARTON FINK, THE BIG LEBOWSKI, THE HUDSUCKER PROXY, INSIDE LLEWYN DAVIS, O BROTHER, WHERE ART THOU?, RAISING ARIZONA.

HAIGH, NANCY

Haigh attended the Massachusetts College of Arts, where she was a Fine Arts 3D major and graduated in 1968. She worked with the art department on *The Hitcher* (1986), Emilio Estevez's *Wisdom* (1986), and Michael Mann's *The Insider* (1999), among others, prior to serving as set decorator for such films as *Earth Girls Are Easy* (1988), *Field of Dreams* (1989), and *The Grifters* (1990). She has worked with Barry Levinson, on *Bugsy* (1991), Robert Zemekis, on *Forrest Gump* (1994), and Terry Gilliam, on *Fear and Loathing in Las Vegas* (1998). For Sam Mendes, she decorated the set for *Road to Perdition* (2002) and *Jarhead* (2005), and for Tim Burton, *Mars Attacks!* (1996) and *Big Fish* (2003). Haigh has been nominated for six Academy Awards for Art Direction, including *Barton Fink* and *True Grit*, and she won the Oscar for Best Art Direction-Set Direction for *Bugsy* (1991), an award she shared with Coen collaborator Dennis Gassner.

Haigh has served as set decorator for Joel and Ethan Coen on ten films. Her first Coen film was *Miller's Crossing* (1990), and she continued to work with the brothers through *Barton Fink* (1991), *The Hudsucker Proxy* (1994), *O Brother, Where Art Thou?* (2000), *Intolerable Cruelty* (2003), *The Ladykillers* (2004), *No Country for Old Men* (2007), *Burn After Reading* (2008), *A Serious Man* (2009), and *True Grit* (2010). On working with Haigh, Joel Coen has commented that she "always shocks us in terms of what she's able to unearth for whatever universe we've chosen to create. She supplies all those small details that make the sets look authentic."

References

Yana Y, "*A Serious Man* Production Notes," *FocusFeatures.com*, *A Serious Man*, In Depth, October 2, 2009. See also *BARTON FINK*, *BURN AFTER READING*, *THE HUDSUCKER PROXY*, *INTOLERABLE CRUELTY*, *THE LADYKILLERS*, *MILLER'S CROSSING*, *NO COUNTRY FOR OLD MEN*, *O BROTHER, WHERE ART THOU?* *A SERIOUS MAN*, *TRUE GRIT*.

HALL, IRMA P. (1935–)

Born June 3, 1935, in Beaumont, Texas, Hall was raised in Chicago. She attended Briar Cliff College for two years prior to graduating from Texas College and taught high school English, Spanish, French, and Latin, primarily in Dallas. Hall first appeared on-screen in *The Book of Numbers* (1973). In 1974, Hall cofounded the Dallas Minority Rep Theater, where she acted, directed, and served as executive director. She then appeared in several made-for-television movies, including *Dallas Cowboy Cheerleaders* (1979) and *Dallas Cowboy Cheerleaders II* (1980) and twice appeared on the television series *Dallas*, in 1978 and 1984. She returned to film in 1986 in *On*

Valentine's Day, an adaptation of Horton Foote's play of the same name. Hall had small parts in Ron Howard's *Backdraft* (1991) and in Arthur Hiller's *The Babe* (1992), and she was cast in a recurring role in the ABC television series *Missing Persons* (1993–1994). She appeared with Robert Duvall and James Earle Jones in *A Family Thing* (1996), with Vanessa Williams in *Soul Food* (1997), and with John Cusack and Kevin Spacey in Clint Eastwood's *Midnight in the Garden of Good and Evil* (1997). She continued her work in television with small parts in *Touched by an Angel* (1998), *Judging Amy* (1999), and recurring roles in *All Souls* (2001) and *Soul Food* (2000–2002), and was cast in *Patch Adams* (1998) and *Bad Company* (2002). Hall appeared with Tom Cruise and Jamie Foxx in Michael Mann's *Collateral* (2004) and twice worked with director Werner Herzog, in *The Bad Lieutenant: Port of Call—New Orleans* (2009) and *My Son, My Son, What Have Ye Done* (2009). She was cast in Billy Bob Thornton's *Jayne Mansfield's Car* (2012) and played more substantial roles in *Hiding in Plain Sight* (2012) and *Lady Luck* (2013).

Hall worked with Joel and Ethan Coen in their 2004 remake of *The Ladykillers*, as Marva Munson, an elderly widow with a room to rent. Her tenant, Professor G. H. Dorr (Tom Hanks), has asked permission for his musical ensemble to practice in her basement, though rather than rehearsing, the group instead is digging a tunnel to the nearby casino riverboat, the *Bandit Queen*. A churchgoing woman, Munson spends much of her time enjoying the choir and preaching at her local church, and while at home, she sits beneath the portrait of her deceased husband, Othar, knitting and talking to her cat, Pickles. Discovering that her boarder has stolen $1.6 million from the casino, Hall demands that they return it and attend church with her, and in return,

the thieves determine she must be killed. As the assailants attempt to murder her, they die one by one, as she is protected by Othar and her faith.

While the *Guardian*'s John Patterson found that Hall's performance "unfortunately recalls the black maid in Tom and Jerry cartoons," Roger Ebert deemed Hall's performance as "the one completely successful comic performance in the movie," and Rex Roberts of *Film Journal International* characterized her as brilliant, "[making] her role wholly her own." Hall won a jury prize at the Cannes Film Festival for her performance in *The Ladykillers* (2004).

References

Roger Ebert, "*The Ladykillers*," *RogerEbert.com*, March 26, 2004; "Biography," *IrmaPHall.com*; John Patterson, "Ealing Hands," *Guardian*, March 28, 2004; Rex Roberts, "*The Ladykillers*," *Film Journal International*. See also THE *LADYKILLERS*.

HANKS, TOM (1956–)

Born July 9, 1956, in Concord, California, Hanks was raised by his father, a chef, from the age of five, following his parents' divorce. He learned to love theatre in high school, appearing in his school's productions of *Night of the Iguana* and *South Pacific*. After graduation, Hanks first attended a junior college and then transferred to California State University, Sacramento, where he studied theatre. During his college years, he spent his summers working with the Great Lakes Shakespeare Festival in Lakewood, Ohio, winning the Cleveland Critics Circle Award for Best Actor in 1978 for his portrayal of Proteus in *Two Gentlemen of Verona*. During the school year, he worked backstage at a theatre in Sacramento. Hanks quit college prior to graduating and moved to New York City, where he briefly appeared in the film *He Knows You're Alone* (1980). Also in 1980, he was cast in the television series *Bosom Buddies* (1980–1982), and during the early 1980s, he appeared in the series *The Love Boat* (1980), *Taxi* (1982), *Happy Days* (1982), and *Family Ties* (1983–1984). When Ron Howard began casting for *Splash* (1984), he recalled Hanks from an appearance on *Happy Days* and asked him to read for a supporting role in the film. While that role went to John Candy, Hanks was cast in the lead role, opposite Daryl Hannah, which led to a series of roles in such films as *Bachelor Party* (1984), *The Man with One Red Shoe* (1985), *The Money Pit* (1986), and *Dragnet* (1987). He was cast in Penny Marshall's *Big* (1988), for which he earned an Oscar nomination for Best Actor and won the Golden Globe for Best Performance by an Actor in a Motion Picture—Comedy or Musical. The role established Hanks as a box-office draw and leading man, and he worked again with Marshall in *A League of Their Own* (1993) and with Nora Ephron in *Sleepless in Seattle* (1993), which garnered him a Golden Globe nomination for Best Actor.

Also in 1993, Hanks appeared in Jonathan Demme's *Philadelphia*, receiving both the Oscar and the Golden Globe for Best Actor, and the following year, he once again took home the Oscar and the Globe for Best Actor for his performance in *Forrest Gump* (1994). Hanks worked again with Ron Howard in *Apollo 13* (1996) and then with Steven Spielberg in *Saving Private Ryan* (1998), for which he earned nominations for both the Golden Globe and Oscar for Best Actor. His next Oscar nod for Best Actor was for his role as a marooned pilot in Robert Zemeckis's *Cast Away* (2000), and though he did not receive the Academy Award, he did win the Golden Globe for his performance. In 2002 he starred in Sam Mendes's gangster film *Road to Perdition*, with Paul Newman and Jude Law, and in 2004, he again worked with Spielberg

in *The Terminal*. Hanks appeared in the adaptation of the Dan Brown novel *The Da Vinci Code* (2006), and he earned a Golden Globe nomination for his performance in *Charlie Wilson's War* (2007) and another for his role in *Captain Phillips* (2013). In 2013, Hanks debuted on Broadway in *Lucky Guy*, written by Nora Ephron and directed by George C. Wolfe; he was nominated for a Tony Award for Best Performance by a Leading Actor in a Play.

Hanks formed the production company Playtone Productions with Gary Goetzman in 1996, producing *That Thing You Do* (1996) and HBO's *From the Earth to the Moon* (1998), which he also co-wrote and hosted on-screen. Additional production credits include HBO's *Band of Brothers* (2001), the films *Cast Away* and *The Polar Express* (2004), in which he appeared, as well as *My Big, Fat Greek Wedding* (2002) and *The Ant Bully* (2006). Hanks continued his production work with HBO, serving as executive producer for the mini-series *John Adams* (2008), *The Pacific* (2010), and *Big Love* (2006–2011). He has directed episodes for *Tales from the Crypt* (1992), *Fallen Angels* (1993), and *Band of Brothers* (2001), and he wrote, directed, and starred in *Larry Crowne* (2011), which costarred Julia Roberts.

Hanks appeared in the Coens' *The Ladykillers* (2004) as Professor G. H. Dorr, longwinded expert in the classics, tenant to Mrs. Marva Munson, and criminal mastermind, plotting to tunnel his way to the local riverboat casino and riches. With a group of misfits hired through the classifieds, Dorr and his "ensemble" meet in the basement of Munson's home not to rehearse music of the Rococo, but to burrow through the Mississippi soil to the underground counting room of the nearby *Bandit Queen*. The role was a change for Hanks, as he has traditionally played sympathetic, if not heroic characters, and

Dorr is "as far from [Forrest] Gump, the holy fool, as an actor can get," says *Rolling Stone*'s Peter Travers.

While the Coens typically write parts with actors in mind, they did not do so with Hanks and Dorr, as the project was originally slated to be directed by Barry Sonnenfeld. When the brothers assumed directorial duties, they thought of Hanks, with whom they were interested in working, and the interest was mutual, as Hanks willingly joined the cast and contributed to the process of designing the professor's costume. Roger Ebert accurately described Dorr as a man "who dresses like Col. Sanders, and who seems to be channeling Tennessee Williams, Edgar Allan Poe and Vincent Price," and *Empire*'s Ian Nathan characterizes Hanks's Dorr as a Forrest Gump who has been "possessed by the spirits of Hannibal Lecter and Stuart Hall." The Vandyke beard and moustache were Hanks's idea, as were the cape and suit, and he created a backstory for the character, who, Hanks suggests, has been on sabbatical for many years, having been fired from the University; studied drinking at the Sorbonne; spent time in jail; and only owns the clothes on his back and the shoes on his feet, which, Hanks suggests, were handmade by a man in Oxford, Mississippi. The professor's laugh, which the Coens called "the rat quiver laugh," was Hanks's idea as well, a description which suits both the laugh and the conniving, duplicitous character of Dorr as well.

References

Roger Ebert, "*The Ladykillers*," *RogerEbert.com*; "Tom Hanks," *Biography.com*; "Tom Hanks," *New York Times*, Movies & TV; Tom Healy, "Tom Hanks, Broadway's New Kid," *New York Times*, February 20, 2013; Ian Nathan, "*The Ladykillers*," *EmpireOnline.com*; Dixie Reid, "Stealing the Show: Tom Hanks and the Coen Brothers Gang Up to Remake *The Ladykillers*," in *The Coen Brothers: Interviews*, ed. William Rodney Allen (Jackson: University Press of Mississippi, 2006); Peter Travers, "*The Ladykillers*," *Rolling Stone*, March 23, 2004. See also *THE LADYKILLERS*.

HARDEN, MARCIA GAY (1959–)

When Donna Isaacson, casting director for the Coen brothers' *Miller's Crossing* (1990), discovered Harden, it was at a college theatre production at the Tisch School of the Arts in New York City. Born August 14, 1959, in La Jolla, California, Harden's family spent her childhood relocating for her father's Navy career. She attended college in Germany and in Baltimore, Maryland, before completing her degree in Theatre at the University of Texas. She was in graduate school at NYU where Isaacson attended a production of *A Comedy of Errors*, in which Harden had a nonspeaking role as Lucy the Fat Pig. Determining that the actress had nerve, Isaacson invited her to audition for the Coen brothers' third film, and she was cast in the role of Verna, girlfriend of the Irish mob boss Leo. After appearing in the film, she earned a Tony nomination for her part in Broadway's *Angels in America* (1993) and in the late 1990s, her film credits include *The Spitfire Grill* (1996), *Meet Joe Black* (1998), and TV movies *Small Vices* (1999) and *Thin Air* (2000). Harden won the Oscar for Best Supporting Actress in *Pollock* (2000) and earned a second Academy Award nomination for Best Supporting Actress for her work in the Clint Eastwood-directed film *Mystic River* (2003). These accolades were followed by an Emmy nomination for her recurring role in *Law and Order: SVU* in 2007 and the Tony for Best Actress in *God of Carnage* (2009) on Broadway. Harden worked with Sean Penn in *Into the Wild* (2007) and had recurring roles in the television series *Damages* (2009), *The Newsroom* (2013), and *The Trophy Wife* (2013).

Gabriel Byrne (left) and Marcia Gay Harden in *Miller's Crossing* (1990)

About working with the Coens, Harden observes that "They hire who they want, and they make the kind of movies they want," an approach that benefitted her directly when they cast the unknown actress as a tough Jewish moll in their 1990 gangster-noir film. Harden had stiff competition for her role in *Miller's Crossing*, including Julia Roberts, Jennifer Jason Leigh, and Demi Moore. She prepared for the audition by reading Dashiell Hammett novels and watching Jean Harlow and Greta Garbo in 1930s gangster films. When *Miller's Crossing* debuted, critics deemed her performance "fresh" and "uncluttered," and a "*femme fatale*, some ten years before her cinematic time," an appropriate assessment, as Ethan Coen has stated that the film is "closer to film noir than to the gangster movie." The role of Verna followed Harden for a time, as she notes she was only offered parts for "tough women with low voices who smoked."

Verna serves as one corner of the film's "heterosexual triangle" of Verna, Leo, and Tom, which the Coens state that they have balanced with a "homosexual triangle," that of Eddie Dane, Mink, and Bernie Bernbaum. Verna is the connective point between these two triangles, as she uses her relationships with Tom (Gabriel Byrne) and Leo (Albert Finney) on behalf of her brother Bernie (John Turturro), a noble but ultimately futile endeavor which culminates in the death of Bernie and the departure of Tom. If Tom, as the film tells us, is the "smart guy" who is in it for the long play, Verna is, perhaps, as Byrne notes, the "source of temptation and actual destruction." While she is not the center of the film, she certainly acts as a force upon Tom, whose role as puppet master is affected by the presence of Harden's Verna.

References

Cassie Carpenter, "Character Studies: Marcia Gay Harden," *Backstage.com*, December 17, 2003; Jean-Pierre Coursodon, "A Hat Blown by the Wind," in *Joel & Ethan Coen: Blood Siblings*, ed. Paul A. Woods (London: Plexus Publishing,

2003); "Marcia Gay Harden," *Biography.com;* Derek Malcolm, *"Miller's Crossing," Guardian,* February 14, 1991; James Mottram, *The Life of the Mind* (Frome, UK: Butler and Tanner, 2000); Ryan Murphy, "'Use'—and Talented 'People' Marcia Gay Harden's Many Faces in a Star Role," *Philly.com,* January 3, 1993. See also *MILLER'S CROSSING.*

HARRELSON, WOODY (1961–)

Born July 23, 1961, in Midland, Texas, Harrelson was raised by his mother in Ohio following his father's conviction for murder. He was involved in high school drama productions and earned a scholarship to Hanover College in Indiana, where he majored in English and Theatre and graduated in 1983. He then moved to New York City to pursue a career in acting, and two years later, he served as an understudy in the Broadway production of Neil Simon's *Biloxi Blues* (1985). That same year, he was cast as Woody Boyd in the television sitcom *Cheers* (1985–1993), a role which would garner Harrelson both name recognition and five Primetime Emmy Award nominations. For the role, he won the Emmy for Outstanding Supporting Actor in a Comedy Series in 1989.

Harrelson's first credited film appearance was in *Wildcats* (1986), with Goldie Hawn and Wesley Snipes, which he followed with several made-for-television movies, including *Killer Instinct* (1988), with Melissa Gilbert, and a small role on the series *Dear John* (1989). He was cast in more substantial roles in the films *Doc Hollywood* (1991), *White Men Can't Jump* (1992), and *Indecent Proposal* (1993), prior to his appearance in Oliver Stone's *Natural Born Killers* with Juliette Lewis. While working on *Cheers* and making films, he continued to appear on stage, in *Brooklyn Laundry* (1991) in Los Angeles, and *Furthest from the Sun* (1993) which Harrelson wrote, directed, and starred in, also in Los Angeles.

He played the title role in Milos Forman's *The People vs. Larry Flynt* (1996), for which he earned both Oscar and Golden Globe nominations, and Harrelson worked with Dustin Hoffman and Robert De Niro in *Wag the Dog* (1997) and with Sean Penn in Terrence Malick's *The Thin Red Line* (1998). In 2001, he returned to television with a recurring role in *Will and Grace,* and in 2004, he was cast in Spike Lee's *She Hate Me.* He appeared in Robert Altman's ensemble project *A Prairie Home Companion* (2006) and the Coens' *No Country for Old Men* (2007), which he followed with roles in films such as *Transsiberian* (2008), *Seven Pounds* (2008), *Zombieland* (2009), and Roland Emmerich's *2012* (2009). Also in 2009, he appeared in *The Messenger,* earning nominations for both a Golden Globe and an Oscar for Best Supporting Actor. In 2012, he earned praise, and a Golden Globe nomination, for his depiction of Steve Schmidt in the mini-series *Game Change* (2012), with Ed Harris and Julianne Moore, which follows John McCain's 2008 presidential campaign and his selection of Sarah Palin as his running mate. Continuing with his stage work, he cowrote *Bullet for Adolph* (2012) with Frankie Hyman, which he directed as well. He played Haymitch Abernathy in *The Hunger Games* (2012) and its sequels *The Hunger Games: Catching Fire* (2013) and *The Hunger Games: Mockingjay Part 1* and *2* (2014, 2015). In 2014, he starred in the HBO series *True Detective* and served as executive producer for one episode of the show. Harrelson received an honorary doctorate of humane letters from his alma mater, Hanover College, in 2014.

As Carson Wells in *No Country for Old Men,* Harrelson appears as a retired Army colonel turned bounty hunter hired by the Mexican drug cartel to bring in a hired gun gone rogue, Anton Chigurh (Javier Bardem). His screen time is limited, but in his scenes with his employer (Stephen Root), Llewelyn Moss (Josh Brolin) and Chigurh, Harrelson's Wells comports himself with studied composure and even wry humor, though he is facing clearly dangerous situations. During production, Harrelson and Bardem took the liberty of rewriting their mutual scene in which Chigurh kills Wells, memorizing the new lines and presenting their version of the exchange for the filmmakers, who declined to incorporate their ideas, with the exception of one line change—Harrelson considered this small change to be a victory. Of working with the Coens, Harrelson enthuses, "I love those guys, just like every other actor. . . . They are among the greatest filmmakers alive," citing their organization and thoroughness in preparing for a film, which he describes as "There was nothing in that movie that they had not thought through a long time before we ever got there."

References

"Woody Harrelson," *Biography.com*; "Woody Harrelson," *BroadwayWorld.com*; David Carr, "Loves the Beach, the Planet and Movies," *New York Times*, November 25, 2007; "Hanover College honors actor Woody Harrelson," *Miami Herald*, April 3, 2014; "Woody Harrelson," *New York Times*, Movies & TV; Owen Wilson, "Woody Harrelson," *InterviewMagazine.com*. See also *NO COUNTRY FOR OLD MEN*.

HEDAYA, DAN (1940–)

Dan Hedaya was born July 24, 1940, in Brooklyn, New York. He earned a Bachelor of Arts degree in Literature from Tufts University, where he first appeared onstage in a University production of *The Crucible*. Following graduation, he taught junior high math and English in New York City, but he subsequently quit teaching to pursue a career in acting. He performed with the New York Shakespeare Festival and appeared in the off-Broadway produc-

tions *The Last Days of British Honduras* (1974), *Museum* (1978), *Conjuring an Event* (1978), and *Henry V* (1984). His on-screen work began with a recurring character on the daytime television series *Ryan's Hope* (1975), and his film debut was in *The Passover Plot* (1976). In the late 1970s and early 1980s, he made one-time appearances in the series *Kojak* (1976), *CHiPs* (1982), and *St. Elsewhere* (1984), among others, and in television movies including *Death Penalty* (1980) and *The Dollmaker* (1984), with Jane Fonda. He worked with Robert De Niro and Robert Duvall in *True Confessions* (1981), with Tom Hanks and Meg Ryan in *Joe Versus the Volcano* (1990), and with Anjelica Huston and Raul Julia in Barry Sonnenfeld's *The Addams Family* (1991).

Much of Hedaya's work has been on television, with recurring roles in *Hill Street Blues* (1981–1984), *Miami Vice* (1984–1986), *The Tortellis* (1987), *Family Ties* (1988–1989), *LA Law* (1988–1990), *Cheers* (1984–1993), and *ER* (1997–2005). He was nominated for a Primetime Emmy for Outstanding Guest Actor in a Drama Series for his performance in *NYPD Blue* (1993). Hedaya appeared in the Oscar-winning film *The Usual Suspects* (1995), in Amy Heckerling's *Clueless* (1995), and in Oliver Stone's *Nixon* (1995). He was cast in John Singleton's remake of *Shaft* (2000) and in David Lynch's *Mulholland Drive* (2001), and lent his voice to the animated feature *Robots* (2005). He appeared as Adrian Monk's father in the television series *Monk* (2006), as Congressman Barney Frank in the made-for-television movie *Too Big to Fail* (2011), and in the 2014 season of Fox's *The Mindy Project*.

Hedaya appeared in one Coen film, their feature debut, *Blood Simple* (1984), as Julian Marty, owner of a dive bar and a suspicious husband who hires a private detective to first shadow and then kill his wife Abby (Frances McDormand) and her lover Ray (John Getz). Marty is double-crossed by the P.I. (M. Emmet Walsh), who shoots but fails to kill him, and Hedaya's Marty meets a memorable end at the hand of Ray, who buries him alive in a West Texas field. *Film Comment*'s Hal Hinson praised Hedaya's performance as one in which he "shows us what a slime the guy is and still makes us feel almost sorry for what happens to him."

References

"Dan Hedaya," *BroadwayWorld.com*; "Dan Hedaya," *New York Times*, Movies & TV; "Dan Hedaya," *Starpulse.com*; Hal Hinson, "Bloodlines," in *The Coen Brothers: Interviews*, ed. William Rodney Allen (Jackson: University Press of Mississippi, 2006). See also *BLOOD SIMPLE*.

HEINRICHS, RICK

Born in San Rafael, California, the son of academics, Heinrichs attended Boston University of Fine Arts, studying sculpting, following which he took classes from cartoonist Will Isner at the Visual Arts Center in New York City. He then studied animation at the Disney School at California Institute of the Arts and was subsequently employed by Disney. While at Disney, he met Tim Burton, with whom he would collaborate on two short films, *Vincent* (1982) and *Frankenweenie* (1984), prior to Burton's directorial debut, *Pee Wee's Big Adventure* (1985), on which Heinrichs served as animated effects supervisor. He worked again with Burton on *Beetlejuice* (1988), as a visual effects consultant, and began working as a set designer on *Ghostbusters II* (1989), followed by Burton's *Edward Scissorhands* (1990). He served as art director on *Batman Returns* (1992), *Last Action Hero* (1993), and *Tall Tale* (1995), and his first job as production designer was for Joel and Ethan Coen's *Fargo* (1996), which he followed with *The Big Lebowski* (1998), *Planet of the Apes* (2001), *Hulk*

(2003), *Captain America: The First Avenger* (2011), and *Frankenweenie* (2012). In 2012, Heinrichs joined Fourth Wall Studios as executive creative director; he directed the mini-series *The Gamblers: The Ledge* for the studio in 2012 as well.

Heinrichs has received three Oscar nominations for Best Achievement in Art Decoration: *Sleepy Hollow* (1999), *Lemony Snicket's A Series of Unfortunate Events* (2004), and *Pirates of the Caribbean: Dead Man's Chest* (2006). He won the Oscar for *Sleepy Hollow*, an award he shared with Peter Young.

For their first collaboration, the Coens asked Heinrichs to serve as production designer on *Fargo*, a film for which they "wanted no design." They recall, "we told him to find the most soul-deadening, flattened locations," which, they note, can be a difficult task. He was, however, responsible for the giant Paul Bunyan statue which dominates the town of Brainerd. In their next collaboration, Heinrichs was production designer for *The Big Lebowski*, which included the Lebowski mansion, the bowling alley, the bungalow, and Maude Lebowski's studio, among other locations. The Coens were clear that they did not want *Lebowski* to look like a "Cheech and Chong movie," so Heinrichs's design for the film incorporated elements of film noir and Brunswick bowling alleys from the 1950s and early 1960s.

Of the Coens, Heinrichs notes that the filmmakers not only write, direct, and produce their projects, but that they are unique because "they are so very visually attuned." Like many of their collaborators, Heinrichs and the Coens have developed a working relationship that requires little discussion, described by Heinrichs as a "process of osmosis. It's a combination of having worked with them now for a couple of pictures, knowing their work very closely."

References

"Rick Heinrichs: Production Designer," *5dInstitute.org*, People; "Rick Heinrichs," *FilmReference.com*; Mark Graser, "Rick Heinrichs Joins Fourth Wall," *Variety*, August 17, 2012; Karen Jaehne, "Ethan Coen, Joel Coen, and *The Big Lebowski*," in *The Coen Brothers: Interviews*, ed. William Rodney Allen (Jackson: University Press of Mississippi, 2006); William Preston Robertson, *The Big Lebowski: The Making of a Coen Brothers Film* (New York: W.W. Norton & Co., 1998). See also *THE BIG LEBOWSKI, FARGO*.

HERRMANN, EDWARD (1943–)

Born July 21, 1943, in Washington, D.C., Herrmann was raised in Grosse Point, Michigan. He attended Bucknell University in Pennsylvania, graduating in 1965, and later studied at London's Academy of Music and Dramatic Art on a Fulbright scholarship. He appeared on stage with the Dallas Theatre Center following his return to the United States, and he began appearing on-screen with the film *The Paper Chase* (1973) and with Robert Redford in both *The Great Gatsby* (1974) and *The Great Waldo Pepper* (1975). His television debut was in the Emmy-winning *Beacon Hill* (1975) and he appeared as Franklin D. Roosevelt in the made-for-television movie *Eleanor and Franklin* (1976), receiving an Emmy nomination for his performance. Herrmann reprised the role the following year, in Daniel Petrie's *Eleanor and Franklin: The White House Years* (1977), again garnering an Emmy nomination. Herrmann's Broadway debut was in *Mrs. Warren's Profession* (1976), for which he received a Tony Award for Best Featured Actor. He starred in the title role in the television movie *A Love Affair: The Eleanor and Lou Gehrig Story* (1978) and worked again with Petrie in *The Betsy* (1978).

Herrmann returned to the Broadway stage in *The Philadelphia Story* (1980), receiving a Tony nomination, which he followed with *Plenty* (1983), and *Love Letters* (1989), both on Broadway. He worked with Warren Beatty in *Reds* (1981) and with John Huston in *Annie* (1982), once again appearing as Franklin Roosevelt. He appeared in Woody Allen's *The Purple Rose of Cairo* (1985) and had a recurring role on the television series *St. Elsewhere* (1984–1986), for which he was Emmy nominated. He played Max in the vampire film *The Lost Boys* (1987) and continued to appear in several made-for-television movies throughout the late 1980s and early 1990s. Herrmann was cast as Nelson Rockefeller in Oliver Stone's *Nixon* (1995) and appeared with Leonardo DiCaprio in Martin Scorsese's *The Aviator* (2004). He narrated six episodes of the PBS documentary *Liberty! The American Revolution* (1997), and additional voice work includes the History Channel's documentary *First Invasion: The War of 1812* (2004), *The Ten Commandments: Part 2—The Laws of Man* (2006), and *Andrew Jackson* (2007), among others. Herrmann has narrated numerous books-on-tape as well, for which he has received several Audie Awards.

Herrmann returned to Broadway in *The Deep Blue Sea* (1998) and continued his work in television with a recurring role in *The Practice* (1997–2001), for which he won the Emmy for Outstanding Guest Actor in a Series—Drama. He appeared in *Grey's Anatomy* (2007) and starred in the series *The Gilmore Girls* (2000–2007), and during this same period, he appeared in the HBO prison drama *Oz* (2000–2003). Nearing age 70, Herrmann continued his television work in both the NBC series *Harry's Law* (2012), with Cathy Bates and *The Good Wife* (2010–2013), with Julianna Margulies. His later films include *Price Check* (2012), with Parker Posey, *Heaven's Door* (2013), and *You Are Here* (2013), with Owen Wilson.

Herrmann has appeared in one film by Joel and Ethan Coen, *Intolerable Cruelty*

(2003), in which he plays the silly, unfaithful Rex Rexroth. His scenes, though limited in number, include the sputtering indignation of a husband wronged and his subsequent red-faced physical attack on a witness of the court; a slumber party involving conductor hats and train whistles; and a courtroom "who's on first" give and take with George Clooney as Miles Massey, and Paul Adelstein's Wrigley.

References

"Edward Herrmann," *AmericanTheatreWing.org,* "Edward Herrmann," *New York Times,* Movies & TV; "Edward Herrmann," *StarPulse.com.* See also *INTOLERABLE CRUELTY.*

HOFFMAN, PHILIP SEYMOUR (1967–2014)

Hoffman was born July 23, 1967, in Rochester, New York, where his mother took him to see a local performance of *All My Sons,* a formative experience in his childhood. He was accepted to the New York State Summer School of the Arts at age seventeen, following which he attended New York's Tisch School of Drama. He began his on-screen career with an appearance on the television series *Law & Order* (1991). His impressive film career began with *Triple Bogey on a Par Five Hole* (1991), and in 1992, he worked with Steve Martin in *Leap of Faith* and with Al Pacino in *Scent of a Woman,* prior to roles in *Nobody's Fool* (1994), *Twister* (1996), and in Paul Thomas Anderson's directorial debut *Hard Eight* (1996). He would work again with Anderson in *Boogie Nights* (1997), *Magnolia* (1999), *Punch Drunk Love* (2002), and *The Master* (2012). Hoffman was nominated for and received the Oscar for Best Performance by an Actor in a Leading Role for his portrayal of Truman Capote in Bennett Miller's *Capote* (2005), for which he also won the Best Actor Golden Globe. Following his Oscar, he was nominated in

quick succession for Best Performance by an Actor in a Supporting Role in *Charlie Wilson's War* (2007), *Doubt* (2008), and *The Master* (2012).

Hoffman's Broadway debut was in Sam Shepherd's *True West* (2000), with John C. Reilly. Reilly and Hoffman each learned both lead parts and periodically switched roles during the play's run, and for their efforts, both received Tony nominations. In 2003, he appeared in the Broadway revival of *Long Day's Journey into Night,* for which he was also Tony nominated. He returned to the stage again in 2012 as Willy Loman in the revival of *Death of a Salesman,* earning his third Tony nomination. Hoffman had extensive stage directing experience as well. In 1999, he directed the off-Broadway *In Arabia, We'd All Be Kings* and directed *Riflemind* by Andrew Upton at the Sydney Theatre Company in Australia and again in London; he served as Artistic Director for Labyrinth Theater Company in New York.

In 2003, Hoffman and Emily Ziff formed the production company Cooper's Town Productions, which went on to produce the Oscar-winning *Capote,* followed by *The Savages* (2007), which starred Laura Linney and Hoffman and was nominated for two Academy Awards for writing and for Linney's performance. Cooper's Town also produced *Jack Goes Boating* (2010), Hoffman's film directorial debut.

Hoffman appeared in the sound play *Sawbones* in 2005, written and directed by Joel and Ethan Coen and scored by Carter Burwell. He appeared in *The Hunger Games: Catching Fire* (2013), and one of his final films, *A Most Wanted Man* (2014), premiered at the Sundance Film Festival. Hoffman died February 2, 2014, in New York City, of a drug overdose.

Hoffman played Brandt, assistant to the Big Lebowski, in the Coens' 1998 cult hit *The Big Lebowski.* Though it was a small part, it would be a role critics and fans alike would reference for decades, as fans addressed him as "Brandt" on the street. "I wasn't thinking about the success, but more about being part of something that would be well done and that funny," he recalls.

References

Andrew Gans, "The Coen Brothers' *Sawbones*—with Buscemi and Hoffman—Broadcast Sept. 2," *Playbill.com*, September 2, 2005; Andy Greene, "Philip Seymour Hoffman Looks Back at *The Big Lebowski*," *RollingStone.com*, February 2, 2014; "Philip Seymour Hoffman," *Biography.com*; "Philip Seymour Hoffman," *Broadway.com*; "Philip Seymour Hoffman," *New York Times*, Movies & TV. See also *THE BIG LEBOWSKI*.

HUDDLESTON, DAVID (1930–)

Born September 17, 1930, in Vinton, Virginia, Huddleston attended a military academy prior to entering the United States Air Force. Following his departure from the military, he attended the American Academy of Dramatic Arts and began his on-screen career at age thirty, in the television series *Shotgun Slade* (1960) and spent over five decades in film and television. His film debut was an uncredited role in *All the Way Home* (1963) followed by a small part in Carl Lerner's *Black Like Me* (1964); he also appeared with John Wayne in Howard Hawks's *Rio Lobo* (1970). His television credits during this time include *Adam-12* (1969), *Cannon* (1971), *McMillan & Wife* (1971), and a recurring role on *Bewitched* (1970–1971). His occasional film appearances in *Fools Parade* (1971) and *Something Big* (1971) punctuated his frequent roles on made-for-television movies and his continued series work including *Bonanza* (1971–1972) and *The Waltons* (1971–1972). Notably, he played Olson Johnson in Mel Brooks's *Blazing Saddles* (1974), John Conn in *Smokey and the Bandit II* (1980), and the title role in *Santa Claus: The Movie*

(1985). Later television work included a lead role in *Hizzoner* (1979), *The Wonder Years* (1990–1992), for which he received an Emmy nomination for Outstanding Guest Actor in a Comedy Series, and *The West Wing* (2000–2002).

Huddleston appeared in the Coens' *The Big Lebowski* (1998), as the title character Jeffrey Lebowski, who appears in contrast to Jeff Bridges's Jeffrey Lebowski, "the Dude." Though wheelchair-bound and financially destitute, Huddleston's Lebowski orchestrates a complicated "kidnapping" scheme, by which he plans to embezzle a million dollars from the Lebowski Foundation, which funds the education of the Little Lebowski Urban Achievers. Ebert characterized Huddleston's performance as "reminding me of no one so much as Major Amberson in *The Magnificent Ambersons*."

The Big Lebowski is attended by his assistant Brandt, played by Philip Seymour Hoffman, a casting choice, suggests Ebert, calculated to suggest to unsuspecting viewers that both the Big Lebowski and Brandt are played by Hoffman, in skillfully applied makeup.

References

Roger Ebert, "*The Big Lebowski*," *RogerEbert.com*, March 10, 2010; "David Huddleston," *New York Times*, Movies & TV. See also *THE BIG LEBOWSKI*.

THE HUDSUCKER PROXY (1994)

DIRECTOR: Joel Coen and Ethan Coen (uncredited). SCREENPLAY: Ethan Coen, Joel Coen, and Sam Raimi. EXECUTIVE PRODUCERS: Eric Fellner and Tim Bevan. PRODUCERS: Ethan Coen and Joel Coen (uncredited); Graham Place (Co-producer). PHOTOGRAPHY: Roger Deakins. EDITING: Thom Noble. MUSIC: Carter Burwell. PRODUCTION DESIGN: Dennis Gassner. ART DIRECTION: Leslie McDonald.

SET DECORATION: Nancy Haigh. COSTUME
DESIGN: Richard Hornung.
CAST: Tim Robbins (Norville Barnes),
Jennifer Jason Leigh (Amy Archer),
Paul Newman (Sidney J. Mussburger),
Charles Durning (Waring Hudsucker),
John Mahoney (Newspaper Chief), Jim
True (Buzz), Bill Cobbs (Moses), Bruce
Campbell (Smitty), Harry Bugin (Aloy-
sius), Steve Buscemi (Bartender), Anna
Nicole Smith (ZaZa), Sam Raimi (Hud-
sucker Brainstormer), Jon Polito (Mr.
Bumstead), Mike Starr (Newsroom
Reporter), Peter Siragusa (Newsroom
Reporter), John Goodman (Newsreel
Announcer, as Karl Mundt).
RUNNING TIME: 111 minutes. Color.
RELEASED THROUGH: Warner Brothers. PRE-
MIERE: March 11, 1994.
DVD: Warner Home Video.

New York City. December, 1958. As the camera wends its way through the city skyline and lightly falling snow, a voice-over narrator informs the viewer that it's New Year's Eve, and people all over the city are celebrating Earth's most recent trip around the sun. Except for Norville Barnes (Tim Robbins), whom we see climb out of the window of a skyscraper, shuffle along the ledge, and prepare to jump. Thus begins *The Hudsucker Proxy*, the fifth major film by Joel and Ethan Coen, released in 1994 with the tagline "A comedy of invention." To learn how Norville came to be in this situation, the film takes us back, thirty days earlier. When Waring Hudsucker (Charles Durning), founder and president of Hud-sucker Industries, leaps to his death from the forty-fourth floor of the building bearing his name, his stock must be sold to the public, a possibility that the Hudsucker Board cannot tolerate. The board, headed by Sidney J. Mussburger (Paul Newman), plots to fill the newly vacated president's chair with a sap, an imbecile, someone sure to tank the value of the company, at which

point they plan to step back in, buy up the stock for pennies, and completely control Hudsucker Industries, where "The Future is Now." The dolt selected for the job is Norville Barnes, fresh off the bus from the Muncie College of Business Administration, Muncie, Indiana, and determined to make his name in the world. Hired to work in the Hudsucker mailroom the very day of Waring Hudsucker's demise, the inexperienced Norville is immediately promoted to president and placed in charge of the company. Mussburger and his associates prepare to celebrate the plummeting value of the company, and for a time, Norville meets all of their very low expectations.

The downfall of "the Hud" is hurried along by the grumblings of dissatisfied investors and the undercover reporting of ambitious, Pulitzer Prize–winning Amy Archer (Jennifer Jason Leigh), who, smelling a rat, imbeds herself in the company as Norville's secretary and pens exposés about the incompetence of Hudsucker's new president. Just as the company and Norville's short-lived career appear set to come crashing down, he pitches his Big Idea, an innovative new toy "for kids," certain to revitalize the company's sales and his own fortunes. Initially, the "extruded plastic din-gus," the hula-hoop, gathers dust on store shelves, but in the hands of one perceptive boy, the colorful plastic circle becomes a smash hit, and Norville and Hudsucker Industries are saved. Success spoils the naive young executive, however, as he indulges in pampering, pay raises, and the attentions of the glamorous ZaZa (Anna Nicole Smith), disappointing and alienating Amy Archer, who has come to believe in his intentions, if not his intelligence.

Undeterred, Mussburger and the board redouble their efforts to unseat Norville, accusing him of stealing the concept for the wildly popular hula-hoop and retaining the services of Dr. Hugo Brofen-brenner, psychiatrist, who declares Norville

Tim Robbins (left) and Paul Newman in *The Hudsucker Proxy* (1994)

mentally incompetent and attempts to have him committed to a mental institution. Further, Mussburger reveals Amy's true identity as a journalist, pits Buzz the elevator operator against Norville, and nearly succeeds in pushing the young president past his limits. Rejected by Amy and beset by an angry crowd on New Year's Eve, an intoxicated Norville stands precariously on the ledge of the Hudsucker building, where the film began, contemplating what he sees as the only option before him. Before he can make the choice to end his life in the same manner Waring Hudsucker did, he slips and rushes toward the very sidewalk where Hudsucker expired. As luck—and the Coens—would have it, Fate intrudes in the form of Moses (Bill Cobbs), the film's narrator and the "guy who knows everything," who tends to the enormous clock atop the Hudsucker Industries building, and who can apparently stop the gears of Time with a broomstick. Norville hangs in midair and is visited by Waring Hudsucker in angel's attire, complete with strumming guitar and shimmering halo. Hudsucker

informs Norville that he has inherited the founder's stock, by virtue of his appointment to the position of company president, and is indeed the rightful head of the corporation. Norville is astonished and pleased. Forty-four stories above, in the gear room behind the enormous clock, Moses battles the forces of evil in the form of Aloysius (Harry Bugin), Mussburger's henchman and the sinister individual who frequently paints, scrapes off, and re-paints executives' names on their frosted glass office doors. Moses emerges victorious, the unharmed Norville seeks out Amy, who receives him gladly, Dr. Brofenbrenner has Mussburger institutionalized, and Norville invents the Frisbee, reassuring the press and the investors that he indeed is deserving of the title of President, Hudsucker Industries.

Though it follows 1990s *Miller's Crossing* and numbers as the fifth Coen film, the *Hudsucker* project had its genesis much earlier in the Coen timeline. In an interview following the release of their first film, *Blood Simple* (1984), the brothers refer to a script that "takes place in the late Fifties in a skyscraper and is about big business. The characters talk fast and wear sharp clothes," describing the picture they would release nearly a decade later, *The Hudsucker Proxy*. Cowritten with Sam Raimi following the filming of *Blood Simple*, but set aside when it would require much more funding than the Coens could generate at that point in their careers, *Hudsucker* is often designated as the Coens' first "big budget" film, costing $25 million to make. When the brothers decided they were ready to pursue funding for the project, their agent Jim Berkus took the project to Joel Silver, producer of what Joel Coen terms "big, glass-shattering action movies" such as the *Matrix* and *Lethal Weapon* films. Silver in turn provided partial funding for the film through his production company Silver Pictures and procured the remainder from a number of other sources, including Working Title Films, whose Tim Bevan and Eric Fellner acted as executive producers, and Warner Brothers, which held the domestic distribution rights.

Coen films prior to this point had ranged in budget from $1.5 million for *Blood Simple* to $11 million for *Miller's Crossing* (1990), but the design for *Hudsucker* included five sound stages at Carolco Studios in Wilmington, North Carolina, and additional shooting on location in Chicago as well as computer-generated effects that were completed in Los Angeles. These factors combined, their vision for the project required a much larger investment than any previous film. The five sound stages held the enormous rooms in which the film was primarily shot, including the board room, the mail room, and Norville's office, and the size of these rooms contributed to the scale of the entire film, which the filmmakers wanted to be "big." And big it was. Production designer Dennis Gassner notes that the table in the boardroom was so large that it had to be made in five pieces and assembled on the set. The scale

of the set is reminiscent of Orson Welles's *Citizen Kane* (1941), as well as other CinemaScope films of the 1950s, including *The Robe* (1953); when Paul Newman, veteran of the immense studio sets of the 1950s, entered the *Hudsucker* set, he said "it was the biggest he'd seen since *The Silver Chalice*," his 1954 film debut. The scope of the project was so large that for the first time, the Coens required a second unit, which *Hudsucker* coauthor Sam Raimi directed in addition to his appearance in silhouette as part of the Hudsucker Industries creative team. The effect of the enormous set was to create an oppressive feel. Gassner compares the office of Mussburger to that of Mussolini, and the mailroom in the bowels of the Hudsucker building was filled with salvaged mail sorters and three hundred fifty thousand pieces of fake mail, which combined to create Norville's claustrophobically busy work area. Gassner further created a 1:24 scale model of the New York skyline for the establishing shots, though the model was never intended to accurately depict New York City. The designers replicated their favorite New York buildings, regardless of their actual locations, and placed them side-by-side in "a fantasy vision of New York," states Gassner.

This fantasy vision originated with the filmmakers themselves, as Joel Coen notes that it was the intent to "create a fairy tale that would be self-consciously artificial, to do everything on stage sets and to push them beyond reality in terms of scale and design." The fantasy encapsulated more than just the arrangement of the skyscrapers, however. The narrator Moses announces that the year is 1958 in New York, and some elements of the film bear out this date, such as lounge singer Vic Tenetta (Peter Gallagher) who is clearly patterned on 1950s crooner Dean Martin. Other details, however, depart from that time and place, as some of the skyline architecture was inspired by buildings in Chicago and costume designer Richard Hornung notes that the clothing is more heavily influenced by the 1930s and 1940s. The Coens were unconcerned with maintaining a realistic depiction of any one era or location and equally unconcerned with contradictions that might manifest themselves as a result of the eclectic approach to design and content. "It's not anachronistic as much as free, partly because of that fairy tale feel, that 'once upon a time' thing," states Ethan Coen. "We almost had to arbitrarily pick a date and say, 'OK, it's 1958', but the period is indeterminate. . . . Nominally, it's New York—but when you see the shots of the buildings, it's more generally Metropolis."

While these anachronisms of authenticity raised the eyebrows of film critics, it was the similarly liberal approach to classic Hollywood references and themes that was more problematic for the film's reviewers. As so often occurs in Coen films, there exist in *Hudsucker* an impressive number of examples of the depth and breadth of the brothers' knowledge of classic film, from Hollywood and abroad. Of *Blood Simple,* a critic wrote "It looks like a movie made by guys who spent most of their lives watching movies, indiscriminately, both in theaters and on TV and for whom, mostly by osmosis, the vocabulary and grammar of film has become a kind of instinctive second language," and that assessment was still as accurate for *Hudsucker* as it was for their first film. In perhaps a more kindly wording of the same concept, Roger Ebert notes in his review of *Hudsucker* that the Coens "seem to be so much in love with old movies that they shape their own ideas into the forms of films made before they were born," and evidence of those old films abounds in this project. John Harkness, in *Sight and Sound,* deems the world of *Hudsucker* to have been created by Fritz Lang, a statement that seems accurate, given Joel Coen's characterization of the city as "Metropolis;" Ian Nathan attributes the machinery of the mailroom to Charlie

Chaplin's *Modern Times* (1936); and Amy Archer seems to be drawn directly from Rosalind Russell's character in Howard Hawks's *His Girl Friday* (1940), "one of those fast-talkin' career gals," as Norville puts it, with dialogue and delivery reminiscent of Katherine Hepburn. *Hudsucker* opened the Cannes Film Festival in 1994, where it was nominated for the Palme d'Or, and while numerous critics marveled at the magnificent design and the beautifully rendered sets, there arose as well the familiar refrain that the latest Coen film was all style and no substance.

John Lyttle of the *Independent* claims that *Hudsucker* "takes the mechanism of old movies and high-style genres . . . but leaves out the engine (the heart, if you please), that ran those mechanisms." Similarly, *Variety*'s Todd McCarthy asserts that the film is an "artificial synthesis of aspects of vintage fare, leaving a hole in the middle where some emotion and humanity should be" and finds the Coens' approach to this film to be "synthetic." Harkness characterizes Coen films, including and especially *Hudsucker*, as the "reduction of characters to trademark gestures and phrases," and Eddie Robson, though more favorable in his overall assessment of the film, characterizes it as a cartoon, in which "Mussburger's perpetual motion toy stops when he commands everything to wait" and "when Byron throws himself at the plexiglass window he doesn't bounce off it—he sticks to it and slowly slides down because it's funnier."

While the historically inaccurate set design and the emphasis on style rather than substance troubled critics of the film, it was the amalgam of thematic elements derived from different, and sometimes opposing, decades of classic Hollywood that seemed to most concern reviewers, typified by Harkness's comment that *Hudsucker* has a story and characters from the thirties in a film with a fifties setting. Echoing the assessment of many critics, Todd McCarthy stated that "*Hudsucker* plays like a Frank Capra film with a Preston Sturges hero and dialogue direction by Howard Hawks." *Hudsucker* does indeed bear some similarity to a number of Capra films, including *It's a Wonderful Life* (1945), in which the main character, George Bailey (Jimmy Stewart), considers throwing himself from a bridge in the opening moments of the film but is saved by the forces of heaven and the timely intervention of an angel, much as Norville's fall is halted by the appearance of Waring Hudsucker's angel and Moses's actions on his behalf. Smaller allusions to the Capra film make their way into *Hudsucker*, in the form of the cop and the cab driver who narrate Norville's first meeting with Amy, who are a nod to characters in *It's a Wonderful Life*, as are the angry citizens who confront both George Bailey and Norville Barnes on the wintery streets of their respective towns. The trials of Norville Barnes are further reminiscent of two additional Capra films from the 1930s: *Mr. Deeds Goes to Town* (1936), in which the foes of Longfellow Deeds (Gary Cooper) attempt to have him deemed insane and reporter Babe Bennett (Jean Arthur) wins Deeds's trust and affection only to write derisive articles about him for her paper; and *Mr. Smith Goes to Washington* (1939), in which Jefferson Smith (Jimmy Stewart) is named to complete the term of a deceased senator, selected because the party's powers believe he will be easily manipulated.

The filmmakers acknowledge the influence of Frank Capra on *The Hudsucker Proxy*, as Ethan Coen notes that "the script, which contains a lot of traditional genre elements, was marked by a kind of heartwarming fantasy element out of Frank Capra, . . . but it was bigger and broader, with physical comedy sequences and a lot of oddball action." Sequences such as Norville's encounter with the flaming trash can in

Mussburger's office and the battle for Norville's future between Moses and Aloysius perhaps qualify as "oddball action" here. Joel Coen adds, however, that "There is Capra in the film, but there's more Sturges. . . . Sturges had more of a satirical undertow. . . . His relationship to business and society is much more sympathetic to our view than Capra is." Sturges's films included *The Great McGinty* (1940), *The Lady Eve* (1941), and *Sullivan's Travels* (1941), which, to some degree, inspired the Coens' *O Brother, Where Art Thou?* (2000), all films filled with irony and satire. The resulting fusion of Capra and Sturges in *Hudsucker* seemed contradictory to reviewers, as the two directors espoused very different worldviews in their films. John Harkness characterizes this difference in terms of romanticism: Capra has "an authentic belief in the romanticism of pure individualism," and his characters battle "the malevolent forces of darkness," a description that clearly applies to Norville's situation, manipulated by the nefarious Sidney J. Mussburger and his henchman Aloysius. Conversely, Sturges is "a romantic wise-guy," who satirizes his heroes, individuals who "do battle with their own limitations," as Norville does, and who is "too in love with the baroque possibilities of the English language to honor the simple decency of a Jimmy Stewart in *Mr. Smith Goes to Washington*," a charge which seems to apply to the ever-present stream of witty banter that pervades *The Hudsucker Proxy*. Simultaneously straddling these two world views is an impossibility, Harkness claims: "A Sturges hero would be eaten alive in Capra's world, which is why *Hudsucker*'s premise doesn't work."

Beset by critics on all fronts and faced with disappointing box office returns—the film grossed under $3 million domestically—the Coens responded to their detractors: "Critics are usually kinder to cheaper movies than to those they perceive to be big Hollywood releases. . . . It's true that a lot of money seems like a stick they want to beat you with. They cut you a lot more slack if you spend less money, which makes no sense." *Hudsucker* went on to gross $12 million internationally, bringing its worldwide gross to just under fifteen million, but the initial domestic response, or lack thereof, would define the film and its place in the Coen canon.

References

Ronald Bergan, *The Coen Brothers* (New York: Thunder's Mouth Press, 2000); John Clark, "Strange Bedfellows," in *Joel & Ethan Coen: Blood Siblings*, ed. Paul A. Woods (London: Plexus Publishing, 2003); Roger Ebert, "*Hudsucker Proxy*," *RogerEbert.com*, March 25, 1994; John Harkness, "The Sphinx without a Riddle," in *Joel & Ethan Coen: Blood Siblings*, ed. Paul A. Woods (London: Plexus Publishing, 2003); John Lyttle, "On Cinema," *Independent*, October 3, 1994; Todd McCarthy, "*The Hudsucker Proxy*," in *Joel & Ethan Coen: Blood Siblings*, ed. Paul A. Woods (London: Plexus Publishing, 2003); Ian Nathan, *Ethan and Joel Coen* (Paris: Cahiers de cinema, 2012); John Naughton, "Double Vision," in *Joel & Ethan Coen: Blood Siblings*, ed. Paul A. Woods (London: Plexus Publishing, 2003); R. Barton Palmer, *Joel and Ethan Coen* (Urbana: University of Illinois Press, 2004); Eddie Robson, *Coen Brothers* (London: Virgin Books, 2003). See also HARRY BUGIN, CARTER BURWELL, STEVE BUSCEMI, BRUCE CAMPBELL, ROGER DEAKINS, CHARLES DURNING, DENNIS GASSNER, JOHN GOODMAN, NANCY HAIGH, JENNIFER JASON LEIGH, JOHN MAHONEY, PAUL NEWMAN, JON POLITO, SAM RAIMI, TIM ROBBINS, MIKE STARR, PETER SIRAGUSA.

HUNTER, HOLLY (1958–)

Born March 20, 1958, in Conyers, Georgia, Hunter began her acting career in a fifth-grade school play as Helen Keller. She attended Carnegie Mellon University, receiving her degree in drama, following which she relocated to New York. There, she first appeared off-Broadway in 1981 in *Battery*, and a chance elevator encounter with playwright Beth Henley led to collaborations between the two women that included the off-Broadway production of *The Miss Firecracker Contest* (1984) and her Broadway debut in *Crimes of the Heart* (1982). Her first film role was in *The Burning* (1981), after which she moved to Los Angeles and was cast in *Swing Shift* (1984). She had a small voice role in the Coens' *Blood Simple* (1984) and a lead role in *Raising Arizona* (1987). Also in 1987, she appeared as Jane Craig in *Broadcast News*, a role for which she received her first Academy Award nomination, and she was twice nominated in 1993 for her roles in *The Firm* (Best Actress in a Supporting Role) and *The Piano* (Best Actress in a Leading Role). She was awarded the Oscar for *The Piano* (1993). The award was followed by a series of less successful films, including *Home for the Holidays* (1995), *Copycat* (1995), and *A Life Less Ordinary* (1997), but she received much critical praise for her work in *Living Out Loud* in 1998, with Danny DeVito and Queen Latifah. With Ed Harris, Amy Madigan, and Beth Henley, among others, Hunter founded the Loretta Theatre in Santa Monica, California in 1996. In 2000, she had a smaller role in the Coen brothers' *O Brother, Where Art Thou?*. Her fourth Oscar nomination was for her 2003 role in *Thirteen* (Best Actress in a Supporting Role), which she also produced, and in 2004, she voiced the character of Elastigirl in the Pixar animated film *The Incredibles*. Her television work includes several made-for-television movies, including *Roe vs. Wade* (1989), *When Billie Beat Bobby* (2001), and *Bonnie and Clyde* (2013), as well as the title role in the TNT series *Saving Grace* (2007–2010). A six-time Emmy nominee, she received the award for Outstanding Lead

Actress in a Miniseries or a Movie for her work in *The Positively True Adventures of the Alleged Texas Cheerleader-Murdering Mom* (1993) and *Harlan County War* (2000).

When casting *Blood Simple*, Joel and Ethan Coen invited Hunter to audition for the part of Abby, but due to her schedule, she was unavailable and suggested to her roommate, Frances McDormand, that she should read for the part. McDormand appeared in the film, her first of many Coen pictures, and Hunter's role was limited to an uncredited voice part on an answering machine. Her second role in a Coen film, *Raising Arizona*, was written specifically for her, that of Ed McDunnough, "a police officer. Who wants a baby," notes Joel Coen. Pauline Kael, writing for the *New Yorker*, described Hunter's Ed as "a huffy little pixie with a quivering pout," and the *Washington Post*'s Rita Kempley characterized her as "tight-lipped, pinched as an American gothic farmwoman's bun."

Joel Coen has said of Hunter, that "she doesn't play it safe, she's always pushing," and following her leading role in *Raising Arizona*, the filmmakers cast her once more in their adaptation of Homer's *Odyssey*, *O Brother, Where Art Thou?*. Hunter appears as Penny, the estranged wife of Ulysses Everett McGill (George Clooney), and while the role is minimal, the character provides the impetus for the plot, as McGill leads his fellow travelers on an adventurous journey through rural Mississippi in attempt to reach Penny and thwart the plans of her bona fide suitor, Vernon T. Waldrip. With seven daughters in tow, Hunter's Penny stoically rejects McGill, only to relent when Waldrip retreats in disgrace and Everett undertakes a heroic quest to prove his worthiness to his bride.

References

Andrew Barker, "Coen Brothers Script Hunter's Career," *Variety*, May 28, 2008; Sheila Dev-aney, "Holly Hunter," *New Georgia Encyclopedia*; "Holly Hunter," *Biography.com*; "Holly Hunter," *New York Times*, Movies & TV; Pauline Kael, "Manypeeplia Upsidownia," *New Yorker*, April 20, 1987; Rita Kempley, "*Raising Arizona*," *Washington Post*, March 20, 1987; Eddie Robson, *Coen Brothers* (London: Virgin Books, 2003). See also *O BROTHER, WHERE ART THOU?*, *RAISING ARIZONA*.

HURST, RYAN (1976–)

Ryan Hurst was born June 19, 1976, in Santa Monica, California, to actor Rick Hurst (*The Dukes of Hazzard*) and Candace Kaniecki, an acting coach who founded the Candace Kaniecki Acting School. The younger Hurst appeared in the television series *Saved by the Bell: The New Class* (1993) as Crunch Grabowski and was also cast in a recurring role in the series *Campus Cops* (1995–1996). He had one-time appearances on such series as *Beverly Hills 90210* (1994), *JAG* (1995), *Boston Common* (1996), and *Wings* (1996). His film debut was in Kevin Costner's *The Postman* (1997), which he followed with Steven Spielberg's *Saving Private Ryan* (1998). He worked with Robin Williams in *Patch Adams* (1998), with Tommy Lee Jones and Samuel L. Jackson in *Rules of Engagement* (2000), and with Denzel Washington in *Remember the Titans* (2000). Hurst was cast in the television mini-series *Taken* (2002) and had a recurring role in the series *Wanted* (2005) and *Medium* (2005–2007). He is perhaps best known for his role as Harry "Opie" Winston in the FX series *Sons of Anarchy* (2008–2012), after which he appeared as Edgar Roy in the TNT series *King & Maxwell* (2013), starring Jon Tenney and Rebecca Romijn.

Hurst served as second unit director for *Remember the Titans*, and in 2004, Hurst founded Los Angeles' Underground Viking Repertory, where he produced and directed, and starred in the debut production of *One*

Flew Over the Cuckoo's Nest (2004), In 2005, Hurst and his wife, actress Molly Cookson, established Fast Shoes Productions.

Hurst appeared in one film by Joel and Ethan Coen, *The Ladykillers* (2004), in which he played Lump Hudson, a college football player and heavy labor/muscle for the gang of thieves recruited by Professor G. H. Dorr (Tom Hanks). Dorr and company plan to tunnel from the basement of Marva Munson's (Irma P. Hall) home to the nearby riverboat casino and clean out the counting room after hours. Lump is tasked with the actual digging, though all of the gang haul away the bags of dirt, and it is also Lump who suggests bribing the casino manager when their plans hit a snag. Lump and Dorr are the last men standing in the film, faced with the choice of returning the money or dividing it, and Lump's lack of intelligence ultimately results in his demise. Hurst's Lump is defined by his size and his IQ, as Dorr describes him as "a hooligan, a goon, an ape—our blunt instrument." Rex Roberts of *Film Journal International* concurs, stating that Hurst has a "thankless role as the dumbest Caucasian ever to trod the gridiron."

References

"Ryan Hurst," *New York Times*, Movies & TV; "Ryan Hurst (Harry 'Opie' Winston)" *Sonsof Anarchy.net*, Cast and Crew; "Ryan Hurst Biography," *StarPulse.com*; Rex Roberts, "*The Lady-killers*," *Film Journal International*. See also *THE LADYKILLERS*.

I

INSIDE LLEWYN DAVIS (2013)

DIRECTOR: Ethan Coen and Joel Coen.
SCREENPLAY: Joel Coen and Ethan Coen.
EXECUTIVE PRODUCERS: Olivier Courson,
Robert Graf, and Ron Halpern. PRODUC-
ERS: Ethan Coen, Joel Coen, and Scott
Rudin; Catherine Farrell (Associate
Producer); Drew P. Houpt (Associate
Producer). PHOTOGRAPHY: Bruno Del-
bonnel. EDITING: Ethan Coen and Joel
Coen (as Roderick Jaynes). MUSIC: T
Bone Burnett (Executive Music Pro-
ducer); Marcus Mumford (Associate
Music Producer). PRODUCTION DESIGN:
Jess Gonchor. ART DIRECTION: Deborah
Jensen. COSTUME DESIGN: Mary Zophres.
CAST: Oscar Isaac (Llewyn Davis), Carey
Mulligan (Jean), Justin Timberlake (Jim),
Ethan Phillips (Mitch Gorfein), Robin
Barlett (Lillian Gorfein), Max Casella
(Pappi Corsicato), Jerry Grayson (Mel
Novikoff), Jeanine Serralles (Joy),
Adam Driver (Al Cody), Stark Sands
(Troy Nelson), John Goodman (Roland
Turner), Garrett Hedlund (Johnny Five),
F. Murray Abraham (Bud Grossman).
RUNNING TIME: 104 minutes. Color.
RELEASED THROUGH: CBS Films. PREMIERE:
May 19, 2013 (Cannes Film Festival).
DVD: Sony Pictures Home Entertainment.
ACADEMY AWARDS: Best Achievement in
Cinematography (nominated: Bruno
Delbonnel); Best Achievement in Sound
Mixing (nominated: Skip Lievsay, Greg
Orloff, Peter F. Kurland).

Set in and inspired by Greenwich Village, New York, 1961, *Inside Llewyn Davis*
depicts the American folk music scene just
prior to the meteoric success of Bob Dylan.
The film chronicles the odyssey of its title
character on a week-long winter journey
through clubs and coffee houses, from New
York to Chicago and back again, much of
it in the company of an orange tomcat and
with frequent performances by Llewyn and
his contemporaries. Structurally, the film
itself is similar to a folk song: the first verse
is followed by a series of verses in which
unfortunate events occur, and at the conclusion, the tale comes back to the first
verse again, though somewhat changed
from its first iteration, and Joel and Ethan
Coen additionally note that the film is
"about a character in a hamster wheel so
it's reflected in how we shape the story."

The film begins and ends in the Gaslight Café, a Village coffee shop and bar
where Llewyn Davis (Oliver Isaac) delivers an acoustic rendition of "Hang Me"
in return for his share of the evening's
tips, and following his set he is beaten by
an angry stranger in the alley behind the
bar, for reasons unknown to the viewer.
Episodic in structure, the film then follows Llewyn as he trudges through the city,
silently enduring the subway and crashing
on a series of couches, each belonging to a
friend, fan, or fellow musician. Dedicated
to his music and seemingly looking for his

Oscar Isaac in *Inside Llewyn Davis* (2013)

big break, Llewyn has no home of his own, relying instead on his worn address book into which he has carefully penned the names and addresses of the people who will host him until he wears out his welcome, which occurs frequently in the film. He begins at the home of Columbia professor Mitch Gorfein (Ethan Phillips) and his wife Lillian (Robin Barlett), where he errantly allows their cat to escape, thus beginning a chase that will continue throughout the film. The recaptured cat accompanies him on his trek to the home of Jim Berkey (Justin Timberlake) and his wife Jean (Carey Mulligan), fellow musicians upon whose couch he regularly sleeps, but in whose home he is not presently welcome. Jean is pregnant, and either Llewyn or Jim could be the father; further, Llewyn's place on the couch has been usurped by newcomer and fellow folk singer Troy Nelson (Stark Sands), and Llewyn must sleep on the floor.

Coatless and perpetually in need of money, Llewyn visits his agent Mel Novikoff (Jerry Grayson), where he hopes for a roy-alty check but instead learns that his solo album is selling poorly, if at all, and Llewyn leaves Novikoff's office with only forty dollars. In his one stroke of good fortune, Jim has arranged for Llewyn to perform as a part of the John Glenn Singers with Jim and Al Cody (Adam Driver), recording "Please Mr. Kennedy." Although the pop-folk song offends his sensibilities, Llewyn takes the gig and the two hundred dollars in payment, money he needs to pay for Jean's abortion. Upon visiting the doctor to make arrangements for the procedure, he discovers that no payment is due, as the last woman for whom he paid to have an abortion did not terminate the pregnancy. Llewyn has a two-year-old child, presumably in Akron, Ohio. Stunned by this news, he learns that in return for his share of the gas money, he can catch a ride to Chicago in the company of the ever-present cat, Roland Turner (John Goodman), and Turner's valet, beat poet Johnny Five (Garrett Hedlund). Turner is a semi-functioning drug addict; Johnny Five is uncommunicative, at best; and Llewyn abandons the car, the cat, and Turner after witnessing Johnny's roadside arrest. He locates his destination, the Gate of Horn, knowing that Troy Nelson has secured an appearance at the renowned Chicago club at the invitation of the club's proprietor, Bud Grossman (F. Murray Abraham), and hoping for some similar arrangement for himself. Llewyn plays for Grossman and is told that he is not commercially viable and, worse, not a good candidate for a solo career. Grossman recommends instead that Llewyn find a partner or perhaps join a trio, an arrangement Llewyn previously enjoyed prior to the suicide of his singing partner, Mike, who threw himself from the George Washington Bridge. Llewyn politely thanks Grossman and hitchhikes back to New York.

Upon his return, Llewyn takes his sister's advice to get a regular job and attempts to return to his former career in the Merchant Marine. He pays his union dues with his remaining cash, only to discover that his pilot's license, which he will need to board the ship on Friday, has been thrown out. Out of options again, Llewyn gets drunk at the Gaslight, where he heckles a fellow musician from Arkansas and gets thrown out of the club. Llewyn plays his own set at the café the following night, again for tips, and again performing not only "Hang Me," but also "Fare Thee Well," a song he had previously recorded as a duet with Mike. Returning to events that parallel those from the film's beginning, Llewyn exits the club to go see his "friend" in the alley, but this time on his way out, he observes a young and as-yet-undiscovered Bob Dylan playing on stage. Llewyn is once again beaten by the stranger, whom we discover is the husband of the Arkansas woman Llewyn heckled, and at the film's conclusion, he watches his assailant drive off in a cab.

In interviews surrounding the release of the film, the Coen brothers openly acknowledge that the inspiration for *Inside*

Llewyn Davis was an amalgam of many people and places in and around Greenwich Village in the early 1960s. Llewyn himself was based loosely on musician Dave Von Ronk, a member of the Village music crowd prior to the discovery of Bob Dylan, and Von Ronk's memoir, *The Mayor of MacDougal Street*, provided details that appeared in Llewyn's story: both Von Ronk and Llewyn hail from the same area and spent time in the Merchant Marine, slept on couches, and played guitar. Von Ronk was represented by Moe Asch of Folkways Records, whose character became Llewyn's agent Mel Novikoff in the film, and Asch once tried to give Von Ronk a coat in lieu of royalties, just as Mel did to Llewyn. Like Llewyn, Von Ronk auditioned for Albert Grossman—Bud Grossman in the film—at the Gate of Horn, and both were rejected and advised to join a trio. In the reality of 1961 Chicago, that trio may allude to Peter, Paul, and Mary, a group that Albert Grossman helped create. Von Ronk's cover photo for his 1963 album *Inside Dave Von Ronk* is nearly identical to that of Llewyn's debut solo album and very similarly named, and some of the songs performed by Llewyn in the film appeared on Von Ronk albums as well.

Beyond the Llewyn Davis/Dave Von Ronk similarities, many of the film's characters are derived or inspired by their real-life counterparts. Pappi Corsicato (Max Casella), proprietor of the Gaslight Café, was based on a combination of Sam Hood, who owned a Village café of the same name, and Mike Porco, who owned Gerde's Folk City, the venue in which a *New York Times* reporter discovered Dylan in October of 1961. John Goodman's Roland Turner was inspired by singer/songwriter Doc Pomus; Troy Nelson sings "The Last Thing on My Mind," which was written and performed by Tom Paxton; and Al Cody, who has changed his name from Arthur Milgram in the film, is reminiscent of Ramblin' Jack Elliott, the cowboy hat–wearing folk singer who was born Elliot Charles Adnopoz. Further, cinematographer Bruno Delbonnel has stated that the visual effects of the film were inspired, in part, by the cover art for *Freewheelin' Bob Dylan.*

Small venues such as the Gaslight Café and Folk City, with musicians like Von Ronk, Paxton, and Elliott, operated in contrast to the jazz clubs that dominated the music scene in New York at this time, offering the talents of Thelonius Monk, Horace Silver, and Herbie Mann, among others. Performers played and sang for tips, rather than a portion of a cover charge, an arrangement which suited the proprietors of the venues: New York's "incidental music" clause permitted fewer than four people, with no accompanying brass, woodwind, or percussion instruments, to entertain restaurant and coffee house patrons without requiring additional licensing or paying fees. The Village folk revival thus operated in the shadows of the commercial folk scene, which featured performers such as The Kingston Trio and Harry Belafonte, "pop folkies," whose songs were playing on the radio. "Please Mr. Kennedy" spoofs this more lucrative approach to folk music, an approach Llewyn scorns, even as he ultimately desires the compensation received by those individuals. This artistic snobbishness, a defining characteristic of Llewyn, was also a characteristic of musicians at this time, claims Ethan Coen: "Such eager devotion to authenticity was a mark of that specific scene . . . and the seriousness and piousness that went with it." Llewyn was intended to reflect this attitude, as "it's kind of a hallmark of the period—against convention, not wanting to sell out, not wanting to be bourgeois," states Ethan.

For the film's music, the Coens returned to former collaborator T Bone Burnett, who had served as music producer for *The Ladykillers* (2004), *O Brother, Where Art Thou?* (2000), its accompanying documentary *Down from the Mountain* (2000), and *The Big Lebowski* (1998). Burnett worked closely with Justin Timberlake, who plays Jim Berkey in the film, and Marcus Mumford, associate music producer for the film and husband of Carey Mulligan, who plays Jean Berkey. Mumford also provides the vocals for Mike, Llewyn's former singing partner, on the song "Fare Thee Well," which appears in the film and on the soundtrack. The film's music was recorded live on the set of the picture, with the exception of "The Auld Triangle," which was recorded in a studio, and the film presents those songs as they were shot, in full, single takes, without editing. Of this approach, Burnett indicates that the filmmakers were interested in achieving a documentary effect, in which "everything you hear [Oscar] play and sing in there is him *actually doing it* right in that moment." For the role of Davis, Oscar Isaac mastered the technique known as Travis Picking, used by Dave Von Ronk and folk musicians of his era, a style of playing pioneered by Arnold Schultz, an African American musician from Kentucky, and popularized by Merle Travis in Nashville. Isaac learned the technique from Erik Frandsen, a contemporary of Dave Von Ronk and opened for Frandsen when he played in Village venues.

In September of 2013, before the film's December release, T Bone Burnett organized a concert to benefit the National Recording Preservation Foundation, which seeks to protect music and radio archives. The concert was held at New York's Town Hall and featured music from the film as well as from the 1960s folk scene and included performances by Oscar Isaac and Marcus Mumford as well as Jack White, Joan Baez, Patti Smith, Gillian Welch, and Dave Rawlings. The concert was filmed and released as a documentary, *Another Day/Another Time: Celebrating the Music of "Inside Llewyn Davis,"* which aired on Showtime in December, 2013, in conjunction with the film's release. The documentary was directed by Chris Wilcha and produced by Joel and Ethan Coen, T Bone Burnett, and Scott Rudin.

Premiering at the Cannes Film Festival, *Inside Llewyn Davis* was nominated for the Palme d'Or and named winner of the Grand Prix, and in the end-of-year award season it received four National Society of Film Critics awards. The film additionally earned three Golden Globe nominations: Best Motion Picture—Musical or Comedy; Best Performance by an Actor in a Motion Picture—Musical or Comedy, for Oscar Isaac; and Best Original Song—Motion Picture, for "Please Mr. Kennedy." The film enjoyed much buzz preceding the Academy Awards nominations, and many critics anticipated nominations for Best Picture, Best Actor, and Best Director. However, when the nominations were announced, the film earned only two Oscar nominations, for Bruno Delbonnel's Cinematography and for the Sound Mixing of Skip Lievsay, Greg Orloff, and Peter F. Kurland.

Named to over 450 top-ten lists for 2013, critics and reviewers overwhelmingly offered praise for *Inside Llewyn Davis.* Tim Blake Nelson, who worked with the Coens in *O Brother, Where Art Thou?,* deemed the film "a beautiful, delicate, work of art" and predicted that it would "both delight and surprise Coen brother fans," and A. O. Scott of the *New York Times* proclaimed it "a brilliant magpie's nest of surrealism, period detail and pop-culture scholarship." More severe, though, were the condemnations of NPR's David Edelstein, who found the tone of the film to be "snotty, condescending, cruel," with a sour worldview, and the film itself "thin," concluding that "only the

Coens could turn that stirring early-'60s era that helped give birth to the best part of the counterculture into a sick joke."

For one group of reviewers, the brothers' depiction of the early 1960s folk scene was especially negative because of the critics' familiarity with and experiences during that place and time. Terri Thal, Dave Von Ronk's former wife, published a piece on *VillageVoice.com* in which she expressed her displeasure with the film on a basis similar to that of NPR's Edelstein, that the film negatively depicted a period of time that she remembered much more positively. From her perspective, the Coens rendered the Village folk scene of the early 1960s as "almost unrecognizable," stating that "what bothers me is that the movie doesn't show those days, those people, that world." She took particular offense at the depiction of Llewyn Davis, whom the Coens loosely based on her ex-husband, characterizing Llewyn as "a not-very smart, somewhat selfish, confused young man for whom music is a way to make a living. It's not a calling, as it was for David and for some others. No one in the film seems to love music." Christine Lavin, a contemporary folk musician, knew Dave Von Ronk personally and concurs with Thal's assessment of the film, stating that she is "outraged that the Coens took such a colorful character and interpreted him as a doofus," and characterizing the Coen worldview as too bleak, a charge which is common to most, if not all, of the brothers' films.

The charge of inaccuracy or lack of authenticity by the film's critics is somewhat ironic, as this is Llewyn's complaint about the pop-folk musicians of his time: his music is somehow more pure, and therefore superior, than that of The John Glenn Singers, or Troy Nelson, or even Jim and Jean, in the same way that the Greenwich Village of Terri Thal and Dave Von Ronk and Christine Lavin was more authentic than the version presented by Joel and Ethan Coen. The Coens, however, have long approached their films by closely approximating a genre, whether gangster, noir, western, or road narrative, and simultaneously altering that genre. Sean Wilentz characterizes the result, in *Inside Llewyn Davis*, as "true enough," in terms of details, "but all mixed up, exaggerated, and refracted," characterizing the Coens' process—and product—as "not unlike that of the finest folk songwriters and performers, in their ability to inhabit the past, touch it, and then reconstruct it, but on their own terms."

Critics additionally commented on the character of Llewyn himself, as Adam Mazmanian of the *Washington Times* proclaimed him "the most fully human character they have yet contrived," a sentiment often echoed by reviewers who simultaneously noted the unsympathetic nature of the man himself. It can be difficult to like Llewyn, who seems to create at least some of his own problems, but at the same time, it is more difficult to stop watching him as he struggles with the forces aligned against him. One reviewer characterized Llewyn's situation as "a Jenga tower of hard knocks that takes its hero . . . piles pain upon pain upon him, then hangs him out to dry. Llewyn . . . starts out homeless and bereaved and goes downhill from there." The Coens acknowledge the beleaguered nature of the character, as Joel comments that "we gave him a lot of crosses to bear," and Ethan adds that they simply find movies about losers more interesting than those about people who succeed. Joel states "there's no drama that's interesting to us in triumph over adversity, or emerging success—unless, of course, it's followed by horrible failure," which seems an accurate characterization of their body of work. The *Guardian*'s Tom Shone contextualizes Llewyn and the film which bears his name as "another of the Coens' idiodysseys, complete with Homeric allusions, in which a blinkered stooge stumbles through a malignant universe, the deck piling up against him, while the brothers try hard to suppress their cackles," referencing the oft-noted tendency of the Coens to gleefully submit their characters to constant sorrows and trials. Even Shone proclaims, however, by the conclusion of his piece, that "*Inside Llewyn Davis* is an exquisite objet d'art."

Oscar Isaac comments on the conclusion of the film, in which Llewyn finds himself beaten, in an alley, with no or few prospects, recognizing that "at the end of the film you don't feel like it's an ending. You imagine this continues and it keeps going and maybe it goes dark, maybe it goes good." The audience, like Isaac, remains uncertain about Llewyn's future, but in an uncharacteristically straightforward comment, Ethan Coen suggests that "How good you are doesn't always matter," adding, "That's what the movie is about." The Coens do not typically comment on the "meaning" of their films, stating often that the film speaks for itself, but here, it would seem, the viewer can assume that regardless of Llewyn's talent, there will be no "emerging success."

References

Kaleem Aftab, "There's Nowt as Queer as Folk: Inside the Coen Brothers," *Independent*, January 8, 2014; "A Conversation with T Bone Burnett," *InsideLlewynDavis*.com; RJ Cubarrubia, "Jack White, Marcus Mumford, to Headline *Llewyn Davis* Benefit," *Rolling Stone*, August 19, 2013; David Edelstein, "Great Soundtrack Aside, *Llewyn Davis* Hits a Sour Note," *NPR.org*, December 6, 2013; Brian Hiatt, "How Oscar Isaac Became Llewyn Davis," *Rolling Stone*, Movies & TV, December 12, 2013; Adam Mazmanian, "Movie Review: *Inside Llewyn Davis*," *Washington Times*, December 20, 2013; Melena Ryzik, "A Folkie Takes Issue with

Llewyn Davis," *The Carpetbagger Blog, Blogs. NYTimes.com*, January 6, 2016; A. O. Scott, "Melancholy Odyssey through the Folk Scene," *New York Times*, December 5, 2013; Catherine Shoard, "The Coen Brothers on Losers, Likability, and *Inside Llewyn Davis*," January 16, 2014; Tom Shone, "*Inside Llewyn Davis*: A Masterpiece 'Anti-musical' from the Coen Brothers," *Guardian*, December 5, 2013; Marlow Stern, "The Coen Brothers on Their Brilliant Folk Film, *Inside Llewyn Davis*, at Telluride," *TheDailyBeast.com*, August 30, 2013; John Jeremiah Sullivan, "Daft Folk," *InsideLlewynDavis. com*; Terri Thal, "Dave Von Ronk's Ex-Wife Takes Us Inside *Inside Llewyn Davis*," *Village Voice* Blogs, *Blogs.VillageVoice.com*, December 13, 2013; Jonathan Valania, "O Brother, Who Art Thou?" *HuffingtonPost.com*, April 3, 2013; Elijah Wald, "Before the Flood: Llewyn Davis, Dave Von Ronk, and the Village Folk Scene of 1961," *InsideLlewynDavis.com*; Sean Wilentz, "That'll Never Happen No More," *InsideLlewynDavis.com*. See also T BONE BURNETT, MAX CASELLA, BRUNO DELBONNEL, ADAM DRIVER, JESS GONCHOR, JOHN GOODMAN, OSCAR ISAAC, CAREY MULLIGAN, JUSTIN TIMBERLAKE, MARY ZOPHRES.

INTOLERABLE CRUELTY (2003)

DIRECTOR: Joel Coen and Ethan Coen (uncredited). SCREENPLAY: Robert Ramsey, Matthew Stone, Ethan Coen, Joel Coen, and John Romano. EXECUTIVE PRODUCERS: Sean Daniel, Robert Graf, and James Jacks. PRODUCERS: Ethan Coen, Joel Coen (uncredited), and Brian Grazer; John Cameron, Grant Heslov, and James Whitaker (Co-producers). PHOTOGRAPHY: Roger Deakins. EDITING: Ethan Coen and Joel Coen (as Roderick Jaynes). MUSIC: Carter Burwell. PRODUCTION DESIGN: Leslie McDonald. ART DIRECTION: Tony Fanning. SET DECORATION: Nancy Haigh. COSTUME DESIGN: Mary Zophres.

CAST: George Clooney (Miles Massey), Catherine Zeta-Jones (Marilyn Rexroth), Geoffrey Rush (Donovan Donaly), Cedric the Entertainer (Gus Petch), Edward Herrmann (Rex Rexroth), Paul Adelstein (Wrigley), Richard Jenkins (Freddy Bender), Billy Bob Thornton (Howard D. Doyle), Julia Duffy (Sarah Sorkin), Jonathan Hadary (Heinz, the Baron Krauss von Espy), Tom Aldridge (Herb Myerson), Stacey Travis (Bonnie Donaly), Jack Kyle (Ollie Olerud), Irwin Keyes (Wheezy Joe), Judith Drake (Mrs. Gutman). RUNNING TIME: 100 minutes. Color. RELEASED THROUGH: Universal Pictures. PREMIERE: September 2, 2003 (Venice Film Festival). DVD: Universal Studios Home Entertainment.

The Coen brothers' tenth feature film, *Intolerable Cruelty* (2003), focuses on the personal and professional dealings of Miles Massey (George Clooney), legendary divorce attorney and partner at the law firm of Myerson, Massey, Sloan and Guralnick. Author of the inviolable Massey Prenup, Miles specializes in securing large settlements for his clients, even in the face of irrefutable physical and video evidence. The film opens with an example of such a case, in which Donovan Donaly (Geoffrey Rush), producer of the soap opera *The Sands of Time*, arrives home early to find his wife, Bonnie (Stacey Travis), in the company of the pool man Ollie (Jack Kyle). As the Donalys have no pool, Donovan correctly assumes that the two are involved and draws a gun on Ollie, who flees. Donaly cleverly takes photographs of the departing Ollie and of the wounds he received at the hand of his wife, certain that such evidence will contribute to his victory in the upcoming division of assets. Miles Massey, however, is Bonnie's attorney, and Miles does

Catherine Zeta-Jones (left) and George Clooney in *Intolerable Cruelty* (2003)

not lose; Bonnie is awarded Donaly's assets in the subsequent divorce case, and Donaly becomes homeless, sleeping in alleys.

Despite his success, Miles is bored. Not content with his tab at the Mercedes dealership, a renovated cabin in Vail, and a man to wax his jet, he seeks a challenge in the midst of his perpetual victories. Death is compromise, he claims, and compromise is essential to both marriage and divorce. Life, however, is complete destruction of the opponent. He finds such a challenge in the case of Rex Rexroth (Edward Hermann), an affluent, married man who is caught on video with his mistress in a motel. Rexroth's wife, Marilyn (Catherine Zeta-Jones), has hired a private investigator, Gus Petch (Cedric the Entertainer) to obtain photographic proof of her husband's indiscretions, and she is confident she will soon be a very wealthy woman. She is in possession of incontestable evidence, and the Rexroths have no prenuptial agreement in place. Rex, however, has hired Miles Massey, who sees the case as the chal-

lenge he desires. Not one to be limited by the law, Miles hires Gus to engage in some sleuthing at the Rexroth home, searching for evidence that will compromise Marilyn's position. He presents that evidence in court via Heinz the Baron Krauss von Espy (Jonathan Hadary), who testifies that Marilyn married Rexroth only for his money, intending from the start to divorce him. She is exposed as a calculating gold-digger and left penniless in the settlement, and Miles has succeeded in the destruction of his opponent.

Not content with his victory, Miles continues in his state of ennui, glimpsing his future in the person of senior partner Herb Myerson, an ancient, frail attorney who raves about hours billed and cases won while hooked up to various medical monitoring devices. Marilyn Rexroth reenters Miles's life, appearing at his office with her fiancé Howard D. Doyle (Billy Bob Thornton), oil tycoon and former tight end for the Texas A&M Aggies, come to obtain a Massey Prenup, her gift to him and a sign of her enduring love for her future groom. Suspicious of Marilyn's intentions, Miles warns her that the Massy Prenup cannot be broken, but Marilyn proclaims her love for Doyle, and the marriage takes place. Following the wedding in an act of devotion to his bride, Howard eats the document, with barbecue sauce, and Miles applauds Marilyn's ingenuity in orchestrating this turn of events. Doyle is now exposed, and should Marilyn divorce him, his fortune becomes hers.

Six months later, Miles Massey arrives in Vegas to deliver the keynote speech for N.O.M.A.N., the National Organization of Matrimonial Attorneys Nationwide, an annual meeting of divorce lawyers, only to discover that Marilyn, too, is in Vegas, celebrating her recent divorce from Doyle and her acquisition of 50 percent of his oil fortune. The two have dinner and commiserate on the emptiness that comes with victory; caught up in his emotion, Miles rushes to Marilyn's room in the middle of the night and proposes to her. They are wed in a Vegas chapel, pausing only to sign a Massey Prenup, but Marilyn, as a sign of her trust in Miles, tears up the document. Miles is to deliver his speech, "How to Nail Your Spouse's Ass," at the conference the following day, but overcome by his recent experience with love, he instead renounces his profession, vowing to work pro bono in Los Angeles, or, well, somewhere. Inspired by his new-found bliss, the crowd of divorce attorneys gives Miles a standing ovation, and leaving the conference, he glimpses a soap opera on the television screen: Howard D. Doyle is not an oil tycoon, but rather an actor, which means that Marilyn has no oil fortune. Upstairs in their room, Marilyn has packed and is leaving Miles, intending to divorce him and claim half of his assets.

Returning to his firm, Miles is berated by Herb Myerson, declared an embarrass-

ment to the partnership, and finds himself sleeping on a colleague's couch, as Marilyn has taken his house. In an act of desperation, Miles hires a hit man, Wheezy Joe (Irwin Keyes) to kill Marilyn, but before the deed can be done, Miles learns that Rex Rexroth has died, and Marilyn has inherited his entire estate. Miles now has an extremely wealthy wife whom he has arranged to be killed, and to stop the hit, he and Wrigley go to the house, where Marilyn has offered the hit man more money to kill Miles. Wheezy Joe dies at the hand of his own pistol, and Marilyn and Miles end up in the conference room of Myerson, Massey, Sloan and Guralnick, negotiating the terms of their divorce and settlement. Miles, who would prefer to be reconciled, offers Marilyn a Massey Prenup to give their marriage another try, and Marilyn is so touched by the offer that she tears up the document and they embrace and kiss. As a postscript, the film offers the opening sequence to a hot new game show, in which Gus Petch plays videos of cheating spouses, presumably collected during his stint as a private detective. Back on top again, the show is produced by Donovan Donaly, no longer homeless, but returned to his former glory as a television producer. Marilyn, it seems, has provided him with the concept for the show, and in return, he gave her the name of "Howard D. Doyle," the actor who so successfully assisted in playing Miles the fool.

Joel and Ethan Coen initially came to *Intolerable Cruelty* as scriptwriters in 1994, as it was their first writing project independent of their own films, never intending to direct the picture. The original story was conceived by John Romano, and the previous version of the script was written by Robert Ramsey and Matthew Stone. Following the completion of the screenplay, the Coens went on to direct their own projects, including *Fargo* (1996), *The Big Lebowski* (1998), *O Brother, Where Art*

Thou? (2000), and *The Man Who Wasn't There* (2001). In the interim, a number of directors were attached to the *Intolerable Cruelty* script, including Ron Howard and Jonathan Demme, as were a variety of actors, such as Julia Roberts and Richard Gere, Julia Roberts and Hugh Grant, and Tea Leoni and Will Smith. When Demme declined to direct and George Clooney signed on as the male lead, the Coens agreed to take the project, with Brian Grazer (*A Beautiful Mind* and *Apollo 13*, among others) producing. The brothers were without a project for the short term, as in 2002, the filmmakers were at work on *To the White Sea*, a picture based on the James Dickey novel *Deliverance* and starring Brad Pitt as a U.S. World War II airman who crashed in Japan. The project fell through, largely because of budgeting concerns, and the Coens were available and willing to take the job because of their familiarity with the *Intolerable Cruelty* script. Julia Roberts continued to be a possibility for the female lead, but the studio announced that Catherine Zeta-Jones, who at that point had appeared in *The Mask of Zorro* (1998), *Traffic* (2000), and *Chicago* (2002), among other films, would star opposite Clooney.

Because producer Brian Grazer was attached to *Intolerable Cruelty*, the process took on new dimensions. Grazer initiated focus group testing of the film, a practice in which the Coens do not typically engage. Carter Burwell, who has written the score for many Coen films, recalls that after screenings with recruited audiences in Los Angeles, Grazer reported that viewers did not immediately realize that the film was a comedy. This development was a problem, given that the intent was that the project would indeed be a comedy. Because of Grazer's insistence that the audience be aware of the tone from the onset, Burwell made some changes to the

score, which satisfied the producer, and the project continued.

Upon the release of the film, reviewers also recognized the Hollywood tenor of *Intolerable Cruelty*, an unusual element in a Coen film and one attributed to the casting of George Clooney and Catherine Zeta-Jones. Though less known in the United States, the Welsh actress was achieving star status by virtue of her recent Academy Award for *Chicago* and her appearance in the Oscar-winning and critically acclaimed *Traffic.* Clooney, as well, was experiencing a similar wave of popularity, largely due to his role in Steven Soderbergh's profitable and high-profile *Ocean's Eleven* (2001). The *Guardian*'s Peter Bradshaw characterized the film's costars as "gold-medalists in the Gorgeous Olympics, an achievement borne with no false modesty whatever," a thought seconded by *Slate*'s David Edelstein, who described the project as one in which "two self-infatuated, perennial *Vanity Fair* cover subjects—George Clooney and Catherine Zeta-Jones—try to psych each other out with their respective gorgeousness." Much of the commentary on *Intolerable Cruelty* focused on the physical attributes of the actors, described as the "impossibly charming George Clooney and impossibly stunning Catherine Zeta-Jones" by *Rolling Stone*'s Peter Travers, but others looked beyond the actors to the characters themselves, who did not fare as well as the film's stars themselves. *USA Today* found Miles and Marilyn "intentionally cartoonish and humorously two-dimensional." The *Hollywood Reporter* took issue with Clooney's performance, in which he "becomes increasingly bug-eyed and goofy as the movie wears on, as if he is playing Miles as another version of his character in the Coens' *O Brother, Where Art Thou?*" This may indeed have been Clooney's intent, as Ethan Coen claims that the star envisioned Miles as a descendent of Ulysses Everett

McGill. One review further found that "Hermann as Marilyn's ex and Paul Adelstein as Massey's worshipful associate are an embarrassment," extending the critique beyond just the principal actors.

Some portion of the reviewers' responses to the characters may be a reaction to the film's genre itself rather than to the Coen picture specifically, as *Intolerable Cruelty* was influenced by such classic screwball comedies as *Adam's Rib* (1949, directed by George Cukor), with Spencer Tracy and Katherine Hepburn, and *The Awful Truth* (1937, directed by Leo McCarey), with Irene Dunn and Carey Grant. Additionally, Coen films are often influenced by those of director Preston Sturges, who was responsible for *The Lady Eve* (1941) and *The Palm Beach Story* (1942), both screwball comedies. While *USA Today* offered faint praise for *Intolerable Cruelty*, designating it as "normal" and "the Coens' most mainstream film yet," and *Empire*'s Damon Wise referenced the "musicality in the lightning-quick dialogue," more often, reviews were negative, including Edelstein's assessment of the picture as "no different from most of the other dumb slapstick spoofs that pass for screwball comedy these days" and Jean Oppenheimer's conclusion that the film was "long on manic, cartoonish behavior and short on intelligence and wit." Other writers seemed disappointed that the film did not possess the qualities that they had come to expect from a Coen film, including Ben Walters, of *Sight & Sound*, who begrudgingly described *Intolerable Cruelty* as "more accessible," though possessed of a "flat, sheeny quality," as if the viewer were offered a "calculatingly packaged consumer product rather than a window into a strange new milieu with its own look, feel, and rules," as previous Coen films had done. Ultimately, most critics found that *Intolerable Cruelty*, while in some ways a "Coen film," was in more ways lacking and seemed to rely too heavily on the attractiveness of its characters and their witty banter, resulting in a sort of empty silliness in the film.

References

Peter Bradshaw, "*Intolerable Cruelty*," *Guardian*, October 24, 2003; *CarterBurwell.com*; David Edelstein, "King George vs. Catherine the Great," *Slate.com*, October 10, 2003; Peter Freed, "Raising *Ladykillers*: Coens Hit Remake Trail with Black Comedy Update," *USA Today*, March 23, 2004; Ian Nathan, *Ethan and Joel Coen* (Paris: Cahiers du cinema Sarl, 2012); Jean Oppenheimer, "*Intolerable Cruelty*," in *Joel & Ethan Coen: Blood Siblings*, ed. Paul A. Woods (London: Plexus Publishing, 2003); Claudia Puig, "*Intolerable Cruelty* Delivers Wicked Fun," *USA Today*, October 9, 2003; Eddie Robson, *Coen Brothers* (London: Virgin Books, 2003); Erica Rowell, *The Brothers Grim: The Films of Ethan and Joel Coen* (Lanham, MD: Scarecrow Press, 2007); Peter Travers, "*Intolerable Cruelty*," *Rolling Stone*, October 9, 2003; Ben Walters, "Bringing Up Alimony," *BFI.org*; Damon Wise, "*Intolerable Cruelty*: Screwball Comedy from the Coen Brothers," *EmpireOnline.com*. See also CARTER BURWELL, CEDRIC THE ENTERTAINER, GEORGE CLOONEY, ROGER DEAKINS, NANCY HAIGH, EDWARD HERRMANN, RICHARD JENKINS, BILLY BOB THORNTON, CATHERINE ZETA-JONES, MARY ZOPHRES.

ISAAC, OSCAR (1980–)

Born March 9, 1980, in Guatamala as Oscar Isaac Hernandez and raised in Miami, Oscar participated in children's and regional theatre, made home movies inspired by Quentin Tarantino, and played with his ska-punk band the Blinking Underdogs. The band enjoyed moderate success, opening for Green Day at one point and playing the Viper Room in Los Angeles. Oscar attended Juilliard beginning in 2001, where he played the title role in *Macbeth* and had small parts in the films *Illtown* (1996) and *All About the Benjamins* (2002). Immediately after graduating from Juilliard, he was cast as Proteus in the Public Theatre's Central Park production of *Two Gentlemen of Verona* (2005). He began using the name Oscar Isaac and appeared in Steven Soderbergh's *Che: Part One* (2008), Ridley Scott's *Body of Lies* (2008), and received positive reviews for his larger role as Prince John in Ridley Scott's 2010 *Robin Hood*. He continued his stage work in off-Broadway productions of *Romeo and Juliet* (2007), as Romeo, and the Manhattan Theatre Club Production of *We Live Here* (2011), while still appearing in films such as *Drive* (2011), Madonna's *W.E.* (2011), and *The Bourne Legacy* (2012). In 2013, Isaac appeared in the title role of Joel and Ethan Coen's *Inside Llewyn Davis*.

Having written the screenplay for their film about the early 1960s folk scene in Greenwich Village, the Coens initiated the process of casting the film's main character, Llewyn Davis. They began by auditioning musicians who could act, but discovered very quickly that because of the amount of screen time and the nature of the character himself, they needed instead to look at actors who were musicians. While acting in a small film in New York, Isaac observed one of the film's extras playing a guitar in a fingerpicking style and upon making his acquaintance, discovered that the extra was Erik Frandsen, a contemporary of Dave Von Ronk and Bob Dylan. Frandsen, who still lived on MacDougal Street above the old Gaslight Club which figured so largely in *Inside Llewyn Davis*, instructed Isaac in the technique, known as Travis Picking, and Isaac opened for Frandsen when he appeared at local Village venues. When Isaac auditioned for the Coens, having played guitar from the age of twelve and trained in acting at Juilliard, the two elements of the character—the music and the acting—came together. The brothers sent Isaac's audition tape to the film's music producer, T Bone Burnett, who, hearing Isaac play, observed that "this guy's actually a better musician than a lot of the studio guys I work with," and Isaac was cast.

Of Isaac's performance, Burnett has stated that "I cannot think of a precedent in the history of civilization for this performance Oscar Isaac gives in this film," and film critics largely concurred. Isaac was nominated for a Golden Globe award for Best Performance by an Actor in a Motion Picture—Musical or Comedy, and he won the Best Actor Award given by the National Society of Film Critics, in addition to being nominated for more than a dozen other Best Actor awards from various cities and countries. The character of Llewyn himself has been alternately described as unsympathetic, a jerk, grumpy, and as "the most fully human character [the Coens] have yet contrived," and is described by Isaac as "such an internal guy. . . . He is an island, shut off from everyone else." Isaac took inspiration for the character from the Coen brothers themselves, stating that "Even though I find them really charming people, they are not people pleasers," a quality which Llewyn manifests throughout the film.

Isaac further characterizes Llewyn as straightforward rather than selfish, a claim that viewers might dispute, given the ways in which he interacts with the film's characters, displaying little emotion toward his former lover Jean when she informs him she's pregnant and heckling a fellow musician on the stage of the Gaslight Café with an alcohol-induced vitriol, resulting in a back-alley beating at the hands of the performer's husband. Donald Clarke of the *Irish Times* concurs with a reading of the character as a man who is blunt and uncompromising, but not a jerk, deeming

Llewyn's lack of personal charm as a sign of his unwillingness to reinvent himself, personally and musically, in the face of the upheaval surrounding him. In a film about a musician who does not make it big, despite his sustained efforts, Llewyn "sees himself as a guy who is never going to make it," Isaac states, adding, "There's a great Van Ronk quote: 'Would I like to have made a little more money? Sure. But I did end up doing what I wanted to do. Even when I wanted to get out, I was pulled back to the music.'" Isaac describes his time on the set as "the most beautiful experience I have had," a sentiment often echoed by actors who work on Coen films.

References

"Cast: Oscar Isaac," *InsideLlewynDavis.com*; Donald Clarke, "*Inside Llewyn Davis* Star Oscar Isaac on Folk, Film, and Working with Cats," *Irish Times*, January 17, 2014; "A Conversation with T Bone Burnett," *InsideLlewynDavis.com*; Manohla Dargis and A. O. Scott, "We Are the Establishment Now: The Coen Brothers Look Wryly at Their Films," *New York Times*, September 4, 2013; Adam Mazmanian, "Movie Review: *Inside Llewyn Davis*," *Washington Times*, December 20, 2013; Bernadette McNulty, "Oscar Isaac Interview for *Inside Llewyn Davis*," *Telegraph*, January 6, 2014; John Jeremiah Sullivan, "Daft Folk," *InsideLlewynDavis.com*. See also *INSIDE LLEWYN DAVIS*.

J

JAYNES, RODERICK

Oscar-nominated editor for his work on *Fargo* (1996) and *No Country for Old Men* (2007), Jaynes hails from Sussex, England, a veteran of British films such as *The Mad Weekend*, with Alistair Sim, *Beyond Mombassa* (1956), and *Operation Fort Petticoat*. Following a lengthy hiatus from the film industry, Jaynes edited *Blood Simple* (1985), and though the filmmakers did not use Jaynes for *Raising Arizona* (1987) or *Miller's Crossing* (1990), he again worked with the brothers on *Barton Fink* (1991) and has edited every Coen film since.

In 2002, Jaynes wrote the introduction for *Collected Screenplays, Vol. 1, Blood Simple; Raising Arizona; Miller's Crossing & Barton Fink*, in which he characterized the brothers as "people patently ignorant of the simplest mechanics of film construction," among other insults directed at their filmmaking abilities. An invention of Joel and Ethan Coen, Jaynes is a pseudonym designed to prevent their names appearing too frequently in the credits of their films. Upon his nomination for *Fargo*, the brothers conspired to have Albert Finney attend the ceremony in disguise, but the Academy rules forbid proxies to accept awards, largely because in 1973 Marlon Brando sent Sacheen Littlefeather, a Native American, to the ceremony. When Brando received his Oscar for Best Actor in *The Godfather*, she read a letter from Brando, in which he complained about the United States' treatment of Littlefeather's people. The true identity of Jaynes was discovered, though the Coens still reference their editor in the third person, filling in bits of his fictional biography. At the 1997 Oscars, the filmmakers indicated that Jaynes was "back at home in Haywards Heath watching cricket," and Billy Bob Thornton, in the DVD commentary on *The Man Who Wasn't There* (2001), expressed his surprise at how tall Jaynes is, having bumped into him at a Los Angeles supermarket.

References

Ronald Bergan, *The Coen Brothers* (New York: Thunder's Mouth Press, 2000); Ian Nathan, *Ethan and Joel Coen* (Paris: Cahiers du cinema Sarl, 2012); Eddie Robson, *Coen Brothers* (London: Virgin Books, 2003); Jada Yuan, "Roderick Jaynes, Imaginary Oscar Nominee for 'No Country,'" *Vulture.com*, January 22, 2008.

JENKINS, RICHARD (1947–)

Born May 4, 1947, in DeKalb, Illinois, Jenkins studied theatre at Illinois Wesleyan University and attended graduate school at Indiana State College, where he studied with Harold Guskin. He was with Rhode Island's Trinity Repertory Company in Providence for fifteen years, serving as artistic director for four years. Jenkins began his on-screen career in the television series *Great Performances* (1974–1975), and his first film appearance was a small part in Lawrence Kasdan's *Silverado* (1985), following which he played a doctor in Woody Allen's *Hannah and Her Sisters* (1986). He worked with Sidney Poitier and River Phoenix in *Little Nikita* (1988) and with Al Pacino and John Goodman in *Sea of Love* (1989).

In the early 1990s, he appeared in several made-for-television movies, including *Challenger* (1990), about the Challenger spaceship, *And the Band Played On* (1993), and *The Boys Next Door* (1996), with Nathan Lane. In 1997, he was cast in Clint Eastwood's *Absolute Power*, and he worked with Sydney Pollack in *Random Hearts* (1999). His 1998 role in *There's Something about Mary* would mark his first picture with Peter and Bobby Farrelly, with whom he would work again on *Me, Myself, & Irene* (2000) and *Hall Pass* (2011). He also appeared in the Farrelly-produced *Outside Providence* (1999) and *Say It Isn't So* (2001). He had a recurring role in HBO's *Six Feet Under* (2001–2005), appeared in *North Country* (2005) with Charlize Theron, and was nominated for Best Actor Oscar for his role in *The Visitor* (2007). He appeared in *Eat, Pray, Love* (2010) with Julia Roberts and Javier Bardem, with Tom Cruise in the crime drama *Jack Reacher* (2012), and was cast in the 2014 HBO mini-series *Olive Kitteridge* with Frances McDormand.

Jenkins began auditioning for Joel and Ethan Coen for *Raising Arizona* (1987) but was not cast until much later, in *The Man Who Wasn't There* (2001), followed by *Intolerable Cruelty* (2003) and *Burn After Reading* (2008). Jenkins played the drunken Walter Abundas in *The Man Who Wasn't There*, a man who immerses himself in his family genealogy rather than in the affairs of his daughter Birdy (Scarlett Johansson). Jenkins was then cast as Freddy Bender in *Intolerable Cruelty*, a divorce attorney for Marilyn Rexroth (Catherine Zeta-Jones), who matches wits with Miles Massey (George Clooney) in the cut-throat

world of high-stakes marriage and divorce. In *Burn After Reading*, Jenkins appeared as Ted, manager of Hardbodies Fitness and former monk who now pines for his employee Linda Litzke (Frances McDormand), a man whom Jenkins characterized as "soulful."

References

Paul Brownfield, "From Supporting Actor to Star, Richard Jenkins Steps Up in *The Visitor*," *Los Angeles Times*, April 6, 2008; "Richard Jenkins," *New York Times*, Movies & TV; "Richard Jenkins," *Starpulse.com*. See also *BURN AFTER READING, INTOLERABLE CRUELTY, THE MAN WHO WASN'T THERE*.

JOHANSSON, SCARLETT (1984–)

Johansson was born November 22, 1984, in New York City to a family well-acquainted with the film industry: her grandfather was a screenwriter and director, and her mother was a producer. With her twin brother, she is the youngest of four children and began acting at an early age, appearing off-Broadway at age eight. She attended Manhattan's Professional Children's School and the Lee Strasburg Institute for Young People, and her first on-screen appearance was in the film *North* (1994), directed by Rob Reiner. Her subsequent films include *Just Cause* (1995) with Sean Connery and Laurence Fishburne, and she appeared with Robert Redford in *The Horse Whisperer* (1998). In 2001 she worked with Thora Birch and Steve Buscemi in *Ghost World*, and in 2002 she graduated from high school. As Charlotte in Sophia Coppola's *Lost in Translation* (2003), Johansson earned a Golden Globe nomination for Best Performance by an Actress in a Motion Picture—Musical or Comedy, a role that escalated her career considerably. She subsequently starred in *Girl with a Pearl Earring* (2003) and *A Love Song for Bobby Long* (2004), receiving Golden Globe nominations for both films as Best Performance by an Actress in a Motion Picture—Drama.

She worked with Woody Allen in *Match Point* (2005), again earning a Golden Globe nomination, and with Brian De Palma in *The Black Dahlia* (2006) and Christopher Nolan in *The Prestige* (2006).

In 2008, Johansson released a vocal album, *Anywhere I Lay My Head*, in which she covers Tom Waits songs, and in 2009, she and Pete Yorn released an album of duets entitled *Break Up*. She debuted on Broadway in Arthur Miller's *A View from the Bridge* (2010), for which she won the Tony Award for Best Featured Actress in a Play, and she subsequently appeared in Broadway's *Cat on a Hot Tin Roof* in 2013. Johansson starred in Woody Allen's *Vicky Cristina Barcelona* (2008) and also in 2008, she appeared as Silken Floss in Frank Miller's adaptation of the comic book *The Spirit*. She would continue working in the genre with roles in *Iron Man 2* (2010), *The Avengers* (2012), and *Captain America: The Winter Soldier* (2014), playing Natasha Rominoff/Black Widow in each film. In 2012, she played Janet Leigh in the biopic *Hitchcock*, and in 2013, she provided the voice of Samantha in the Oscar-nominated *Her*, which starred Joaquin Phoenix.

Johansson has appeared in one film by Joel and Ethan Coen, their neo-noir *The Man Who Wasn't There* (2001), as Birdy Abundas. Birdy has enchanted the film's protagonist, Ed Crane (Billy Bob Thornton), who makes it his mission to see Birdy become an accomplished classical pianist. Anthony Lane deems Johansson a "minx" in the film, and *Rolling Stone*'s Peter Travers describes her performance as "wonderfly sly," though Johansson herself characterizes Birdy's relationship with Ed Crane as "purely innocent." The Coens have commented that they were intimidated by the young actress during production, as she appeared to have no self doubt, and Billy Bob Thornton claims that the filmmakers and he were afraid of the young actress because of "how together she was for her age." Johansson notes, however, that their impression can be attributed to her cockiness at age fifteen.

References

Carlo Cavangna, "Profile & Interview: Scarlett Johansson," *AboutFilm.com*, February, 2004; "Scarlett Johansson," *Biography.com*; "Scarlett Johansson," *BroadwayWorld.com*; "Scarlett Johansson" *Broadway.com*; A. J. Jacobs, "Scarlett Johansson Is the Sexiest Woman Alive, 2006," *Esquire.com*, October 31, 2006; Anthony Lane, "Her Again," *New Yorker*, March 24, 2014; "Scarlett Johansson," *New York Times*, Movies & TV; "Scarlett Johansson: A New Bacall?" *Today*, December 15, 2003; Peter Travers, "*The Man Who Wasn't There*," *Rolling Stone*, November 2, 2001. See also THE MAN WHO WASN'T THERE.

JONES, TOMMY LEE (1946–)

Born in San Saba, Texas, September 15, 1946, Jones first appeared on stage in the second grade, as Sneezy, in a school production of *Snow White and the Seven Dwarves*. He attended St. Mark's School of Texas in Dallas, prior to earning a football scholarship to Harvard University, where he majored in English and was roommate to Al Gore, future vice president of the United States. He participated in Harvard drama productions, playing the lead in Shakespeare's *Coriolanus* and appearing with John Lithgow in the University's production of *The Lady's Not for Burning* (1967). Jones graduated *cum laude* from Harvard in 1969 and relocated to New York City, where ten days after graduation, he appeared off-Broadway in *Patriot for Me*. Jones was then cast in his first film role, *Love Story* (1970), and he played a recurring role on *One Life to Live* (1971–1979), as Dr. Mark Toland. He moved to Los Angeles in 1975, where he appeared in a number of small parts in television series, including *Barnaby Jones* (1975), *Baretta* (1975), and *Charlie's Angels* (1976), and was cast in a leading role in *Jackson County Jail* (1976). He worked with Faye Dunaway in *Eyes of Laura Mars* (1978), with Laurence Olivier in *The Betsy* (1978), and with director Mike Figgis in *Stormy Monday* (1988). A veteran of television movies, his credits include *Cat on a Hot Tin Roof* (1984), the mini-series *Lonesome Dove* (1989), for which he earned a Golden Globe nomination for Best Supporting Actor, and *The Good Old Boys* (1995), which he adapted from Elmer Kelton's novel of the same name and directed and starred in as well.

Jones's name recognition increased significantly following his role in Oliver Stone's *JFK* (1991), for which he was nominated for the Best Supporting Actor Oscar, and in *The Fugitive* (1993), for which he received the Oscar for Best Supporting Actor as well as the Golden Globe for Best Supporting Actor. He worked with Oliver Stone again in *Heaven and Earth* (1993) and *Natural Born Killers* (1994), and he continued to appear in high-profile films, with his role as Harvey Dent/Two Face in Joel Schumacher's *Batman Forever* (1995). He also appeared with Will Smith in the summer blockbuster *Men in Black* (1997) and its sequels *Men in Black II* (2002) and *Men in Black 3* (2012). In 2005, he directed *The Three Burials of Melquiades Estrada*, in which he also starred, with Barry Pepper and Dwight Yokum. He appeared with Samuel L. Jackson in HBO's adaptation of the Cormac McCarthy play, *The Sunset Limited*, which he directed, and he wrote, directed, and starred in *The Homesman* (2014).

In addition to his Oscar-winning appearance in *The Fugitive*, Jones received a Primetime Emmy for his portrayal of convicted murderer Gary Gilmore in *The Executioner's Song* (1982). Additionally, he was nominated by the Academy for Best Supporting Actor in *JFK*, Best Actor in Paul Haggis's *In the Valley of Ellah* (2007), and

Best Supporting Actor in Steven Spielberg's *Lincoln* (2012). Also in 2012, Jones received the Harvard Arts Medal, an award that honors a Harvard or Radcliffe graduate who has achieved excellence in the arts and contributed to education or the public good.

As Sheriff Ed Tom Bell, Jones played an aging lawman, beset by his own insecurities and tracking a serial killer Anton Chigurh (Javier Bardem). Jones was selected early in the casting process, as the Coens considered a very short list of actors; they wanted an individual who would appear a native Texan, and as Ian Nathan declared, Jones is "Texan to his core." The *New York Times*' A. O. Scott said his quality of "craggy, vinegary warmth is well suited to the kind of righteous, decent lawman he has lately taken to portraying," continuing, "he gives the movie a grace above its lashing violence." Peter Travers of *Rolling Stone* stated that Jones played Bell with "the kind of wit and assurance that reveals a master actor at the top of his game," and the Screen Actors Guild concurred, nominating him for the Award for Outstanding Performance by a Male Actor in a Supporting Role. As a part of the cast, Tommy won the SAG Award for Outstanding Performance by a Cast in a Motion Picture.

References

"Tommy Lee Jones," *Biography.com*; Ian Nathan, "*No Country for Old Men*: Heaven Be Praised, the Brothers Go Grim Again," *EmpireOnline.com*; "Tommy Lee Jones," *New York Times*, Movies & TV; A. O. Scott, "He Found a Bundle of Money, and Now There's Hell to Pay," *New York Times*, November 9, 2007; Peter Travers, "*No Country for Old Men*," *Rolling Stone*, November 1, 2007; Colleen Walsh, "Tommy Lee Jones Receives Arts Medal," *Harvard Gazette*, April 26, 2012; Bernard Weinraub, "Tommy Lee Jones Snarls His Way to the Pinnacle," *New York Times*, August 1, 1993. See also *NO COUNTRY FOR OLD MEN*.

K

KIND, RICHARD (1956–)

Born November 22, 1956, in Trenton, New Jersey, Kind was raised in Pennsylvania and attended Northwestern University, graduating in 1978 with a degree in Pre-Law. At the advice of a family friend, Kind turned his attention to acting, and after a brief stint in New York, he began working with Chicago's Practical Theatre Company, founded by Julia Louis-Dreyfus, Brad Hall, and Gary Kroeger. He later joined the Second City improv group, also in Chicago, where he appeared in *How Green Were My Values*, and *John, Paul, Sartre, and Ringo*, among others. Kind's stage career has included *Candide* at the New York City Opera, and on Broadway, *The Tale of the Allergist's Wife* (2000), *The Producers* (2001), *Bounce* (2003 and 2006), *Dirty, Rotten Scoundrels* (2005), *The Best Little Whorehouse in Texas* (2006), and *The Big Knife* (2013), for which he earned a Tony Award nomination for Best Performance by an Actor in a Featured Role in a Play.

Kind first appeared on-screen in the made-for-television movies *Two Fathers' Justice* (1985) and *Bennett Brothers* (1987), which he followed with one-time parts in the television series *Hooperman* (1987), *My Sister Sam* (1988), and *Mr. Belvedere* (1988), among others. He was then cast in a recurring role in the series *Unsub* (1989), following which he appeared on Carol Burnett's *Carol & Company* (1990) and *The Carol Burnett Show* (1991) and in recurring roles in *Blue Skies* (1994), *The Commish* (1993–1995), and *A Whole New Ball Game* (1995). Kind is best known for his roles in *Mad About You* (1992–1999), as Dr. Mark Devanow, *Spin City* (1996–2002), as Paul Lassiter, and *Scrubs* (2003–2004), as Harvey Corman. He also appeared periodically as Cousin Andy on *Curb Your Enthusiasm* (2002–2009).

Kind's film work began in *Vice Versa* (1988) with Judge Reinhold, and subsequent films include *Mr. Saturday Night* (1992) with Billy Crystal, *Stargate* (1994) with Kurt Russell and James Spader, George Clooney's *Confessions of a Dangerous Mind* (2002), Thomas McCarthy's *The Station Agent* (2003) and *The Visitor* (2007), and the Oscar-winning *Argo* (2012), produced by close friend George Clooney. Kind has lent his voice to numerous animated projects, including the films *A Bug's Life* (1998), *Garfield* (2004), *Cars* (2006), *Toy Story 3* (2010), and *Cars 2* (2011). His television voice work includes *Oswald* (2001–2002), *Kim Possible* (2003–2007), *Dora the Explorer* (2009), *American Dad* (2005–2010), and *The Penguins of Madagascar* (2009–2011).

In the Coens' 2009 *A Serious Man*, Kind plays Uncle Arthur, brother to the film's lead character, Larry Gopnik (Michael Stuhlbarg). Arthur appears periodically in the film, first monopolizing the

Gopnick's couch and bathroom, where he drains his sebaceous cyst, then at the hotel, where he shares a room with Larry, whose wife has evicted him from their home; Arthur, meanwhile, continues working on his mentaculus, a system by which he proposes to decipher the universe. His later contributions to Larry's chaos include encounters with the law for illegal gambling and solicitation, bringing the local authorities to Larry's home on more than one occasion. As one of the only recognizable actors in the film—most of the cast comes from a stage background—Kind received mention in many reviews, praising him for his performance. Of working with the Coens, Kind commented that "I love to talk things out, but I have a feeling they don't," referencing their approach to his character as well as the meaning of the film. He adds, "And yet they're very specific, very concerned and thoughtful about what they want. So it's a contradiction."

References

"Richard Kind," *BroadwayWorld.com*, "Richard Kind," *FocusFeatures.com*, *A Serious Man*, Cast & Crew; "Richard Kind," *New York Times*, Movies & TV; Naomi Pfefferman, "Get *Serious*: The Coen Brothers," *JewishJournal.com*, September 2, 2009; "Richard Kind Biography," *StarPulse .com*. See also *A SERIOUS MAN*.

L

THE LADYKILLERS (2004)

DIRECTOR: Ethan Coen and Joel Coen. SCREENPLAY: Joel Coen, Ethan Coen, and William Rose. PRODUCERS: Ethan Coen, Joel Coen, Tom Jacobson, Barry Josephson, Barry Sonnenfeld; John Cameron (Co-producer); David Diliberto and Robert Graf (Associate Producers). PHOTOGRAPHY: Roger Deakins. EDITING: Ethan Coen and Joel Coen (as Roderick Jaynes). MUSIC: Carter Burwell. EXECUTIVE MUSIC PRODUCER: T Bone Burnett. PRODUCTION DESIGN: Dennis Gassner. ART DIRECTION: Richard Johnson. SET DECORATION: Nancy Haigh. COSTUME DESIGN: Mary Zophres.
CAST: Tom Hanks (Professor G. H. Dorr), Irma P. Hall (Marva Munson), Marlon Wayans (Gawain MacSam), J. K. Simmons (Garth Pancake), Tzi Ma (The General), Ryan Hurst (Lump Hudson), Diane Delano (Mountain Girl), George Wallace (Sheriff Wyner), John McConnell (Deputy Sheriff), Jason Weaver (Weemack Funthes), Stephen Root (Fernand Gudge).
RUNNING TIME: 104 minutes. Color.
RELEASED THROUGH: Buena Vista Pictures.
PREMIERE: March 26, 2004.
DVD: Touchstone Home Entertainment.

The eleventh feature film by Joel and Ethan Coen was a remake of the 1955 Ealing Studios film of the same name, *The Ladykillers,* originally written by William Rose, directed by Alexander Mackendrick, and starring Alec Guinness, Peter Sellers, and Cecil Parker. In the 2004 Coen film, Professor Goldthwait Higginson (G. H.) Dorr (Tom Hanks), ostensibly on sabbatical from the University of Mississippi at Hattiesburg, has rented a room from the widow Marva Munson (Irma P. Hall). Dorr, an eloquent and refined figure in a cape and off-white suit, claims to have a passion for music of the Cinquecento and arranges to have his ensemble—playing music that originated no earlier than the Rococo—practice in the basement of the Munson home. The group meets in the dank room under the guise of rehearsing and devises a plan to tunnel from the home's basement to the nearby *Bandit Queen,* a riverboat casino. For the task, Dorr has assembled a team of experts, each possessing a specialized skill, and together, the group will execute a break-in and robbery of the underground offices and counting room of the Mannix Corporation, which owns and operates the *Bandit Queen.*

The team consists of Dorr, the mastermind of the plan; Gawain MacSam (Marlon Wayans), the inside man who works as a janitor for the casino; The General (Tzi Ma), tunneling expert and donut store proprietor; Lump (Ryan Hurst), "muscle" for the group and college football player; and Garth Pancake (J. K. Simmons), demolitions specialist and consultant for television

Tom Hanks (left) and Marlon Wayans in *The Ladykillers* (2004)

commercials. As the narrative progresses, the erstwhile musicians/would-be thieves meet regularly for practice, digging a sizeable hole through the earth and hauling the excess dirt to a bridge where it is dropped onto a garbage barge; Mrs. Munson attends a series of church services; and Pickles, the ever-present housecat, watches the proceedings through knowing eyes. The plan encounters a number of obstacles, including Gawain's termination from his position on the *Bandit Queen*; Garth's disclosure of the impending heist to his girlfriend, Mountain Girl (Diane Delano), a decision that meets with much disapproval from the team; the arrival of the sheriff at the home of Mrs. Munson, during which Professor Dorr is nearly discovered by the lawman; and a premature explosion in the basement that threatens to expose the entire plan.

The thieves are, however, successful in breaching the counting room and spiriting away $1.6 million, replacing the bricks and re-plastering the wall, leaving no trace of their presence and an impenetrable mys-

tery. The caper has reached its end only to be thwarted by the unexpected arrival home of Mrs. Munson, who hears the final explosion sealing the tunnel and erasing all trace of the endeavor. Munson is joined by ladies from the church who have come to have tea and listen to the musical stylings of Professor Dorr and his fellow musicians. Following a stirring oration by Dorr, in which he recites "To Helen," by Edgar Allen Poe, the widow confronts the team, demanding an explanation. Dorr attempts to weave a clever story to placate her, but Mrs. Munson is not deceived and threatens to call the authorities to report the group. Upon hearing the truth, she issues an ultimatum: Dorr and his accomplices will return the money and attend church with her or she will turn them all in. The thieves confer and determine that the widow needs to be killed, drawing straws to designate an assassin. Gawain is unable to fulfill his duties as executioner and is shot and killed in a struggle with Garth over the gun; Garth attempts to abscond with the cash, only to be apprehended by the General; the General then is appointed to the task of removing Mrs. Munson from the equation, but as he bends to strangle her in her sleep, he is startled and falls down the stairs to his death. Only the Professor and Lump remain, and having dumped the rest of the bodies off of the bridge, Lump accidently shoots himself, leaving Dorr in sole possession of the cash, which is stacked neatly in the basement. However, a raven dislodges the head of a stone gargoyle on the bridge, knocking Dorr unconscious; he falls to his death, landing on the garbage barge. All the members of the team, then, make their final repose on garbage island, while the widow Munson is assured by the skeptical members of the sheriff's department that she can keep the cash, which she intends to donate to Bob Jones University.

The Coen approach to *The Ladykillers* marks a departure from the filmmakers' earlier projects, as they had not previously engaged in remaking films in such a direct manner, though their prior film viewing experiences always influence their current projects. Their involvement with the film was initially limited to the rewriting of the screenplay, as Barry Sonnenfeld was scheduled to direct the film, and the brothers assumed the role of directors when Sonnenfeld withdrew from the project. A remake would not have been the sort of project the filmmakers would undertake, Joel Coen has stated, but when the situation developed, they agreed to make the film. In doing so, they shared directing, writing, and producing credits for the first time, as previously, they shared only writing credits, while Joel served as director and Ethan served as producer.

The 1955 *The Ladykillers* from which the Coens remade their 2004 film was produced by England's Ealing Studios and told the story of one Professor Marcus (Alec Guinness), who rents a room in the home of Mrs. Louisa Alexandra Wilburforce (Katie Johnson). In Alexander Mackendrick's black comedy, Marcus brings his string quartet to Mrs. Wilburforce's home to plan an armed-car robbery in post–World War II London. The gang plans to make an unwitting accomplice of the elderly woman, using her to move the cash they have successfully stolen and ultimately determining that she should be killed, but, as in the Coen version, the thieves are unable to bring about her demise and she remains alive while the gang members meet their end one by one. The ensemble cast included Peter Sellers, Cecil Parker, Danny Green, and Herbert Lom, and the story was said to be based on a dream that screenwriter William Rose had during a particularly unproductive time in his career. Rose received an Oscar nomination for his screenplay.

In remaking the film, the Coens relocated the action from post–World War II London to the Deep South at the beginning of the twenty-first century, where a bridge, a trash barge, and garbage island take the place of the railroad yards that served as the dumping ground for the bodies that pile up near the end of the film. Reviewers largely applauded the change of setting as a means by which to update the film, as the new locale offered a timelessness to the picture, and the Coens added an element of the Southern Gothic in their remake, notes *Empire*'s Ian Nathan. The execution of the plot, however, did not meet with such approval. Nathan characterizes the film as "off-kilter and lethargic, stuffed with forced jollity and broad mishap," and Charles Taylor, writing for *Salon*, notes that the film is "structured like a *Mad* magazine parody where there's a promised joke in each frame. It doesn't add up to a movie." The comedic elements, in particular, were found to be wanting, as *New York*'s Peter Rainer found that "at times we might be watching *Dumb and Dumber* with a college degree." More specifically, claims Rex Roberts of *Film Journal International,* "a half-century ago, audiences delighted in jokes that took five minutes to unfold," whereas "today, moviegoers are treated to a dog suffocating in a gas mask in a bit of contemporary humor typically mean-spirited and gratuitous." *Rolling Stone*'s Peter Travers, in a comment that gained consensus among the film's reviewers, notes that "the film means to evoke giggles out of the grotesque. But you'll have to watch the original film to see it done right."

One element that the Coens inserted into their new *Ladykillers* is religion, which did not appear in Mackendrick's original but makes its way into the 2004 version through the character of Marva Munson, a devout churchgoer who quotes scripture and regularly donates to charity. In turn, the religion of Mrs. Munson leads to some of the film's most powerful music, the performances by the choir at Munson's church, including "Let the Light from the Lighthouse Shine on Me" and "Come, Let Us Go Back to God." While the plot and comedy of the Coens' remake may have suffered in the opinion of film critics, they wrote much more enthusiastically about the film's music, a collaboration between Carter Burwell, who composed the original music in the score, and T Bone Burnett, who served as executive music producer for the film. The film combines hip-hop (referred to by Mrs. Munson as "hippity-hop music"), which accompanies members of the gang and more specifically Gawain MacSam; the gospel music that occurs in Marva Munson's church; and the baroque compositions that the group is ostensibly creating in the basement. Particularly effective are the sequences in which the action crosscuts from the Casino, to the church, to the tunnel, and back again, while the music simultaneously moves

from hip-hop to gospel to baroque and again to hip-hop. The music further correlates to the philosophical positions of the characters, who affiliate themselves with materialism, as found in the lyrics of the hip-hop songs; faith, as championed by the hymns; and classical refinement, communicated through the music of the Renaissance, so dramatically savored by the effete Professor Dorr.

The Coens' Professor Dorr, as depicted by Hanks, is described by *Empire*'s Ian Nathan as "exquisite," a villain who has "slithered straight out of the pages of a Mark Twain novel, flush with a fey gentlemanly delicacy, mud-brown fangs and a magician's sprig of a beard." The role was unusual for Hanks, who has made a career of playing likeable, often heroic characters, which include Forrest Gump, Jim Lovell (*Apollo 13*), Captain Miller (*Saving Private Ryan*), and Woody (*Toy Story*), but Hanks eagerly accepted the part, contributing to the wardrobe design and creating the wheezy laugh used by the Professor to awkwardly mask his criminal intentions. Casting the film was an unusual process for the Coens, as they had not intended to direct the film and therefore did not engage in their common practice of writing the characters with actors in mind. While the cast, specifically Hanks and Hall, garnered much praise for their performances, the characters themselves did not fare as well. The *Guardian*'s John Patterson characterized the gang of thieves as "five transcendently stupid crooks," suggesting that the film reaches a point at which "you cannot wait for them all to die, so that you can finally go home." This idiocy is by design, however, as Joel Coen claims that their criminals are typically "knuckleheads," which renders them amusing, and elements of this design can be observed in the fugitives of *O Brother, Where Art Thou?* (2000), the nihilists of *The Big Lebowski* (1998), and the entire ensemble of *Burn After Reading* (2008). The charge of unsympathetic, unintelligent characters was not limited to Patterson, however. Though not as direct in his assessment, Roger Ebert similarly categorized the group as "over-the-top in a way rarely seen outside Looney Tunes." Ebert did, however, reserve praise for the performance of Irma P. Hall, as "the one completely successful comic performance in the movie," though still a caricature, but one that is recognizable as human. The others, he claims, are comic strip creations.

The Coens' *Ladykillers* remake does not typically find itself atop the best-of Coen lists, though viewers will occasionally sing its praises as an underrated film. Despite its status as a "lesser" Coen film, the picture was nominated for the Palme d'Or at the Cannes Film Festival, and Irma P. Hall was awarded a Jury Prize at Cannes for her performance as Marva Munson. Regardless, the Coens have not remade another film since *The Ladykillers*—their 2010 *True Grit* is characterized as a re-adaptation rather than a remake of the 1969 Henry Hathaway film—perhaps an indication that this sort of project was less satisfying than their previous pictures.

References

Roger Ebert, "*The Ladykillers*," *RogerEbert.com*, March 26, 2004; David Edelstein, "Thieves Like Us," *Slate.com*; Peter Freed, "Raising *Ladykillers*: Coens Hit Remake Trail with Black Comedy Update," *USA Today*, March 23, 2004; Shawn Levy, "The British Are Going to Crucify Us," *Guardian*, May 9, 2004; Ian Nathan, "*The Ladykillers*," *EmpireOnline.com*; John Patterson, "Ealing Hands," *Guardian*, March 28, 2004; Peter Rainer, "Low Country," *New York*; Rex Roberts, "*The Ladykillers*," *Film Journal International*; Erica Rowell, *The Brothers Grim: The Films of Ethan and Joel Coen* (Lanham, MD: Scarecrow Press, 2007); Jeff Stafford, "*The Ladykillers*," *TCM.com*; Charles Taylor, "*The Ladykillers*," *Salon.com*, March 26, 2004; Peter Travers, "*The Ladykillers*," *Rolling Stone*, March 23, 2004. See also CARTER BURWELL, T BONE BURNETT, ROGER DEAKINS, DENNIS GASSNER, NANCY HAIGH, IRMA P. HALL, TOM HANKS, RYAN HURST, STEPHEN ROOT, J. K. SIMMONS, BARRY SONNENFELD, MARLON WAYANS, MARY ZOPHRES.

LEIGH, JENNIFER JASON (1962–)

Born in Los Angeles, California, on February 5, 1962, Leigh is the daughter of actor Vic Morrow and screenwriter Barbara Turner. She became a member of the Screen Actors Guild at age nine and left high school prior to graduation to study at the Lee Strasberg Institute in New York City. She began her professional acting career with small roles on television series such as *Baretta* (1977), *Family* (1978), and *The Waltons* (1981), and continued with larger parts in made-for-television movies including *The Killing of Randy Webster* (1981) and *The Best Little Girl in the World* (1981). Known as a method actor, Leigh made her debut film appearance in *Eyes of a Stranger* (1981), which she followed with *Fast Times at Ridgemont High* (1982). Her work in the 1990s included such films as *Backdraft* (1991), *Single White Female* (1992), Robert Altman's *Short Cuts* (1993), and *Delores Claiborne* (1995), and in 1998 she made her debut on Broadway in the revival of *Cabaret*, where she worked with Alan Cumming. Leigh and Cumming then wrote and directed the 2001 film *The Anniversary Party*, following which she returned to the stage as the lead in the Broadway production of *Proof* (2001). Leigh worked with her husband, director Noah Baumbach, on *Margot at the Wedding* (2007) and they cowrote *Greenberg* (2010), prior to their divorce. She had a recurring role on the Showtime series *Weeds* (2009–2012) as well as on ABC's *Revenge* (2012), and she received a Golden Globe nomination for her role in the film *Mrs. Parker and the Vicious Circle* (1994). She has appeared in two Coen films: *The Hudsucker Proxy* (1994), as journalist Amy Archer, and *The Man Who Wasn't There* (2001), in an uncredited role as a female inmate.

In *The Hudsucker Proxy*, Leigh's character first schemes to expose newly appointed Hudsucker executive Norville Barnes (Tim Robbins) as a fraud, but soon discovers that he is instead a patsy for the real swindlers, Sidney J. Mussburger (Paul Newman) and the Hudsucker Board. Despite her journalistic intentions, Archer develops feelings for Barnes, realizing his aw-shucks manners and idealistic approach to management are genuine. It appears, however, that she may be too late to save Norville from the corporate culture that first rockets him to success and then strands him on the brink of self-destruction, but Norville is rescued by Fate, Time, and an angel, allowing him a second chance at love and leading Hudsucker Industries.

Roger Ebert deemed Leigh's performance as reminiscent of Rosalind Russell in *His Girl Friday* (1940), a perfect portrayal of the "hard-bitten, fast-talking girl reporter who sits on your desk, lights a cigarette, and lays down the law," a description that is not very different from Norville's description of Amy, as "one of these fast talkin' career gals, thinks she's one of the boys." To prepare for the part, Leigh read old fan magazine articles about Jean Arthur and Rosalind Russell, who starred in Hollywood films of the 1930s and whose performances and attitudes shaped the development of her character, Amy Archer. Her accent closely replicates that of Katherine Hepburn, with a delivery characterized by the *New York Times*' Caryn James as "delightfully perfect," though Joe Brown of the *Washington Post* found Leigh's Amy a performance in which her "panicky straining quickly becomes tiring."

References

Joe Brown, "*The Hudsucker Proxy*," *Washington Post*, March 25, 1994; John Clark, "Strange Bedfellows," in *Joel & Ethan Coen: Blood Siblings*, ed. Paul A. Woods (London: Plexus Publishing, 2003); Roger Ebert, "*Hudsucker Proxy*," *Rogerebert.com*, March 25, 1994; Caryn James, "*The Hudsucker Proxy*: Reviews/Film: Sniffing Out the Truth about Instant Success," *New York Times*, March 11, 1994; "Jennifer Jason Leigh," *Biography.com*; "Jennifer Jason Leigh," *New York Times*, Movies & TV; Eddie Robson, *Coen Brothers* (London: Virgin Books, 2003). See also *THE HUDSUCKER PROXY*, *THE MAN WHO WASN'T THERE*.

LENNICK, SARI

Born in Miami, Lennick attended the University of Southern California, where she earned her bachelor of arts degree in theatre and philosophy in 1997. While at USC, she received the Eileen Stanley Award for Outstanding Talent and the Ruth & Albert McKinley Award for Outstanding Performance. Lennick then studied at the Actors Studio at The New School in New York City, where she earned her MFA and the Bob Hope Fellowship for Excellence in Comedy. She acted for a time in New York, with roles in *I'm Not Sorry*, a solo show, and *Fat Men in Skirts*. Lennick and her husband moved to the Minneapolis area, where she stopped acting; fourteen years later, the Coens cast her in their 2009 film *A Serious Man*.

As Judith Gopnik, Lennick plays a 1960s suburban wife who, early in the film, informs her husband Larry (Michael Stuhlbarg) that she wants a divorce. The picture's narrative then follows the fall-out that develops from that request, as Judith and her companion, Sy Ableman (Fred Melamed), convince Larry that he should move out of his own house, for propriety's sake, and, following Sy's death, that Larry should pay for the funeral expenses. The

Village Voice's Ella Taylor describes Lennick's Judith as "a stout matron with all her discontent lodged in her curled lip," a role for which Lennick gained weight and dyed her blonde hair dark brown. Of the character, Lennick sees Judith as "someone who has made some decisions, and some very clear decisions," who has likely experienced a "lot of disappointment," much of it related to her marriage. On working with the Coens, Lennick states, "once you step on the set with them, they hand you ownership of the role, which makes it this incredible work experience," taking place in "an extraordinary work environment." She adds, "it's like the best boss you've ever had. . . . They believed in me, which made me want to make them proud every single day."

Lennick continued to live in Minneapolis following her role in *A Serious Man*; in 2014, she was cast in Shelli Ainsworth's film *Stay Then Go*.

References

"Sari Lennick," *FocusFeatures.com*, *A Serious Man*, Cast & Crew; Jessica Sick, "Local Actress Gets *Serious*," *NBCMiami.com*, October 23, 2009; Mordecai Specktor, "The Way We Were Midwest Jews," *American Jewish World*, September 30, 2009; Ella Taylor, "For *A Serious Man*, Coen Brothers Aim Trademark Contempt at Themselves," *Village Voice*, September 29, 2009. See also *A SERIOUS MAN*.

LERNER, MICHAEL (1941–)

Born June 22, 1941, in Brooklyn, New York, Lerner attended Brooklyn College and the University of California before receiving a Fulbright scholarship at the London Academy of Music and Dramatic Art. He performed with the San Francisco American Conservatory Theatre and made his small screen debut in the television series *The Good Guys* (1969), which he followed with appearances in *The Brady Bunch* (1969), *The Doris Day Show* (1969–

1970), and *Ironside* (1971–1972), among others. Lerner is often cast in made-for-television movies, including such biographical roles as Pierre Salinger in *The Missiles of October* (1974), Jack Ruby in *Ruby and Oswald* (1978), and Hollywood studio head Harry Cohn in *Rita Hayworth: The Love Goddess* (1983). His first film appearance was in *Alex in Wonderland* (1970), which he followed with several small roles prior to his roles in *The Postman Always Rings Twice* (1981) with Jack Nicholson and Jessica Lange, *Eight Men Out* (1988) with John Cusack, and *Harlem Nights* (1989) with Eddie Murphy. He earned an Oscar nomination for Best Actor in a Supporting Role for his role as studio head Jack Lipnick in the Coens' *Barton Fink* (1991). Additional films include *Godzilla* (1998), Woody Allen's *Celebrity* (1998) with *Barton Fink* actress Judy Davis, the Coen film *A Serious Man* (2009), and the Snow White adaptation, *Mirror Mirror*, with Julia Roberts, in 2012.

While Lerner's *Barton Fink* character of Jack Lipnick was inspired by some combination of Louis B. Mayer, Jack Warner, and Harry Cohn, according to the Coens, Lerner based his role on Mayer, head of MGM Studios, stating "I even found a pair of glasses in a junk shop that were identical to the ones he wore. As soon as I put them on, I felt like Mayer." As Lipnick, he played Capitol Pictures' studio head, who first adores, then rejects writer Barton Fink, a performance, states Daniel DiMattei, that "borders between hilarious and horrifying." He blithely assigns Fink a Wallace Beery wrestling picture, but not a B picture, he emphasizes, demanding a treatment at the end of the week. Though his screen time as Lipnick was limited, Lerner was nominated for Best Actor in a Supporting Role by the Academy.

In *A Serious Man* (2009), Lerner plays Solomon Schultz, an attorney who has been tasked with assisting Larry Gopnik (Michael Stuhlbarg) with a property line dispute. The role of Schultz is remarkable only in that he suffers a heart attack just as he prepares to deliver good news to Gopnik regarding the borders of his yard, which have been trespassed upon by his neighbor.

References

Daniel DiMattei, "*Barton Fink*: A Review," *Examiner.com*, August 3, 2012; Courtney Howard, "*Mirror Mirror's* Michael Lerner Talks Visionary Directors, Newsies, & Career Beginnings," *Veryaware.com*, March 28, 2012; Michael Lieberman, "An Actor Clears His Bookshelves: The Michael Lerner Collection at Bonhams," *Seattlepi.com*, April 10, 2012; Andy Marx, "Michael Lerner Still Slipping into Larger-Than-Life Character Roles," *Los Angeles Times*, August 31, 1991; "Michael Lerner Bio," *Tribute. ca*; "Michael Lerner," *Turner Classic Movies*. See also *BARTON FINK, A SERIOUS MAN*.

MACDONALD, KELLY (1976–)

Born February 23, 1976, in Glasgow, Scotland, Macdonald grew up an avid fan of Doris Day, particularly the film *Calamity Jane* (1953), which she would watch daily. She attended an open call for Danny Boyle's film *Trainspotting* (1996) and was cast to play Ewan McGregor's love interest. Boyle has said "Kelly has that thing Ewan McGregor has, indefinable star quality, yet they're ordinary people." Her subsequent film appearances include *Elizabeth* (1998), *Gosford Park* (2001), and *The Hitchhiker's Guide to the Galaxy* (2005), and her television work includes the BBC mini-series *State of Play* (2003) and *Boardwalk Empire* (2010–2013), where she appeared with Coen regular Steve Buscemi and for which she was nominated for an Emmy Award. She was cast as Helena Ravenclaw in *Harry Potter and the Deathly Hallows: Part 2* (2011) and as Dolly in *Anna Karenina* (2012), and she lent her voice to *Brave*'s Merida (2012).

As Carla Jean Moss in the Coen adaptation of Cormac McCarthy's *No Country for Old Men* (2007), Macdonald played the wife of Llewelyn Moss (Josh Brolin), a country boy who finds himself in over his head when he finds the missing money from a Mexican drug deal gone wrong. Carla Jean spends much of the film worrying over her husband, now on the run, and at the film's conclusion, she comes face to face with Anton Chigurh (Javier Bardem), an expressionless serial killer with an unshakeable code. When casting for the film, the Coens were looking for an American to play the Texas native Carla Jean, but when they viewed her audition tape, in which she used a perfect West Texas accent, they gave her the part.

References

"Kelly Macdonald," *Biography.com*; Amy Raphael, "Kelly's Grace," *Guardian*, November 7, 2008. See also *NO COUNTRY FOR OLD MEN*.

MACY, WILLIAM H. (1950–)

Born March 13, 1950, in Miami, Florida, Macy acted in high school prior to attending Bethany College, where he majored in veterinary medicine. He then transferred to Goddard College to study theatre, studying under playwright David Mamet. Upon receiving his degree, he became a member of Mamet's St. Nicholas Company in Chicago, appearing in Mamet's *American Buffalo* (1975), which was nominated for two Tony Awards. In 1978 Macy relocated to New York, where he did some commercial voice-work and appeared in the television mini-series *The Awakening Land* (1978). He appeared in small film roles in *Somewhere in Time* and *Foolin' Around*, both in 1980, followed by a number of made-for-television movies in the mid-1980s. In 1985 he and Mamet formed

William H. Macy in *Fargo* (1996)

the Atlantic Theater Company, for which Macy directed Mamet's *Radio: An Evening of Sketches* and Chekov's *Three Sisters*. He appeared in Mamet's film directorial debut *House of Games* (1987) and Mamet's subsequent films *Homicide* (1991) and *Oleanna* (1994), as well as Woody Allen's *Radio Days* (1987). In the late-1990s, Macy's credits include roles in *Air Force One* (1997), *Boogie Nights* (1997), *Pleasantville* (1998), and Gus Van Sant's 1998 remake of Alfred Hitchcock's *Psycho*. He appeared in Paul Thomas Anderson's *Magnolia* (1999), where he met his future wife Felicity Huffman. His recurring television roles include *ER* (1994–2009), *Sports Night* (1999–2000), and *Shameless* (2011–2013). Macy won the Emmy Award for Outstanding Lead Actor in a Motion Picture Made for Television for *Door to Door* (2002), for which he also received a Golden Globe nomination. Additional Globe nominations include Best Performance by an Actor in a Supporting Role in a Motion Picture for his part in *Seabiscuit* (2003) and Best Performance by an Actor in a Motion Picture Made for Television for *The Wool Cap* (2004), which he also wrote. In 2007 Macy appeared in *Wild Hogs* with John Travolta, Martin Lawrence, and Tim Allen, and his first feature directorial project was *Rudderless* (2014), with Selena Gomez, Laurence Fishburne, and Felicity Huffman.

As a writer, Macy penned the television movie *A Slight Case of Murder* (1999), and his 2002 project *Door to Door*, cowritten with Steven Schachter, won the Emmy for Outstanding Writing for a Motion Picture Made for Television. Also with Schachter, he cowrote the 2008 romantic comedy *The Deal*, which starred Macy and Meg Ryan. He produced the television movie *The Wool Cap* (2004) and the 2005 film *Transamerica*, which featured his wife Felicity Huffman.

Macy has appeared in one film by Joel and Ethan Coen, their 1996 Oscar-winning *Fargo*, which received the award for Best

Screenplay; cast as Jerry Lundegaard, he was nominated for the Academy Award for Best Actor in a Supporting Role. Jerry was the only major part not written with an actor in mind—Marge was written for Frances McDormand and the kidnappers were penned for Steve Buscemi and Peter Stormare—and Macy auditioned twice for the role: first in Los Angeles, following which he flew to New York and unexpectedly showed up for the auditions there. The Coens had envisioned Jerry as "a sloven, uncomfortable in his body, a little overweight," and had to reimagine the character as the uptight, repressed car salesman ultimately portrayed by Macy, described by one reviewer as resembling Mr. Potato Head and behaving like Mr. Milquetoast. He plays Jerry with precision; the Coens recall that he refused to shoot a single scene without his lapel pin which signified five years of service to his father-in-law's car dealership. Roger Ebert characterizes Macy's Jerry as exhibiting "the unbearable agony of a man who needs to think fast, and whose brain is scrambled with fear, guilt and the crazy illusion that he can somehow still pull this thing off." The Coens were similarly interested in the character as an individual who cannot for a moment "project himself into the future and evaluate the consequences of his decisions," and Jerry's anger and frustration at his eventual capture in a North Dakota hotel demonstrate his inability to accept the inevitability and finality of his failure.

References

Emma Brockes, "William H. Macy: May I Be Frank?" *Guardian*, June 3, 2011; "William H. Macy," *Biography.com*; Michel Ciment and Hubert Niogret, "Closer to Life Than the Conventions of Cinema," in *The Coen Brothers: Interviews*, ed. William Rodney Allen (Jackson: University Press of Mississippi, 2006); Barbara Cramer, *Films in Review*, 47.5/6 (1996); Roger Ebert, "Fargo," *RogerEbert.com*, March 8, 1996; Lizzie Francke, "Hell Freezes Over," in *Joel & Ethan Coen: Blood Siblings*, ed. Paul A. Woods (London: Plexus Publishing, 2003); "William H. Macy," *New York Times*, Movies & TV; Eddie Robson, *Coen Brothers* (London: Virgin Books, 2003). See also *FARGO*.

MAHONEY, JOHN (1940–)

Born June 20, 1940, in Blackpool, Lancashire, England, and raised in Manchester, England, Mahoney was one of eight children and the son of a baker. He relocated to the United States at the age of nineteen, where he joined the Army and gained his citizenship. He attended Quincy College in Illinois and earned his master's degree at Western Illinois University, where he taught English prior to moving to Chicago in 1970. There, Mahoney edited a medical journal until determining that he needed to make a mid-life career change; at age thirty-seven, he began acting lessons at David Mamet's St. Nicholas Theatre, appearing in *The Water Engine* and *Ashes* with John Malkovich. Mahoney was recruited to the Steppenwolf Theatre Company by Malkovich shortly thereafter, first appearing in *Philadelphia, Here I Come* in 1978. His screen debut was in *Hudson Taylor* (1981), which he followed with appearances in television movies such as *Lady Blue* (1985) and *Trapped in Silence* (1986), as well as series that included *Saturday Night Live* (1987), *Cheers* (1992), *3rd Rock from the Sun* (1996), and a recurring role on *H.E.L.P* (1990). In 1993, he was cast as Martin Crane, father of Frasier Crane, on the series *Frasier*.

While he appeared in numerous films, including *Moonstruck* (1987) with Cher, *Say Anything* (1989) with John Cusack, *In the Line of Fire* (1993) with John Malkovich, and Ed Burns's *She's the One* (1996), Mahoney often returned to the stage for Steppenwolf productions of *The Drawer Boy* (2001), *I Never Sang for My Father* (2004), *The Seafarer* (2008), and *The Birthday Party* (2013), among others. He won a Tony award for his role in the Broadway production of *House of Blue Leaves* (1986) and was nominated for two Golden Globes, two Emmys, and ten Screen Actors Guild Awards, all for his role as Martin Crane in *Frasier*. As a member of the *Frasier* cast, he jointly received the SAG Award for Outstanding Performance by an Ensemble in a Comedy Series in 2000.

Mahoney appeared in two films by Joel and Ethan Coen: *Barton Fink* (1991) and *The Hudsucker Proxy* (1994). In *Barton Fink*, he played writer W.P. Mayhew, whom Fink calls "the finest novelist of our time," a character directly inspired by William Faulkner, according to Joel Coen. Mahoney was chosen for the role because of his physical resemblance to Faulkner, though Faulkner successfully navigated Hollywood in a way that Mahoney's Mayhew did not. In a performance described by Vincent Canby of the *New York Times* as "superb," Mahoney plays a Southern writer, fond of the bottle, who is little help to the struggling Fink. His secretary and muse, Audrey Taylor (Judy Davis) has resorted to writing Mayhew's screenplays and novels, and Mayhew stumbles and hums his way through his scenes, ultimately meeting his demise at the hands of Madman Karl Mundt, played by John Goodman.

As the chief of the city desk for *The Manhattan Argus* daily newspaper, Mahoney's role in *The Hudsucker Proxy* was limited, but in his scenes he barked assignments to reporters and demanded a piece on the "human angle," a behind-the-scenes story on the "Idea Man," Norville Barnes (Tim Robbins), which sets in motion the investigative reporting of Amy Archer (Jennifer Jason Leigh) and one of the primary subplots of the film.

References

Vincent Canby, "*Barton Fink*," *New York Times*, August 21, 1991; Rick Kogan, "The Curse of John Mahoney," *Chicago Tribune*, May 17, 1996; Kathryn MacNeil, "Actor John Mahoney finds his muse," *Times of Northwest Indiana*, November 14, 2011. See also *BARTON FINK*, *THE HUDSUCKER PROXY*, JOHN MALKOVICH.

MALKOVICH, JOHN (1953–)

The two-time Oscar nominated actor was born December 9, 1953, in Christopher, Illinois, and attended Illinois State University, where he experienced the stage for the first time. He so enjoyed acting that he joined the Steppenwolf Theatre in Chicago in 1976, which had been founded by his friend Gary Sinise. To make ends meet, Malkovich worked several jobs, including at an office supply store, driving a school bus, painting, and landscaping. His role in *True West*, a Sam Shepherd play, took him to New York in 1982, where he won an Obie and Steppenwolf made its name. Malkovich appeared on Broadway in 1984 with Dustin Hoffman in Arthur Miller's *Death of a Salesman* and also appeared on screen that same year in *The Killing Fields* and *Places in the Heart*, earning his first Academy Award nomination. His most well-known films include *Dangerous Liaisons* (1988), *In the Line of Fire* (1993), for which he received his second Oscar nomination, *Con Air* (1997), and *Secretariat* (2010). In 1999, Malkovich appeared as himself in the Spike Jonze film *Being John Malkovich*, in which the film's characters discover a secret tunnel to the interior of John Malkovich's head, and in 1998, he formed the production company, Mr. Mudd, with partners Lianne Halfon and Russell Smith. The company produced such films as *Ghost World* (2001), *Juno* (2007), and *The Perks of Being a Wallflower* (2012). His directorial debut was *The Dancer Upstairs* (2002), starring Javier Bardem, also a Mr. Mudd production. He has appeared in one Coen brothers film, *Burn After Reading* (2008).

Malkovich has the reputation of playing characters who are malevolent in some way, and while he has played numerous roles that are not, audiences remember most those "combined acting roles" which "add up to a cross between Hannibal Lecter and Casanova." The character of Osborne Cox, in *Burn After Reading*, is less Casanova than Malkovich's role in *Dangerous Liaisons*, for example, but the volatility and seething anger manifested in roles such as *In the Line of Fire* and *Con Air* are certainly present in the Coen spy thriller spoof. The *New Yorker*'s David Denby characterized Malkovich's role as "scenes of slowly mounting ire, complete with baroque insults and fervent profanity, [that] move through time like a series of slow-motion Olympic dives," and Malkovich himself describes Cox's anger as a "slow burn." His anger is not righteous, nor his cause just, however, as Malkovich characterizes Cox as "an ass . . . an idiot," as are most of the characters in the film. Though he had met the Coens only once prior to the film, the role of Cox was written with Malkovich in mind, as it was for many of the cast members, and such a part gave Malkovich and company a unique opportunity to revel in the nonsense of the characters and the film's plot, which Malkovich sees as "a comedy with meanness."

References

David Denby, "Storm Warnings," *New Yorker*, September 15, 2008; Ian Nathan, *"Burn After Reading:* Concoctions of Two Dangerous Minds," *EmpireOnline.com*; John Patterson, "Big Bad John," *Guardian*, November 29, 2002; Susan Wloszczyna, "Feel the 'Burn' with the Coen Brothers," *USA Today*, September 12, 2008; Gaby Wood, "A Multitude of Malkovich," *TheGuardian.com*, September 29, 2001. See also *BURN AFTER READING*.

THE MAN WHO WASN'T THERE (2001)

DIRECTOR: Joel Coen and Ethan Coen (uncredited). SCREENPLAY: Joel Coen and Ethan Coen. EXECUTIVE PRODUCERS: Tim Bevan and Eric Fellner. PRODUCERS: Ethan Coen and Joel Coen; John Cameron (Co-producer); Robert Graf (Associate Producer). PHOTOGRAPHY: Roger Deakins. EDITING: Ethan Coen and Joel Coen (as Roderick Jaynes) and Tricia Cooke. MUSIC: Carter Burwell. PRODUCTION DESIGN: Dennis Gassner. ART DIRECTION: Chris Gorak. SET DECORATION: Chris L. Spellman. COSTUME DESIGN: Mary Zophres.

CAST: Billy Bob Thornton (Ed Crane), Frances McDormand (Doris Crane), Michael Badalucco (Frank), James Gandolfini (Big Dave Brewster), Katherine Borowitz (Ann Nordlinger Brewster), Jon Polito (Creighton Tolliver), Scarlett Johansson (Birdy Abundas), Richard Jenkins (Walter Abundas), Tony Shalhoub (Freddy Riedenschneider), Peter Siragusa (Bartender), Jennifer Jason Leigh (female inmate—uncredited).

RUNNING TIME: 116 minutes. Black and White.

RELEASED THROUGH: USA Films. PREMIERE: May 13, 2001 (Cannes International Film Festival).

DVD: USA Entertainment.

ACADEMY AWARDS: Best Cinematography (nominated: Roger Deakins).

The ninth feature film by Joel and Ethan Coen was the black and white drama *The Man Who Wasn't There*, starring Billy Bob Thornton and Frances McDormand, with Michael Badalucco, James Gandolfini, and Scarlett Johansson in supporting roles. In the film, Thornton plays Ed Crane, a barber who works for his brother-in-law, Frank Raffo (Badalucco), at Guzzi's barbershop. Crane, an impassive, quiet man, cuts the hair, while Frank talks incessantly and an

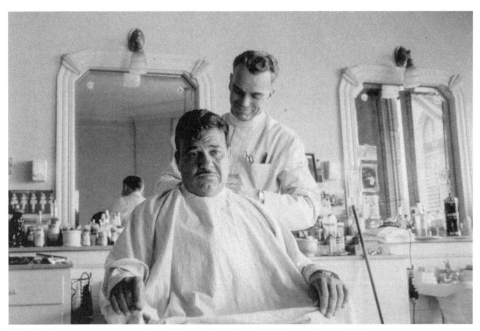

Billy Bob Thornton (top) and Jon Polito in *The Man Who Wasn't There* (2001)

unending series of nameless men and boys cycle through their stations. Crane lives in a little bungalow on Napa Street with his wife, Doris (McDormand), who keeps the books at Nirdlinger's, a department store run by Big Dave Brewster (Gandolfini) and owned by his wife, Ann (Katherine Borowitz), and her family. Life for Ed and Doris is comprised of uneventful days and nights, during which they attend Tuesday night bingo at the Catholic Church and entertain Ann and Big Dave, with whom Doris is having an affair, a sameness pervading their daily existence.

The tedium of Ed's days is altered with the entrance of Creighton Tolliver (Jon Polito), a traveling entrepreneur who visits the barber shop in need of a quick trim and a venture capitalist: Tolliver has arrived in Santa Rosa seeking a $10,000 investment to begin a dry cleaning business. Big Dave is unwilling to contribute to the venture, as he plans to open a haberdashery of his own, and as Tolliver explains the innovative business opportunity, Crane ponders

what this enterprise could mean to his own future. He determines that a partnership in Tolliver's dry cleaning shop could get him out of Frank's employ at the barbershop and place him in control of his own destiny. To obtain the $10,000, Crane blackmails Big Dave, sending him an anonymous, type-written demand for cash. If Dave fails to comply, the note threatens, Ed Crane and Ann Brewster will be informed about the affair with Doris, and Brewster will be ruined.

Distraught about the attempted extortion, Big Dave asks Ed for his advice regarding the situation, stating only that he is being blackmailed for his involvement with a married woman without stating that the woman in question is Doris, a fact that both men know but do not reveal in the conversation. To come up with the cash, Dave enlists the assistance of Doris, who fixes the Nirdlinger books and makes the funds available. Once delivered, Ed passes the money along to Tolliver, signing the necessary papers and becoming a silent partner in the dry cleaning business. The exchange seems to have gone as planned, and Ed can look forward to 50 percent of the profits and a new direction in his life. Doris, however, sees her world crumbling around her, becomes drunk at a family wedding, and upon arriving home, passes out. Dave phones Ed, asking him to come to the department store, as the two men need to talk. Dave confronts Ed, accusing him of blackmail and attacking him in the darkened office, and in the struggle, Ed stabs Big Dave in the neck. Bleeding out onto the office floor, Dave dies from his wounds. In their investigation, the police discover the irregularities in the store books, conclude that Doris murdered Dave in an attempt to avoid prosecution for embezzlement, and charge Doris with Big Dave's murder.

Surprised that Doris is behind bars, rather than himself, Ed approaches Frank with the situation. Frank secures a loan on the barbershop and uses the funds to hire Freddy Riedenschneider (Tony Shalhoub), a sharp, fast-talking attorney from Sacramento. During an interview with Riedenschneider and Doris, Ed confesses to the murder and explains his motive, but the lawyer determines that the story isn't flashy enough and that the jury won't buy it. Riedenschneider instead concocts an elaborate story involving Big Dave's service record and a blackmail plot by an unknown person who sought to expose Dave as a fraud rather than a war hero. Before the case can come before the jury, however, Doris hangs herself in her cell, having discovered that she is pregnant with Big Dave's child.

Ed continues to cut the hair, hiring a new barber to replace Frank, who has gone to pieces over Doris's suicide. Looking for meaning in his life, Ed first visits a psychic, whom he determines to be a fraud, and then takes an interest in Birdy Abundas (Scarlett Johansson), the adolescent daughter of a family friend, who Ed thinks plays the piano beautifully. Unwilling to watch Birdy let life slip away from her, as Ed feels his has, he takes her to visit a renowned music teacher who mentors child prodigies, hoping that Birdy will realize her potential as a world-famous musician. Ed will serve as her manager, for a small fee, he supposes. Birdy, however, is not destined to become a world-famous pianist, as she lacks the necessary passion, news which so disappoints and angers Ed that on the drive home, Birdy attempts to give him oral sex. Shocked, Ed drives the car down an embankment, breaking Birdy's collarbone and injuring himself as well.

While in the hospital, Ed is visited by two policemen who inform him that he is under arrest for the murder of Creighton Tolliver, whose car and body were found in a local lake along with the partnership papers that indicated that Ed had delivered $10,000 in return for half of the business. The police have concluded that Ed forced Doris to embezzle the money and then he beat Tolliver to death to prevent him from exposing the origin of the funds. Freddy Riedenschneider represents Ed in court, which ends in a mistrial. In the subsequent trial, Ed is represented by the county defender, who throws Ed upon the mercy of the court. The court, however, sentences Ed to death by electric chair, and at the film's conclusion, Ed's sentence is carried out, his final thoughts about what he will say to Doris, should he find her in another life.

The concept for *The Man Who Wasn't There* originated from a poster used on the set of *The Hudsucker Proxy* (1994), on which different kinds of haircuts were illustrated: "the butch," "the executive contour," "the junior contour," the styles listed by Ed Crane in the opening scenes of the film. The Coens began thinking about the cuts and the person responsible for executing them, and "The Barber Project" was born. They began working on the script but set it aside to shoot *The Big Lebowski* (1998), and though the screenplay was complete prior to *O Brother, Where Art Thou?* (2000), they filmed *O Brother* first because of George Clooney's availability. As is common to Coen projects, they wrote some of the parts for specific actors: Doris was written for Frances McDormand, as was Frank for Michael Badalucco, but the rest of the actors were selected during the casting process. The Coens contacted Billy Bob Thornton for the lead role, telling him the film was about "a barber who wants to be a dry cleaner," and Thornton accepted without reservation or further explanation of the film or the role.

The Man Who Wasn't There is set in Santa Rosa, California, in 1949, the same era and location as Hitchcock's *Shadow of a Doubt* (1943), Joel Coen's favorite Hitchcock film. The project received its final title at a late date, just prior to its premiere at the Cannes Film Festival: previously, it was referenced as "The Barber Project," the name by which it had been known for some years. The new title is reminiscent of Alfred Hitchcock's *The Man Who Knew Too Much* (1956) but also reflects how Ed Crane sees himself, as a ghost, and how others see him, failing to remember his name or recognize him outside of the barbershop. Of the title, Ethan Coen states, "There is something pulpy about the movie that helps the title work. It's consistent with the fact that he's writing this story for a men's magazine." The pulpy characteristics of the film originate not only in the men's magazine for which Ed is writing but also in the sources that contributed to the film's creation. Reviewers often note that the picture has a film noir sensibility about it, noting the film's Medical Examiner whose name is Dietrichson—the name of Barbara Stan-

wyck's character in Billy Wilder's film *Double Indemnity*.

The Coens, however, would point to literature rather than film as the primary influence for *The Man Who Wasn't There*, as demonstrated by the film's Nirdlinger's Department Store, which shares its name with the *femme fatale* in the James M. Cain novel *Double Indemnity*. Cain's hardboiled detective stories often serve as inspiration for the brothers, as they did for writers and directors in 1940s Hollywood. Cain's novels were adapted into such films as *Double Indemnity* (1944), *Mildred Pierce* (1945), and *The Postman Always Rings Twice* (1946), and the filmmakers cite Cain as a significant source for their first feature film, *Blood Simple* (1984). Joel Coen explains, "What intrigues us about Cain is that the heroes of his stories are nearly always schlubs—loser guys involved in dreary, banal existences," a description which certainly applies to many of the Coens' protagonists, including Ed Crane, *Fargo*'s Jerry, and *A Serious Man*'s Larry, among others. In addition to films noir and hardboiled detective literature, the culture of the 1950s also served as an influence on the film. The filmmakers drew upon school health movies, civil defense films, and public information cinema, as well as early fifties' science fiction films, which manifested themselves in the picture's UFO references. The resultant tone of the film replicates that of the period as well, characterized by Joel Coen as paranoid and filled with existential dread.

The temptation to compare the film to classic noir was difficult for reviewers to resist, and *The Man Who Wasn't There* did not always hold up well in those comparisons. The UK's *Daily Mail* concluded that "however cleverly it may imitate the style of a *Double Indemnity*, it doesn't have the power of the originals," referencing the film's characters as the reason for the film's failures. It found them unsympathetic, "mean, greedy, squalid and defeated by life," and the common accusation of the Coens' privileging of style over substance was raised. French critic Michel Ciment, in Roger Ebert's "*The Man Who Wasn't There*," having viewed the film at its Cannes premiere, characterized the picture as "a 90-minute film that plays for two hours," and one viewer remarked, "I guess their problem is that basically they don't have anything to say." *Salon*'s Andrew O'Hehir offers that perhaps "the Coens want it to be about something that can't be described or defined," which would be appropriate to a film that centers around a man who doesn't talk much. The picture was, however, championed by other reviewers, as the *Guardian*'s Peter Bradshaw deemed it "the best American film of the year," describing it as "stunning" and "mesmeric." *Rolling Stone*'s Peter Travers enthused "*Man* is steadily engrossing and devilishly funny, and, o brother, does it look sharp," pointing to the technique used by cinematographer Roger Deakins during filming and post-production.

The brothers chose to release the picture in black and white, a decision that met with much approval from reviewers. Roger Ebert describes the effect as elegant, reminding the viewer of "a 1940s station wagon—chrome, wood, leather and steel all burnished to a contented glow." To achieve this effect, Deakins shot the film in color, as the Coens were contractually obligated to release the film color in Europe, though ultimately it remained in black and white for most of its international release as well. Deakins further states that outdated technology prompted him to shoot in color, as black-and-white film stock hadn't been updated in years, and color allowed him to maintain a better quality of image. His goal was to produce a more modern look for the film, rather than an homage to the black and white films of the 1940s, though critics did not necessarily differentiate between the intent and the homage, as the *New York Times*' A. O. Scott praised Deakins's work as reminiscent of "old Hollywood masters like the prolific James Wong Howe and like Gregg Toland, who shot *Citizen Kane* and *The Best Years of Our Lives*." Ultimately, the choice had its desired effect, if in a thematic way, as Ian Nathan wrote, "Black and white isn't just about style or movie history, it is narrative: Ed sees the world in monochrome," yet another Coen loser, trapped in his mundane life.

References

Peter Bradshaw, "*The Man Who Wasn't There*," *Guardian*, October 25, 2001; Kyle Buchanan, "From *Shawshank* to *Skyfall*, How Master Cinematographer Roger Deakins Got These Ten Shots," *Vulture.com*, February 21, 2013; Roger Ebert, "*The Man Who Wasn't There*," *RogerEbert.com*, November 2, 2001; Todd McCarthy, "Review: *The Man Who Wasn't There*," *Variety*, May 13, 2001; James Mottram, "Joel and Ethan Coen: *The Man Who Wasn't There*," *BBC.co.uk*; Smitri Hundhra, "Interview with Joel Coen," *IGN.com*, November 2, 2001; "*The Man Who Wasn't There*," *DailyMail.co.uk*; "*The Man Who Wasn't There*," *Guardian*, October 25, 2001; Ian Nathan, *Ethan and Joel Coen* (Paris: Cahiers du cinema Sarl, 2012); Andrew O'Hehir, "*The Man Who Wasn't There*," *Salon.com*, October 31, 2001; Gerald Peary, "Joel and Ethan Coen," in *The Coen Brothers: Interviews*, ed. William Rodney Allen (Jackson: University Press of Mississippi, 2006); Eddie Robson, *Coen Brothers* (London: Virgin Books, 2003); A. O. Scott, "*The Man Who Wasn't There*," *New York Times*, October 31, 2001; Andrew Simon, "Roger Deakins: Imagemaker," *TheHollywoodInterview.com*, December 10, 2012; Peter Travers, "*The Man Who Wasn't There*," *Rolling Stone*, November 2, 2001. See also MICHAEL BADALUCCO, KATHERINE BOROWITZ, CARTER

BURWELL, ROGER DEAKINS, JAMES GANDOLFINI, DENNIS GASSNER, RICHARD JENKINS, SCARLETT JOHANSSON, JENNIFER JASON LEIGH, FRANCES MCDORMAND, JON POLITO, TONY SHALHOUB, PETER SIRAGUSA, BILLY BOB THORNTON, MARY ZOPHRES.

MARVEL, ELIZABETH (1969–)

An accomplished theatre actress, Marvel was born on November 27, 1969, in Los Angeles, California, and raised in Pennsylvania. She attended high school at the Interlochen Arts Academy in Michigan, followed by the Juilliard School in New York. She began her onstage career off-Broadway as an understudy for *The Seagull* (1992), appeared in *Troilus and Cressida* (1995), *King Lear* (1996), and *Henry V* (1996), and moved to Broadway with *Taking Sides* in 1996, where she has appeared steadily since. Marvel is a four-time Obie Award winner for her off-Broadway work, and her notable stage roles include Blanche DuBois in *A Streetcar Named Desire* (1999), the title role in *Hedda Gabler* (2004), and Rosemary Sidney in *Picnic* (2013). Her first on-screen appearance was in the television series *Homicide: Life on the Streets* (1998), which she followed with small roles in *New York Undercover* (1999), *Law and Order: Criminal Intent* (2001–2005), and a recurring role in *The District* (2000–2004). Her debut film appearance was in *Ten Hundred Kings* (2000), and her subsequent on-screen roles were, for a time, a mix of small parts in films, including Charlie Kaufman's *Synecdoche, New York* (2008), and one-time television series appearances, including *30 Rock* (2009) and *The Good Wife* (2009). She was cast in recurring roles in the Showtime series *Nurse Jackie* (2009–2010), the CBS series *Person of Interest* (2012), and NBC's *Law and Order: Special Victims Unit* (2010–2014). She has additionally worked with directors Steven Spielberg, in *Lincoln* (2012); Tony Gilroy, in *The Bourne Legacy* (2012); and Roger Michell, in *Hyde Park on Hudson* (2012) and has appeared in two films by Joel and Ethan Coen: *Burn After Reading* (2008), and *True Grit* (2010).

In *Burn After Reading*, Marvel plays Sandy Pfarrer, successful author of children's books featuring Oliver the Cat, and wife of Harry Pfarrer (George Clooney), a philandering federal marshal. Marvel appears only periodically in the film, as Sandy is perpetually on a book tour, but near the film's conclusion, we learn not only that she has hired a private investigator to follow Harry and therefore is aware of his affairs but also that she is involved with a man in Seattle as well.

Marvel appears as the middle-aged Mattie Ross in the Coen re-adaptation of Charles Portis's novel *True Grit* (2010) and serves as the picture's narrator as well, providing a voice-over at the beginning of the film. On-screen, she travels by train to visit Rooster Cogburn (Jeff Bridges), whom she has not seen in many years. Arriving to find him already deceased, she has his body transported to her home in Yell County, Arkansas. An elderly Mattie visits his grave at the film's conclusion, and the story ends, as it began, with her voice.

References

"Elizabeth Marvel," *Broadway.com*; "Elizabeth Marvel," *BroadwayWorld.com*; "Elizabeth Marvel," *FocusFeatures.com*, *Hyde Park on Hudson*, Cast and Crew. See also BURN AFTER READING, TRUE GRIT.

McDORMAND, FRANCES (1957–)

Frances McDormand's lengthy and impressive career began by way of her college friend, Holly Hunter, who auditioned for Joel and Ethan Coen's *Blood Simple* (1984), but, unable to take the part, recommended that McDormand read for the lead role of Abby. Born in Chicago, Illinois, on June 23,

1957, McDormand and her family moved frequently during her childhood, as her father was a Disciples of Christ preacher. In high school, she encountered acting for the first time as Lady Macbeth in her school production, and she subsequently attended Bethany College in West Virginia, majoring in theatre. She then earned her master's of fine arts from the Yale Drama School, following which she moved to New York, where she roomed with Hunter and acted with the O'Neill Playwright's Conference. After her role in *Blood Simple*, McDormand appeared in another Coen project, *Crimewave* (1985), written by Joel and Ethan Coen and directed by Sam Raimi. Also in the mid-1980s, McDormand worked in a number of made-for-television movies including *Scandal Sheet* (1985) and *Vengeance: The Story of Tony Cimo* (1986), and television series including *Hunter* (1985), *Spenser: For Hire* (1986), and a recurring role on *Hill Street Blues* (1985).

When McDormand auditioned for the part of Abby in *Blood Simple*, her initial impression of the brothers Coen was that they were "weird, geekish, intellectual," she recalls. For their part, the Coens were impressed by McDormand's audition and asked her to return to read with an actor who had already been cast. She declined, stating that her boyfriend was in a soap opera, and she had promised to watch it. "Nobody ever says something like that when you're starting to offer them a job," says Joel Coen. "We really liked that. It was so guileless—just what we wanted for Abby." Of making the film, she recalls, "When you look at the movie now, where other people think I made the choice of looking dumb—that was me. I stood paralyzed until they told me what to do." Following the completion of the film, McDormand and Joel Coen would become a couple, marrying in 1984; in 1995, they adopted a son, Pedro.

McDormand appeared in a smaller role in the Coen comedy *Raising Arizona* (1987), which also starred Hunter and Nicolas Cage, and the following year, she appeared with Gene Hackman and Willem Dafoe in the southern Civil Rights drama *Mississippi Burning* (1988), for which she received an Academy Award nomination for Best Actress in a Supporting Role. Also in 1988, she appeared as Stella Kowalski in the Broadway revival of *A Streetcar Named Desire*, earning a Tony Award nomination, and in 2011 she won the Tony for Best Actress in a Play for her work with *Good People*. Additional Broadway credits include the revivals of *Awake and Sing!* (1984) and *The Country Girl* (2008), both by Clifford Odets.

Miller's Crossing (1990) featured McDormand in a cameo role as the mayor's secretary, and she worked with Robert Altman in the ensemble film *Short Cuts* (1993). In 1996, she played Police Chief Marge Gunderson in the Oscar-winning *Fargo*, for which she won for Best Actress in a Leading Role and Joel and Ethan Coen received the award for Best Screenplay. In a part written specifically for her, McDormand plays Marge Gunderson, a small-town police chief, tasked with solving a triple homicide in Brainerd, Minnesota. Marge gamely follows the clues which eventually reveal a series of criminal acts, many of them violent: kidnapping, several murders, embezzlement, and grand theft auto, among others. Seven months pregnant, McDormand's Marge demonstrates insightfulness that the audience might not initially anticipate, correctly assessing the events that transpired at the scene of the murders and deftly interviewing witnesses and suspects alike as she nears the troubling truth: Jerry Lundegaard (William H. Macy) has hired two kidnappers, one of them ineffectual and one of them surprisingly violent, to abduct his wife. As Jerry's plan goes terribly wrong and Marge must piece together the various narrative strands of the plot, she determines that she and her husband, as they await the arrival of their child, are "doin' pretty good."

Fargo's reviewers found McDormand's performance and the character as written by the Coens more than just pretty good. The *Village Voice* pronounced Marge "one of the great creations of American cinema," and Rita Kempley of the *Washington Post* deemed her "the most endearing, hilarious and wholly feminine heroine since Thelma or Louise." Janet Maslin, referring to one of the more remarkable set pieces of the film, writes that "the camera gazes balefully at a huge statue of Paul Bunyan, but it's Marge who is this film's idea of a folk hero." While Marge would act as the center of the film, when *Fargo* was adapted for television in 2014, the series creators opted to retain the Brainerd setting but did not attempt to replace McDormand. The series, executive produced by Joel and Ethan Coen, focused instead on an insurance salesman whose life is affected by a drifter who wanders into Fargo.

Also in 1996, McDormand appeared in two other Oscar-nominated films, *Primal Fear*, with Richard Gere and Edward Norton, and *Lone Star*, with Stephen Mendillo and Chris Cooper. Her work in *Almost Famous* (2000), as the mother of aspiring journalist William Miller, earned McDormand an Academy Award nomination for Best Actress in a Supporting Role, and she received positive reviews for her role in *Wonder Boys*, also in 2000. She worked again with the Coens in *The Man Who Wasn't There* (2001), appearing as Doris Crane, wife of Ed Crane (Billy Bob Thornton), bookkeeper at Nirdlingers' Department Store, and mistress to Big Dave Brewster (James Gandolfini). In the Coens' take on neo-noir, *The Man Who Wasn't There* presents a complicated plot

in which Ed blackmails and then kills Dave, and Doris is tried for the murder of her lover, which was committed by her husband. While the film itself received mixed reviews, McDormand's performance was generally well-received: *Salon*'s Andrew O'Hehir described Doris as "a vain and damaged woman, pathologically laden with undergarments, cosmetics and high-style accessories, but in McDormand's admirable hands she is never a cartoon bitch," and *Rolling Stone*'s Peter Travers stated "You can't take your eyes off McDormand, who makes Ed's two-timing clotheshorse of a wife a vulnerable woman awakening late to her own sexuality."

McDormand's fourth Oscar nomination came in 2005, for Best Performance by an Actress in a Supporting Role for *North Country*, and in 2008, she appeared with Brad Pitt, George Clooney, and John Malkovich in the Coens' *Burn After Reading*. As Linda Litzke, McDormand plays a middle-aged fitness instructor at Hardbodies Fitness, who, in an attempt to attract suitors in the Washington, D.C., online dating community, is planning a full-body, cosmetic surgery makeover. To pay for the procedures, Linda and her colleague Chad Feldheimer (Brad Pitt) attempt to blackmail a former CIA analyst Osborne Cox (John Malkovich), sell sensitive information to the Russians, and conduct surveillance missions, which go very wrong. While some devoted Coen fans deemed the film a success, *Burn After Reading* was generally not well-received, and the negative reviews extended to the character of Linda as well as McDormand's performance. Sukhdev Sandhu, writing for the *Telegraph*, commented that "McDormand's Linda, a functioning neurotic with a vocal delivery at once pedantic and whiny, never for a moment resembles a woman who would break the law just to improve her jaw structure."

McDormand appeared with Coen regular John Turturro in *Transformers: Dark of the Moon* (2011) and with Tilda Swinton in Wes Anderson's *Moonrise Kingdom* (2012). Also in 2012, McDormand lent her voice to the animated film *Madagascar 3: Europe's Most Wanted* (2012) and appeared in Gus Van Sant's *Promised Land*, with Matt Damon. She was scheduled to appear in HBO's 2014 mini-series *Olive Kitteridge*, with Bill Murray and Richard Jenkins.

References

"Frances McDormand," *Biography.com*; Rita Kempley, "Coens' *Fargo*: How Swede It Is," *Washington Post*, March 8, 1998; Andrew O'Hehir, "*The Man Who Wasn't There*," *Salon.com*, October 31, 2001; Janet Maslin, "*Fargo*," *New York Times*, March 8, 1996; Eddie Robson, *Coen Brothers* (London: Virgin Books, 2003); Sukhdev Sandhu, "Brad Pitt and George Clooney Star in *Burn After Reading*: Review," *Telegraph*, October 17, 2008; Ella Taylor, "For *A Serious Man*, Coen Brothers Aim Trademark Contempt at Themselves," *VillageVoice.com*, September 29, 2009; Peter Travers, "*The Man Who Wasn't There*," *Rolling Stone*, November 2, 2001. See also *BLOOD SIMPLE, BURN AFTER READING, FARGO, RAISING ARIZONA, THE MAN WHO WASN'T THERE*.

MELAMED, FRED (1956–)

Born May 13, 1956, in New York City, New York, Melamed is the son of Louis Melamed, who produced television's *Car 54, Where Are You?* (1961–1962). Fred Melamed received his bachelor's degree from Hampshire College, following which he attended the Yale School of Drama in the company of Coen regulars Francis McDormand, John Turturro, and Katherine Borowitz. He earned his master's of fine arts in 1981 and debuted on Broadway in *Amadeus* shortly thereafter but found that he did not enjoy stage work. He left the theatre and began working in commercials, where he provided voice-overs for Mercedes Benz, National Geographic, and the USA Network. His first film appearance was in *Lovesick* (1983), with Dudley Moore and Elizabeth McGovern, and he was cast in small roles in the Woody Allen films *Hannah and Her Sisters* (1986), *Radio Days* (1987), *Another Woman* (1987), and *Crimes and Misdemeanors* (1989), among others. Melamed's television work includes appearances in the series *One Life to Live* (1981–1982) and *Another World* (1989) and announcing for *USA Up All Night* (1987–1989), *Silk Stalkings* (1993), and *Biography* (1998). He lent his voice to the animated series *Courage the Cowardly Dog* (2000–2001) and *The Wonder Pets* (2006) and to such video games as *The Multipath Adventures of Superman* (1999), *Grand Theft Auto: San Andreas* (2004), and *Grand Theft Auto V* (2013).

Melamed returned to Broadway in 2011 to appear in *Relatively Speaking*, a trio of one-act plays directed by John Turturro, which included *Talking Cure*, written by Ethan Coen. Prior to the production's opening night, however, Melamed left the show, citing scheduling conflicts and creative differences with Ethan Coen regarding Melamed's character. His later television work includes appearances on *Law and Order* (2010), *Curb Your Enthusiasm* (2011), *The Good Wife* (2011), and *30 Rock* (2012), and he appeared on film with Sacha Baron Cohen in *The Dictator* (2012) and as movie trailer voice-over actor in *In a World . . .* (2013).

In 2009, Melamed appeared in the Coens' *A Serious Man* as Sy Ableman, described by the film's characters as the titular "serious man" and by the *Guardian* as "a smug and mellifluous widower." Ableman has designs on Judith Gopnik (Sari Lennick), wife of Larry Gopnik (Michael Stuhlbarg), and convinces Larry to move out of his own house and grant his wife

Judith a ritual divorce, allowing Ableman to marry her. Melamed characterizes Ableman as "evil," explaining that he viewed the character as "someone who gets people to give up control by this very hypnotic way of behaving, by convincing them that everything's going to be fine." Melamed has stated that he was the first actor cast for the film, but as the Coens were making *Burn After Reading* (2008) prior to *A Serious Man*, Ethan informed Melamed that he would not be needed for a year and a half. Melamed responded "That's fine, because I'm trying to bring the pompous, Jewish, overweight, rabbinic figure back to the center of American sexuality, where I feel it belongs. That should take me at least a year." For his performance, Melamed received widespread praise, the *New York Times*' A. O. Scott deeming him "splendidly unctuous."

References

Peter Bradshaw, "*A Serious Man*," *Guardian*, November 19, 2009; Bilge Ebiri, "*A Serious Man*'s Fred Melamed: 'I'm Trying to Bring the Pompous, Jewish, Overweight, Rabbinic Figure Back to the Center of American Sexuality,'" *Vulture.com,* January 21, 2010; Adam Hetrick, "Fred Melamed Departs Broadway's *Relatively Speaking*," *Playbill.com*, October 6, 2011; Susan King, "Fred Melamed Is Well-Versed *In a World*," *Los Angeles Times*, August 14, 2013; "Fred Melamed," *BroadwayWorld.com*; "Fred Melamed," *FocusFeatures.com*, *A Serious Man*, Cast & Crew; A. O. Scott, "Calls to God: Always a Busy Signal," *New York Times*, October 1, 2009. See also *A SERIOUS MAN*.

MILLER'S CROSSING (1990)

DIRECTORS: Joel Coen and Ethan Coen (uncredited). SCREENPLAY: Joel Coen and Ethan Coen. EXECUTIVE PRODUCER: Ben Barenholtz. PRODUCER: Ethan Coen and Joel Coen (uncredited); Graham Place (Line Producer); Mark Silverman (Co-producer). PHOTOGRAPHY: Barry Sonnenfeld. EDITING: Michael R. Miller. MUSIC: Carter Burwell. PRODUCTION DESIGN: Dennis Gassner. ART DIRECTION: Leslie McDonald. SET DECORATION: Nancy Haigh. COSTUME DESIGN: Richard Hornung.

CAST: Gabriel Byrne (Tom Reagan), Marcia Gay Harden (Verna), John Turturro (Bernie Bernbaum), Jon Polito (Johnny Caspar), J. E. Freeman (Eddie Dane), Albert Finney (Leo O'Bannon), Mike Starr (Frankie), Al Mancini (Tic Tac), Steve Buscemi (Mink), Michael Badalucco (Driver).

RUNNING TIME: 115 minutes. Color.

RELEASED THROUGH: 20th Century Fox. PREMIERE: September 21, 1990 (New York Film Festival).

DVD: 20th Century Fox Home Entertainment.

Miller's Crossing, selected to open the 1990 New York Film Festival, is the Coen brothers' third feature picture, a treatment of 1930s gangster films with overtones of 1940s films noir. Set in a nameless American city in the late 1920s, *Miller's Crossing* follows two rival gangsters: Leo (Albert Finney), the Irish boss who controls the city's liquor, police, and politicians; and Italian mobster Johnny Caspar (Jon Polito), who arranges and bets on fixed fights. The film opens with Caspar's views on "ethics, character, and friendship," as he lays out his case to kill Bernie Bernbaum (John Turturro), a Jewish bookie who is selling information about Caspar's fixed fights: "You can't trust a fix, what can you trust?" laments Caspar. Leo, unmoved by Caspar's pleas, opposes this logic and the plan to punish Bernie's betrayal, reaffirming Bernie's protected status and setting off a mob war that includes the local police department, the mayor, and all of gangland. Tom

Albert Finney (left) and Gabriel Byrne in *Miller's Crossing* (1990)

Reagan (Gabriel Byrne), Leo's lieutenant and an inveterate gambler, attempts to convince Leo that the smart play would be to give up the crooked bookie, only to discover that Leo's motive for protecting Bernie is his relationship with Bernie's sister, Verna (Marcia Gay Harden). Tom's revelation of his own involvement with Verna results in his ouster from Leo's organization, at which point Tom joins Caspar's cause, now serving as the Italian's right-hand man, ostensibly.

The turf war between opposing factions, clad in fedoras and topcoats, continues to escalate. The crooked police alternately raid first Caspar's, then Leo's Prohibition-era drinking and gambling clubs, and Leo survives a memorable assassination attempt at his home, played out to the swelling strains of "Danny Boy" and innumerable rounds from Tommy guns. Tom proves his loyalty to Caspar by giving up Bernie and then proves his loyalty to Leo by choosing not to execute Bernie

in the woods of Miller's Crossing, a decision that haunts him later in the film, as Bernie returns to town and attempts to blackmail Tom into killing Caspar. Eddie Dane (J. E. Freeman), Caspar's henchman, believes Tom to be too smart by half and, correctly suspecting that Tom did not actually kill Bernie, nearly succeeds in executing Tom on a return trip to Miller's Crossing. The Dane finds instead the unidentifiable, decaying body of Mink (Steve Buscemi), sometime "amigo" to both Dane and Bernie, and Tom is spared. Refusing offers from Leo, Caspar, and Bernie to pay off his gambling debts, Tom asserts his responsibility for his own losses and maintains that "Nobody knows anybody," adhering to his firmly entrenched principles and hidden motivation to do whatever he has to in order to protect Leo. Joel Coen has noted, however, that those principles are "in conflict with themselves," and we see Tom achieve his goal by lying to and manipulating Caspar, Verna, Bernie, Leo himself, and the Dane, among others. His deft marshaling of the film's events results in the elimination of the Dane and a final early-morning showdown, culminating in the shooting deaths of power-hungry Caspar and the perpetually untrustworthy Bernie Bernbaum, the only fatal shot that Tom fires, an hour and forty-five minutes into the film. At the film's conclusion, Tom has successfully returned Leo to his former position of authority, with Verna on his arm, leaving Tom alone in the overcast, muted treescape of Miller's Crossing.

Miller's Crossing began as an image for the Coen brothers, the idea of "big guys in overcoats in the woods—the incongruity of urban gangsters in a forest setting." The complicated plot became problematic during the writing process, to the point that they suspended work on the screenplay for two months and instead composed *Barton Fink*, their fourth film, which they completed entirely during this break. *Miller's Crossing* is indebted to Dashiell Hammett's *Red Harvest* and *The Glass Key* and gangster films of the 1930s generally, which Ethan Coen calls "dirty town movies;" specifically, elements of *The Third Man* (1949), *On the Waterfront* (1954), and *The Godfather* (1972) are clearly evident in the film. Released the same year as *The Godfather III*, *Goodfellas*, and *Dick Tracy*, *Miller's Crossing* was obscured by a spate of gangster films and earned just over $5 million. In an unusual deal negotiated by Circle Films' Ben Berenholtz, 20th Century Fox financed the reportedly $14 million budget entirely, though the Coens estimate that the production costs were closer to $11 million. The second in a three-picture deal with Circle Films, Fox had the option to produce *Miller's Crossing*, based first on a two-line description of the story, and then a "yes" or "no" option upon viewing the completed script. Fox chose to finance the film but had no input regarding any cre-

ative decisions, including the script itself and the casting, which includes cameos by Sam Raimi as a member of the police-force-for-hire, Francis McDormand as the mayor's secretary, and Michael Badalucco as Caspar's driver.

Critics alternately saw *Miller's Crossing* as a successful homage to gangster films or as a hollow approximation of them, replete with the familiar tropes of 1930s and 1940s mob films: Tommy guns, fedoras, witty slang, and the gangster's moll. Roger Ebert deemed the film "a movie that is constantly aware of itself . . . an over-stylized version of the gangster film," and the *New Yorker* considered it "not so much a gangster movie as an extended, elaborate allusion to one." While some saw the complexity of the plot as a sign of brilliance, others saw it as impenetrable. Not all viewers, however, found the film lacking; *Empire* deemed the story to be of "Shakespearean stature—a timeless tale of humanity." Taking the middle ground, Peter Travers of *Rolling Stone* notes that "the plot's not the point. Action, atmosphere and humor are." Despite the range of responses to the film, the dominant impression was that it was visually striking. According to Barry Sonnenfeld, cinematographer for the first three Coen pictures including *Miller's Crossing*, Ethan Coen described the look they wanted for the film as a "handsome movie with men in hats," and "handsome" characterizes the film nicely. In an interview, Sonnenfeld used such terms as "beautiful," and "manly," to describe the film; he also characterized the shooting of the film as the "perfect experience."

The visual details of the film invite detailed analysis, as viewer logic dictates that the exquisitely designed and decorated sets—too perfect, perhaps, according to Roger Ebert—are so meticulously planned that they must be significant down to the last detail. Specifically, the significance of the hat, which rolls and bounces through the film, garnered much attention. Viewed alternately as emotional camouflage, a symbol of masculinity, fear, or unrequited love, Tom's hat tumbles across the leaf-strewn ground of Miller's Crossing, leads Tom on a continual chase through bars and bedrooms, and is knocked from Tom's head repeatedly throughout the film. Tom and Verna discuss the hat, in the film's overt nod to symbolism, as Tom recounts his dream of chasing his hat, which Verna then predicts will symbolically transform into something wonderful. Tom, however, like the Coens themselves, quashes the idea; the hat remains just a hat. There is, after all, "nothing more foolish than a man chasing his hat." Asked repeatedly about the subject, the brothers maintain that the hat bears no secret meaning or profound symbolism; it is just a hat, an image that serves as "a kind of practical guiding thread, but there's no need to look for deep meanings," claims Joel. This principle extends to a reading of the film on a broader level, as Ethan notes that their "movies speak for themselves."

While classic Hollywood gangster films have previously addressed the tension between the Italian and Irish mobs, *Miller's Crossing* takes the ethnic conflict a step further, encompassing both Irish and Italian "families" and adding the stereotype of a Jewish bookie who is also a homosexual; his sister, the gangster's moll; as well as "the Dane." This diversity is reflected in the dialogue, replete with ethnic labels such as "potato eater," "Guinea," "Dago," "Sheeney," and "Schmada," slang terms that equally malign all of the racial groups represented in the film. The dialogue also includes language recognizable from the genre—terms such as "bumped off" and Verna's lament that "we're a couple o' heels, Tom." But commingled with this familiar gangster-speak, the Coens con-

tributed their own hard-boiled phrases: "What's the rumpus?," "the high hat," and "the kiss-off," among others, delivered in turn by the characters and often repeated throughout the film. In a pattern established in *Blood Simple* (1984), repeated in *Miller's Crossing*, and continued throughout their films, the genre at hand is replicated and simultaneously altered in their pictures. The Coen version of the mob film not only alters the characters' language and the ethnic makeup, but also shifts the building blocks of the classic gangster films, even if only slightly. Caspar begins the film with his treatise on the ethics of an inherently unethical profession, and when encouraged to double-cross Tom, he cannot bring himself to do so. "Ya double cross once, where does it all end? An interesting ethical dilemma," he muses. The irony here, of course, is that Tom is indeed double-crossing Caspar, an action he can justify because it fits into his master plan of saving Leo from himself.

Beyond the shifts in language and principle, the very structure of the film is based on establishing a system—the dominance of Leo and his inviolate commands—and then walking back that system scene by scene, until Johnny Caspar has placed himself, visually and practically, on Leo's throne. In the first half of the film, Leo raids Caspar's gambling hall, hosts the mayor and the police chief in his office, and consults with his best man, Tom. Near the mid-point of the film, Leo is forced from his bed by an assassination attempt in the night, and though he emerges unscathed, still the master of the Tommy gun, from this point on Leo is nearly absent from the film, as Caspar raids Leo's club, entertains the mayor and police chief in his office, and seeks the advice of Tom, Leo's former lieutenant. Within this symmetry of plot, scenes involving Tom are duplicated as well: the "assassination" of Bernie Bernbaum and Tom's march to near-death take place among the swaying trees of Miller's Crossing; Bernie's two appearances in Tom's apartment in the middle of the night, lying in wait for him in the dark; Tom's two visits to Verna, both of which conclude with Tom and Verna in bed together. The symmetry of the plot extends to the film's end, which finds Leo once more in charge of the city, its politicians, police, and liquor, though Tom himself chooses not to return to his position as right-hand man.

Even as one of the Coen brothers' earlier films, *Miller's Crossing* remains an excellent example of the techniques and themes that would come to define their films: careful attention to detail, eccentric characters, a complicated plot with surprising and sometimes bizarre twists, and random, supposedly meaningless elements that entice the viewer to interpretations not intended by the filmmakers.

References

Vincent Canby, "In *Miller's Crossing*, Silly Gangsters and a Tough Moll," *New York Times*, September 21, 1990; Kenneth Chanko, "Ben Barenholtz," *Films in Review* 41.8/9 (1990); Jean-Pierre Coursodon, "A Hat Blown by the Wind," in *Joel & Ethan Coen: Blood Siblings*, ed. Paul A. Woods (London: Plexus Publishing, 2003); Roger Ebert, "*Miller's Crossing*," *RogerEbert.com*, October 5, 1990; Steven Levy, "Shot by Shot," in *The Coen Brothers: Interviews*, ed. William Rodney Allen (Jackson: University Press of Mississippi, 2006); DVD Special Features, *Miller's Crossing*, 20th Century Fox Home Entertainment, 2003; Terrence Rafferty, "*Miller's Crossing*," *New Yorker*, The Film File; Erica Rowell, *The Brothers Grim: The Films of Ethan and Joel Coen* (Lanham, Maryland: Scarecrow Press, 2007); Scott Russon, "*Miller's Crossing*," *EmpireOnline.com*; Peter Travers, "*Miller's Crossing*," *Rolling Stone*, September 22, 1990. See also CARTER BURWELL, STEVE BUSCEMI, GABRIEL BYRNE, ALBERT FINNEY, DENNIS GASSNER, NANCY HAIGH, MARCIA GAY HARDEN, JON POLITO, BARRY SONNENFELD, MIKE STARR, JOHN TURTURRO.

MOORE, JULIANNE (1960–)

Born December 3, 1960, at Fort Bragg in North Carolina, Moore grew up in a military family that often relocated when she was a child, and she recalls being bullied for her freckles, experiences that prompted her as an adult to write a *New York Times* bestselling children's book series titled *Freckleface Strawberry* (2007). She attended high school in Germany, and upon returning to the United States, she studied at Boston University's School of Performing Arts. Moore graduated in 1983 and then moved to New York City to pursue a career in acting. In 1985, she was cast in a recurring role and occasionally played twins in *As the World Turns* (1985–2010), for which she won a Daytime Emmy Award in 1988. In the late 1980s, she appeared in the television series *The Edge of Night* (1984) and *B.L. Stryker* (1990), in the mini-series *I'll Take Manhattan* (1987), and in several made-for-television movies. Prior to working in film, she appeared off-Broadway in *Serious Money* (1987) and *Ice Cream with Hot Fudge* (1990), and she debuted on the big screen in 1990 in *Tales from the Darkside: The Movie*, which she followed with *The Hand That Rocks the Cradle* in 1992. She worked with Madonna in *Body of Evidence* (1993), with Johnny Depp in *Benny & Joon* (1993), with Harrison Ford in *The Fugitive* (1993), and appeared as part of the ensemble cast in Robert Altman's *Short Cuts* (1993).

Moore's commercial film career gained momentum in the mid-1990s with her roles in Todd Haynes's *Safe* (1995), with Hugh Grant in *Nine Months* (1995), and in *Vanya on 42nd Street* (1995). She then worked with Steven Spielberg in *The Lost World:*

Jurassic Park (1997) and appeared in *Boogie Nights* (1997), for which she received her first Academy Award nomination for Best Actress in a Supporting Role. She was nominated by the Academy as Best Actress in a Leading Role for the 1999 adaptation of Graham Greene's *The End of the Affair*. She worked with Gus Van Sant in the remake of Alfred Hitchcock's *Psycho* (1998) and with Ridley Scott in *Hannibal* (2001), the sequel to 1991's *The Silence of the Lambs*. In 2002, she appeared in *Far from Heaven* and *The Hours*, garnering Oscar nominations for Best Actress in a Leading Role and Best Actress in a Supporting Role, respectively. She returned to the theatre in Broadway's *The Vertical Hour* with Bill Nighy in 2006, and her additional films include *Children of Men* (2006), *The Kids Are All Right* (2010), and *Carrie* (2013), in which she reprises the Sissy Spacek role of the mother of the title character. On the small screen, she portrayed presidential candidate Sarah Palin in the HBO movie *Game Change* (2012), and from 2009–2013, she had a recurring role on the NBC comedy *30 Rock*.

Moore has appeared in one Coen brothers film, *The Big Lebowski* (1998), as Maude Lebowski, a fluxus artist and daughter to Jeffrey "the Big" Lebowski (David Huddleston), a character described by Janet Maslin of the *New York Times* as "a feminist artist who has successfully reduced sex to an intellectual exercise." She initially appears in the film when her associates break into the Dude's (Jeff Bridges) bungalow to recover a valuable rug, and in the Dude's visit to her studio, he observes her careening from the ceiling, supported by wires and slinging paint onto a canvas. Maude later appears in a Busby Berkeley-like dream sequence with the Dude, in Valkyrie attire and amid women sporting bowling-pin headdresses. Speaking about her performance, Ethan Coen characterizes Moore's accent

as a "vague, non-specific geographically, swell finishing school for girls in Switzerland accent," which Moore created for the part. She "intuitively grasped that there should be something horribly regal about the character." On the film's tenth anniversary, Moore appeared with Bridges, John Goodman, John Turturro, and Steve Buscemi at Lebowski Fest, where she commented that fans still approach her on the street to comment on the film.

References

Simon Hattenstone, "Julianne Moore: 'Can We Talk about Something Else Now?'" *Guardian*, August 9, 2013; *LebowskiFest*.com; Janet Maslin, "*The Big Lebowski* (1998) film review; A Bowling Balls-Eye View of Reality," *New York Times*, March 6, 1998; "Julianne Moore," *Biography.com*; "Julianne Moore," *New York Times*, Movies & TV; Elaine Lipworth, "Julianne Moore: Still Fabulous at 50, Interview," *Telegraph*, August 7, 2011; Eddie Robson, *Coen Brothers* (London: Virgin Books, 2003). See also *THE BIG LEBOWSKI*.

MULLIGAN, CAREY (1985–)

Born in London on May 28, 1985, Mulligan's family moved to Germany when she was three and back to London again when she was eight, due to her father's job as a hotel manager. Her first acting role was at elementary school, playing a boy in the school production of *The King and I*. She attended convent school from age eight to eleven, and at seventeen she informed her parents she didn't want to attend university, but she instead wanted to go to drama school. Her parents discouraged this career, so she wrote letters to both Kenneth Branagh and screenwriter Julian Fellowes, looking for support. Fellowes met with Mulligan, and, impressed with her passion for acting, made arrangements that led to her role as Kitty in *Pride and Prejudice* (2005). She subsequently appeared in several television series in England, including *Bleak House* (2005) and *The Amazing Mrs. Pritchard* (2006), as well as an episode of *Dr. Who* (2007). Her breakout role was in Lone Scherfig's *An Education* (2009), for which she received both an Oscar nomination and a Golden Globe nomination for Best Performance by an Actress in a Leading Role. She has appeared in Oliver Stone's *Wall Street: Money Never Sleeps* and *Never Let Me Go*, both in 2010, *Drive* and *Shame* in 2011, as Daisy Buchanan in Baz Luhrmann's *The Great Gatsby* (2013), and in Joel and Ethan Coens' *Inside Llewyn Davis* (2013). Her husband, Marcus Mumford, served as assistant music producer on *Inside Llewyn Davis* and appeared on the soundtrack in a quartet with Justin Timberlake, among others.

Often compared to Audrey Hepburn, Mulligan's early roles were primarily as sweet and likeable young women, factors that influenced Joel and Ethan Coen when they intentionally cast her against type as *Inside Llewyn Davis*'s Jean, whom they characterize as a "harpy." The narrative of the film covers one week in the life of folk singer Llewyn Davis (Oliver Isaac), and his friends and acquaintances—one of whom is Jean—in the Greenwich Village of the early 1960s. Tom Shone of the *Guardian* praises Mulligan's performance, in which she "seizes on the part of Jean, seething with ever-escalating fury, as if plucking the petals one by one from her reputation of an English rose." During filming, the Coens encouraged her to swear more, scream louder, and be nastier in her role as Jean, which Mulligan describes as "brutal," a "dense and brilliantly written" part.

On working with the Coens, Mulligan states "I love the way they work," noting especially the organization with which they approach their shoots: "you get a shot list, and it's storyboarded. So you know you'll be the third shot of the day, and they'll shoot a mid shot, and that's it . . . they just shoot what they're going to use." The result of this approach is that there were days when the shoot finished at four or five o'clock and the cast and crew went home: "I'd never experienced that. I've always experienced shoots where you run over by an hour and the crew all hate you."

As did all of the actor-musicians in the film, Mulligan sang the *Inside Llewyn Davis* songs live, which were recorded on set as a part of the film. An experienced singer, Mulligan was comfortable with the idea of singing, and she approached the musical performances as an outgrowth of her character. Having recently discovered that she is pregnant and knowing that the father could be either her husband, Jim (Justin Timberlake) or the talented but indigent Llewyn, Jean comports herself quite differently on stage while singing, Mulligan notes: "you can see the split between how she presents herself to the world and how she actually is with Llewyn," referring to the seething, cursing exchanges she hurls at the musician.

References

Robbie Collin, "*Inside Llewyn Davis:* The Ballad of Carey Mulligan and Justin Timberlake," *Telegraph*, January 18, 2014; Simon Hattenstone, "The Dark Side of Carey Mulligan," *Guardian*, January 17, 2014; "Carey Mulligan," *New York Times*, Movies & TV; Steve Pond, "Carey Mulligan on the Coen Brothers: They Pushed Me to Be Nastier and Say More Swear Words," *TheWrap.com*, December 30, 2013; Tom Shone, "*Inside Llewyn Davis*: A Masterpiece 'Anti-musical' from the Coen Brothers," *Guardian*, December 5, 2013. See also *INSIDE LLEWYN DAVIS*.

NELSON, TIM BLAKE (1964–)

Actor/director/singer Nelson played one of three lead roles in *O Brother, Where Art Thou?* (2000), as Delmar O'Donnell. Born May 11, 1964, and raised in Tulsa, Oklahoma, by his geologist father and activist mother, Nelson majored in classics at Brown, followed by four years at Juilliard. His first play, *The Grey Zone*, premiered off-Broadway, and received both an Obie and an Oppenheimer Award, and his film career began with small parts in films such as *This Is My Life* (1992), *Donnie Brasco* (1997), and *The Thin Red Line* (1998). An accomplished character actor, he is most recognized for his roles in *O Brother*, *The Good Girl* (2002), *Holes* (2003), and *The Incredible Hulk* (2008). From the other side of the camera, Nelson has directed *Eye of God* (1997), which he also wrote, and which appeared off-Broadway in 2009; *O* (2001), an adaptation of Shakespeare's *Othello*, set at a preparatory school in the South; *The Grey Zone* (2001), an adaptation of his off-Broadway play; and *Leaves of Grass* (2009, also written by Nelson), starring Edward Norton as identical twins. He has twice worked with Steven Spielberg, in *Minority Report* (2002) and *Lincoln* (2012), and has often appeared in television series, including *Chaos* (2011) and *CSI* (2009).

Joel and Ethan Coen have commented that Nelson was likely the only person in *O Brother* who had read Homer's *Odyssey*, a statement that should be questioned in light of the classical allusions in the film, but it was his knowledge of the classics that ostensibly brought Nelson into the project. Nelson, who knew the Coens personally prior to being cast in the film, was initially asked by Joel to read the script and offer advice, and Nelson read the screenplay as an adaptation of the epic poem. Ultimately, however, rather than soliciting his input on the Homeric connections, the Coens offered Nelson the part of Delmar, whose character is most often described by critics as sweet, simple, and childlike. Certainly the least-assertive of the three, Delmar acts alternately as the straight man, for comic relief, and as peacemaker between the conniving Everett (George Clooney) and Pete (John Turturro). While Nelson characterizes himself as an imitative rather than natural singer and is without extensive formal vocal training, he nonetheless recorded "In the Jailhouse Now" on the *O Brother* soundtrack, which won a Grammy for Album of the Year. He cites Lefty Frizzell and Levon Helm as influencing his vocal performance in the film.

References

Melissa Merli, "Nelson a Man of Constant Talents," *News-Gazette* (Champaign, Illinois), April 25, 2013; "Tim Blake Nelson Biography," *New York Times*, Movies and TV; Jonathan Valania, "O Brother Who Art Thou? A Q&A with Actor/

Writer/Director Tim Blake Nelson," *Huffington Post*, April 3, 2013. See also *O BROTHER, WHERE ART THOU?*

NEWMAN, PAUL (1925–2008)

Born near Cleveland, Ohio, January 26, 1925, Newman performed in school plays while growing up and joined the U.S. Navy Air Corps following high school. His goal was to be a pilot, but because he was colorblind, he instead served as a radio operator during World War II. He attended Kenyon College after the war, playing football on an athletic scholarship until he was arrested and kicked off the football team, at which point, he became a theatre major. Graduating with a degree in English, he appeared in summer stock theatre in Wisconsin and married his first wife, Jacqueline Witte. When his father died in 1950, Newman moved home to Ohio to run the family business but soon handed over the business to his brother and moved his family to Connecticut, where he attended the Yale School of Drama for a year. He then moved to New York and studied with Lee Strasberg at the Actor's Studio, along with fellow actors Marlon Brando and James Dean. He debuted on Broadway in *Picnic* (1953), where he met Joanne Woodward, who would become his second wife some time later.

He worked in television in the early 1950s, appearing in series such as *Tales of Tomorrow* (1952) and *Suspense* (1952), with recurring appearances in *You Are There* (1953) and *The Web* (1952–1953). His first film role was in *The Silver Chalice* (1954), which was not well received, and he played Rocky Graziano in the film *Somebody Up There Likes Me* (1956) and Brick in the film adaptation of Tennessee Williams's *Cat on a Hot Tin Roof* (1958), with Elizabeth Taylor, for which he received his first Academy Award nomination. In 1958, divorced from his first wife, he married Joanne Wood-

ward, with whom he appeared in *The Long Hot Summer* (1958), and in 1961, he received his second Academy Award nomination for his role in *The Hustler*. His third and fourth Oscar nominations soon followed, for *Hud* (1963) and *Cool Hand Luke* (1967). His directorial debut, *Rachel, Rachel* (1968), which starred Woodward, received four Academy Award nominations, including one for Best Picture. Newman teamed up for the first time with Robert Redford in *Butch Cassidy and the Sundance Kid* (1969) and again in *The Sting* (1973), which was nominated for ten Oscars, and won seven, though not for acting. He was again nominated for Academy Awards for *Absence of Malice* (1981) and *The Verdict* (1982), and in 1986 the Academy gave him an honorary award for his contributions to film. In 1987, he won the Oscar for Best Actor for his role in Martin Scorsese's *The Color of Money*, and the Academy awarded him the 1993 Jean Hersholt Humanitarian Award. Almost seventy, Newman continued to act, in *Nobody's Fool* in 1994 and *Road to Perdition* in 2002, both roles garnering him Oscar nominations for Best Supporting Actor. In 2005, he received a Golden Globe Award and an Emmy for his supporting role in the television mini-series *Empire Falls*, which he also executive produced and which starred his wife, Joanne Woodward.

Early in his career, Newman bought out his contract with Warner Brothers for the sum of $500,000, a move that allowed him more input in the roles he would play, and in 1969, he cofounded First Artists, a production company, with Barbra Streisand and Sidney Poitier; Steve McQueen and Dustin Hoffman later joined the venture. The enterprise was designed to give the actors creative control over their pictures, and each star agreed to make three pictures with the company. The company produced the Newman vehicles *Pocket Money* (1972), *The Life and Times of Judge*

Roy Bean (1972), and *The Drowning Pool* (1975), and the venture folded in late 1979.

Offscreen, Newman was a social activist, committed to the civil rights movement and opposed to the Vietnam War. He campaigned with Woodward for 1968 Democratic Presidential candidate Eugene McCarthy, earning him a place on President Nixon's "enemies list," about which he was most proud. Newman created a number of "Hole-in-the-Wall" summer camps, so named for Butch Cassidy's gang, to provide free vacations for ill children, and he created an antidrug foundation and camp to prevent substance abuse. The antidrug cause was prompted by the overdose death of his son, Scott, in 1978. In 1982, he established Newman's Own, a company that originally produced sauces and salad dressings from Newman's home recipes and grew to include many different varieties of foods, the profits of which are donated entirely to charity, totaling hundreds of millions of dollars.

In 1969, he appeared in *Winning*, a film about the Indianapolis 500 race that introduced him to race car driving, an interest he would maintain for much of his life. In 1979 his team competed in the twenty-four-hour LeMans race, placing second, and he completed the Daytona 500 race in 1995, age 70, the oldest person to do so; his team placed third. He continued racing into 2005, and in 2006 he provided the voice for the retired racecar Doc Hudson in the Pixar film *Cars*.

Newman appeared in one Coen film, *The Hudsucker Proxy* (1994), as Sidney J. Mussburger, fast-talking corporate executive reminiscent of Edward Arnold. With the Hudsucker Industries Board of Directors, Mussburger cleverly devises a plan to depreciate the stock of Hudsucker Industries in order to then buy up the worthless stock and maintain a controlling interest in the company. Mussburger selects Nor-ville Barnes (Tim Robbins) as the patsy who will facilitate the demise of Hudsucker Industries, and while it seems that Norville will do exactly that, his invention of the hula hoop, which Mussburger calls "the dingus," rallies the company's stock and thwarts Mussburger's attempt at a takeover. Ultimately, Mussburger is institutionalized by the psychiatrist he hired to commit Norville, and Norville basks in the company's success. In his approach to Mussburger, Newman took an unusual perspective; rather than playing the character as the bad guy to Norville's good guy, he played Mussburger as a hero, claiming that "Every character every actor plays has to be the hero." Newman's performance received mixed reviews from the film's reviewers: Roger Ebert characterized his Mussburger as "right on target . . . the gray eminence behind the scenes," and the *New York Times'* Caryn James deems the casting of Newman as "inspired," while the *Washington Post*'s Joe Brown asserts that "Newman does a lot of hand-rubbing and harrumphing, but never seems to be in the same movie as everyone else."

In 2007, Paul Newman announced his retirement from acting, and at the age of eighty-three, he died of cancer in 2008.

References

Brian Baxter, "Paul Newman: Obituary," *Guardian*, September 27, 2008; "Paul Newman," *Biography.com*; Joe Brown, "The Hudsucker Proxy," *Washington Post*, March 25, 1994; Roger Ebert, "Hudsucker Proxy," *RogerEbert.com*, March 25, 1994; Pamela G. Hollie, "First Artists Movie Company Folds," *Day* (New London, Connecticut), December 27, 1979; Caryn James, "*The Hudsucker Proxy*: Reviews/Film: Sniffing Out the Truth about Instant Success," *New York Times*, March 11, 1994; Josh Levine, *The Coen Brothers: Two American Filmmakers* (Toronto: ECW Press, 2000); "Paul Newman," *New York Times*, Movies & TV; Jeffrey Ressner and Kenneth

P. Vogel, "Paul Newman, Actor and Activist, Dies," *Politico*, September 27, 2008; Lynn Smith, "Actor Paul Newman Dies at 83," *Los Angeles Times*, September 28, 2008. See also *THE HUDSUCKER PROXY*.

NO COUNTRY FOR OLD MEN (2007)

DIRECTORS: Ethan Coen and Joel Coen. SCREENPLAY: Joel Coen and Ethan Coen, adapted from the novel by Cormac McCarthy. EXECUTIVE PRODUCERS: Robert Graf and Mark Roybal. PRODUCERS: Ethan Coen, Joel Coen, and Mark Rudin. MUSIC: Carter Burwell. PRODUCTION DESIGN: Jess Gonchor. ART DIRECTION: John P. Goldsmith. SET DECORATION: Nancy Haigh. COSTUME DESIGN: Mary Zophres.

CAST: Tommy Lee Jones (Ed Tom Bell), Javier Bardem (Anton Chigurh), Josh Brolin (Llewelyn Moss), Woody Harrelson (Carson Wells), Kelly Macdonald (Carla Jean Moss), Garret Dillahunt (Wendell), Tess Harper (Loretta Bell), Stephen Root (Man who hires Wells).

RUNNING TIME: 122 minutes. Color.

RELEASED THROUGH: Miramax Films. PREMIERE: May 19, 2007 (Cannes International Film Festival).

DVD: Miramax Home Entertainment.

ACADEMY AWARDS: Best Motion Picture of the Year: Scott Rudin, Ethan Coen, and Joel Coen; Best Performance by an Actor in a Supporting Role: Javier Bardem; Best Achievement in Directing: Ethan Coen and Joel Coen; Best Writing, Adapted Screenplay: Joel Coen and Ethan Coen; Best Achievement in Cinematography (nominated: Roger Deakins); Best Achievement in Film Editing (nominated: Ethan Coen and Joel Coen, as Roderick Jaynes); Best Achievement in Sound Mixing (nominated: Skip Lievsay, Craig Berkey, Greg Orloff, Peter F. Kurland); Best Achievement in Sound Editing (nominated: Skip Lievsay).

The twelfth film by Joel and Ethan Coen, *No Country for Old Men* is based on the novel of the same name by Cormac McCarthy, published in 2005. Set in West Texas, the film follows the fallout from a violent drug deal and the men who become involved in it. The opening sequence of the film pans across various features of the Texas landscape: plains, fences, and windmills, accompanied by a voice over narration by Ed Tom Bell (Tommy Lee Jones), Sheriff of Terrell County, as he reminisces about lawmen from his youth, wondering what they would make of the profession these days. As the voice-over concludes, the viewer is introduced first to Anton Chigurh (Javier Bardem), an ominously silent, dark-haired man who has been taken into custody by the local authorities, only to violently strangle the deputy and escape. The narrative then shifts to Llewelyn Moss (Josh Brolin), who, while hunting, discovers the scene of a drug deal gone wrong, a man dying of gunshot wounds, and, eventually, a satchel full of drug money: he estimates it at $2 million.

Having hidden the satchel at home, Llewelyn returns to the desert in the middle of the night with a jug of water for the dying man and is joined by Mexicans who have come to collect the drugs and money; though he outruns them, he is wounded in the process. Returning home, he and his wife, Carla Jean (Kelly Macdonald), vacate their trailer home, as he will be easily located by anyone who researches the tags on his truck, now abandoned in the desert. Chigurh does precisely this, seeking the money now in Llewelyn's possession. In the third strand of the narrative, Sheriff Ed Tom Bell begins to piece together the events that have transpired, and while Llewelyn sends Carla Jean to the safety of her mother in Odessa, both Chigurh and Ed Tom visit the Moss home in search of Llewelyn and the money. Llewelyn heads

Tommy Lee Jones (left) and Garret Dillahunt in *No Country for Old Men* (2007)

for the south Texas town of Del Rio, and Chigurh follows, locating him via an electronic transponder hidden in the cash, but Chigurh is not alone in pursuing Llewelyn and the money, as several Mexicans who also have a receiver are lying in wait in Llewelyn's hotel room. Chigurh eliminates his competition, and Llewelyn, alerted by the gunshots, escapes with the satchel, hitchhiking to the border town of Eagle Pass, Texas.

In addition to Chigurh, Llewelyn, and Ed Tom Bell who are tracking the money and each other, the corporate arm of the drug trade has enlisted the services of Carson Wells (Woody Harrelson), a retired army colonel who moonlights as a bounty hunter. Wells is commissioned with locating Chigurh, now deemed a rogue by management, and returning the money to the interested parties. In the Eagle Hotel, Llewelyn finds and removes the transponder in the satchel, and when he is injured in a shoot-out with Chigurh, Llewelyn crosses the border into Mexico, throwing the satchel into the bushes next to the river. Chigurh, also injured, robs a pharmacy,

taking medical supplies to remove the bullets from his own leg. In Odessa, Sheriff Bell visits Carla Jean, assuring her that he can keep Llewelyn safe if he knows where he is, and Wells visits Llewelyn in his hospital room in Mexico, telling Llewelyn that he has no idea whom he's dealing with in the person of Chigurh. Wells, who has discovered the money hidden in the brush, is shot by Chigurh in the Hotel Eagle before he can recover the funds. Chigurh then presents Llewelyn with an ultimatum: if he returns the money, Carla Jean will be spared, but if not, she will die, as will Llewelyn, a proposition that Llewelyn rejects.

The parties converge in El Paso, Texas, where Llewelyn is to give Carla Jean the satchel, freeing him to hunt down Chigurh. Carla Jean, in turn, phones Ed Tom to tell him of the plan and Llewelyn's whereabouts, and Ed Tom and Carla Jean both arrive to find that the Mexicans have gunned down Llewelyn. In an inspection of Llewelyn's hotel room, the Sheriff observes that Chigurh has already come and gone, removing the satchel of money from the air conditioning duct. Returning to Sanderson,

Ed Tom resigns, feeling defeated and over-matched by the criminal forces that oppose him, and in Odessa, Carla Jean returns from her mother's funeral to find Chigurh waiting for her. The film implies that she is killed, and while driving away from the murder, Chigurh is hit by a car that runs a red light. He limps away, his arm in a homemade sling, before the police arrive. In the film's final scene, the retired Ed Tom sits morosely at his kitchen table, uncertain how to fill his days. He tells his wife of his dreams the night before, in which he and his father were riding on horseback, over a mountain pass in the snow and cold. His father passed him, going ahead with a horn full of fire, to make a fire in the dark and cold, and Ed Tom knew that when he arrived at camp, his father would be there. As the screen cuts to black, a clock ticks in the background and the credits roll.

Cormac McCarthy's novel *No Country for Old Men* was published in 2005, but a year prior to its publication, producer Scott Rudin purchased the film rights for the book and sent Joel and Ethan Coen the galley proofs. The brothers agreed to make the film, provided they maintained control of the project, as per their usual agreement. They warned Rudin that the film would be violent, and with his blessing they proceeded. The Coens' adaptation was released in late 2007, a brief two years after the book's publication. While Coen films are often influenced by literature, specifically that of Raymond Chandler (*The Big Lebowski*, 1998), Dashiell Hammett (*Miller's Crossing*, 1990), and James M. Cain (*Blood Simple*, 1984), this would be their first direct adaptation. The brothers have explained their adaptation process as one in which Ethan holds the book and Joel types, and while the film is very close to the novel in many aspects, including dialogue, tone, characters, and much of the plot, there are

departures as well, revealing the Coens' fingerprints on the project.

As the filmmakers thought about the cast for the film, Tommy Lee Jones was a natural choice. Joel Coen explains that Jones was immediately placed on the short list of actors for the role, as "he's one of the sort of great American actors of a certain age and who can convincingly be from that area." Jones is indeed from the area, near Marfa, Texas, where part of the film was shot. Jones and Bardem were first to be cast, and the brothers describe the Spanish actor as "fantastic." Bardem had reservations about the role, telling the filmmakers "I cannot do this movie. I can't. I don't drive, I don't speak English, and I hate violence. And they said: You're perfect." He became perfect, that is, after his appearance had been significantly altered. While researching for the film, costume designer Mary Zophres located a picture of a man at a bar in West Texas, circa 1979. Examining the hair and clothes, the Coens thought, "Well, he looks like a sociopath"; using the man as a model, the transformed Javier Bardem became Anton Chigurh, a sociopathic serial killer. The filmmakers were then faced with a problem, as casting the third leading role would require someone who could "be an equal in the movie with those two guys," Ethan explains. Josh Brolin was not someone the Coens initially considered for the part of Llewelyn, but his agent was persistent in putting him forward for the part. When he read for the role, the brothers cast him immediately, but just prior to shooting, Brolin was involved in a motorcycle accident and badly injured his shoulder. The injury caused him considerable pain during filming, particularly in the scene when he is running from the drug dealers' dog and swimming the river.

The film was shot primarily in Santa Fe, Albuquerque, and Las Vegas, New Mexico, with additional scenes in Mexico and some landscape filming near Marfa, Texas. Upon its release, reviewers responded by writing in superlatives: Roger Ebert characterized the film as "startlingly beautiful, stark and lonely," Philip French of the *Guardian* declared it "the best of their career so far," and Peter Travers of *Rolling Stone* wrote that the film "offers an embarrassment of riches." Many reviewers compared it to what they considered the finest films in the Coen canon: the *New Yorker* likened it to "their best work, in *Blood Simple* and *Miller's Crossing.*" *Rolling Stone* added *Barton Fink* and *The Big Lebowski* to the list of comparisons, for reasons not clarified in the review, and *Empire* and the *New York Times* draw parallels between *No Country* and *Fargo*, based on the winding plot and the small-town setting, with a sheriff in a leading role. The Coens maintain that while the similarities do indeed exist, they did not realize it at the time. Joel Coen admits, "These things really should seem obvious to us," but the brothers assert that when they move from one project to the next, they do not make these connections, nor do they engineer the patterns that fans and scholars locate in their works.

Nominated for eight Academy Awards, *No Country* won four Oscars, including Best Picture, Best Directing, Best Adapted Screenplay, all for Joel and Ethan Coen, and Best Actor for Javier Bardem. But for all of the praise of its cinematography and acting, viewers also found the story, and particularly the character of Anton Chigurh, to be very grim. A. O. Scott described the film as "bleak, scary and relentlessly violent;" the *Guardian* found it "a dark, violent and deeply disquieting drama;" and of Chigurh, the *New Yorker* declared him "less a person than a conceit: an angel of death, stalking the landscape like a plague." These observations apply to McCarthy's novel as well

as to the Coens' adaptation, and they additionally echo comments that reviewers have been making about the Coens since their debut film, *Blood Simple.*

In his review for the *New Yorker*, Anthony Lane comments that *No Country for Old Men* "is not telling a tale—the plot remains open-ended—but reinforcing the legend of a place, like a poem adding to an oral tradition," and the legend to which Lane refers has to some degree been fostered by cinematic westerns. Most Coen films are an exercise in genre, to some degree, and *No Country* might be considered a western, when examined in light of cinematic traditions. The Coens describe their three characters as a "good guy," Sheriff Bell; a "bad guy," Anton Chigurh; and "guy in between," Llewelyn Moss; and these categories appear to work within the western genre. The good guy/bad guy dichotomy is the bread and butter of the classic western, and the man in the middle represents the citizen whose well-being depends on the success of the lawman. Set in a small town in Texas with its sweeping shots of the horizon, complete with windmills and fences, the film visually references the genre as well: boots, hats, horses, and western wear, and the proliferation of guns, as well as the Texas accent of both Llewelyn and Ed Tom Bell round out the western-like characteristics of the film.

The Coens, however, "didn't particularly look at this movie as a Western," as "it's hard to know exactly what a traditional western means," says Joel. Their assessment of McCarthy's narrative in this regard seem correct, as despite its setting and costumes, the characters, upon closer examination, do not fit the stereotypes of the traditional white hat/black hat scenario. Ed Tom Bell, while Sheriff of Terrell County, would not be considered a hero, in the tradition of Marshal Dillon of *Gunsmoke*

(1955–1975). Bell never actually faces down the bad guy, and Chigurh not only lives, but he gets away with the money and kills the citizen, Llewelyn Moss. Bell seems ineffectual, at best, and he admits that he is "overmatched" by the forces aligned against him. The film's final image is of Bell's face, drooping with age and defeat, and the star that he wore for decades has no meaning, no power in the face of the new breed of villain that has manifested itself in the West. This villain, Chigurh, is clearly meant to be viewed as an evil man, with his dark clothes, his sinister black ostrich-skin boots, and his helmet-like hair. Javier Bardem describes Chigurh as "everything but a human being. It's more an idea of what violence means." He personifies evil, rather than just acting as an agent of evil, and he seems undefeatable, unlike the mortal, dark-clothed bad guys of the traditional western. He survives his encounters with both the law and the lawbreakers, and he lurks in the distance at the close of the film, damaged but not defeated.

The final man in this triangle is Llewelyn Moss, described by *Rolling Stone* as "a cowboy in a world with no more room for cowboys." He represents the citizen, but his greed sets in motion the events that lead to his own death, and one might view him as culpable for his demise, a pawn in the larger battle between the ineffectual law and the other-worldly menace that challenges it. Brolin describes Llewelyn as a "backwoods country boy who never had any money," and while the Coens shy away from social and political interpretations of their films, McCarthy may indeed have had created Moss as a commentary on the perils of greed in the Reagan era. A unique entry in the Coen canon, *No Country for Old Men* stands as a celebrated piece of filmmaking but does not easily fit into their catalog of heavily stylized genre pieces. The brothers have played this one straight, remaining faithful to McCarthy's vision, and have been amply rewarded for their departure from their own well-established cinematic tradition.

References

Peter Bradshaw, "*No Country for Old Men*," *Guardian*, January 17, 2008; Roger Ebert, "*No Country for Old Men*," *RogerEbert.com*, November 8, 2007; Philip French, "*No Country for Old Men*," *Guardian*, January 20, 2008; David Gritten, "*No Country for Old Men*: Are the Coens Finally Growing Up?" *Telegraph*, January 12, 2008; "Interview with Javier Bardem on 'Biutiful' Acting Career," *NPR.org*, February 3, 2011; Anthony Lane, "Hunting Grounds," *New Yorker*, November 12, 2007; Rebecca Murray, "Filmmaking Brothers Joel and Ethan Coen Talk *No Country for Old Men*," *Movies.About.com*; Ian Nathan, *Ethan and Joel Coen* (Paris: Cahiers du cinema Sarl, 2012); Ian Nathan, "*No Country for Old Men*: Heaven Be Praised, the Brothers Go Grim Again," *Empire Online.com*; A. O. Scott, "*No Country for Old Men*," *New York Times*, November 9, 2007; Sonya Topolnisky, "For Every Tatter in Its Mortal Dress: Costume and Character in *No Country for Old Men*," in *From Novel to Film: "No Country for Old Men*," ed. Lynnea Chapman King, Rick Wallach, and Jim Welsh (Lanham, MD: Scarecrow Press, 2009); Peter Travers, "*No Country for Old Men*," *Rolling Stone*, November 1, 2007; Pat Tyrer and Pat Nickell, "'Of What Is Past, or Passing, or to Come': Characters as Relics in *No Country for Old Men*," in *From Novel to Film: "No Country for Old Men*," ed. Lynnea Chapman King, Rick Wallach, and Jim Welsh (Lanham, MD: Scarecrow Press, 2009). See also JAVIER BARDEM, JOSH BROLIN, CARTER BURWELL, JESS GONCHOR, NANCY HAIGH, WOODY HARRELSON, TOMMY LEE JONES, KELLY MACDONALD, STEPHEN ROOT, MARY ZOPHRES.

O BROTHER, WHERE ART THOU? (2000)

DIRECTOR: Joel Coen and Ethan Coen (uncredited). SCREENPLAY: Joel Coen and Ethan Coen. EXECUTIVE PRODUCERS: Tim Bevan and Eric Fellner. PRODUCERS: Ethan Coen and Joel Coen (uncredited); John Cameron (Co-producer); Robert Graf (Associate Producer). PHOTOGRAPHY: Roger Deakins. EDITING: Ethan Coen and Joel Coen, as Roderick Jaynes, and Tricia Cooke. ORIGINAL MUSIC: T Bone Burnett. PRODUCTION DESIGN: Dennis Gassner. SET DECORATION: Nancy Haigh.

CAST: George Clooney (Ulysses Everett McGill), John Turturro (Pete Hogwallop), Tim Blake Nelson (Delmar O'Donnell), John Goodman (Big Dan Teague), Holly Hunter (Penny), Chris Thomas King (Tommy Johnson), Charles Durning (Menelaus "Pappy" O'Daniel), Michael Badalucco (George "Baby Face" Nelson), Wayne Duvall (Homer Stokes).

RUNNING TIME: 106 minutes. Color.

RELEASED THROUGH: Buena Vista Pictures. PREMIERE: May 13, 2000 (Cannes International Film Festival).

ACADEMY AWARDS: Best Cinematography (nominated: Roger Deakins), Best Writing, Screenplay Based on Material Previously Produced or Publisher (nominated: Ethan Coen and Joel Coen).

DVD: Touchstone Home Video.

Filmed on location across rural Mississippi and on set in Los Angeles, the Coen brothers' eighth film chronicles the adventures of three escaped convicts, Ulysses Everett McGill, Pete Hogwallop, and Delmar O'Donnell, as they journey toward home and hidden treasure. Everett (George Clooney), the self-appointed leader of the group, has lured Pete (John Turturro) and Delmar (Tim Blake Nelson) away from a penal farm chain gang with promises of nearly a half a million dollars each, but time is of the essence, as the money lies hidden in what will soon be a nine thousand-hectare lake, flooded by the Tennessee Valley Authority to produce electricity. Encouraged onward by a blind railroad man, reminiscent of the mythical Tiresias, and beaten by a Cyclops-like one-eyed Bible salesman, Big Dan Teague (John Goodman), enticed by Sirens, and set upon by a Satanic sheriff, the men traverse their way through 1930s Mississippi, ever hurried by the upcoming deadline. They are joined by bank robber and aspiring celebrity George "Babyface" Nelson (Michael Badalucco) and Tommy Johnson (Chris Thomas King), a guitarist who sold his soul to the devil at a crossroads, a nod to the Southern Depression-era bluesman Robert Johnson, who claimed to have done the same.

Also traveling the countryside are Homer Stokes (Wayne Duvall), the Reform candidate in the upcoming gubernatorial

George Clooney (left) and Holly Hunter in *O Brother, Where Art Thou?* (2000)

election and sometime KKK wizard, and the incumbent governor, Menelaus "Pappy" O'Daniel (Charles Durning), who frequent the roads, stages, and radio airwaves of Mississippi. Their collective journeys are punctuated by frequent musical numbers, often worked into the narrative: living room radio entertainment of an evening, songs of salvation to salve the soul, political endorsements by down-home folks, and sorrowful campfire songs reflecting the despondency and struggles of the travelers. Lured by the offer to "sing into a can" for money, the boys and Tommy, as the Soggy Bottom Boys, visit a 25-watt radio station, where they record "Man of Constant Sorrow," a blues number that becomes an instant hit, unbeknownst to the quartet. For their efforts, they earn ten dollars apiece, funds that allow them to continue toward their destination and the riches awaiting them. They become separated from Tommy, only to find and rescue him from a lynch mob of Klansmen, in a fiery, intricately choreographed nighttime scene.

Together, the four reach their destination, where, at the end of the road lies not a treasure borne of armed robbery, but instead the real reason for the escape and journey: Everett's wife, Penny (Holly Hunter), is set to marry Vernon T. Waldrip (Ray McKinnon), a bona fide man of means. With a live Soggy Bottom Boys' performance of "Man of Constant Sorrow," Everett and the boys secure a different kind of treasure: the governor's pardon grants them freedom, fame, and legitimacy, Everett wins back Penny and their seven daughters, and Stokes is run out of town on a rail. At the conclusion of the film, while procuring the ring for the upcoming nuptials, the group is caught in, and survives, the flooding of the valley, a sign of the new age of technology and progress that has engulfed the land.

O Brother claims, at its outset, to be "based on the *Odyssey* by Homer," taking its episodic, narrative structure and some characters—Ulysses, Penny, Menelaus, the Cyclops, and the Sirens—from the classic epic poem, which follows Odysseus and his men on their post–Trojan War journey to their homeland. Other sources, however, influence the film, perhaps to a greater degree. *O Brother* takes its name from the 1941 Preston Sturges film, *Sullivan's Travels*, in which the title character, played by Joel McCrea, travels rural America to make a serious, social commentary in his film *O Brother, Where Art Thou?*, finding instead that audiences prefer comedy. In addition to the borrowed title, several scenes in the Coen film clearly originate in Sturges's picture: the hair-raising ride in Washington Hogwallop's car, driven by his young son; the entrance of the chain gang into the darkened theatre for a night at the movies, and the ominous presence of the sheriff and his hound. The Coens give visual nods, as well, to *The Wizard of Oz* (1939), *Moby Dick* (1956), *The Grapes of Wrath* (1940), early chain gang films, Busby Berkeley choreography, as well as other familiar tropes of road and buddy films.

The enormously popular soundtrack to *O Brother* received Grammies for Album of the Year and Best Compilation Sound Track Album for a Motion Picture, Television, or Other Visual Media; T Bone Burnett won Producer of the Year, Non-Classical; and Dan Tyminsky ("Man of Constant Sorrows") and Ralph Stanley ("O Death") each received a Grammy for their individual efforts. An amalgam of country, gospel, bluegrass, and folk music, and reminiscent of Harry Smith's *Anthology of American Folk Music*, the soundtrack features a vintage prison chain gang recording, "Po Lazarus," collected by Alan Lomax in 1959, which accompanies the film's opening sequence. A number of songs in the film are voiced by musicians who appear as characters: Delmar/Tim Blake Nelson, "In the Jailhouse Now"; Tommy/Chris Thomas King, "Hard Time Killing Floor Blues"; and the grave diggers/The Fairfield

Four, "The Lonesome Valley." Those numbers not voiced by actors were recorded by such musicians as Norman Blake, Alison Krauss, Emmylou Harris, Gillian Welch, the Cox Family, and the Whites; Gillian Welch made a cameo appearance in the film as a woman trying to buy the record "Man of Constant Sorrow" at a general store. The soundtrack sold more than eight million copies, spent more than two weeks at number one on Billboard's Top 200 Albums chart, and spawned a corresponding live concert album entitled *Down from the Mountain* (2000) and its accompanying documentary of the same name, as well as a touring show. The soundtrack was rereleased on its tenth anniversary, in 2011, in expanded form.

O Brother, Where Art Thou? was the first completely digitized, Digital Intermediate (DI), film. The process was necessary because the Mississippi countryside in which *O Brother* was filmed was overly green during the summer shooting, and the Coens wanted ochre tones, reminiscent of the Depression and Dust Bowl era, with "the look of an old tinted photograph or a postcard," according to Joel Coen. The task of de-saturating the colors was left to Roger Deakins, cinematographer for the film, who achieved the desired effect by scanning the film and then color correcting to arrive at the "brown and dirty and golden" color.

O Brother did only moderately well at the box office, initially, earning just over $45 million domestically, with a production budget of $26 million. Critical reception was mixed, with comments ranging from full-throated endorsements to descriptions of the film as thin and hokey. All of the reviews and analyses, however, addressed the soundtrack of the film, about which critics were overwhelmingly positive. They were less certain what to make of the film: is *O Brother*, as it purports to be, an adaptation of Homer's *Odyssey*? A fulfillment of

Sullivan's dream to make a social commentary? A road or buddy film? Interpreting the film is further complicated by the Coen brothers themselves, who are, as always, little help in resolving these tensions. Ethan Coen noted that *O Brother* "pretends to be a big important movie . . . but the grandiosity is obviously a joke. It is what it is, it's a comedy," and this quotation captures the film accurately: much pretending is going on here. The film points us in one direction while simultaneously referencing another, and the result is a complicated set of messages that, by Coen design, leaves the viewer looking for answers.

Everett McGill twice in the film comments that people, like the film's viewers, are "looking for answers," a perspective that is seconded by Big Dan Teague, the one-eyed Bible salesman and Klansman, and during the social upheaval of the American Depression of the 1930s, this phrase characterizes the national mind-set accurately. There are many places to look for those answers in this film: religion, science, politics, technology, tradition, and myth populate the rural Mississippi countryside through which the characters travel. From the outset, the film's classical references to Homer in the epigraph and the attribution of source material to the *Odyssey* encourage the viewer to follow the breadcrumbs toward an adaptation of the classical epic poem: Cyclops, Sirens, Greek columns in the firelight, the blind seer who accurately predicts the events of the film, and Everett's journey through the known world with the fate of his family resting on his shoulders, in epic hero tradition. "Ulysses" Everett McGill's story is indeed the *Odyssey*. Or is it? The Coens claim to have never read Homer's epic poem, though the film's narrative and allusions, and actor Tim Blake Nelson, call that claim into question. Perhaps it is, instead, a picture of Christian salvation, the tale of

sinners seeking redemption. Pete and Delmar dash willingly into riverside baptism, while Everett observes that "hard times flush the chump," scoffing at the newfound religion of his companions. Many of the songs performed by characters throughout the narrative are renditions of old-time gospel hymns, and the film is replete with references to salvation and redemption. Even "Babyface" Nelson announces to the crowd at the bank that "Jesus saves, but George Nelson withdraws," and the Devil incarnate, the bespectacled sheriff (Daniel von Bargen), tells the boys that he will meet them in the "sweet by and by." At the film's conclusion, Everett, faced with certain death, looks upward in confession and asks God to spare him for the sake of his friends and family, embracing the baptism by flood that he had earlier scorned. However, having survived the flood, Everett embraces the technology that will result from the nine-thousand-hectare lake, as a "brave new world . . . an age of reason," right before he observes the foretold cow on a cotton shed, completing the mythical circle and pointing the viewer back to the classical Tiresias and his prediction early in the film. Everett claims that "fate was smiling on him," and finding the ring following the flood was "foreordained." Thus, mythology and Christianity weave their way through the narrative seamlessly, and the viewer is again left wondering which direction to look for meaning in this film.

The intersection of authentic and false, as well, is emphasized repeatedly, visually, symbolically, and politically in the film. Most notably, the Soggy Bottom Boys assume false identities from their time in the radio station through their performance at the political rally at the conclusion of the film. Donning false beards at one point and blackface at another and finally assuming the role of Pappy O'Daniel's "brain trust," the Boys fish about for whatever identity will suit them best at the moment. The memorable KKK rally of the film, as well, emphasizes the relationship between appearances and reality, as not only are the Klansmen in disguise, but Everett and companions are also, concealing themselves in the garb of the color guard in an effort to rescue Tommy. The Bible salesman, Big Dan Teague; the aspiring governor, Homer Stokes; and a host of other Klansmen perform an elaborate Busby Berkeley–like dance while chanting eeny-meeny-miny-moe, making a tragic and serious portion of American history a farce in the process. Characters are concerned with appearances throughout, as Everett obsesses about his coiffure, Penny seeks a man with bona fides, and Pete dreams of owning a restaurant where he can be the maitre d', dressing up every day for work to earn the respect of his wealthy diners. Everett is sent up to the penal farm for practicing law without a license, plans to have a fellow print him up a dentist license, and tells Penny he wants to be "what you want me to be." Finding a genuine, authentic character in this tale is difficult indeed, as concern with appearance dominates the film. Underlying those appearances, however, is a slippery set of deceits, betrayals, and shifting identities. The answers are difficult to locate.

In the midst of the dissonance, however, there is indeed social commentary to be found. The film foregrounds the chicanery of politicians, abetted by the technology of the day and pandering campaign teams. The Klansmen are simultaneously terrifying in their intent to lynch Tommy and rendered ridiculous by the choreography of their ritual observances. The images of poverty and desolation convey the desperation of a period of American history that comedy cannot alleviate. Though the Coens assert that the film is a comedy, and in many ways it is, it is also a tribute to the nation's history, cinematic history, and a very American form of art: the bluegrass, folk, and gospel music that sustained a nation in its most troubled times.

References

Ronald Bergan, "On the Run with Joel and Ethan," *Guardian*, August 14, 2000; Sean Chadwell, "Inventing That 'Old Timey Style,'" *Journal of Popular Film & Television* 31.1 (2004); Randy Lewis, "'O Brother,' Is It 10 Already?" *Los Angeles Times*, August 23, 2011; Douglas McFarland, "Philosophies of Comedy in *O Brother Where Art Thou?*" in *The Philosophy of the Coen Brothers*, ed. Mark T. Conard (Lexington: The University Press of Kentucky, 2009); James Mottram, *The Life of the Mind* (Frome, UK: Butler and Tanner, 2000); Jim Ridley, "Brothers in Arms," in *The Coen Brothers: Interviews*, ed. William Rodney Allen (Jackson: University Press of Mississippi, 2006); Jonathan Romney, "Double Vision," *Guardian*, May 18, 2000; Margaret Toscano, "Homer Meets the Coen Brothers: Memory as Artistic Pastiche in *O Brother Where Art Thou?*" *Film and History* 39.2 (2009). See also MICHAEL BADALUCCO, T BONE BURNETT, GEORGE CLOONEY, ROGER DEAKINS, *DOWN FROM THE MOUNTAIN*, CHARLES DURNING, DENNIS GASSNER, JOHN GOODMAN, NANCY HAIGH, HOLLY HUNTER, TIM BLAKE NELSON, *SULLIVAN'S TRAVELS*, JOHN TURTURRO.

PARIS, JE T'AIME: "TUILERIES" (2006)

The first of two short films by the Coens—the other is *World Cinema* (2007)—*Tuileries* is the Coens' contribution to the larger project, *Paris, je t'aime*, a collection of eighteen short films set in Paris. Each filmmaker in the project received the same prompt, described by the *New York Times* as "Make a five-minute film set in a Paris arrondissement that reflects the spirit of the neighborhood, the city and the nature of love itself." The collection was produced by Emmanuel Benbihy, who selected largely foreign directors, as "The French see in Paris something more quotidian, problematic, existential. Foreign directors are interested in what the city gives off and what it inspires." The Coen segment stars Steve Buscemi, Julie Bataille, Axel Kiener, and Franckie Pain and captures an encounter between Buscemi's American tourist and Bataille, who unexpectedly kisses him on the platform of a Paris Metro station.

References

Kristin Hohenadel, "Find the Soul of Love and Paris. You Have Five Minutes. Go!" *New York Times*, August 27, 2006; Ian Nathan, *Ethan and Joel Coen* (Paris: Cahiers du cinema Sarl, 2012). See also STEVE BUSCEMI.

PEPPER, BARRY (1970–)

Pepper was born April 4, 1970, in British Columbia, where his family had lived for many generations; from age five to age ten, he and his family built and lived aboard a fifty-foot sailboat, sailing in the Islands of the South Pacific. Pepper and his siblings were homeschooled, though they attended public schools when opportunity allowed. Returning from these travels, he attended high school in British Columbia, where he participated in drama, and following graduation, he enrolled in the Vancouver Actors Studio, where he worked with Mel Tuck, and he appeared in the Vancouver television series *Madison* (1993–1996). He later moved to Los Angeles to pursue a career in Hollywood. Throughout the 1990s, Pepper was cast in television series, including *M.A.N.T.I.S.* (1994), *Highlander* (1995), *Lonesome Dove: The Series* (1995), and *Lonesome Dove: The Outlaw Years* (1996); he also appeared in the made-for-television movies *Titanic* (1996), *Dead Silence* (1997), and *61** (2001), directed by Billy Crystal, for which Pepper earned Golden Globe and Emmy nominations for Best Actor in a Mini-series. He worked with Steven Spielberg in *Saving Private Ryan* (1998), with Tony Scott in *Enemy of the State* (1998), with Spike Lee in *25th Hour* (2002), and with Clint Eastwood in *Flags of Our Fathers*

(2006). In 2011, he played Bobby Kennedy in the television mini-series *The Kennedys*, for which he won the Emmy for Outstanding Lead Actor in a Mini-Series. Pepper appeared in Gore Verbinski's *The Lone Ranger* (2013), with Johnny Depp and Armie Hammer.

In Joel and Ethan Coen's re-adaptation of the Charles Portis novel *True Grit* (2010), Pepper plays Lucky Ned Pepper, train robber and leader of a gang of outlaws. Ned serves as the antagonist to Jeff Bridges's Rooster Cogburn and Hailee Steinfeld's Mattie Ross, as they seek to capture and bring to justice the murderer Tom Chaney (Josh Brolin). As Lucky Ned, whom *Empire* described as a "revolting treat," Barry Pepper is a dirty, disheveled, snaggle-toothed bandit, a role that included a set of broken prosthetic teeth and wooly chaps, which Pepper notes had not appeared on-screen since the days of Buster Keaton. His character is simultaneously a violent, calculating outlaw harboring much hate for Rooster Cogburn, who shot Ned in the face in a previous encounter, and a kinder man who speaks in a civilized manner to Mattie, discussing his fate and hers. On working with the Coens, Pepper offers praise, characterizing them as possessing "an effortless grace as filmmakers," who provide a "calm, cool, collected environment on the set."

References

Angie Errigo, "*True Grit*: The Dude Bests The Duke in a New Coens Masterpiece," *EmpireOnline.com*; "Barry Pepper," *New York Times*, Movies & TV; "Biography," *BarryPepper.com*; Todd Gilchrist, "Barry Pepper on His Understated *True Grit* Role," *Speakeasy: Wall Street Journal*, blogs.wsj.com, December 28, 2010; Julie Miller, "*True Grit*'s Barry Pepper on the Coen Brothers and 'Lucky' Ned's Mangled Teeth," *Movieline.com*, June 7, 2011. See also *TRUE GRIT*.

PITT, BRAD (1963–)

Born December 18, 1963, in Shawnee, Oklahoma, and raised in Missouri, Pitt studied journalism at the University of Missouri, planning to become an advertising art director. In his last semester of college, he dropped out of school and moved to Los Angeles, working as a chauffeur prior to securing an acting agent. His career began with television roles, followed by his breakthrough role in Ridley Scott's *Thelma and Louise* (1991), in which he had a small role as a hitchhiker; he then appeared in Robert Redford's 1992 fly-fishing drama, *A River Runs Through It*, in a much larger role. He then cemented his position as a leading man in such films as *Legends of the Fall* (1994), *Interview with the Vampire* (1994), and *Se7en* (1995). Best known for *Fight Club* (1999), the *Ocean's Eleven, Twelve,* and *Thirteen* films (2001, 2004, 2007), *Mr. & Mrs. Smith* (2005), and Quentin Tarantino's *Inglourious Basterds* (2009), he has been nominated for five Golden Globes and three Academy Awards for acting, winning the Globe for his role in Terry Gilliam's *Twelve Monkeys* (1995). His Oscar nominations include *Twelve Monkeys*, *The Curious Case of Benjamin Button* (2008), and *Moneyball* (2011), which he also produced and which was nominated by the Academy for Best Motion Picture of the Year. He began producing films in 2006, and his production credits include *The Departed* (2006), *The Assassination of Jesse James by the Coward Robert Ford* (2007), *World War Z* (2013), and the Oscar-winning Best Motion Picture of the Year, *12 Years a Slave* (2013).

Pitt has appeared in one film by Joel and Ethan Coen, as Chad Feldheimer in the 2008 spy thriller/comedy, *Burn After Reading*. As Feldheimer, Pitt sports too-tight T-shirts, a goofy grin, and a memorable hairstyle, "a kind of sculpted butterscotch pudding shot through with a splash of cream," as described by *The Nation*'s Stuart Klawans. A trainer at Hardbodies Gym, Feldheimer is pulled into the labyrinthine plot of the film when he finds a CD containing what he supposes is top-secret information. With Francis McDormand's Linda Litzke, he plans to cash in on the find and attempts first to extort money from CIA agent Osborne Cox (John Malkovich), to whom the CD belongs, and then to sell the classified material to the Russians. Pitt's Chad, however, is clearly outmatched in the world of covert affairs, in a performance characterized by *Salon*'s Andrew O'Hehir as Pitt "pretending to be a dumb ass who's pretending to be a guy who knows what he's talking about," and by *Empire*'s Ian Nathan as "a gym-cute bubble-head bounding into the world of espionage like a puppy." Although the film itself is not widely considered the Coens' best work, Pitt fared well in a number of reviews, including that of the *Daily Mail*'s Chris Tookey, who concluded that "the film is an ensemble piece, but it's stolen by Brad Pitt."

References

Stuart Klawans, "Burned Out," *Nation*, October 6, 2008; Ian Nathan, "*Burn After Reading*: Concoctions of Two Dangerous Minds," *EmpireOnline.com*; Andrew O'Hehir, "No Country for Human Beings," *Salon.com*, September 12, 2008; "Brad Pitt," *Biography.com*; Chris Tookey, "*Burn After Reading*: Pitt the Halfwit Steals the Show with the Greatest Ever Portrayal of Stupidity," *Daily Mail*, October 17, 2008. See also BURN AFTER READING.

POLITO, JON (1950–)

Born December 29, 1950, in Philadelphia, Pennsylvania, Polito was the son of a Westinghouse factory worker. He attended Villanova University on a drama scholarship prior to relocating to New York, where he spent his twenties, which he characterizes as the "theatre years." During this time he played various roles, influenced by Lon Chaney characters, "the guy who changes faces and changes body stuff." After six years in the theatre, he won the 1980 Best Actor Obie for a series of five off-Broadway performances.

Polito began his on-screen career in a genre that would figure largely in his work, that of the gangster film. He appeared first in the television mini-series *The Gangster Chronicles* (1981), followed closely by *The Clairvoyant* (1982), in which he played a detective, the other type of role which would dominate his career. He continued his work on stage, and though he was initially considered for the part of Biff, Willy's son, in the 1984 Broadway production of *Death of a Salesman,* he appeared as Howard, Willy's boss, a part for which he lobbied heavily. The production was then adapted for television, with Polito again playing Howard. The following year he played Detective Bedsoe in the cult film, *Highlander* (1986). In 1990, he worked with Marlon Brando and Matthew Broderick in *The Freshman*, one of his many gangster films, and in 1993 he began a recurring role as Detective Crosetti on *Homicide: Life on the Street* (1993–1994). Once again, he was called to audition for one role, and having done so, asked to be considered for a different part, in which he was ultimately cast, that of Crosetti. Following his time with *Homicide*, Polito appeared on various television series, including *NYPD Blue* (1995), *Seinfeld* (1998), *The Chronicle* (2001–2002), *Desperate Housewives* (2005), and *Raising the Bar* (2008–2009), among others. His gangster films continued with *The Last Godfather* (2010), a spoof on films about the mob and *Gangster Squad* in 2013.

Polito's first Coen film was 1990's *Miller's Crossing*, in which he appeared as the apoplectic Italian mob boss Johnny Caspar, who challenged the authority of Albert Finney's Leo. In a memorable monologue that opens the film, Caspar waxes philosophical about the role of "ethics, character, friendship" in gangland, all the while lobbying for permission to kill a local bookie, Bernie Bernbaum (John Turturro), who is selling information on Caspar's fixed fights and thus negatively impacting Caspar's profits. Having seen Polito in *Death of a Salesman*, the Coens contacted him to audition for the part of the Dane, Caspar's enforcer, but Polito insisted on reading for Caspar. Initially, they declined to have him audition, as another actor was in negotiations for the part; however, as casting concluded, Polito was called back to read for Johnny Caspar, and, after reading the entire role for the brothers, he was cast. Polito points to this role as the part that led to the rest of his career.

His second Coen film, *Barton Fink* (1991), finds Polito as the sycophantic Lou Breeze, a part that the Coens purportedly wrote for him. He resisted accepting the part, as he wanted the role of Jack Lipnick, which went to Michael Lerner, but Frances McDormand appealed personally to Polito, and he agreed to play Breeze. Following a brief cameo in *The Hudsucker Proxy* (1994), Polito's next Coen role was that of Da Fino, a private detective who drives a Volkswagen Beetle, in *The Big Lebowski* (1998), a film experience he characterizes as "magical," despite the fact that Jeff Bridges "looked like he smelled." In 2001, Polito appeared in *The Man Who Wasn't There*, as the entrepreneur Creighton Tolliver, whose quest for a venture capitalist sets in motion the film's plot. The Coens have commented that looking back at the film, "We realized a few years too late that Jon Polito's character in *The Man Who Wasn't There* should have been named Larry London. I can't even

remember what name we gave him. But it was the wrong one."

Polito has commented, on working with the Coen brothers, "They sort of seduce you into doing what they want by just making you think that you've thought of it," adding that he has "really been able to have a career based on the fact that what they touch is gold and I just keep holding onto them and touching them."

References
Alec Campagna, "Interview with Jon Polito," *TheCelebrityCafe.com*, August 3, 2011; Nathan Rabin, "Jon Polito," *AVClub.com*, August 11, 2011; Damon Wise, "Uncut Interview: Joel and Ethan Coen," *Uncut.co.uk*. See also BARTON FINK, THE BIG LEBOWSKI, THE MAN WHO WASN'T THERE, MILLER'S CROSSING.

PRESNELL, HARVE (1933–2009)
Born September 14, 1933, in Modesto, California, Harve Presnell rode in rodeos prior to attending the University of Southern California. There, a music teacher encouraged him to pursue a career in opera, which he did, noting that he went into the music business "because it was easier than being a jock." A baritone, he trained vocally in Europe and sang with the Roger Wagner Chorale and the San Francisco Opera. Composer Meredith Willson heard Presnell perform in Berlin and subsequently created the role of "Leadville" Johnny Brown, husband of Molly Brown, in *The Unsinkable Molly Brown* (1960); he reprised the role in the 1964 film version of the same name, opposite Debbie Reynolds. In 1965 he was awarded the Golden Globe award for Most Promising Newcomer—Male, and for over forty years, Presnell worked steadily on stage, film, and television, alternating between the three. He came to Hollywood as film musicals declined in popularity, appearing in *When the Boys Meet the Girls*

(1965) and in *Paint Your Wagon* (1969), with Clint Eastwood and Lee Marvin, in which he sang "They Call the Wind Maria" and for which he received positive reviews. His television debut was in *Alfred Hitchcock Presents* (1956), and his work on television series includes *The Red Skelton Hour* (1965), *Ryan's Hope* (1984), and *The Client* (1995), though he appeared very little on screen from the mid-1970s to the mid-1990s. During this time, however, he toured with stage productions of *Annie Get Your Gun* (1977), *Carousel,* and a musical version of *Gone with the Wind* (1972) in London. In 1979, he assumed the role of Daddy Warbucks in the Broadway musical *Annie,* following which he toured with the show for a decade.

In 1996, he returned to the big screen following a hiatus of over two decades. He appeared in the Oscar-winning Coen film *Fargo* as Wade Gustafson, the wealthy and tight-fisted father-in-law of Jerry Lundegaard (William H. Macy), a role that reinvigorated his waning career. That year he also had parts in *Larger Than Life* (1996) and *The Chamber* (1996), and the increased visibility resulted in many television series appearances, including *Nash Bridges* (1996), *Star Trek: Voyager* (1996), and a recurring role on *Lois & Clark: The New Adventures of Superman* (1995–1997). He appeared in made-for-television movies such as *The Guardian* (1997), *The Pretender 2001* (2001), and *Jackie, Ethel, Joan:*

The Women of Camelot (2001), and his additional film work included *Saving Private Ryan* (1998), *The Legend of Bagger Vance* (2000), *Old School* (2003), and Clint Eastwood's *Flags of Our Fathers* (2006). He continued to make television appearances until his death in 2009.

As Wade Gustafson, Presnell played a businessman who intimidates his son-in-law, criticizes his daughter's parenting of his grandson, and, when the ransom demand arrives for the safe return of his daughter, considers counter-offering half a million dollars, rather than handing over the million dollars. Janet Maslin of the *New York Times* considered Presnell well cast, as he has "just the gruff, booming manner to explain why Mr. Macy, as his son-in-law, looks scared to death," and Ben Walters of *Sight and Sound* describes Presnell as "boomingly effective."

References

Ronald Bergan, "Obituary: Harve Presnell," *Guardian,* July 7, 2009; Adam Bernstein, "Leading Man Traveled from Broadway to *Fargo,*" *Washington Post,* July 3, 2009; Janet Maslin, "*Fargo* (1996) film review; Deadly Plot by a Milquetoast Villain," *New York Times,* March 8, 1996; Robert Simonson, "Harve Presnell, Enduring Daddy Warbucks in *Annie,* Dies at 75," *Playbill.com,* July 2, 2009; Ben Walters, "*Glengarry Glen Ross/Fargo,*" *Sight and Sound,* 18.1 (2008). See also *FARGO.*

RAIMI, SAM (1959–)

Producer, director, writer, and actor, Raimi has played many roles at all levels in the film industry, in a career that spans more than three decades. Born October 23, 1959, near Detroit, Michigan, his interest in film dates to his childhood and stems from his father's love of home movies. As a teen, he made 8 mm movies with his friends, and following high school, he attended Michigan State University for a time. Raimi quit college to devote himself fully to film, forming Renaissance Pictures with friends Bruce Campbell and Robert Tapert. In an approach to funding that would be emulated by the Coen brothers, Raimi, Campbell, and Tapert approached local professionals in the Detroit area, previewing twenty minutes of film footage and asking each for a $5,000 investment in their first film. They raised almost $400,000, which funded the 1981 break-out horror film *The Evil Dead*, written, directed, and produced by Raimi, and on which Joel Coen served as an assistant film editor. Though the original *Evil Dead* initially experienced a slow box-office start, it ultimately gained a cult following, and Hollywood producer Dino Di Laurentiis funded the 1987 sequel, *Evil Dead II*. The third film in the series was *Army of Darkness* (1992), which Raimi also wrote, directed, and produced. The film spawned a touring production, *Evil Dead—The Musical*, and was remade in 2013 by Fede Alvarez.

Raimi first appeared on screen in *It's Murder* (1977) and has made numerous cameos since then, but he is better known for his role behind the camera. In 1985, he directed *Crimewave*, which he wrote in conjunction with Joel and Ethan Coen, who appear briefly in the film, and in which Frances McDormand also makes an appearance. Raimi then wrote and directed *Darkman* (1990) and its two sequels, which went straight to video, and directed the western *The Quick and the Dead* (1995), starring Sharon Stone, Gene Hackman, and Russell Crowe. Subsequent directing projects included *A Simple Plan* (1998) with Billy Bob Thornton and the film adaptation of *Spider-Man* (2001) and its sequels *Spider-Man 2* (2004) and *Spider-Man 3* (2007). The Spider-Man series was then handed over to director Mark Webb for a reboot, and Raimi directed *Drag Me to Hell* (2009), starring Alison Lohman and Justin Long, and *Oz the Great and Powerful* (2013), starring James Franco and Michelle Williams.

Raimi's television work includes the creation of the series *Spy Game* (1997) and *M.A.N.T.I.S.* (1994–1997), both of which he wrote for, and extensive production credits that include a series of made-for-television Hercules movies (1994–1995) and the subsequent series *Hercules: The Legendary Journeys* (1995–1999), *American Gothic* (1995–1996), *Jack of All Trades*

(2000), *Xena: Warrior Princess* (1995–2001), *Zombie Roadkill* (2010), and *Spartacus: War of the Damned* (2010–2013).

In 2002, Raimi established a production company, Ghost House Pictures, with Robert Tapert in conjunction with Mandate Pictures, created specifically to foster the development of horror films. Ghost House produced *The Grudge* (2004), *The Grudge 2* (2006), *Boogeyman* (2005), and its sequels *Boogeyman 2* (2007) and *Boogeyman 3* (2008), *30 Days of Night* (2007), *Drag Me to Hell* (2009), and *The Possession* (2012), among others, as well as television series *Devil's Trade* (2007), *13: Fear Is Real* (2009), *Legend of the Seeker* (2009–2010), and *Zombie Roadkill* (2010). Ghost House Pictures launched a new horror banner, Spooky Pictures, dedicated to producing family horror films such as a remake of 2007's Danish film *The Substitute*.

Raimi's relationship with the Coen brothers began with Joel Coen's work as assistant film editor on *The Evil Dead*, and the working relationship continued with their collaboration as writers for *Crimewave*. When Joel and Ethan Coen began making their own films, they were heavily influenced by the filmmaking techniques of Sam Raimi, which are easily identified in their first film, *Blood Simple*. The "shaky-cam" technique, which Raimi used extensively in *The Evil Dead* films, appears in both *Blood Simple* and *Raising Arizona* (1987). To achieve the shaky-cam effect, an apparatus is built that attaches the camera to the center of a twelve-foot board with handles on each end. Grips then carry the board, sometimes running, to achieve the unusual effects for which the filmmakers would become known. The connection between the three filmmakers is such that Anne Billson, when reviewing *Blood Simple* (1984) referenced Raimi's rules for filmmaking: (1) the innocent must suffer; (2) the guilty must be punished; (3) you must

taste blood to be a man. She applies these three rules to the Coen film, as well, though for the Coens, she adds (4) the dead must walk.

In the period following the release of the Coens' *Blood Simple* (1984), the brothers lived with Raimi in Los Angeles while they were promoting the film. During that time, the Coens and Raimi cowrote the screenplay for *The Hudsucker Proxy* (1994), which would be released almost a decade later. While working on *Hudsucker*, which had a much larger budget and an immense production design, the Coens tapped Raimi to direct the second unit for *The Hudsucker Proxy*, due to the size of the project. He also appears in silhouette as a member of the Hudsucker Industries' creative team. Raimi appeared again in a cameo as a gunman in *Miller's Crossing* (1991).

References

Anne Billson, "Simply Bloody," in *Joel & Ethan Coen: Blood Siblings*, ed. Paul A. Woods (London: Plexus Publishing, 2003); Marc Graser, "Spooky Haunts Family Audiences," *Variety*, October 1, 2009; Mark Horowitz, "Coen Brothers A–Z: The Big Two-Headed Picture," in *Joel & Ethan Coen: Blood Siblings*, ed. Paul A. Woods (London: Plexus Publishing, 2003); "Sam Raimi," *Biography.com*; "Sam Raimi," *New York Times*, Movies & TV. See also *BLOOD SIMPLE, CRIMEWAVE, THE HUDSUCKER PROXY*, BILLY BOB THORNTON.

RAISING ARIZONA (1987)

DIRECTOR: Joel Coen and Ethan Coen (uncredited). SCREENPLAY: Ethan Coen and Joel Coen. EXECUTIVE PRODUCER: James Jacks. PRODUCERS: Ethan Coen and Joel Coen (uncredited); Deborah Reinisch (Associate Producer); Mark Silverman (Co-producer). PHOTOGRAPHY: Barry Sonnenfeld. EDITING: Michael R. Miller. MUSIC: Carter Burwell.

PRODUCTION DESIGN: Jane Musky. ART DIRECTION: Harold Thrasher. SET DECORATION: Robert Kracik. COSTUME DESIGN: Richard Hornung.

CAST: Nicolas Cage (H.I. McDunnough), Holly Hunter (Edwina "Ed" McDunnough), Trey Wilson (Nathan Arizona), John Goodman (Gale Snoats), William Forsythe (Evelle Snoats), Sam McMurray (Glen), Frances McDormand (Dot), Randall "Tex" Cobb (Leonard Smalls), M. Emmet Walsh (Machine Shop Employee), William Preston Robertson (Amazing Voice).

RUNNING TIME: 94 minutes. Color.

RELEASED THROUGH: Twentieth Century Fox Film Corporation. PREMIERE: March 6, 1987 (New York City).

DVD: 20th Century Fox Home Entertainment.

The second film by Joel and Ethan Coen, *Raising Arizona* begins with a voice-over narration by H.I. McDunnough (Nicolas Cage), as he is being processed into the county lockup in Tempe, Arizona. H.I., a repeat offender, robs convenience stores with an unloaded gun for a living and cycles through jail, parole hearings, and convenience stores, unable to "fly straight" because of the current Reagan administration, he claims. On one of his trips through the system, he slips a ring on to the finger of Edwina "Ed" (Holly Hunter), a police officer with whom he has fallen in love during his many visits to the county jail. Promising to live responsibly and earn an honest wage, H.I. marries Ed at the local VFW and takes a job at a factory putting holes in sheet metal. Ed's father gifts them a "starter home," a trailer nestled in the scrub brush of the Arizona desert. These are the salad days, H.I. claims, in which the couple enjoy a respectable and peaceful existence.

The honeymoon ends, however, when Ed discovers that she cannot bear children, a fact that renders her inconsolable. Adoption is not an option, given H.I.'s criminal record, and so, when they see on the news that Florence Arizona (Lynne Kitei), wife to unpainted furniture tycoon Nathan Arizona (Trey Wilson), has given birth to the "Arizona Quints," Harry, Barry, Larry, Garry, and Nathan Jr., Ed determines that one of those babies should be theirs. Rationalizing that the Arizonas have more than they can handle and that they're doing the right thing, H.I. and Ed strap an extension ladder to the top of their car and visit the Arizona home, where Ed sneaks in through the nursery window, returning with "the best one," Nathan Jr. The McDonnoughs welcome the new addition to their family with festive signage and stuffed animals, preserving the moment with a family picture and settling into family life.

Within twenty-four hours, however, conflict interrupts this domestic bliss in the form of brothers Gale (John Goodman) and Evelle (William Forsythe) Snoats, friends of H.I. and former inmates of the local correctional facility, who have released themselves on their own recognizance. Despite Ed's protests referencing respectability and the good of their family, Gale and Evelle avail themselves of the divan, H.I.'s beer, and the McDunnough's breakfast cereal. H.I. is torn between his duty to his family and his prison-forged bond with the fugitives, and in the night, he dreams of the Lone Biker of the Apocalypse (Randall "Tex" Cobb), a frightening, bearded, giant of a man who rides a Harley Davidson, guns, grenades, and baby shoes strapped to his leather vest and a skull tattoo emblazoned with "Mama didn't love me." H.I. fears that he has released this specter on his family but awakens to find all is well, though their houseguests remain a point of contention. With the visit of family friends Glen (Sam McMurray) and Dot (Frances McDormand), and their gaggle of

From left: Holly Hunter, Nicolas Cage, and T. J. Kuhn in *Raising Arizona* (1987)

severely misbehaving children, and with the talk of college funds, life insurance, and immunizations, H.I. begins to feel the pressure of responsibility weighing on him after a mere twenty-four hours of parenthood and longs for his former, carefree life.

When approached by Gale and Evelle with a plan to rob the Farmers and Mechanics Bank of LaGrange, H.I. consents and writes a good-bye letter to Ed, explaining that he is not the kind of man who can be a responsible husband and father and that by leaving Ed and Junior, he hopes to spare them from the menace he feels approaching, the ever-nearer Lone Biker. Before they can depart on their criminal endeavor, however, Glen arrives at the McDunnough household, announcing that he knows that the baby is the missing Nathan Jr., and H.I. has one day to prepare Ed for the news that Glen and Dot will be adding the baby to their family. Gale and Evelle overhear the discussion, and realizing the toddler is worth $25,000 in reward money, tie H.I. to a chair and take the child.

The presence of Nathan Jr., however, does not deter the fugitives from their plan to rob the bank, and though the heist is successful, in the ensuing chaos the baby is left behind, sitting contentedly in his car seat in the middle of the highway.

The parties converge in LaGrange: H.I. and Ed, searching for the missing baby; Gale and Evelle, returning for the lost toddler; and the Lone Biker Leonard Smalls, tracking Gale and Evelle, Nathan Jr., and H.I. and Ed. Smalls reaches the baby first, placing the car seat and child on the front of his motorcycle and tossing a grenade into the McDunnough's car. Ed recovers Nathan Jr., and H.I. and Smalls battle one another, a contest that ends with H.I. pulling the pin on a grenade and Smalls exploding in a shower of leather and baby shoes. H.I. and Ed return the child to the Arizona home, where Nathan Sr. discovers them, but upon hearing their story, he sends them on their way without calling the authorities. In the film's final sequence, H.I. dreams again, this time of

Gale and Evelle, who return to prison; the reunited Arizona family; Glen; Nathan Jr. as a teen; and an old couple surrounded by their children and grandchildren, in a land where "all parents are strong and wise and capable, and all children are happy and beloved," perhaps Utah.

Following the relative success of *Blood Simple*, Joel and Ethan Coen set up shop in a New York office and planned their second film, one that they intended to be completely different from their first, with a lighter sense of humor and a faster pace. The brothers wanted to write a character for Holly Hunter, whom they knew previously and had hoped to cast as Abby in *Blood Simple* (1984), the part played instead by Frances McDormand when Hunter was unavailable. The character of Ed began for the writers with an image, that of Hunter in uniform, "hurling orders at the prisoners," and that snapshot set the script in motion for them. The characters were the focus for this project, rather than the plot, which came as the characters developed. As they combined Hunter's character, the image of her in uniform barking orders at prisoners, and the goal of a quicker pace for this film, they developed a story based on characters who "rebound, and collide, and simply their speed of movement. We tried to refine the spirit of animation you find in pinball machines," recalls Ethan Coen. To this, they added the baby. In an interview with David Edelstein for *American Film*, Joel explains this choice: "a baby's face is movie fodder. You just wanna take elements that are good fodder and do something different with them." Placing the baby in imminent danger at regular intervals, on the front of a motorcycle, on the center stripe of a highway, in the midst of a bank robbery, they worked this "fodder" into a script that included kidnapping, a prison break-out, high-speed chases, and the Lone Biker of the Apocalypse.

While the film centers on Ed's desire to have a child, the brothers weren't particularly concerned with issues of infertility or parenting; as Joel Coen notes, "This movie is about parenting and neither of us is a parent. But we're not really intimately acquainted with murder, either, and we made a movie about killing people." Barry Sonnenfeld, friend of the Coens and cinematographer on their first three films, claims that "topics are incredibly unimportant to them—it's structure and style and words. If you ask them for their priorities, they'll tell you script, editing, coverage, and lighting."

With the pieces of the film falling in place, the brothers worked in allusions to films and literature that influenced the project, including authors John Steinbeck, William Faulkner, and Flannery O'Connor, and films such as *Bringing Up Baby* (1938), *Bonnie and Clyde* (1967), *Fellini's Roma* (1972), and *Mad Max 2: The Road Warrior* (1981). The filmmakers thought of Gale and Evelle Snoats as a sort of Laurel and Hardy, Joel has noted, and reviewers regularly noted the similarity of the film itself to the Road Runner cartoons, as the action of the picture certainly mimics the antics of Wile E. Coyote and his prey. While the Coens' first film seemed to fit nicely into the genre of thriller or film noir, Joel Coen suggests that *Raising Arizona* "seems more absurd, an amalgam of genres."

While Hunter's character was written specifically for her, the filmmakers turned to auditions to round out the rest of the cast. They initially offered the part of H.I. to Kevin Costner, who turned it down, but when Nicolas Cage read the script, he was most enthusiastic about the role. The Coens were uncertain that Cage was right for the part, as he had traditionally played more urban characters in such films as *Fast Times at Ridgemont High* (1982), *Valley Girl* (1983), and *The Cotton Club* (1984), but Cage convinced them to let him test for the part, and ultimately he was cast. On the set, Cage was interested in contributing his own ideas to the character, but the Coens, who meticulously complete their scripts and create detailed storyboards from which to shoot, were less interested in altering their ideas for the character. Edelstein, who visited the set of *Raising Arizona*, characterized the relationship between the actor and the filmmakers as "bumpy but respectful," though the Coens spoke only positively about Cage's performance. The quintuplets were cast during an open casting call in Scottsdale, Arizona, in which more than 400 toddlers were considered. The Coens selected fifteen babies to rotate through the kidnapping scene where H.I. removes all five babies from their crib and they escape, one by one. The fifteen selected were chosen because they didn't cry when their mothers left them, and during filming, some of the toddlers took their first steps on the set, at which point they were fired from the film. Though they had planned to cast twins for the part of Nathan Jr., TJ Kuhn Jr. appeared in the entire film. James Jacks, executive producer for the film, commented "TJ just did what he was supposed to do. He appeared to be smarter than any adult in the movie."

Jacks's comment perhaps refers to the working relationship between Randall "Tex" Cobb and the filmmakers. Cobb's character, Leonard Smalls, is so named as a reference to John Steinbeck's Lennie Small, from *Of Mice and Men*, and doubles as the Lone Biker of the Apocalypse in H.I.'s dream. The Coens imagined the menacing biker as H.I.'s perception of "The Evil One," come to avenge the kidnapping of Nathan Jr. and punish H.I. for his crime. Joel explains, "Being from the Southwest, he'd see him in the form of a Hell's Angel." Cobb, a former boxing champion who made his name brawling on Texas streets,

was described by Joel Coen as "less an actor than a force of nature. Not really someone it's easy to work with." Physically, Cobb looked the part, a large man with an unruly beard and hair, but he was unable to effectively ride the motorcycle and didn't take direction well: his lack of biking experience caused him to miss his mark regularly, resulting in added takes, and he fell off the motorcycle in one take and skidded along the ground. Joel has rather diplomatically stated that Cobb "posed problems," and the Coens commented that they didn't intend to cast Cobb again anytime soon. The remaining characters were cast without event, and John Goodman, in particular, earned praise for his first role in a Coen film and would play much more substantive parts in both *Barton Fink* (1991) and *The Big Lebowski* (1998).

While *Blood Simple* was made with $1.5 million raised by private investors, the budget for their second film was $6 million. Circle Films, headed by Ben Barenholtz, had distributed the Coens' first film and subsequently signed the brothers to an additional three-picture contract, of which *Raising Arizona* was the first. Circle contributed $3 million to the project, and 20th Century Fox provided the balance in return for distribution rights. Again, the filmmakers exercised complete control over the project, with no input from the studios. The film was shot on set at Carefree Studios in Greater Phoenix and on location in the Phoenix area. Joel and Ethan Coen and cinematographer Barry Sonnenfeld spent ten weeks testing locations in the area, having learned during the filming of *Blood Simple* that a location may appear to be conducive to filming, while in reality, it may not be so. Following the location scouting, the storyboards were prepared, and J. Todd Anderson began working with the brothers as their storyboard artist, a partnership they would maintain in future films. The three would create detailed storyboards of the shots, often frame by frame, with which they would plan and execute the on-set shooting; this approach resulted in economy of both time and money, as there was no need for alterations during the shooting day.

Technically, *Raising Arizona* is known for its fast-forward tracking shots, which were again achieved by using the shaky-cam, a technique they used in *Blood Simple*. The shaky-cam apparatus is built by attaching the camera to the center of a twelve-foot board with handles on each end. Grips then carry the board through streets, up ladders and into the nursery window, most memorably, achieving the unusual effects for which the filmmakers would become known. The brothers were intent on creating an unusual experience for the viewer, as Barry Sonnenfeld, in *Film Comment*, recalls, "Every time I put on a lens, Joel and Ethan would ask, 'Does it look wacky enough?'"

The choice to make the film look "wacky" was met with both praise and derision. Vincent Canby, writing for the *New York Times*, characterized the film as "mostly a film-school affectation," that is full of "technical expertise but has no life of its own," concluding that "the direction is without decisive style." Dave Kehr of the *Chicago Tribune* concurs, adding that the Coens "use a half-dozen separate shots where a more assured filmmaker would cover the action in one," resulting in a picture that appears to have been directed "by an amphetamine-crazed Orson Welles," and is "consistently smug, snide and show-offy." Sheila Benson of the *Los Angeles Times*, however, deemed the cinematography "miraculously adept technically," and David Edelstein found those same techniques resulted in a film that was "galloping instead of languorous, sunny instead of lurid, genial and upbeat instead of murder-

ous and cynical," which was precisely the effect the brothers sought to achieve.

The characters themselves garnered much comment from reviewers, as Benson charged that the filmmakers "don't cherish the McDonnoughs as fellow human beings—they manipulate them like cartoon figures and it's hard to cherish a cartoon," and Roger Ebert claimed that the film "cannot decide if it is about real people, or comic exaggerations." Benson further claimed that the film is "swathed in a caul of superiority toward its characters, just plain folk," a claim that writers would often make about characters in subsequent Coen films, and during production, the script was leaked to a Tempe newspaper, which expressed outrage at the way in which the locals were portrayed in the film. Ethan Coen responded that as they wrote the characters, their approach to them was deliberately inaccurate, implying that they indeed were comic exaggerations, as Ebert claimed, and Joel Coen has further noted that the characters were supposed to be sympathetic. Critics were surprised by the film's conclusion, which some deemed to be overly sentimental and uncharacteristic in light of the bleakness of *Blood Simple*. The brothers explain, however, that H.I.'s warm, glowing dream and voice-over description of a future in which he and Ed welcome their children and grandchildren to their home does not reflect the Coens' attitude toward life, but that of H.I.: "It fits with his ideas about life, what he dreams of accomplishing in the future."

In *Raising Arizona*, viewers began to see emerging patterns in the filmmakers' style, which included clever dialogue and camera use, frequent allusions to cinema and literature, and characters whose ineptitude would be their defining characteristic. The film earned over $29 million worldwide, and this success would allow the Coens to move on to a larger project, their

Dashiell Hammett-inspired gangster film, *Miller's Crossing* (1991).

References

Sheila Benson, "2 Unlikely Love Affairs: *Raising Arizona*: Farcing around with Parenthood," *Los Angeles Times*, March 20, 1987; Vincent Canby, "Film: *Raising Arizona*, Coen Brothers Comedy," *New York Times*, March 11, 1987; Michel Ciment and Hubert Niogret, "Interview with Joel and Ethan Coen," in *The Coen Brothers: Interviews*, ed. William Rodney Allen (Jackson: University Press of Mississippi, 2006); Roger Ebert, "*Raising Arizona*," *RogerEbert.com*, March 20, 1987; David Edelstein, "Invasion of the Baby Snatchers," in *The Coen Brothers: Interviews*, ed. William Rodney Allen (Jackson: University Press of Mississippi, 2006); Steve Jenkins, "*Raising Arizona*," in *Joel & Ethan Coen: Blood Siblings*, ed. Paul A. Woods (London: Plexus Publishing, 2003); Dave Kehr, "Furious Pace of *Raising Arizona* Leads Nowhere," *Chicago Tribune*, March 20, 1987; Ian Nathan, *Ethan and Joel Coen* (Paris: Cahiers du cinema Sarl, 2012); Eddie Robson, *Coen Brothers* (London: Virgin Books, 2003). See also CARTER BURWELL, NICOLAS CAGE, RANDALL "TEX" COBB, JOHN GOODMAN, HOLLY HUNTER, FRANCES MCDORMAND, BARRY SONNENFELD, M. EMMET WALSH, TREY WILSON.

REID, TARA (1975–)

Born in Wyckoff, New Jersey, on November 8, 1975, Reid acted as a young child, appearing in commercials for Jell-O and McDonalds. She attended the Professional Children's School in New York City, and in 1982 she was cast in a recurring role in the CBS game show *Child's Play*; her big screen debut was a small part in *A Return to Salem's Lot* (1987). After graduating from high school, Reid moved to Los Angeles, where she appeared in *Saved by the Bell: The New Class* (1994) and was cast in a recurring role in NBC's *Days of Our Lives* (1995). She appeared as Bunny Lebowski in Joel and Ethan Coens' *The Big Lebowski* (1998), which she followed with *American Pie* (1999) and its sequels *American Pie 2* (2001) and *American Reunion* (2012). Reid has most often appeared in comedies and romantic comedies such as *My Boss's Daughter* (2003) and *Last Call* (2012), and in horror and suspense films, including *Devil's Pond* (2003), *Alone in the Dark* (2005), and *Incubus* (2006). Her later television work has included a recurring role on *Scrubs* (2003–2005) and an appearance in the made-for-television movie *Sharknado* (2013).

References

"Tara Reid," *Biography.com*. See also *THE BIG LEBOWSKI*.

ROBBINS, TIM (1958–)

Robbins was born October 16, 1958, in West Covina, California, the son of singer Gil Robbins and actress Mary Robbins, and raised in Greenwich Village, New York, where he acted as a teen with the Theatre for the New City. He attended the State University of New York at Plattsburgh and then the University of California, Los Angeles, following which he was the founding artistic director of The Actor's Gang.

His on-screen career began with a series of television roles, including appearances on *St. Elsewhere* (1982), *Hardcastle and McCormick* (1984), and *The Love Boat* (1984), prior to his debut film role in *Toy Soldiers* (1984). He had small parts in *Top Gun* (1986) and *Howard the Duck* (1986), among others, but his breakout role came as "Nuke" LaLoosh in the 1988 baseball film *Bull Durham*. On set, he met Susan Sarandon, who would be his partner for twenty-three years and with whom he has two children. Robbins was cast as the lead in Robert Altman's *The Player* (1992), for which he won a Best Actor Golden Globe and the award for Best Actor at the

Cannes Film Festival. That same year, he wrote, directed, and starred in *Bob Roberts*, a political mockumentary that parodies right-wing politics. He appeared in *The Shawshank Redemption* in 1994, and in 1995, he directed his first feature film, *Dead Man Walking*, starring Sarandon and Sean Penn, for which Robbins received an Academy Award nomination and Sarandon was awarded the Oscar for Best Actress. His follow-up directorial project was *Cradle Will Rock* (1999), starring Hank Azaria and Ruben Blades, which was nominated for the Palme d'Or at the Cannes Film Festival, and in 2001 he directed the music video "Dead Man Walking" for *Bruce Springsteen: The Complete Video Anthology 1978–2000*. He received the Best Supporting Actor Oscar for his portrayal of Dave Doyle in Clint Eastwood's *Mystic River* (2003), for which he also won a Golden Globe, and he appeared in *War of the Worlds* (2005), with Tom Cruise. His additional directorial projects include the pilot episode for *Queens Supreme* (2003), the made-for-television movie *Possible Side Effects* (2009), and two episodes of the HBO series *Treme* (2011–2012).

Robbins has been an outspoken political and social activist; at the 1993 Academy Awards, where he and Sarandon were presenters, they spoke on camera about HIV-positive Haitian refugees who were detained by the United States at Guantanamo Bay. The refugees were released as a result, but Robbins and Sarandon were banned from the Awards ceremony the following year. He supported Ralph Nader's presidential bid in 2000 and was an outspoken critic of the Bush administration, appearing on the television program *Politically Incorrect* and attending an anti–Iraq War rally in London in 2003.

In the Coen's 1994 film *The Hudsucker Proxy*, Robbins plays naive Norville Barnes, from Muncie, Indiana, come to the big city to make his fortune. Having arrived, however, he finds that there is no demand for an inexperienced young graduate of the Muncie College of Business Administration. He lands a job in the mailroom at Hudsucker Industries, only to be promoted to president of the company by the nefarious Sidney J. Mussburger, who seeks to depreciate the company's stock and blame it on Norville. The film follows the travails of Norville as he first surprises and then succumbs to the evils of late-1950s corporate culture, and, when it appears that he will die at his own hand as a victim of Mussburger's greed and ambition, Fate steps in, or rather Time, and Norville is saved. Robbins, like more and more actors at the time, was interested in the part, as "when I finished *The Player* (1992) I said what I wanted to do next was to work with the Coen brothers. It's great that it happened," he commented. The character offered more, however, than just a chance to work with the Coens: "I jumped at the chance to do a guy who isn't an evil son-of-a-bitch," he said, "a guy who had heart. And Norville's not dumb—he's just ill-equipped to get by in a fiercely competitive world." Caryn James of the *New York Times* concurred with Robbins's assessment of the character, stating "Norville is not dumb, but he sure looks that way when he glances at a quickly changing board that advertises job openings." While James characterizes Robbins's performance as having "a goofy appeal," John Harkness, writing for *Sight and Sound* deems Robbins as having been miscast, and finds the actor too tall, and not "lovable" enough to play the naif Norville, instead describing the performance as "broad mugging."

References

Patt Diroll, "Social Activism," *Los Angeles Times*, June 17, 2001; John Harkness, "The Sphinx without a Riddle," in *Joel & Ethan Coen: Blood*

Siblings, ed. Paul A. Woods (London: Plexus Publishing, 2003); Caryn James, "*The Hudsucker Proxy*: Reviews/Film: Sniffing Out the Truth about Instant Success," *New York Times*, March 11, 1994; "Tim Robbins," *Biography.com*; "Tim Robbins," *New York Times*, Movies & TV; Eddie Robson, *Coen Brothers* (London: Virgin Books, 2003). See also *THE HUDSUCKER PROXY*

ROOT, STEPHEN (1951–)

Born November 17, 1951, in Sarasota, Florida, Root attended the University of Florida, where he earned a degree in acting and broadcasting. Following college, he toured with the National Shakespeare Company for three years before relocating to New York City, where he debuted off-Broadway in *Journey's End* (1980). Root appeared on Broadway in *So Long on Lonely Street* (1986), and *All My Sons* (1987) and shortly thereafter began his work in film with small roles in *Crocodile Dundee II* (1988) and *Monkey Shines* (1988). In 1989 his long and frequent television career began with appearances in the made-for-television movie *Cross of Fire*, following which he appeared in such series as *Roseanne* (1990), *Star Trek: The Next Generation* (1991), *LA Law* (1990–1994), *NYPD Blue* (1994), and *Seinfeld* (1996). His best-known recurring roles include Jimmy James in *Newsradio* (1995–1999), Eddie Gauthier in *True Blood* (2008–2009), Gaston Means in *Boardwalk Empire* (2012–2013), and Judge Mike Reardon in *Justified* (2010–2014). Root has lent his voice to such television and film projects as *Buzz Lightyear of Star Command* (2000), *Ice Age* (2002), *Finding Nemo* (2003), *King of the Hill* (1997–2010), and *Rango* (2011).

An accomplished character actor, he has appeared in such films as *Ghost* (1990), *Office Space* (1999), *Dodgeball: A True Underdog Story* (2004), the George Clooney–directed film *Leatherheads* (2008), Clint Eastwood's *J. Edgar* (2011), and *The Lone Ranger* (2013). He has appeared in three Coen films: *O Brother, Where Art Thou?* (2000), *The Ladykillers* (2004), and *No Country for Old Men* (2007).

As the blind radio station manager in *O Brother*, Root appears only twice in the film, first as the Soggy Bottom Boys record "Man of Constant Sorrow," and then when he learns that the song he recorded for them has become a hit. In *The Ladykillers*, Root plays Fernand Gudge, manager of the riverboat casino the *Bandit Queen* and employer of Gawain MacSam (Marlon Wayans), a racist who is not above taking bribes. In another brief appearance, Root appears as the administrative representative of the Mexican drug trade, hiring Carson Wells (Woody Harrelson) to track down the dangerously elusive Anton Chigurh (Javier Bardem). See also *THE LADYKILLERS, NO COUNTRY FOR OLD MEN, O BROTHER, WHERE ART THOU?*

Reference

"Stephen Root," *New York Times*, Movies & TV.

RUDRÜD, KRISTIN (1955–)

Born May, 23, 1955, in Fargo, North Dakota, Rudrüd participated in theatre in high school. She attended college at Morehead State University, earning a bachelor of arts degree in Theatre, following which she studied acting at the London Academy of Music and Dramatic Art, where she appeared on stage in *The Merchant of Venice* and *The Misanthrope*. She relocated to New York, where she appeared in the Broadway production of *Amadeus* (1980) with Ian McKellen and with Al Pacino in a public theater reading of *Othello*, as well as off-Broadway in *A Midsummer Night's Dream* (1981). She left performing and returned to Fargo, where she learned that Joel and Ethan Coen were casting for a film. She was cast as Jean Lundegaard in the Oscar-winning *Fargo* (1996), following which she appeared in *Pleasantville* (1998), *Drop Dead Gorgeous* (1999), and *Herman U.S.A.* (2001). Her television work includes *Chicago Hope* (1997), and she helped to found the Fargo Film Festival.

As *Fargo*'s Jean Lundegaard, Rudrüd has little screen time; her character is kidnapped near the beginning of the film, a scene in which Jean valiantly—though comically—attempts to evade the intruders. She appears again briefly when the kidnappers bring her to their lake house hideaway, where she again seeks to escape in an equally comic scene. She then spends the rest of the film tied to a chair with a bag over her head. Though her role is minor, John Simon of *National Review* describes her performance as "a perfect cameo: simperingly unbearable in domesticity, she becomes heartbreakingly poignant in danger."

References

"Kristin Rudrüd," *BroadwayWorld.com*; "Kristin Rudrüd," *A Prairie Home Companion: With Garrison Keillor*, Special Guests, December 8, 2001; John Simon, "Forgo *Fargo*," *National Review*, April 22, 1996. See also *FARGO*.

S

A SERIOUS MAN (2009)

DIRECTOR: Ethan Coen and Joel Coen. SCREENPLAY: Joel Coen and Ethan Coen. EXECUTIVE PRODUCERS: Tim Bevan, Eric Fellner, and Robert Graf. PRODUCERS: Ethan Coen and Joel Coen. PHOTOGRAPHY: Roger Deakins. EDITING: Ethan Coen and Joel Coen (as Roderick Jaynes). MUSIC: Carter Burwell. PRODUCTION DESIGN: Jess Gonchor. SET DECORATION: Nancy Haigh. COSTUME DESIGN: Mary Zophres.

CAST: Michael Stuhlbarg (Larry Gopnik), Richard Kind (Uncle Arthur), Fred Melamed (Sy Ableman), Sari Lennick (Judith Gopnik), Aaron Wolff (Danny Gopnik), Jessica McManus (Sarah Gopnik), Peter Breitmayer (Mr. Brandt), David Kang (Clive Park), Ari Hoptman (Arlen Finkle), Alan Mandell (Rabbi Marshak), Amy Landecker (Mrs. Samsky), George Wyner (Rabbi Nachtner), Michael Tezla (Dr. Sussman), Katherine Borowitz (Friend at Picnic), Steve Park (Clive's Father), Allen Lewis Rickman (Shtetl Husband), Yelena Shmulenson (Shtetl Wife), Fyvush Finkel (Reb Groshkover), Simon Helberg (Rabbi Scott), Adam Arkin (Divorce Lawyer), Michael Lerner (Solomon Schlutz).

RUNNING TIME: 106 minutes. Color.

RELEASED THROUGH: Focus Features. PREMIERE: September 12, 2009 (Toronto Film Festival).

DVD: Universal Studios Home Entertainment.

ACADEMY AWARDS: Best Motion Picture of the Year (nominated: Joel and Ethan Coen); Best Writing—Original Screenplay (nominated: Joel Coen and Ethan Coen).

The fourteenth feature film by Joel and Ethan Coen, *A Serious Man* begins with a quote from the Jewish sage Rashi: "Receive with simplicity everything that happens." The film's prologue is set in nineteenth-century Poland, where Velvel (Allen Lewis Rickman) returns home to his wife with a story: on his journey, his wagon lost a wheel, and he was assisted by a man, Reb Groshkover (Fyvush Finkel), whom he has invited to the house for soup. His wife Dora (Yelena Smulenson) is horrified, convinced that God has cursed them, as Reb Groshkover has been dead for three years. Reb Groshkover arrives, however, appearing very much alive. When he will eat no soup, Dora is convinced he is a dybbuk, the soul of a dead person that inhabits a living person, and stabs him with an ice pick to prove she is correct. Groshkover initially only laughs, but as he turns to go, he bleeds through his shirt, where the ice pick remains.

The film then transitions to the primary narrative, in which Larry Gopnik (Michael Stuhlbarg), a professor of

Michael Stuhlbarg in *A Serious Man* (2009)

physics, lives in a very typical house in a typical suburban neighborhood with his wife, Judy (Sari Lennick), and their two children, Sarah (Jessica McManus) and Danny (Aaron Wolff). Danny attends Hebrew school in the afternoons, where he listens to his transistor radio rather than the teacher, and Sarah spends her spare time washing her hair and hanging out at The Hole with her friends. Larry's life appears to be very normal: his recent physical exam demonstrates that he is in good health. At work he is in the process of tenure review and teaches such principles as Schrodinger's paradox and Heisenberg's uncertainty principle. At home, domestic drama abounds within acceptable boundaries, as his children complain about the television reception, Danny is preparing for his bar mitzvah, and his brother Arthur (Richard Kind) sleeps on the couch and commandeers the bathroom, where he drains his sebaceous cyst. This normalcy is shattered, however, when Larry's wife announces that she wants a ritual divorce, a get, as she plans to marry Sy Ableman (Fred Melamed); his Korean student, Clive (David Kang), leaves an envelope of money on Larry's desk, presumably a bribe to change a failing test grade, and when Larry attempts to return it, Clive denies it is his; the chair of the tenure committee drops by Larry's office to inform him that the committee has been receiving letters of complaint suggesting moral turpitude on Larry's part; and his neighbor, Mr. Brandt, has begun mowing part of Larry's lawn and is thus claiming it as his own.

Larry begins sleeping on a cot in the den and, at the suggestion of Sy Ableman, moves to the Jolly Roger Hotel, where he and Arthur share a room. He retains a divorce lawyer (Adam Arkin), whom he also consults about the disputed property line, and makes an appointment to see the junior rabbi, Rabbi Scott (Simon Helberg), who suggests that he look at life with a new perspective, to see God in the situation. Adding to Larry's stress, a representative of Columbia Records Club calls his office daily, insisting that he owes four months of payments, and he is visited at his home by Clive's father (Steve Park), who threatens to sue because Larry kept the envelope of money. While driving from the Jolly Roger to the college one day, Larry is in a car accident, and he later learns that Sy Ableman was in an accident at the same time; Sy, however, dies, and Judy asserts that Larry should pay for Sy's funeral.

Visiting the second rabbi, Rabbi Nachtner (George Wyner), Larry inquires as to the meaning of the double car crashes. Is Larry Sy? Is this a sign? In response, the rabbi tells him the story of Dr. Sussman and the Goy's teeth, in which the dentist finds mysterious Hebrew letters that read "help me" etched into the back of a patient's teeth and wonders himself, what does this sign mean? The rabbi tells Sussman, as he tells Larry, that the answer is unknown, that we can't know everything; perhaps the answer is to help others. Following Sy's funeral, the police arrive at Larry's house to issue a warning to Arthur, who has been participating in illegal gambling. Compounding his tribulations, Larry discovers that Judy has cleaned out his bank account in preparation for the divorce. In an act of neighborly generosity, he offers the attractive Mrs. Samsky (Amy Landecker) his assistance, as her husband travels, and Larry is trying to "help others," as the rabbi encouraged. After he and Mrs. Samsky smoke marijuana together, he returns to his home to find that the police have Arthur in handcuffs, picked up on charges of solicitation and sodomy.

In a visit with his lawyer, Larry learns that his property line dispute may be decided in his favor, only to watch the lawyer tasked with the issue die of a heart attack in the conference room. The chair of the tenure committee visits Larry's office to inform him that the committee has received more letters of complaint. In an attempt to gain some wisdom and perspective on his situation, he visits a third rabbi, Marshak (Alan Mandell). He explains his situation to the rabbi's secretary, who informs him that the rabbi is busy thinking. At his son's bar mitzvah, there is a moment during which Larry and the gathered crowd fear that Danny will be unable to complete the required reading of the Torah, as he has been smoking marijuana in the bathroom prior to the event. The trajectory of Larry's life changes there in the synagogue, as Danny successfully reads the text, Judy apologizes for their marital problems, and he learns that he has been approved for tenure. The reasons for celebration are short-lived, however, as he receives a $3,000 bill from the lawyer he has retained on behalf of Arthur, and to pay the attorney's fees, he must use the cash from Clive's envelope and change the failing grade, which he does. He then receives a call from his doctor, asking him to come to the office right away, as they need to discuss the results of his X-rays. As the film closes, a tornado is bearing down on the Hebrew school, where his son Danny is in class.

Following the release of a film that so directly addresses the Jewish experience, the Coens anticipated that the community would respond negatively, much as some natives of the Minneapolis area were outraged by *Fargo* (1994) and Arizonans took umbrage with *Raising Arizona* (1987). Ethan Coen comments, "Whenever you're specific with ethnicity or religion, people find reason to take offence," though the filmmakers assert that they create characters who represent individuals, rather than entire ethnicities or regions. As if on cue, the *Boston Globe* wrote, "The brothers toy with the fire of ethnic stereotypes in ways that at times seem calculated to offend," but the Jewish community itself viewed the film positively, for the most part. Michael Fox, of *American Jewish News* suggested the movie be "required viewing for all

American Jews above the age of, well, 17," referencing the film's R rating, and Jesse Tisch, of *InterFaithFamily.com* deemed it "a superb movie, a clever, cerebral, darkly comic fable that contains an entire Jewish world—a world that enfolds you like a good novel." Joel Coen says, "Part of the pleasure of making a movie, of actually putting the movie together, is creating a world that's specific to the movie," and the Coens assert that the world is largely fictional, though informed by their upbringing.

Because *A Serious Man* takes place in the Midwest and focuses on the lives of a Jewish family in the late 1960s, many reviewers theorized it was somewhat autobiographical. The action is set in 1967, the year that Joel Coen turned thirteen and had his own bar mitzvah, and a rumor circulated that the character of Larry was based on Joel and Ethan's father, Ed, who was a professor of economics at the University of Minnesota. The brothers were quick to respond that Larry was a fictional character, for which their father was not the model, though they did note that, like Sarah, their sister Debbie did spend much of her adolescence in the bathroom, washing her hair. They describe the film as "reminiscent" of their childhood, having been "filmed in the context [of] our own youth in St. Louis Park, but with a made-up story." Joel and Ethan had long considered writing a film focusing on a character similar to Danny, Joel says: "Years ago we considered making a short subject about a bar mitzvah boy who goes to see an ancient rabbi." Ethan adds, "The rabbi was loosely based on a sagelike figure we'd seen as kids, a Semitic Wizard of Oz. He never spoke, but he had great charisma," a model for the film's third rabbi. To the disappointment of reviewers, then, *A Serious Man* was intended to be "a very affectionate look at the community and is a movie that will show aspects of Judaism which are not usually seen," rather

than an exposé of the Coen household in the late 1960s.

A Serious Man was cast with unknown actors, a choice that placed the focus of the picture on the characters and their misadventures, rather than on high-profile actors like George Clooney, Brad Pitt, and John Malkovich in *Burn After Reading* (2008). Michael Stuhlbarg, an actor with few film credits but experience on the stage, was cast in the primary role. The Coens state that they "were determined to use as many local Jews as we could instead of resorting to the usual Hollywood ethnic type," a choice they had not made in previous films, having cast John Turturro as a Jew in *Barton Fink* (1991). Roger Deakins returned to work with the brothers for this project, having been otherwise committed when they made *Burn After Reading*, and they called upon Carter Burwell for the film's music, which uses a combination of Judaic harmonics, Yiddish songs, Jimi Hendrix, and Jefferson Airplane. Stylistically, A. O. Scott of the *New York Times* described the film as having been written and structured as a farce, while it was shot, scored, and edited as a horror movie, and though the *New Yorker*'s David Denby wrote a scathing review of the film, he found it "fascinating" as a "piece of moviemaking craft." Though these technical aspects of the film garnered some discussion, as is common for Coen pictures, the primary focus of reviewers was on the central character's search for answers and the Jewish community in which it is situated.

The prologue of the film, which squarely positions the action within that Jewish world, historically and religiously, raises questions for the viewer: are the Polish Jews to be seen as ancestors of Larry Gopnik? Are they representative of Jewish people in some larger way? Joel Coen explains that the purpose of the prologue is that it "tells you upfront. This is a story about a Jewish community and Jews," not just "a story about the Midwest," or "'a piece of Americana' in 1967." Ethan adds, "It's a cliché, but when you see them in the long black coats and the sidelocks, that's putting your face in it. And we thought that was a good thing." The brothers add that the prologue further serves to situate the narrative within the context of storytelling, to say "Here's another folk tale, here's another Jewish story." The film, then can be read as "part of the whole Yiddishkeit, part of the whole Jew storytelling thing." The prologue's tale, invented by the Coens, is open-ended, leaving the viewer to decide if Reb Groshkover is indeed a dybbuk, a choice one writer found "discomfiting." Joel Coen was pleased: "The 'discomfiting' thing is nice to hear . . . that means the opening was doing its job." He adds, "We just thought a Yiddish ghost tale would be a good ambassador for what comes after."

The theme of storytelling is repeated throughout the film, most notably in the story of "The Goy's Teeth," a tale imbedded into the narrative and told by Rabbi Nachtner (George Wyner), as well as in the comparisons of the film to the Book of Job, which operates on a larger level as the structure of the film. Both stories foreground the questions of the picture, queries that Larry asks throughout: "Why is this happening to me?" "Why does he (Hashem, God) make us feel the questions, if he's not going to give us the answers?" Like the dentist, Dr. Sussman (Michael Tezla), Larry is consumed by his search for meaning and remains unable to understand the circumstances in which he finds himself or to locate someone who can provide him with answers. Ethan Coen addresses Larry's ordeals from the brothers' perspective, saying, "the fun was inventing new ways to torment Larry," though the film's credits claim that "No Jews were harmed in the making of this motion picture." Reviewers found Larry's persecutions familiar, likening him to another Coen protagonist, Barton Fink, whom the filmmakers tormented "like a bug under a magnifying glass," and critics compared him to Schrodinger's cat, a subject in an experiment conducted by Joel and Ethan Coen, from which the viewer is not certain he will survive. Jesse Tisch concludes, "The vital question, the filmmakers seem to be suggesting, is *vat* to do when life falls apart, not *vhy* it's fallen apart."

A Serious Man was made on budget of $7 million and grossed $31 million worldwide. It was nominated for two Oscars—Best Picture and Best Original Screenplay—and Michael Stuhlbarg earned a Golden Globe nomination for his performance. The general opinion about the Coens was that they were continuing the trajectory set by their Oscar-winning *No Country for Old Men*, as Kenneth Turan characterized this film as "one of the ones that count . . . a work of cruel comic genius," and the *Guardian* declared the brothers "America's pre-eminent film-makers" of the decade. It was, as Todd McCarthy of *Variety* said, "the kind of picture you get to make after you've won an Oscar."

References

Peter Bradshaw, "*A Serious Man*," *Guardian*, November 19, 2009; Ty Burr, "*A Serious Man*," *Boston Globe*, October 9, 2009; "The Coen Brothers Discuss *A Serious Man*," *TimeOutLondon.com*; David Denby, "Gods and Victims," *New Yorker*, October 5, 2009; Bilge Elbiri, "*A Serious Man*'s Fred Melamed," *Vulture.com*; Michael Fox, "Review: *A Serious Man* Unspools Funny and Foreboding Bubbe Meises," *American Jewish World*, September 30, 2009; Neal Karlen, "For Jews in St. Louis Park, Minn., *A Serious Man* Is a Homecoming," *Washington Post*, October 11, 2009; Liel Libovitz, "Taking It Seriously," *TabletMag.com*, October 2, 2009; Franz Lidz, "Biblical Adversity in a 60s Suburb," *New*

York Times, September 23, 2009; Todd McCarthy, "Review: A Serious Man," Variety, October 1, 2009; Ian Nathan, Ethan and Joel Coen (Paris: Cahiers du cinema Sarl, 2012); Andrew O'Hehir, "Goys, God, Dentistry and A Serious Man," Salon.com, October 1, 2009; Naomi Pfefferman, "Get Serious: The Coen Brothers," JewishJournal.com, September 2, 2009; A. O. Scott, "Calls to God: Always a Busy Signal," New York Times, October 1, 2009; Jesse Tisch, "A Different View of Movie Jews: A Serious Man," InterFaithFamily.com, November 18, 2009; Kenneth Turan, Movie Review: A Serious Man," Los Angeles Times, October 2, 2009. See also CARTER BURWELL, ROGER DEAKINS, JESS GONCHOR, NANCY HAIGH, RICHARD KIND, SARI LENNICK, MICHAEL LERNER, FRED MELAMED, MICHAEL STUHLBARG, MARY ZOPHRES.

SHALHOUB, TONY (1953–)

Born October 9, 1953, in Green Bay, Wisconsin, Shalhoub began his acting career at age six as an extra in his sister's high school production of The King and I. He attended the University of Southern Maine and Yale University's School of Drama, following which he worked with the American Repertory Theater in Cambridge, Massachusetts, for four seasons. He then relocated to New York, where he appeared on Broadway in productions of The Odd Couple (1985), and The Heidi Chronicles (1989) and received a Tony nomination for his role in Conversations with My Father (1992). His work on television began with appearances on The Equalizer (1986), Spenser: For Hire (1987), The X Files (1995), and Frasier (1996); his first major recurring role was as Antonio Scarpacci on the television series Wings (1991–1997), a role that he played for six seasons.

Though he appeared in small roles in films such as Longtime Companion (1989), Searching for Bobby Fischer (1993), and Addams Family Values (1993), it was not until 1996 that Shalhoub was cast in a lead role in Big Night (1996) by Stanley Tucci, with whom he had worked on Broadway. Though he has appeared frequently in films including Men in Black (1997), Primary Colors (1998), and the Spy Kids films (2001, 2002, 2003), he is perhaps best known for playing the title role in the USA Network's hit television show Monk (2002–2009), for which he won three Primetime Emmy Awards for Outstanding Lead Actor in a Comedy Series (2003, 2005, 2006), and one Golden Globe Award for Best Performance by an Actor in a Television Series (2003). Shalhoub returned to Broadway to appear in Lend Me a Tenor (2010), Golden Boy (2012), for which he was nominated for Best Performance by an Actor, and Act One (2014).

Shalhoub has appeared in two films by Joel and Ethan Coen: in Barton Fink (1991), as movie producer Ben Geisler, and in The Man Who Wasn't There (2001), as attorney Freddy Riedenschneider. As Geisler, Shalhoub played a slick, fast-talking movie producer who offers Barton Fink (John Turturro) platitudes and dismissive advice in rapid-fire fashion, leaving the novice screenwriter in a greater state of distress than prior to the conversation. The Man Who Wasn't There's Riedenschneider was a larger part, though no less voluble than Shalhoub's prior Coen role. The attorney is brought in to defend Doris Crane (Frances McDormand) on murder charges, a crime that the audience and her husband Ed (Billy Bob Thornton) know she did not commit. Peter Travers of Rolling Stone proclaimed, "for sheer scene-stealing bravado, nobody beats Tony Shalhoub," a sentiment seconded by Tim Robey of the Telegraph, who characterized Shalhoub's performance as one of "tremendous swagger . . . which should net him an Oscar nomination." While he did not receive the Oscar nod, the New Yorker's Anthony Lane declared that Shalhoub stole the picture as Riedenschneider.

References

Anthony Lane, "*The Man Who Wasn't There*," *New Yorker*, November 12, 2001; "Tony Shalhoub," *New York Times*, Movies & TV; Tim Robey, "The Film That Wasn't Really There," *Telegraph*, October 26, 2001; Peter Travers, "*The Man Who Wasn't There*," *Rolling Stone*, November 2, 2001. See also *BARTON FINK, THE MAN WHO WASN'T THERE*.

SIMMONS, J. K. (1955–)

Born January 9, 1955, in Detroit, Michigan, Jonathan Kimble (J. K.) Simmons attended the University of Montana, where he received a degree in music. He began acting on the stage and moved to New York in 1983, where he appeared off-Broadway in *Birds of Paradise* (1987) and on Broadway in *Peter Pan* (1991), as Captain Hook. Simmons's first film appearance was in Ted Demme's *The Ref* (1994), which he followed with small roles in the television series *New York News* (1995) and *Homicide: Life on the Street* (1996). Returning to film, he had a small part in *The First Wives Club* (1996) and more substantive roles in *The Jackal* (1997), with Bruce Willis and Richard Gere, and Gore Verbinski's *The Mexican* (2001), with Brad Pitt and Julia Roberts. Simmons had a recurring role in the television series *Law and Order* (1994–2010), as Dr. Emil Skoda, a character he also played on *New York Undercover* (1996–1998), *Law and Order: Special Victims Unit* (2000–2001), and *Law and Order: Criminal Intent* (2002). During his early *Law and Order* years, he also appeared regularly on the HBO prison drama *Oz* (1997–2003).

Simmons appeared in Sam Raimi's *For the Love of the Game* (1999) and worked again with Raimi in his adaptation of *Spider-Man* (2002) as J. J. Jameson, a role that raised his profile considerably and that he would reprise for *Spider-Man 2* (2004), and *Spider-Man 3* (2007). He then appeared in the critically acclaimed films *Juno* (2007) and *Up in the Air* (2009). He has lent his voice to a number of animated television shows, including *Justice League* (2004–2006), *The Simpsons* (2006–2007), *Kim Possible* (2007), *The Avengers: Earth's Mightiest Heroes* (2012), and *Ultimate Spider-Man* (2012–2013), among others. In 2014, he costarred in the film *Whiplash*, which premiered at the Sundance Film Festival, a performance for which he received much praise. Simmons has appeared in three Coen films: *The Ladykillers* (2004), *Burn After Reading* (2008), and *True Grit* (2010), as the voice of Lawyer J. Noble Daggett.

In *The Ladykillers*, Simmons plays Garth Pancake, safety expert for the team of thieves who conspire to tunnel their way to the counting room of the *Bandit Queen*, a riverboat casino. *Slate*'s David Edelstein describes Simmons's Garth as "the demolitions expert for whom safety comes second only to holding forth on the subject of safety," and Rex Roberts, writing for *Film Journal International*, deems him as "the funniest of the lot."

Simmons plays a smaller role of a CIA Superior in *Burn After Reading*, who, when presented with the baffling details of the film's plot, wonders aloud, "what did we learn?" He determines that they "learned not to do it again," though he is uncertain exactly what the CIA did, a conclusion that the film's reviewers extended to the film's complicated plot as a whole.

References

David Edelstein, "Thieves Like Us," *Slate*, March 26, 2004; "J. K. Simmons," *BroadwayWorld.com*; "J. K. Simmons," *New York Times*, Movies & TV; Rex Roberts, "*The Ladykillers*," *Film Journal International*. See also *BURN AFTER READING, THE LADYKILLERS*, SAM RAIMI.

SIRAGUSA, PETER

Born in Boston, Massachusetts, Siragusa attended Boston College, where he began his stage career in the college production of *Arsenic and Old Lace*. He first appeared on-screen in the made-for-television movie *Parole* (1982), and in 1990, he had a bit part in the John Hughes Christmas film *Home Alone*. Siragusa's film work includes small roles in the remake of *Miracle on 34th Street* (1994), *While You Were Sleeping* (1995), and *Dunston Checks In* (1996), but his television work is far more extensive, including a recurring role in *Night Stand* (1995), appearances on *Frasier* (1995), *Walker, Texas Ranger* (2001), *NYPD Blue* (2004), and HBO's *Entourage* (2009), among others, and roles in numerous made-for-television movies. His voice work includes *Dinosaur* (2000), *Home on the Range* (2004), *Cloudy with a Chance of Meatballs* (2009), and *Cloudy with a Chance of Meatballs 2* (2013). In addition to his screen work, Siragusa maintained an active role in a number of Chicago theatres: Drury Lane Theatre, the Goodman Theatre, and Court Theatre. He has appeared in over three thousand performances of *Shear Madness*, a murder-mystery, in Boston, Philadelphia, and Chicago, and has performed at the Pasadena Playhouse in California.

Siragusa appeared in small roles in three films by Joel and Ethan Coen: *The Hudsucker Proxy* (1994), as a newsreel reporter; *The Big Lebowski* (1998), as Gary the bartender; and in *The Man Who Wasn't There* (2001), again as a bartender.

References

Clifford Terry, "Bottom's Up: Peter Siragusa Is Ready to Tackle Shakespeare," *Chicago Tribune*, Arts and Entertainment, March 17, 1991. See also THE BIG LEBOWSKI, THE HUDSUCKER PROXY, THE MAN WHO WASN'T THERE.

SONNENFELD, BARRY (1953–)

Born April 1, 1953, in New York City, Sonnenfeld met Joel Coen while they were both attending film school at NYU. Like the Coens, he had saved up to buy his own Super 8 camera, with which he shot industrial films, documentaries, and two pornographic movies. He was first credited as cinematographer on the Oscar-nominated documentary film *In Our Water* (1982), which he followed with the made-for-television movie *How to Be a Perfect Person in Just Three Days* (1983). He was then recruited by Joel Coen to film the two-minute trailer for *Blood Simple* (1984), which Joel would then shop around the Minneapolis suburbs where he and Ethan were raised, raising funds to make the film. Sonnenfeld served as director of photography for Penny Marshall's *Big* (1988), *When Harry Met Sally,* (1989), and *Misery* (1990), as well as the first three Coen films, *Blood Simple, Raising Arizona* (1987), and *Miller's Crossing* (1990), before moving on to directing. He directed *The Addams Family* (1991), *Get Shorty* (1995), *Men in Black* (1997), and its sequels *Men in Black II* (2002) and *Men in Black 3* (2012), among others. In 1995, he began producing as well, and has served as executive producer for the television series *Fantasy Island* (1998–1999), *Secret Agent Man* (2000), *The Tick* (2001–2002), and HBO's *Pushing Daisies* (2007–2009), for which he won a Primetime Emmy. He was credited as producer on the Coens' *The Ladykillers*, and he appeared as an extra in *Blood Simple* (Marty's vomiting voice), in *Barton Fink* (page calling for Barton Fink), and in several of his own films, including *Get Shorty* and all three *Men in Black* films.

References

"Barry Sonnenfeld," *New York Times*, Movies & TV; Ian Nathan, *Ethan and Joel Coen* (Paris: Cahiers du cinema Sarl, 2012). See also BLOOD SIMPLE, THE LADYKILLERS, MILLER'S CROSSING, RAISING ARIZONA.

STARR, MIKE (1950–)

Born July 29, 1950, in Queens, New York, Starr studied drama on a scholarship at Hofstra University. His early film work included small roles in *Squeeze Play* (1979) and *Cruising* (1980), following which he appeared in *The Natural* (1984), *The Money Pit* (1986), and *Lean on Me* (1989). Standing over six feet in height, Starr has often played cops and tough guys, appearing in gangster films such as Martin Scorsese's *Goodfellas* and the Coens' *Miller's Crossing*, both in 1990. He was cast in John Turturro's directorial debut, *Mac* (1992), worked again with the Coens in *The Hudsucker Proxy* (1994), and has twice worked with director Spike Lee, in *Clockers* (1995) and *Summer of Sam* (1999). Best known for his work in *Mad Dog and Glory* (1993) and *Ed Wood* (1994), his television work includes recurring roles on *Hardball* (1994), *EZ Streets* (1996–1997), *Ed* (2000–2002), and *Chicago Fire* (2013). He has appeared in two daytime soap operas, *Days of Our Lives* (2010) and *The Young and the Restless* (2011–2012).

As Johnny Caspar's (Jon Polito) henchman Frankie in *Miller's Crossing*, Starr spends much of the film threatening and intimidating members of the mob, though when the opportunity presents itself to bring physical harm to rival gangster Tom Reagan (Gabriel Byrne), Frankie retreats in pain and brings in reinforcements, a comedic moment, given Starr's size. His appearance in the Coens' *The Hudsucker Proxy* was limited to only one scene, as a newspaperman.

References

"Mike Starr," *New York Times*, Movies & TV. See also THE HUDSUCKER PROXY, MILLER'S CROSSING.

STEINFELD, HAILEE (1996–)

After an exhaustive search in which fifteen thousand actresses auditioned for the part of Mattie Ross in the Coens' 2010 adaptation of *True Grit*, Hailee Steinfeld was cast in the part. Ellen Chenoweth, casting director for the film, began her search in the South, intending to cast an actress from the region of the country in which the film is set. Steinfeld, however, born December 11, 1996, is from Thousand Oaks, California, and was thirteen when the film was made. Prior to her role as Mattie, Steinfeld's on-screen work was limited to bit parts in the television shows *Back to You* (2007) and *Sons of Tucson* (2010), the title role in the short film *Heather: A Fairy Tale* (2008), and a lead role in the short film *She's a Fox* (2009). Steinfeld had also done some commercial work, including the "Blingitude" ad for Kmart. Since appearing in *True Grit*, she has continued to appear in short films, and she worked with Keira Knightley in *Can a Song Save Your Life?* (2013) and with Kristen Wiig and Guy Pierce in *HateshipLoveship* (2013). Steinfeld was cast as Juliet in Carlo Carlei's *Romeo and Juliet* (2013) and as Petra in the 2013 adaptation of *Ender's Game*.

Steinfeld earned the part of Mattie because of her ability to master the unusual language of Portis's novel, Joel Coen has stated. Gwynne Watkins of *New York* magazine characterizes Steinfeld's Mattie as "solid and unnervingly tense," and Richard Corliss of *Time* magazine states that Steinfeld "fully resides inside the skin of a 19th century character," the prevailing opinion of critics regarding her performance. To prepare for the part, she viewed Henry Hathaway's 1969 film *True Grit*, which starred John Wayne and in which Kim Darby played Mattie Ross. Steinfeld was inspired by the fact that Darby "held her own next to all these guys and the Duke," stating that she wanted, in turn, to hold her own with the Dude, Jeff Bridges. *Empire*'s Angie Errigo concluded that Steinfeld did just that, describing the chemistry between

Bridges and the young actress as "magical." Steinfeld, whom Corliss deems "the heart, star and glory of *True Grit*," was nominated for an Academy Award for Best Performance by an Actress in a Supporting Role.

References

David Carr, "The Coen Brothers, Shooting Straight," *New York Times*, December 10, 2010; Richard Corliss, "*True Grit*: Trading the Dude for the Duke," *Time*, December 25, 2010; Angie Errigo, "*True Grit*: The Dude Bests the Duke in a New Coens Masterpiece," *EmpireOnline.com*; Gwynne Watkins, "True West," *New York*, November 21, 2010. See also *TRUE GRIT*.

STORMARE, PETER (1953–)

Born August 27, 1953, in Arbrå, Gävleborgs län, Sweden, Stormare acted with the Royal National Theatre of Sweden, where he appeared in *Don Juan* and *The Curse of the Starving Class*, and where he also wrote original plays. He first appeared in film in Ingmar Bergman's *Fanny and Alexander* (1982). He worked in Swedish film and television until 1990, when he accepted a position as associate artistic director at the Tokyo Globe Theatre. Also in 1990, he appeared with Robert De Niro and Robin Williams in the American film *Awakenings*, which he followed with a role in *Damage* (1993) with French director Louis Malle. After his appearance in *Fargo* (1996), he began to work more in Hollywood films, including *The Lost World: Jurassic Park* (1997) and *Armageddon* (1998). He appeared in the Coens' *The Big Lebowski* (1998) and in Joel Schumacher's *8MM* (1999), followed by Oscar-nominated films *Dancer in the Dark* (2000) and *Chocolat* (2000). He worked with Tom Cruise in Steven Spielberg's *Minority Report* (2002), with director Terry Gilliam in *The Brother's Grim* (2005), and with Jack Black in 2006's *Nacho Libre*. Stormare has played recurring roles in the Fox television series *Prison Break* (2005–2006), HBO's *Entourage* (2009), and Showtime's *Weeds* (2010), and has contributed his voice to several animated series, including *Transformers: Animated* (2008), *Adventure Time* (2010), and *Phineas and Ferb* (2013).

Stormare's first appearance in a film by Joel and Ethan Coen was in *Fargo* (1996), as Graear Grimsrud, one of a pair of kidnappers hired by Jerry Lundegaard (William H. Macy) to abduct his wife Jean (Kristen Rudrüd). For their share of the ransom, Graear and Carl Showalter (Steve Buscemi) take Jean from her home and keep her captive in a lake house, awaiting the promised money. As the big, quiet partner, Grimsrud appears first to be sullen and ill-tempered, but as events unfold, the "Marlboro man" demonstrates his proclivity toward violence, killing first a state trooper and eventually Jean. His performance was described as "awesomely granitic," in a role that was written specifically for Stormare. The Coens had known him for some time, and they considered it interesting to cast a Swedish actor in a film set in the upper-Midwest.

In *The Big Lebowski*, Stormare appears as leader of the Nihilists and sometime adult film star, Uli Kunkel, who visits the Dude (Jeff Bridges) at his bungalow, and later at the bowling alley. Chasing money that does not exist, Stormare's Uli and his henchmen resort to extraordinary measures to extort money from the Big Lebowski (David Huddleston), but their ineffectual threats remain unfulfilled throughout the course of the film. Of the role, Stormare states that on "every movie set, someone always comes up to me and asks me to say I'm going to cut off their johnson," referring to one of Uli's lines from the film, and adding that he planned to attend a Lebowski Fest and sing a "Cut Off Your Johnson song," which he was writing for the event. He calls the Coens "really good friends," stating that the filmmakers have indicated they would like to work with him again. Stormare turned down a part in *Miller's Crossing*, that of "the Swede," which eventually became "the Dane," because of a commitment to a stage play in Sweden.

References

"Peter Stormare," *New York Times*, Movies & TV; Eddie Robson, *Coen Brothers* (London: Virgin Books, 2003); Owen Williams, "Rogues Gallery: Peter Stormare," *EmpireOnline.com*. See also *THE BIG LEBOWSKI*, *FARGO*.

STUHLBARG, MICHAEL (1968–)

Born July 5, 1968, in Long Beach, California, Stuhlbarg began acting at the age of eleven, when he appeared in the chorus of a community production of *Bye Bye Birdie*. He attended the University of California, Los Angeles, studying in the School of Theater, Film, and Television, but after two years, he transferred to The Juilliard School, where he earned a bachelor of fine arts degree in drama. In 1993, he made his Broadway debut in *Saint Joan*, which he followed with *Three Men on a Horse* (1993), *Timon of Athens* (1993), *The Government Inspector* (1994), *Taking Sides* (1996), and *Cabaret* (1998). Stuhlbarg's first on-screen appearance was in the television series *Prey* (1998), and his film debut was *A Price Above Rubies*, also in 1998. He appeared in Tim Blake Nelson's play *The Grey Zone* and the film adaptation of the same name (2001), and returned to Broadway in *The Invention of Love*, also in 2001. Stuhlbarg had limited roles in the television series *Law and Order: Criminal Intent* (2006), *Studio 60 on the Sunset Strip* (2006–2007), and *Damages* (2007), and in 2005, he was Tony nominated for his role in Broadway's *The Pillowman*. His subsequent films include small parts in Ridley Scott's *Body of Lies* (2008) and Sophie Barthes's *Cold Souls* (2009), with Paul Giamatti.

In 2010, Stuhlbarg was cast in a recurring role in the HBO series *Boardwalk Empire* (2010–2013), created by Terence Winter, starring Steve Buscemi, and executive produced by Martin Scorsese, among others. Scorsese directed the first episode of the series, and Stuhlbarg would work with the director again in *Hugo* (2011). He worked with Barry Sonnenfeld in *Men in Black 3* (2012), with Colin Farrell and Woody Harrelson in *Seven Psychopaths* (2012), with Steven Spielberg in *Lincoln* (2012), with Anthony Hopkins and Helen Mirren in *Hitchcock* (2012), and with Woody Allen in *Blue Jasmine* (2013). Stuhlbarg has appeared in one film by Joel and Ethan Coen, *A Serious Man* (2009).

When auditioning for the Coen film, Stuhlbarg read for three parts: the Polish man in the film's prologue; Uncle Arthur, played in the film by Richard Kind; and Larry Gopnik, the part in which he was ultimately cast. In the lead role, Stuhlbarg's Larry endures various domestic and professional crises, including his wife's request for a divorce, his ouster from his own home, the harping of his teenage children regarding the television antenna, and his brother's arrest and upcoming court appearance, among others. The *New York Times*' Franz Lidz describes Larry as "a physics professor in desperate need of a metaphysician," and of his performance, Roger Ebert states that Stuhlbarg "doesn't play Gopnik as a sad-sack or a loser, a whiner or a depressive, but as a hopeful man who can't believe what's happening to him." Prior to filming, he asked the filmmakers to suggest films he should watch to prepare for the part; the brothers suggested *The Graduate* (1967). Stuhlbarg speculates that "Perhaps something about the time period resonated with them, and Dustin Hoffman's journey, in terms of feeling baffled by events thrown at him—there was a similar sense of being adrift." For his performance, Stuhlbarg was nominated for a Golden Globe for Best Performance by an Actor in a Motion Picture—Comedy or Musical.

References

Roger Ebert, "*A Serious Man*," *RogerEbert.com*, October 7, 2009; Franz Lidz, "Biblical Adversity in a 60's Suburb," *New York Times*, September 23, 2009; Scott Macaulay, "How to Cast a Coen Brothers Film," *FocusFeatures.com*, Overview, October 23, 2009; Naomi Pfefferman, "Get *Serious*: The Coen Brothers," *JewishJournal.com*, September 2, 2009; "Michael Stuhlbarg," *Biography.com*; "Michael Stuhlbarg," *BroadwayWorld.com*. See also STEVE BUSCEMI, TIM BLAKE NELSON, *A SERIOUS MAN*, BARRY SONNENFELD.

SULLIVAN'S TRAVELS (1941)

DIRECTOR: Preston Sturges. WRITER: Preston Sturges. EXECUTIVE PRODUCER: Buddy G. DeSylva (uncredited). PRODUCERS: Paul Jones (Associate Producer) and Preston Sturges (uncredited). CINEMATOGRAPHY: John F. Seitz . EDITING: Stuart Gilmore . MUSIC: Charles Bradshaw and Leo Shuken. ART DIRECTION: Hans Dreier and Earl Hedrick. COSTUME DESIGN: Edith Head.

CAST: Joel McCrea (John Sullivan); Veronica Lake (The Girl); Robert Warwick (Mr. LeBrand); Margaret Hayes (Secretary).

RUNNING TIME: 90 minutes.

RELEASED THROUGH: Paramount Pictures.

DVD: The Criterion Collection.

John L. Sullivan (Joel McCrea), rising Hollywood director, is on a campaign to make lofty, symbolic, socially significant films that "hold a mirror up to life," specifically a film called *O Brother, Where Art Thou?* a Capra-esque project meant to capture the human suffering of early 1940s America.

His producers, instead, want a musical, something "with a little sex in it," comprised of "laughter and music and lace." Armed with appropriate attire from the wardrobe department and joined by an aspiring actress fallen on hard times, Sullivan hitchhikes, jumps trains, and sleeps in hobo camps and shelters in order to learn about the common man and "real life." After Sullivan becomes separated from his traveling companion, he is attacked, robbed, and presumed dead by Hollywood, following which he is arrested for trespassing and assault upon a railroad employee and sentenced to six years of hard labor. In the labor camp, he learns about real human suffering and determines that he would prefer to make films that make people laugh because in the reality of the common man, laughter is "all some people have."

Clearly a source for the Coen's 2000 *O Brother, Where Art Thou?*, *Sullivan's Travels* appears periodically in the Coen film, specifically the young boy in a car who helps Sullivan outrun his entourage, the ascent of Sullivan into the freight train car, the sheriff and hound dog who pass judgment on Sullivan, and the visit of the chain gang to the picture show. Joel Coen notes that *O Brother* is the realization of the film Sullivan wanted to make, "The important movie. The one that takes on the big, important themes," though one should note that it is also the film Sullivan didn't want to make: a musical comedy with a little sex in it, wrapped in Homeric allusions.

One of Sturges' earlier films, *Sullivan's Travels* is one of only fourteen films directed by Sturges, beginning with *The Great McGinty* in 1940 and concluding with 1955's *The French, They Are a Funny Race*. His writing credits, however, are much more extensive and include *Remember the Night* (1940), which is referenced in the Coen brothers' *The Hudsucker Proxy* (1994).

References

Jim Ridley, "Brothers in Arms," in *The Coen Brothers: Interviews*, ed. William Rodney Allen (Jackson: University Press of Mississippi, 2006). See also *O BROTHER, WHERE ART THOU?*; *THE HUDSUCKER PROXY*.

SWINTON, TILDA (1960–)

English actor Katherine Mathilda Swinton was born in London on November 5, 1960, and attended Cambridge University, earning a degree in social and political science. After graduation, however, she pursued a career in acting and performed with the Royal Shakespeare Company in London prior to moving on to film roles. Her first film appearance was in Derek Jarman's *Caravaggio* (1986), which she followed with additional Jarman films, *The Last of England* (1988) and *The Garden* (1990). Her role as Queen Isabella in Jarman's *Edward II* (1992) was well-received and earned her the Best Actress award at the Venice Film Festival. In addition to roles in several independent films, including *Orlando* (1992) and *The Deep End* (2001), her commercial films include *The Chronicles of Narnia: The Lion the Witch and the Wardrobe* (2005), *Constantine* (2005), *Michael Clayton* (2007), and *The Curious Case of Benjamin Button* (2008). She has been nominated for a Golden Globe three times, for *The Deep End*, *Michael Clayton*, and *We Need to Talk about Kevin* (2011), and she received an Oscar for Best Supporting Actress for her role as Karen Crowder in *Michael Clayton*. She appeared in the Coen brothers' film *Burn After Reading* in 2008.

Swinton's role in *Burn After Reading* was not written specifically for her, unlike other parts in the film that were written for Brad Pitt, George Clooney, and John Malkovich. Regardless, she is credited for playing pediatrician Katie Cox with cold precision, the word "icy" appearing in reference to Swinton more often than not in reviews of the film. Opposite the bombastic idiocy of Clooney and Malkovich, Swinton's Katie is brutally precise, eviscerating all within earshot and emasculating her husband on a regular basis with what Peter Travers describes as "a delicious look of contempt that could freeze lava." Chris Tookey of the *Daily Mail* describes Katie as "a woman with the warmth and interpersonal skills of the speaking clock," and Ross Douthat of *National Review* characterizes her as "the world's most terrifying pediatrician."

References

"Tilda Swinton," *Biography.com*; Ross Douthat, "Burn before Watching," *National Review*, October 20, 2008; "Tilda Swinton," *New York Times*, Movies & TV; Chris Tookey, "*Burn after Reading*: Pitt the Halfwit Steals the Show with the Greatest Ever Portrayal of Stupidity," *MailOnline.com*, October 17, 2008; Peter Travers, "*Burn after Reading*," *Rolling Stone*, September 12, 2008. See also *BURN AFTER READING*.

THORNTON, BILLY BOB (1955–)

Born August 4, 1955, in Hot Springs, Arkansas, Thornton came to love rock music at an early age, when he discovered Elvis Presley and the Beatles. He began playing drums at the age of nine and played with local bands while working in construction, operating heavy equipment, and in a screen-door factory. He briefly studied psychology at Henderson State University in Arkansas, and in his twenties worked as a roadie for touring groups. He attempted a career in music in New York prior to relocating to Los Angeles, where he became interested in acting. Thornton began his screen appearances with small parts in television series, including *Matlock* (1987), *Evening Shade* (1990), and *Knots Landing* (1992), and a recurring role on *The Outsiders* (1990) and *Hearts Afire* (1992–1995), while playing similarly small parts in films such as *South of Reno* (1988), *For the Boys* (1991), *Indecent Proposal* (1993), and *Tombstone* (1993). With Tom Epperson, he wrote the script for *One False Move* (1992), in which he appeared with Bill Paxton, and in 1994, he wrote and starred in the short film *Some Folks Call It Slingblade*. He later lengthened the script and directed the feature *Slingblade* (1996), and for his portrayal of Karl Childers, he was nominated for two Oscars: Best Actor in a Leading Role and Best Adapted Screenplay, which he won. His additional directorial projects include *All the Pretty Horses* (2000), *Daddy and Them* (2001), and *The King of Luck* (2011), a documentary about the life of Willie Nelson.

Following the success of *Slingblade*, Thornton appeared in *The Apostle* (1997) with Robert Duvall, in *Primary Colors* (1998) with John Travolta and Emma Thompson, and with Bruce Willis in *Armageddon* (1998). He received Oscar and Golden Globe nominations for his role in Sam Raimi's *A Simple Plan* (1998), and he played leading roles in *Monster's Ball* (2001), *Levity* (2003), and *The Alamo* (2004). He has appeared in two Coen films, *The Man Who Wasn't There* (2001), and *Intolerable Cruelty* (2003), as well as *Bad Santa* (2003), which was executive-produced by Joel and Ethan Coen.

Thornton's first appearance in a Coen film was in *The Man Who Wasn't There*, a neo-noir drama that focuses on a barber who wants to be a dry cleaner. Ed Crane is a barber; he cuts the hair, and he lives in a little bungalow on Napa Street with his wife Doris (Frances McDormand), and over the course of the film, Ed's life moves from a tedious predictability to a bizarre melodrama that includes UFOs and multiple murder trials, all precipitated by Ed's decision to blackmail his wife's lover. Both Thornton and Michael Badalucco, who plays Frank, trained for the part and actually cut hair on the set, though Ethan Coen has noted "The sad thing is that Billy Bob thinks he's good." The filmmakers claim that they had to make arrangements for professionals to recut hair after Thornton was finished with the extras, as he produced "some pretty gruesome haircuts."

Though the part was not written with Thornton in mind, his performance as Ed Crane garnered much praise among film critics. A. O. Scott describes Thornton as the film's "Pole Star—or perhaps the black hole—around which everything else turns," and the *Guardian* deems his performance "a stunning achievement." Ethan Coen compares Thornton to Montgomery Clift, both "soulful" actors; "If this movie was being made in 1949, when it's set, Clift would have been the man to do it. He had the same quality that Billy Bob has." Returning the compliment, Thornton describes working with the Coens: "The thing is," he says, "they just don't suck." Prior to the making of this film, the Coens were familiar with Thornton, though they had not worked together previously. Thornton had, however, recently worked with Coen friend and collaborator, Sam Raimi, in *A Simple Plan* (1998).

Thornton played a smaller role in his next Coen film, as Howard D. Doyle in *Intolerable Cruelty*. Thornton appears as an actor playing an oil tycoon, part of a plan by Marilyn Rexroth (Catherine Zeta-Jones) to entrap the wealthy Miles Massey (George Clooney). Doyle, a former tight end for the Texas A&M Aggies, is "so flashy he seems to have stepped out of a 1950's stage musical," notes Elvis Mitchell of the *New York Times*. Thornton concludes his role as Doyle by eating a prenuptial agreement dipped in barbeque sauce, while proclaiming his love for Marilyn at their wedding.

References

"Billy Bob Thornton," *New York Times*, Movies & TV; "*The Man Who Wasn't There*," *Guardian*, October 25, 2001; Elvis Mitchell, "*Intolerable Cruelty*: Film Review: A Lawyer's Good Teeth Help in Love and Court," *New York Times*, October 10, 2003; Ian Nathan, *Ethan and Joel Coen* (Paris: Cahiers du cinema Sarl, 2012); Gerald Peary, "Joel and Ethan Coen," in *The Coen Brothers: Interviews*, ed. William Rodney Allen (Jackson: University Press of Mississippi, 2006); Eddie Robson, *Coen Brothers* (London: Virgin Books, 2003); A. O. Scott, "*The Man Who Wasn't There*," *New York Times*, October 31, 2001. See also *INTOLERABLE CRUELTY*, *THE MAN WHO WASN'T THERE*, SAM RAIMI.

TIMBERLAKE, JUSTIN (1981–)

Born January 31, 1981, in Memphis, Tennessee, Timberlake first appeared on-screen in *The New Mickey Mouse Club* (1993–1995) prior to joining the immensely popular boy band 'N Sync, with which performed from 1995 to 2001. In 2002 he released his first solo album, *Justified*, and began appearing in films, including *Alpha Dog* (2006) with Bruce Willis, *The Love Guru* (2008) with Mike Myers, David Fincher's *The Social Network* (2010), and *Trouble with the Curve* (2012) with Clint Eastwood. He also lent his voice to such films as *Shrek the Third* (2007), *Yogi Bear* (2010), as BooBoo, and the Fox television show *The Clevelands* (2011). Timberlake has earned eleven Grammy nominations and received three Grammy Awards: in 2003 for Best Pop Vocal Album for *Justified*; in 2007 for Best Rap/Sung Collaboration, with T.I., for "My Love"; and in 2008 for Best Male Pop Vocal Performance for "What Goes Around Comes Around." As executive producer, Timberlake has produced not only music-related concert videos and television movies, but also the 2013 golf documentary *The Short Game* and the MTV reality television series *The Phone* (2009). Timberlake played Jim Berkey in the Coens' *Inside Llewyn Davis* (2013).

As the buttoned-down Jim Berkey in *Inside Llewyn Davis*, Timberlake plays husband and singing partner to Carey Mulligan's Jean Berkey. The couple sing in Greenwich Village coffee houses and bars and host fellow folk musicians on their couch, including Oscar Isaac's Llewyn Davis and Stark Sands's Troy Nelson. Timberlake and Mulligan recorded several songs live on set for the film, as did many of the film's actors, including Isaac and Sands. Timberlake worked extensively with the film's music producer T Bone Burnett, and, along with Burnett, Ed Rush, George Cromarty, and Joel and Ethan Coen, he co-authored the Golden Globe-nominated song "Please Mr. Kennedy (Don't Shoot Me into Outer Space)," which he performs on-screen with Oscar Isaac and Adam Driver in perhaps the film's most overtly comedic moment. The song was based on the 1962 Goldcoast Singers tune of the same name, "Please Mr. Kennedy," which begs the president not to send the singer to Vietnam, though the Goldcoast song is less bouncy than the Coen version. Timberlake also appears on the soundtrack's "The Auld Triangle" as part of a quartet with The Punch Brothers and Marcus Mumford.

Timberlake describes his character Jim Berkey as a folk singer who isn't as talented as the film's lead, Llewyn Davis, but who is willing to capitalize on a transition that is taking place in the American music scene just prior to Bob Dylan's entrance and success. Extremely principled musicians such as Llewyn choose not to compromise their approach to the music and as a result are perceived as failures and forced to eke out

a living on tips from basket houses. Jim, whose character writes the sell-out pop-folk song, "doesn't have the chops to be a Bob Dylan . . . which leads to the 'Please Mr. Kennedy' song. To me, Jim represents the transition," Timberlake states.

References

"Justin Timberlake," *Biography.com*; Jake Coyle, "Timberlake Finds Harmony in *Llewyn Davis*," *TheSpectrum.com*, January 16, 2014; Andrew O'Hehir, "Justin Timberlake: I'm a Mediocre Folk Singer!" *Salon.com*, May 21, 2013. See also *INSIDE LLEWYN DAVIS*.

TO EACH HIS OWN CINEMA: "WORLD CINEMA" (2007)

In 2007, the Cannes Film Festival presented *Chacun son cinema* (*To Each His Own Cinema*), described by the Festival as "35 directors, from 5 different continents and 25 countries, all universally recognised, pay tribute, in 3 minutes each, to the motion picture theatre, that magical venue of communion par excellence of film lovers the world over." The project was conceived by Gilles Jacob, president of the Cannes Festival, to commemorate the festival's sixtieth anniversary. All contributors were asked to create a piece that reflected their "state of mind of the moment as inspired by the motion picture theater." The Coen contribution to this project was the short film *World Cinema*, written and directed by Joel and Ethan Coen and starring Josh Brolin as a cowboy who contemplates which film he should see in Los Angeles. Just over three minutes in length, the piece is described as "light and whimsical" by the *New York Times*, which served as a contrast to many of the other contributions, which focused on "the neglect or disrepute into which contemporary cinema, as a collective viewing experience, has fallen."

References

"*To Each His Own Cinema,*" *Festival-Cannes.fr*, Official Selection; "*Chacun son cinema,*" *New York Times*, Review Summary. See also JOSH BROLIN.

TRUE GRIT (2010)

DIRECTOR: Ethan Coen and Joel Coen. SCREENPLAY: Joel Coen, Ethan Coen, and Charles Portis. EXECUTIVE PRODUCERS: David Ellison, Megan Ellison, Robert Graf, Paul Schwake, and Steven Spielberg. PRODUCERS: Ethan Coen, Joel Coen, and Scott Rudin. PHOTOGRAPHY: Roger Deakins. EDITING: Ethan Coen and Joel Coen (as Roderick Jaynes). MUSIC: Carter Burwell. PRODUCTION DESIGN: Jess Gonchor. ART DIRECTION: Stefan Dechant and Christy Wilson (Supervising Art Director). SET DECORATION: Nancy Haigh. COSTUME DESIGN: Mary Zophres.

CAST: Jeff Bridges (Rooster Cogburn), Hailee Steinfeld (Mattie Ross), Matt Damon (LaBoeuf), Josh Brolin (Tom Chaney), Barry Pepper (Lucky Ned Pepper), Dakin Matthews (Col. Stonehill), Paul Rae (Emmitt Quincy), Domhnall Gleeson (Moon), Elizabeth Marvel (forty-year-old-Mattie), Roy Lee Jones (Yarnell), Ed Corbin (Bear Man), J.K. Simmons (J. Nobel Daggett, voice).

RUNNING TIME: 110 minutes. Color.

RELEASED THROUGH: Paramount Pictures.

PREMIERE: December 14, 2010, New York City.

DVD: Paramount Home Entertainment.

ACADEMY AWARDS: Best Motion Picture (nominated: Ethan Coen, Joel Coen, and Scott Rudin), Best Performance by an Actor in a Leading Role (nominated: Jeff Bridges), Best Performance by an Actress in a Supporting Role (nominated: Hailee Steinfeld), Best Achievement in Directing (nominated: Ethan Coen and Joel Coen), Best Writing, Adapted Screenplay (nominated: Joel Coen and Ethan Coen), Best Achievement in Cinematography (nominated: Roger Deakins), Best Achievement in Costume Design (nominated: Mary Zophres), Best Achievement in Sound Mixing (nominated: Skip Lievsay, Craig Berkey, Greg Orloff, Peter F. Kurland), Best Achievement in Sound Editing (nominated: Skip Lievsay and Craig Berkey), Best Achievement in Art Direction (nominated: Jess Gonchor and Nancy Haigh).

Many Coen fans, upon learning that *True Grit* would be the fifteenth feature film by Joel and Ethan Coen, incorrectly assumed that the film would be a remake of the 1969 film starring John Wayne and directed by Henry Hathaway. Instead, the filmmakers returned to the Charles Portis 1968 novel of the same name, intending to re-adapt the novel rather than remake the previous film. In the Coen *True Grit*, which adheres more closely to the novel than did the Hathaway production, Mattie Ross (Hailee Steinfeld), age fourteen, has arrived in Fort Smith, Arkansas, to collect her father's body and his personal possessions. Frank Ross has been fatally shot by his former hired hand, Tom Chaney (Josh Brolin), who has then fled to the Indian Territory, where the local sheriff has no authority. Learning that the law has no intention of bringing her father's killer to justice in any timely manner, Mattie determines to set about the task herself. A straightforward young woman with no time or inclination for the emotional devastation that one might expect from a young teen, she attends a hanging, passes the night at the local undertakers, and engages in a shrewd and spirited horse-trading session.

Mattie searches for a U.S. marshal to assist her in the manhunt, and at the suggestion of the sheriff, she decides upon Reuben "Rooster" Cogburn (Jeff Bridges), the meanest, toughest of the available

Jeff Bridges (left) and Hailee Steinfeld in *True Grit* (2010)

marshals. Observing Cogburn's testimony in Judge Parker's court, she approves of what she sees and approaches him with her proposal: to pay him fifty dollars cash to locate, apprehend, and return Tom Chaney to the authorities. Cogburn is slightly amused and certainly not interested, dismissing her almost immediately. Mattie is subsequently approached at her boarding house by LaBoeuf (Matt Damon), a Texas Ranger who seeks to capture Chaney and escort him to Texas, where he is wanted in the shooting death of a Texas senator. LaBoeuf will receive a sizable reward for his successful efforts, but Mattie, not interested in having Chaney hang in Texas, informs the ranger that she is employing Cogburn and together they will bring Chaney to be hanged in Fort Smith, Arkansas. She visits Cogburn in his room behind the Chinese grocery, where the hungover and slovenly marshal first rebuffs her attempts to hire him and then, seeing that she has cash money, agrees to hunt down Chaney for the fee of $100, though he is displeased with

the prospect of having Mattie accompany him on the journey.

Mattie arrives to collect Cogburn and begin their adventure the next morning, only to discover that he and LaBoeuf have left without her. She pursues, riding her horse Little Blackie across a sizeable river, and joins the men in their search for the fugitive. They pass the first night before a campfire, at which the men exchange heated words about the unworthiness of the other, and in the morning an argument about their respective service in the Civil War demonstrates that continuing on together would be untenable. They agree to part ways, and Mattie presses on in the company of Rooster Cogburn. At the suggestion of a traveling veterinarian/dentist/doctor, they plan to spend the night at the dugout of the Original Greaser Bob, and arriving at the dugout, discover that it is occupied. Rooster flushes two men from the dwelling and learns that Lucky Ned Pepper (Barry Pepper) and his gang, with whom Tom Chaney has likely joined forces, are due to arrive that very night. Cogburn and Mattie lie in wait in the rocks above the dugout, observing first LaBoeuf and then Ned Pepper's gang arriving at the meeting place. LaBoeuf is injured in the subsequent shootout, and Lucky Ned escapes, though not all of his gang is so fortunate.

Mattie, Cogburn, and LaBoeuf continue on into the mountains but are unable to locate Ned Pepper and his henchmen. At camp that night the men argue once more, and LaBoeuf departs, leaving Mattie with the drunken marshal and a cold trail. The following morning while getting water at the stream, Mattie sees and confronts Tom Chaney, shooting him in the side with her father's pistol. The wounded Chaney captures Mattie and takes her to the gang's camp, and Cogburn agrees to leave the area in return for her safety. Short a horse, Ned and his gang leave Mattie in Chaney's care, promising to send a man back with a horse, and the frustrated murderer is stopped by LaBoeuf seconds before he kills Mattie. Looking down upon the valley floor below them, Mattie and LaBoeuf watch as Cogburn rides across the plain, reins in his mouth and Navy six shooters firing, taking on Ned and his three companions. Three men are felled, leaving only the wounded Ned and the marshal, who has fallen beneath his dead horse. In a miraculous display of marksmanship, LaBoeuf shoots and kills Ned, only to be struck in the head by Chaney, who has regained consciousness. Mattie stands face-to-face with her father's killer and does not hesitate when she pulls the trigger, sending Chaney off a precipice to his death. Mattie, set off balance by the recoil of the gun, falls into a pit where she becomes entangled in vines and discovers a nest of hibernating rattlesnakes. She is rescued by the combined efforts of Cogburn and LaBoeuf, and, as she is snake bit, Cogburn rides throughout the night to see her to safety. She loses part of her arm

as a result of the bite and does not see either man alive again.

At the conclusion of the Coen film, the middle-aged Mattie embarks upon a train ride to see the former marshal, at his invitation, as he is traveling with an Old-West show in the company of Frank James and Cole Younger. Arriving to find that Cogburn has died three days previously, she removes his body from the Confederate cemetery where he was buried and brings him to her home. In the film's final scene she visits his grave.

Comparisons to Hathaway's earlier adaptation of Portis's novel are inevitable, as are discussions of the actors who appeared in both adaptations. Critics widely praised the film's casting, and in particular, Hailey Steinfeld's performance: *Texas Monthly* deemed her the "beating heart and driving force" of the film, and Kenneth Turan of the *Los Angeles Times* states that "LaBoeuf is beautifully realized by Damon." Some reviewers found Jeff Bridges's line delivery to be problematic and difficult to understand, while others saw echoes of *The Big Lebowski*'s Dude in his rendering of Cogburn. Bridges was, however, nominated for the Best Actor Oscar, and many reviewers, including Roger Ebert and *Empire*'s Angie Errigo, considered Bridges's performance to be equal, if not superior, to that of John Wayne in the role.

The film does depart from the Portis novel in some aspects, as the brothers added the portion of the film in which Cogburn and Mattie are traveling by horseback and encounter first a man hanging from a tree, then a Native American who takes and then sells the body, and finally the man clothed in a bear skin who attempts to sell the body back to them. The entrance of the bear/man on horseback is a decidedly Coen touch, one that regular viewers of their films will recognize as appropriate to their films, as surreal as the dream/dance sequences in *The Hudsucker Proxy* (1994) and *The Big Lebowski* (1998) and the KKK rally or the sirens scenes in *O Brother, Where Art Thou?* (2000). *Empire's* Angie Errigo characterized the film as "unmistakably Coen-esque," while Christopher Kelly of *Texas Monthly* is more specific in his assessment, stating, "The writer-directors imbue this movie with bursts of bloodshed, surreal whimsy, and distinctly Coen-esque humor—the 'grit,' in other words, that went missing from Hathaway's polished, bordering-on-synthetic version." Manohla Dargis of the *New York Times* concludes that despite the "Coen" touches, the filmmakers, who "like to play with genre, often with giggles and winks, haven't mounted an assault on the western." Critics were not inclined to label this Coen western a parody or spoof of the genre but instead, a more straightforward presentation of the experiences of three individuals as they travel through the American West.

The film was shot in Texas and New Mexico, which represented a shift from Hathaway's earlier adaptation, filmed largely in Colorado and therefore incongruent with the Arkansas and Oklahoma landscapes of Portis's book. In keeping with the generic traditions of Western films, Roger Deakins presented the viewer with sweeping landscapes that render the characters insignificant by comparison, emphasizing the forces of nature against which Mattie and company must struggle as they continue their quest. The harshness of those landscapes, described by Kenneth Turan of the *Los Angeles Times* as a West that is "visually arid, an unsettling Big Empty where only bitterness and bile thrive," gives the Coen film an appropriate tone, one that is in keeping with the bleakness of the Portis novel. When filming, the filmmakers employed a "straightforward presentation," says Joel Coen, in which the "default

position was more pretty, more classical," a departure for the Coens, who typically create more stylized films with a signature all their own. Audiences responded well to *True Grit*, as the film, which cost $38 million to make, earned over $100 million domestically and a total of $250 million worldwide.

Upon the release of *True Grit*, the film's reviewers gave special attention to the language used by the film's characters, as no contractions are used in their speech, resulting in an almost biblical formality. The language, though, which Matt Damon describes as "amazing," is Portis's; the book's characters speak in this way, and the Coens, in adapting the novel, did so quite faithfully in terms of both dialogue and plot. Reviewers likewise expressed their surprise at the "feel good" nature of the film, often referring to it as a family film, a designation unusual for Coen pictures. When asked about this shift in tone and the more accessible style of the film, Ethan Coen replied, "It's not our fault. . . . It was based on the novel. That's the good thing about adapting novels. You blame it on the book." Josh Brolin further noted, "I don't think they thought a lot about how the film might land," a statement that seems likely to be true, as the Coens have made clear that they are more interested in the making of their films than how audiences will respond to them.

The film's three characters invite a reading that examines the relationships and tensions between the concepts of law, vengeance, and justice, with each character identifying with one or more of the ideas. LaBoeuf, as a legal agent and representative of the law, relies heavily on the prestige of his position, discussing at length the policies and regulations of the Texas Rangers with whom he serves. He appears, however, to be more concerned with the reward he will collect when he returns Tom Chaney to

Texas than embracing a purely philosophical idea of justice. The law serves as an end to enhance his own reputation and his bank account, and while he toys with the meanings of Latin legal terms in a conversation with Mattie, the discussion appears to have more to do with showing off his knowledge and linguistic skills than with demonstrating a passion for the concepts themselves. He proudly reminds all who will listen of his legal status and regales his traveling companions with tales of his previous journeys, boasting of drinking muddy water from a hoof print. He conspicuously wears jangling spurs, which do not aid in his stealthiness, and his final words in the film are "ever stalwart," referring to the reputation and duties of a Texas Ranger. In his capacity as lawman, he successfully assists in apprehending Tom Chaney, and he does indeed save Mattie from the lawless and violent murderer, but he is incapacitated in return, and the combined efforts of Cogburn and LaBoeuf are necessary to facilitate her final rescue from the pit. He fails in his mission to return Chaney to the court for hanging, thus forfeiting his reward. The law alone does not appear to be the concept that dominates this film.

True Grit opens with a voice-over narration by Mattie, now middle-aged, recalling the events of the film: "People do not give it credence that a fourteen-year-old girl could leave home and go off in the wintertime to avenge her father's blood but it did not seem so strange then." The quotation, which is verbatim from Portis's novel, immediately connects Mattie to the concept of vengeance, as it is her stated goal from the outset. She initially appears to be closely aligned with the law as well, repeatedly referring to her lawyer in her dealings with the horse trader, discussing the nuances of Latin terms and their application to the situation at hand with LaBoeuf, and offering Tom Chaney an affidavit regarding his

behavior, should he let her go free. The law, however, is a means to an end—vengeance—for Mattie, just as LaBoeuf's legal position is a means to a financial end. Her goal is to see Chaney hang in Fort Smith for the murder of her father, and her motivation might be best characterized as a righteous anger, shored up by her absolute faith that a biblical retribution awaits Chaney, an eye for an eye—at her own hand, if necessary. If the legal system can assist her in that pursuit, then she will wield it to her benefit; if it cannot, then she will serve as the agent of vengeance—and of righteousness. As she travels the wilds of Indian Territory with Cogburn and LaBoeuf, she learns that these men, appointed by the law, cannot bring about Chaney's capture and trial, and she turns to avenging her father's death herself, as she said she would, shooting Tom Chaney in the absence of either the Texas Ranger or the U.S. marshal. Mattie, then, is not singularly representative of just one of these concepts; she moves from affiliating herself with the law in order to achieve justice and ultimately metes out vengeance for her father's death.

Rooster Cogburn, though formally a lawman, is lawful in title only. From the beginning of the film, Cogburn is more concerned with serving justice than the means by which he achieves it, having killed twenty-three men in his four years of service as a U.S. marshal. His testimony in Judge Parker's court clearly demonstrates that he believes he was in the right in these killings, as he sees them as justified, rather than as acts of murder. Like LaBoeuf, Cogburn seeks monetary compensation for his "good" deeds in capturing or killing criminals, but he also demonstrates a sense of internal justice, as he tells Mattie that he robbed a high-interest bank, which he finds acceptable, as you "can't rob a thief." He states that he has "never robbed a citizen, never took a man's watch," and while the legal system would not condone his definition or execution of justice, it makes perfect sense to him, and he lives by it. Mattie is aware of his tarnished reputation, having observed his testimony early in the film, and for this very reason, she selects him for her mission. Cogburn gets his man, though not always alive, and not always legally in a technical sense, and Cogburn's system of justice appears to be working for him, to some degree. As an agent of the court, he can confiscate liquor to support his drinking habit, he is above the efforts of the attorney to point out his ethical and legal transgressions, and while he leaves behind him a trail of unsuccessful marriages and business ventures, he appears to be comfortable with the code that dictates his actions. In the end, Cogburn's version of justice prevails over Ned's gang, though the lawman LaBoeuf is responsible for the death of Ned himself, and Mattie, with her desire for vengeance, kills Tom Chaney.

No one of these three concepts, then, rises above the other in the film. Each individual and the principles for which he or she stands emerge victorious in some way: LaBoeuf makes the shot he could not make earlier in his pursuit of Chaney, accurately shooting at Ned from four hundred yards. Mattie does indeed avenge her father's killer, though at the foot of a cliff, rather than through the trapdoor of the gallows. And Rooster Cogburn relives his glory days in his four-against-one ride across the flats and goes on to protect a child and her future in a way he could not for Horace, his long-abandoned son.

References

David Carr, "The Coen Brothers, Shooting Straight," *New York Times*, December 10, 2010; Manohla Dargis, "Wearing Braids, Seeking Revenge," *New York Times*, December 21, 2010; Roger Ebert, "*True Grit,*" *RogerEbert. com*, December 21, 2010; Angie Errigo, "*True Grit*: The Dude Bests the Duke in a New Coens Masterpiece," *EmpireOnline.com*; Christopher Kelly, "Best Western," *Texas Monthly*, 39.1 (2011); Kenneth Turan, "Movie Review: *True Grit*," *Los Angeles Times*, December 22, 2010. See also JEFF BRIDGES, JOSH BROLIN, CARTER BURWELL, MATT DAMON, ROGER DEAKINS, JESS GONCHOR, NANCY HAIGH, ELIZABETH MARVEL, BARRY PEPPER, J. K. SIMMONS, HAILEE STEINFELD, MARY ZOPHRES.

TURTURRO, JOHN (1957–)

Born in Brooklyn, New York, on February 28, 1957, John Turturro attended the State University of New York, New Palz, where he earned a bachelor's degree in science. He then attended graduate school at the Yale School of Drama and appeared off-Broadway in *Danny and the Deep Blue Sea*, for which he won an Obie Award. In 1980, his first film role was in Martin Scorsese's *Raging Bull*, followed by *The Exterminator 2* in 1984. His Broadway debut was in *Death of a Salesman* in 1984, and he had small roles in the films *Desperately Seeking Susan* (1985), *The Color of Money* (1986), and Woody Allen's *Hannah and Her Sisters* (1986). Spike Lee's *Do the Right Thing* (1989) featured him in the role of the racist Pino, a performance that raised Turturro's public profile considerably. He then appeared in two consecutive Coen films: *Miller's Crossing* (1990) and *Barton Fink* (1991). He worked again with the Coens on *The Big Lebowski* (1998) and *O Brother, Where Art Thou?* (2000) and again with Spike Lee in *Jungle Fever* (1991), *Mo' Better Blues* (1990), *Clockers* (1995), *Girl 6* (1996), *He Got Game* (1998), *Summer of Sam* (1999), *She Hate Me* (2004), and *Miracle at St. Anna* (2008). He appeared in *Transformers* (2007) and its two sequels, *Transformers: Revenge of the Fallen* (2009) and *Transformers: Dark of the Moon* (2011).

In addition to his acting work on film and Broadway, Turturro has written and directed several projects. His first turn at directing was *Mac* (1992), a film informed by the life of Turturro's father, who was a builder; for this film, he won a Camera d'Or Award for Best First Picture at the Cannes Film Festival. He wrote and directed *Illuminata* (1998), and *Romance and Cigarettes* (2005), which he began composing on the set of the Coens' *Barton Fink*. As his character Barton was filmed typing on-screen, Turturro was generating scenes for his own film; *Romance and Cigarettes* was, in turn, produced by Joel and Ethan Coen. In 2010, he directed a documentary about the music of Naples, *Passione*, and in 2011, he directed three one-act plays on Broadway, one of which, *Talking Cure*, was written by Ethan Coen. His 2013 *Fading Gigolo* starred Woody Allen as a pimp to Turturro's gigolo. In keeping with the character of Barton Fink and his aspirations to write for the common man, Turturro's own films focus on builders and blue-collar workers, and the common man; Turturro told the *Guardian* in 2006, "I am Barton Fink."

As Bernie Bernbaum in *Miller's Crossing*, Turturro's character serves as the catalyst for the film's plot: the point of contention between rival mob bosses. Johnny Caspar (Jon Polito) wants him dead; Leo (Albert Finney), the reigning Irish gangster, refuses to grant permission for the hit, as Bernie is the brother of Leo's girl, Verna (Marcia Gay Harden). Bernie appears in darkened rooms throughout the movie, and Turturro's performance in the woods of Miller's Crossing, begging for his life at the hands of his would-be assassin, was described as a "tour de force" by Peter Travers of *Rolling Stone*, and Vincent Canby of the *New York Times* designated Turturro's performance the most interesting of the film.

In his second Coen film, Turturro assumed the lead role in *Barton Fink*: a Broadway writer whose first play garners much praise from elegantly dressed theatergoers and the *Herald* theatre critic. Barton accepts a writing position for Capitol Pictures in Hollywood, and the film follows his ensuing battles with writer's block, his encounters with industry moguls, and his interactions with the Hotel Earle's only other inhabitant, Charlie Meadows (John Goodman). At the film's conclusion, Barton finds himself a captive to his studio contract, his script rejected, and his dream of creating "the theatre of the common man" retreating with the tide. In preparation for the part, Turturro attended secretarial school and read the 1940 journal of author Clifford Odets, a Broadway playwright who also wrote for motion pictures and upon whom the character Barton Fink is loosely based. Turturro also read *Jews without Money*, Michael Gold's account of the origins of the socially conscious writers of the 1930s, and when Turturro is at last typing his wrestling picture script on his typewriter in his hotel room, Joel Coen notes that the style of the scene is meant to replicate that of Odets. For his portrayal of Barton Fink, Turturro received the Best Actor Award at the Cannes Film Festival.

The Big Lebowski featured Turturro in the small but memorable role of Jesus, the bowling pederast, described by Desson Howe of the *Washington Post* as "a hotdog whose tight, high-waisted bowling uniform shows a little too much of everything." David Bennun, writing for *Uncut* magazine, describes Turturro's Jesus as "hissing, in a voice halfway between Speedy Gonzalez and Kaa the python," and Roger Ebert proclaims the character "a man who has converted himself into an artwork in his own honor."

Turturro's fourth Coen film was *O Brother Where Art Thou?*, the chain-gang, buddy road movie in which three escaped convicts run from the law and toward hidden treasure. In his role as Pete Hogwallop, Turturro's "face is stuck in an expression of baffled disapproval, his jaw twisted round to make his face shaped like a J," writes Peter Bradshaw of the *Guardian*. Pete joins George Clooney's Everett McGill and Tim Blake Nelson's Delmar O'Donnell as a member of the Soggy Bottom Boys. Together, they record the hit "Man of Constant Sorrow," evade an ominous Sheriff, and become engulfed in a flood of biblical proportions.

In the twenty-plus years of working with the filmmakers, Turturro and the Coens have developed a working relationship that transcends verbal communication: Ethan Coen has stated "Somebody once asked us about [John] Turturro, if we developed a shorthand with him working together over the course of all these movies. And we said, 'It's beyond shorthand. We don't even talk to him!'"

References

David Bennun, "The Coen Brothers," in *The Coen Brothers: Interviews*, ed. William Rodney Allen (Jackson: University Press of Mississippi, 2006); Peter Bradshaw, "*O Brother, Where Art Thou,*" *Guardian*, September 14, 2000; Vincent Canby, "In *Miller's Crossing*, Silly Gangsters and a Tough Moll," *New York Times*, September 21, 1990; Michel Ciment and Hubert Niogret, "A Rock on the Beach," in *Joel & Ethan Coen: Blood Siblings*, ed. Paul A. Woods (London: Plexus Publishing, 2003); Roger Ebert, "*The Big Lebowski,*" *RogerEbert.com*, March 10, 2010; Desson Howe, "*The Big Lebowski*: Rollin' a Strike," *Washington Post*, March 6, 1998; Mark Kermode, "John Turturro," *Guardian.com*, March 23, 2006; Sean Levy, "'The British Are Going to Crucify Us,'" *Guardian*, May 9, 2004; Sean O'Neal, "John Turturro," *AVClub*.com, June 28, 2011; Eddie Robson, *Coen Brothers* (London: Virgin Books, 2003); Peter Travers, "*Miller's Crossing,*" *Rolling Stone*, September 22, 1990. See also *BARTON FINK, THE BIG LEBOWSKI, MILLER'S CROSSING, O BROTHER, WHERE ART THOU?*

WALSH, M. EMMET (1935–)

Born on March 22, 1935, in Ogdensburg, New York, Walsh attended the Tilton School in New Hampshire prior to enrolling at Clarkson University. Though he graduated with a degree in marketing, he discovered acting and attended the American Academy of Dramatic Arts. He then appeared on stage in summer stock and regional theatre in New England, and in 1967 he appeared off-Broadway in *The Death of the Well-Loved Boy* (1967). His Broadway debut was *Does a Tiger Wear a Necktie* (1969), with Al Pacino and Hal Holbrook. That same year, he was cast in small parts in *Midnight Cowboy* and *Stiletto*, and he appeared in a larger role in *Alice's Restaurant* (1969), as Sergeant of Group W. Walsh developed a reputation as a character actor, appearing in such films as *Little Big Man* (1970) and *Escape from the Planet of the Apes* (1971), and in the 1970s, he began to work in television as well, with small parts in *Ironside* (1971), *Bonanza* (1971), and *The Waltons* (1975). He was cast in a recurring role in the series *Nichols* (1971–1972) and *The Sandy Duncan Show* (1972). He worked with Peter Bogdanovich in *What's Up Doc?* (1972), with Al Pacino in *Serpico* (1973), and with Jack Lemmon in *Airport '77* (1977).

In the 1980s, Walsh worked with Robert Redford in *Brubaker* (1980), *Ordinary People* (1980), and *The Milagro Beanfield War* (1988), and he appeared in Ridley Scott's *Blade Runner* in 1982. In 1984, Walsh appeared in a larger role in Joel and Ethan Coen's *Blood Simple*, following which he was cast in *Fletch* (1985) and the Coens' *Raising Arizona* (1987). He played various roles in the PBS documentary mini-series *The Civil War* (1990) and twice appeared on the Tim Allen television series *Home Improvement* (1994). He worked with Baz Luhrmann in *Romeo + Juliet* (1996) and with Barry Sonnenfeld in *Wild, Wild West* (1999), and he starred in Evan Aaronson's *Baggage* (2003). He returned to the stage periodically, at the LaJolla Playhouse in *Sweet Bird of Youth* (1999), at the Geffen Playhouse in *Third* (2007), and at the Freud Playhouse in Los Angeles, where he appeared in *Carousel* (2010), among others. Walsh has lent his voice to such animated series as *The Wild Thornberrys* (1999), *What's New, Scooby Doo?* (2002), *Adventure Time* (2012–2013), and *Pound Puppies* (2010–2013).

The part of Loren Visser in the Coens' *Blood Simple* (1984) was written with Walsh in mind, as the brothers had seen him in Ulu Grosbard's *Straight Time* (1978). When they sent him the script, Walsh agreed to take the part, intending to develop a character for the film that he could use in a future role; he was convinced that the movie would not be a success: "at best, it would be the third bill at

WAYANS, MARLON ■ 195

an Alabama drive-in," he recalls. The film, however, set the cinematic trajectory for the Coens and earned Walsh positive reviews. Hal Hinson of *Film Comment* writes that Walsh "gives his character a mangy amorality," and Anne Bilson states that Walsh plays Loren Visser "with all the sordid and slimy panache of a walking social disease." Walsh was cast in a small part in the Coens' second film, *Raising Arizona* (1987), as a worker in a sheet metal factory, alongside H.I. McDunnough (Nicolas Cage).

References

Anne Bilson, "Simply Bloody," in *Joel & Ethan Coen: Blood Siblings*, ed. Paul A. Woods (London: Plexus Publishing, 2003); Hal Hinson, "Bloodlines," in *The Coen Brothers: Interviews*, ed. William Rodney Allen (Jackson: University Press of Mississippi, 2006); "M. Emmitt Walsh," *BroadwayWorld.com*; "M. Emmitt Walsh," *FilmBug.com*; "M. Emmitt Walsh," *New York Times*, Movies & TV; "M. Emmitt Walsh," *StarPulse.com*; Eddie Robson, *Coen Brothers* (London: Virgin Books, 2003). See also *BLOOD SIMPLE*.

WAYANS, MARLON (1972–)

Born July 23, 1972, in New York City, Marlon Wayans is the youngest of ten siblings that include Keenan, a writer, director, and actor; Damon, an actor and producer; Kim, an actress; and Shawn, an actor and writer. Marlon attended the Fiorello H. La Guardia High School of Music & Art and Performing Arts and began his on-screen career with a bit part in *I'm Gonna Git You Sucka* (1988), directed by his brother Keenan Ivory Wayans. He then appeared in *Mo Money* (1992), written by brother Damon, and *Above the Rim* (1993), starring Tupac Shakur. With his brother Shawn, he wrote and starred in *Don't Be a Menace to South Central While Drinking Your Juice in the Hood* (1996), and he lent his voice to the animated television series *Waynehead* (1996–1997). He cocreated and costarred in *The Wayans Bros.*

(1995–1999), and he regularly appeared in *In Living Color* (1992–2001), created by his brother Keenan. He played heroin addict Tyrone C. Love in Darren Aronofsky's *Requiem for a Dream* (2000), wrote and appeared in *Scary Movie* (2000) and its sequel *Scary Movie 2* (2001), and wrote and starred in *White Chicks* (2004). Wayans worked with Eddie Murphy in *Norbit* (2007), with Dennis Quaid and Channing Tatum in *G.I. Joe: The Rise of Cobra* (2009), and with Sandra Bullock in *The Heat* (2013).

Marlon Wayans appeared in the 2004 Coen remake of *The Ladykillers*, originally released in 1955 by the UK's Ealing Studios. As Gawain McSam, Wayans plays a member of the team of thieves who tunnel into the counting room of the *Bandit Queen* Casino, stealing $1.6 million. A. O. Scott, writing for the *New York Times*, describes Wayans's Gawain as "full of hippety-hop attitude," a sentiment seconded by Rex Roberts of *Film Journal International*, who characterizes Gawain as "Snoop Puppy, a gold-clad cliché who launches into profanity at the slightest provocation." Gawain's attitude, combined with his language, serve as a point of conflict with the widow Marva Munson (Irma P. Hall) as well with coconspirator Garth Pancake (J. K. Simmons), but ultimately, Gawain is unable to kill the widow, as she reminds him of his grandmother. On working with the Coen brothers, Wayans has commented that the filmmakers approach films like crossword puzzles: "The Coens know all the answers before they even start, very organized and laid out," contrasting their approach with that of his brother Keenan: "We kinda figure it out as we go. We know what we want but we have fun and play around with it more."

References

"*The Ladykillers* Interview: Marlon Wayans," *Hollywood.com*; "Marlon Wayans," *Biography.com*; Rex Roberts, "*The Ladykillers*," *Film Jour-*

nal International; A. O. Scott, "*The Ladykillers* (2004): Film Review," *New York Times*, March 26, 2004. See also *THE LADYKILLERS*.

WILSON, TREY (1948–1989)

Born January 21, 1948, in Houston, Texas, Wilson's full name was Donald Yearnsley Wilson III. Wilson attended Bellaire High School, where he participated in drama under the instruction of Cecil Pickett, following which he studied acting at Trinity University and Houston Baptist University. At Astroworld, he played a snake-oil salesman, and while there, met Randy Quaid, with whom he developed a comedy show called Quaid and Wilson. Wilson moved to Los Angeles for a time to try his hand at film and television acting, but he was forced to move back to Texas when he was no longer able to support himself in California.

He appeared on Broadway in *Peter Pan* (1979) with Sandy Duncan, in *Tintypes* (1980) as Teddy Roosevelt, in *The First* (1981) as Leo Durocher, and in *Foxfire* (1982) with Hume Cronyn and Jessica Tandy. His first on-screen role was a small part in *Drive-In* (1976), which he followed with *Three Warriors* (1977), with Randy Quaid. He appeared in the television series *What Really Happened to the Class of '65?* (1978), *Dallas* (1978), *Another World* (1981), and *The News Is the News* (1983). He had small parts in the 1978 film adaptation of *The Lord of the Rings* and *Places in the Heart* (1984), and he played Jimmy Hoffa in the television mini-series *Robert Kennedy & His Times* (1985). His career as a character actor continued to grow, and he worked with Tim Robbins in *Bull Durham* (1988), with Michelle Pfeiffer in *Married to the Mob* (1988), and with Arnold Schwarzenegger and Danny DeVito in *Twins* (1988). He appeared again with Tim Robbins in *The Miss Firecracker Contest* (1989), which starred Holly Hunter, and with Kris Kristofferson in *Welcome Home* (1989).

Wilson appeared in the second Coen film, *Raising Arizona*, as Nathan Arizona, an unpainted furniture tycoon and father to quintuplets. When H.I. (Nicolas Cage) and Ed (Holly Hunter) kidnap Nathan Arizona Jr., Wilson's Arizona makes a public plea on television for the safe return of his child, and, to cover all his bases, hires Leonard Smalls (Randall "Tex" Cobb) to track the kidnappers and the missing toddler. Vincent Canby of the *New York Times* claims that Nathan Arizona "has the Coens' best lines and, as played by Trey Wilson, exemplifies the implacable nuttiness that's missing in much of the rest of the film." The *Houston Chronicle*, in a twenty-year retrospective on the film, states that Wilson "brought proud, frenzied and compassionate life to that character," in one of "the great comic performances in American cinema: fluid, nuanced, physical, witty, cerebral, surprising and at the end of the film, touching."

The Coens subsequently cast Wilson as Leo in their 1990 gangster film *Miller's Crossing*, but just prior to the start of production, Wilson died, and the part was given to Albert Finney. Wilson died from a cerebral hemorrhage at the age of forty, in 1989. His final role was as Sam Phillips, owner of Sun Records, in the Jerry Lee Lewis bio-pic *Great Balls of Fire* (1989). Following his death, the films *Miss Firecracker* (1989) and *The Silence of the Lambs* (1991) were dedicated to his memory, as was a Broadway production of *Guys and Dolls*.

References

"Trey Wilson," *BroadwayWorld.com*; Vincent Canby, "Film: *Raising Arizona*, Coen Brothers Comedy," *New York Times*, March 11, 1987; Andrew Dansby, "Houston's Trey Wilson: Best Actor You've Never Heard Of," *Houston Chronicle*, January 21, 2007; "Trey Wilson, 40, Dies: A Stage and Film Actor," *New York Times*, January 17, 1989. See also *RAISING ARIZONA*.

Z

ZETA-JONES, CATHERINE (1969–)

Born September 25, 1969, in Wales, Zeta-Jones became a performer early in life, taking dance lessons at age four and leaving school at fifteen to tour with a production of *The Pajama Game*. At age seventeen, she appeared in *42nd Street* in London's West End, which she followed with a role in *Street Scene* (1989), also in the West End. There, she came to the attention of French director Philippe de Broca, who cast Zeta-Jones in his film *Les 1001 nuits* (1990), as Scheherazade. In 1992, she appeared in *Christopher Columbus: The Discovery*, with Marlon Brando and Tom Selleck. She was cast in the British television series *The Darling Buds of May* (1991–1993), in the mini-series *The Cinder Path* (1994), and the made-for-television movie *Catherine the Great* (1996). Her break-through role in Hollywood was in *The Mask of Zorro* (1998), with Antonio Banderas and Anthony Hopkins, which she followed with *Entrapment* (1999) and *High Fidelity* (2000), with John Cusack. She was nominated for a Best Supporting Actress Golden Globe for her performance in Steven Soderbergh's *Traffic* (2000), and in 2002, she won the Oscar for Best Actress in a Supporting Role for Rob Marshall's adaptation of *Chicago*. In 2004, she worked again with Soderbergh in *Ocean's Twelve*, starring George Clooney, Brad Pitt, Julia Roberts, and Matt Damon, among others. Her subsequent films include *The Legend of Zorro* (2005), the musical comedy *Rock of Ages* (2012), and *Red 2* (2013), with Bruce Willis, Helen Mirren, and John Malkovich. In 2009, she appeared in the Broadway revival of *A Little Night Music.*

Zeta-Jones has appeared in one film by Joel and Ethan Coen, *Intolerable Cruelty* (2003), which costarred George Clooney, Geoffrey Rush, and Billy Bob Thornton. As Marilyn Rexroth, Zeta-Jones spends the film scheming to marry and divorce a series of ever-richer husbands, and while the reviews of the film varied widely, the consensus was that the casting of Zeta-Jones for the role was a home run. Much of the film's plot relies on the exceptional beauty and composure of Marilyn and the consequent effect that her presence has on men, and in the role, Zeta-Jones "is the epitome of languorous glamour, somehow managing to blend a remote, icy-goddess quality with a limpid-eyed innocence," writes Claudia Puig of *USA Today*. While the character invites adjectives such as calculating, manipulating, and greedy, Zeta-Jones saw Marilyn differently, commenting in an interview, "she really has no idea how much chaos she can create. She is like the eye of the storm. The tornado—all this craziness that happens around her—she just waltzes through it."

References

"Catherine Zeta-Jones," *Biography.com*; "Catherine Zeta-Jones," *BroadwayWorld.com*; "Catherine Zeta-Jones," *New York Times*, Movies & TV; David Michael, "Catherine Zeta-Jones: *Intolerable Cruelty*," *BBC.co.uk*, October, 2003; Claudia Puig, "Intolerable Cruelty Delivers Wicked Fun," *USA Today*, October 9, 2003. See also *INTOLERABLE CRUELTY*.

ZOPHRES, MARY (1964–)

Born on March 23, 1964, in Fort Lauderdale, Florida, of Greek and Italian heritage, Zophres attended Vassar College, where she earned a degree in Art History and Studio Art. She initially worked in the fashion industry, as a designer for Norma Kamali and Esprit, prior to moving to the film industry with her foray as extras wardrobe supervisor for Oliver Stone's *Born on the Fourth of July* (1989). Zophres has stated that she selected costume design partially due to the fact that her parents owned a clothing store while she was growing up; she has described herself as a "vintage clothing brat" during her college years. Zophres worked with Richard Hornung, who served as costume designer on *Raising Arizona* (1987), *Barton Fink* (1991), *Miller's Crossing* (1990), and *The Hudsucker Proxy* (1994). She was assistant costume designer to Hornung on *Hudsucker*, and when he became too ill to commit to *Fargo* (1996), he recommended Zophres to the Coens. She has acted as costume designer for the Coens on every film since *Fargo*: *The Big Lebowski* (1998), *O Brother, Where Art Thou?* (2000), *The Man Who Wasn't There* (2001), *Intolerable Cruelty* (2003), *The Ladykillers* (2004), *No Country For Old Men* (2007), *Burn After Reading* (2008), *True Grit* (2010), and *Inside Llewyn Davis* (2013). Zophres earned an Oscar nomination for Best Achievement in Costume Design for her work on *True Grit* (2010).

Zophres describes her relationship with Joel and Ethan Coen as more like family, noting that the filmmakers are "very prepared and very collaborative." Regarding Zophres' approach to their films, Joel Coen has commented that "What we like about Mary is she reads the script and she goes, 'Okay, it's this story; it's these characters.'" He continues, "It's not like she brings some signature thing. What she brings is a sensitivity to what [the story] should be." While Zophres takes her cues from a film's script to dress a character, "Sometimes you have to costume based in part on what's written on the page, and in part based on what the actor they cast brings to it."

Though she is widely known as the Coens' costume designer, Zophres has also worked with Steven Spielberg on *Catch Me If You Can* (2002), *The Terminal* (2004), and *Indiana Jones and the Kingdom of the Crystal Skull* (2008); with the Farrelly brothers on *Dumb and Dumber* (1994), *Kingpin* (1996), and *There's Something About Mary* (1998); again with Oliver Stone on *Natural Born Killers* (1994) and *Any Given Sunday* (1999); with Robert Redford on *Lions for Lambs* (2007); with Jon Favreau on *Iron Man 2* (2010) and *Cowboys and Aliens* (2011); and with Christopher Nolan on *Interstellar* (2014), among others.

References

Alec Banks, "ESQ&A: Talking with Mary Zophres, Costume Designer for *Gangster Squad*," *Esquire.com*, January 11, 2013; Sarah Haight, "Dressing the Part," *WMagazine.com*, April 2008; "Talking with Mary Zophres, Costume Designer of *True Grit*," *FrockTalk.com*, February 14, 2011; "Mary Zophres," *FocusFeatures.com*, A Serious Man, Cast & Crew. See also *THE BIG LEBOWSKI, BURN AFTER READING, FARGO, INSIDE LLEWYN DAVIS, INTOLERABLE CRUELTY, THE LADYKILLERS, THE MAN WHO WASN'T THERE, NO COUNTRY FOR OLD MEN, O BROTHER, WHERE ART THOU?, TRUE GRIT*.

Inside Llewyn Davis. Written, directed, edited, and produced by Joel and Ethan Coen. CBS Films, StudioCanal, Anton Capital Entertainment, 2013. Sony Pictures Home Entertainment, 2014. DVD.

True Grit. Written, directed, edited, and produced by Joel and Ethan Coen. Paramount Pictures, Skydance Productions, Scott Rudin Productions, Mike Zoss Productions, 2010. Paramount Pictures, 2011. DVD.

A Serious Man. Written, directed, edited, and produced by Joel and Ethan Coen. Focus Features, StudioCanal, Relativity Media, Mike Zoss Productions, Working Title Films, 2009. Universal Studios Home Entertainment, 2010. DVD.

Burn After Reading. Written, directed, edited, and produced by Joel and Ethan Coen. Focus Features, StudioCanal, Relativity Media, Mike Zoss Productions, Working Title Films, 2008. Universal Studios Home Entertainment, 2008. DVD.

To Each His Own Cinema, "World Cinema" segment. Directed by Joel and Ethan Coen. Cannes Film Festival, Elzévir Films, 2007. Deltamac, 2007. DVD.

No Country for Old Men. Directed, edited, produced, and adapted from the novel by Cormac McCarthy by Joel and Ethan Coen. Paramount Vantage, Miramax Films, Scott Rudin Productions, Mike Zoss Productions, 2007. Miramax Home Entertainment, 2008. DVD.

Paris, je t'aime, "Tuileries" segment. Written and directed by Joel and Ethan Coen. Victoires International, Pirol Stiftung, Filmazure, Canal+, Arrival Cinema, 2006. First Look International, 2007. DVD.

The Ladykillers. Directed, edited, produced, and screenplay written by Joel and Ethan Coen. Touchstone Pictures, Mike Zoss Productions, 2004. Touchstone Home Entertainment, 2004. DVD.

Intolerable Cruelty. Directed by Joel Coen, Ethan Coen uncredited. Produced by Ethan Coen, Joel Coen uncredited. Edited by Ethan and Joel Coen. Screenplay by Robert Ramsey and Matthew Stone, and Ethan and Joel Coen. Universal Pictures, Imagine Entertainment, Alphaville Films, Mike Zoss Productions, 2003. Universal Studios Home Entertainment, 2004. DVD.

The Man Who Wasn't There. Written by Joel and Ethan Coen. Directed by Joel Coen, Ethan Coen uncredited. Produced by Ethan Coen, Joel Coen uncredited. Edited by Ethan Coen, Joel Coen, and Tricia Cooke. Good Machine, Grammercy Pictures, Mike Zoss Productions, The KL Line, Working Title Films, 2001. USA Entertainment, 2002. DVD.

O Brother, Where Art Thou? Written by Homer and Joel and Ethan Coen. Directed by Joel Coen, Ethan Coen uncredited. Produced by Ethan Coen, Joel Coen uncredited. Edited by Ethan Coen, Joel Coen, and Tricia Cooke. Touchstone Pictures,

Universal Pictures, StudioCanal, Working Title Films, Mike Zoss Productions, 2000. Touchstone Home Video, 2001. DVD.

The Big Lebowski. Written by Joel and Ethan Coen. Directed by Joel Coen, Ethan Coen uncredited. Produced by Ethan Coen, Joel Coen uncredited. Edited by Ethan Coen, Joel Coen, and Tricia Cooke. PolyGram Filmed Entertainment, Working Title Films, 1998. Universal Studios Home Entertainment, 2007. DVD.

Fargo. Written by Joel and Ethan Coen. Directed by Joel Coen, Ethan Coen uncredited. Produced by Ethan Coen, Joel Coen uncredited. Edited by Ethan and Joel Coen. PolyGram Filmed Entertainment, Working Title Films, 1996. MGM Home Entertainment, 2002. DVD.

The Hudsucker Proxy. Written by Joel and Ethan Coen and Sam Raimi. Directed by Joel Coen, Ethan Coen uncredited. Produced by Ethan Coen, Joel Coen uncredited. Edited by Thom Noble. PolyGram Filmed Entertainment, PolyGram Filmproduktion, Silver Pictures, Warner Bros., Working Title Films, 1996. Warner Home Video, 1999. DVD.

Barton Fink. Written by Joel and Ethan Coen. Directed by Joel Coen, Ethan Coen uncredited. Produced by Ethan Coen, Joel Coen uncredited. Edited by Ethan Coen and Joel Coen. Circle Films, Working Title Films, 1991. 20th Century Fox Home Entertainment, 2003. DVD.

Miller's Crossing. Written by Joel and Ethan Coen and Dashiell Hammett. Directed by Joel Coen, Ethan Coen uncredited. Produced by Ethan Coen, Joel Coen uncredited. Edited by Michael R. Miller. Circle Films, Twentieth Century Fox Film Corporation, 1990. 20th Century Fox Home Entertainment, 2003. DVD.

Raising Arizona. Written by Joel and Ethan Coen. Directed by Joel Coen, Ethan Coen uncredited. Produced by Ethan Coen, Joel Coen uncredited. Edited by Michael R. Miller. Circle Films, 1987. 20th Century Fox Home Entertainment, 1999. DVD.

Blood Simple. Written by Joel and Ethan Coen. Directed by Joel Coen, Ethan Coen uncredited. Produced by Ethan Coen, Joel Coen uncredited. Edited by Ethan Coen, Joel Coen, and Don Wiegmann. River Road Productions, Foxton Entertainment, 1984. MGM Home Entertainment, 2008. DVD.

ADDITIONAL ACTING CREDITS

Spies Like Us (1985) Joel Coen, Drive-In Security Guard.

Crimewave (1985) Joel Coen and Ethan Coen, Reporters at Execution.

ADDITIONAL EDITING CREDITS

The Evil Dead (1981) Joel Coen, assistant film editor.

Fear No Evil (1981) Joel Coen, assistant editor.

ADDITIONAL PRODUCING CREDITS

Fargo (2014) (FX television series). Ethan Coen and Joel Coen. executive producers.

Another Day Another Time: Celebrating the Music of "Inside Llewyn Davis" (2013). Ethan Coen and Joel Coen, producers.

Romance & Cigarettes (2005). Ethan Coen and Joel Coen, executive producers.

Bad Santa (2003). Ethan Coen and Joel Coen, executive producers.

Down from the Mountain (2000). Ethan Coen and Joel Coen, executive producers.

ADDITIONAL WRITING CREDITS

Unbroken (2014). Joel Coen and Ethan Coen, screenplay (with Richard LaGravanese and William Nicholson, adapted from the novel by Laura Hillenbrand).

Women or Nothing (2013). Written by Ethan Coen (drama).

The Day the World Ends (2012). Written by Ethan Coen (poetry collection).

Gambit (2012). Joel Coen and Ethan Coen, screenplay (based on a short story by Sidney Carroll).

Happy Hour (2012). Written by Ethan Coen (three one-act plays).

Talking Cure (2011). Written by Ethan Coen (one-act play).

A Woman, A Gun and a Noodle Shop (2009). Directed by Zhang Yimou (adapted from the 1984 *Blood Simple* screenplay by Ethan Coen and Joel Coen).

Offices (2009). Written by Ethan Coen (three one-act plays).

Almost an Evening (2008). Written by Ethan Coen (three one-act plays).

The Drunken Driver Has the Right of Way (2001). Written by Ethan Coen (poetry collection).

The Gates of Eden (1998) Written by Ethan Coen (short story collection).

Crimewave (1985). Written by Ethan Coen, Joel Coen, and Sam Raimi, screenplay.

TELEVISION COMMERCIALS

Reality Coalition/Alliance for Climate Protection Campaign (2009).

Parisienne: "Parisienne People" (2003).

H&R Block: "Desk" (2002).

Gap: "Two White Shirts" (2002).

Alltell Campaign (1999).

Honda: "Family Negotiations Campaign" (1999).

Parisienne Cigarettes: "Parisienne" (1999).

Honda: "Office" (1996).

Olympus: "Tourist" (1995).

SELECTED BIBLIOGRAPHY

Allen, William Rodney, ed. *The Coen Brothers Interviews*. Jackson: University Press of Mississippi, 2006.

Bergen, Ronald. *The Coen Brothers*. New York: Thunder's Mouth Press, 2000.

Conard, Mark T. *The Philosophy of the Coen Brothers*. Lexington: University Press of Kentucky, 2009.

King, Lynnea Chapman, Rick Wallach, and Jim Welsh, eds. *No Country for Old Men: From Novel to Film*. Lanham, MD: Scarecrow Press, 2009.

Korte, Peter, and Georg Seesslen. *Joel and Ethan Coen*. New York: Proscenium Publishers, 2001.

Levine, Josh. *The Coen Brothers: The Story of Two American Filmmakers*. Toronto: ECW Press, 2000.

Mottram, James. *The Coen Brothers: The Life of the Mind*. Dulles, VA: Brassey's, 2000.

Nathan, Ian. *Joel and Ethan Coen*. Paris: Cahiers du cinema Sarl, 2012.

Palmer, R. Barton. *Joel and Ethan Coen*. Urbana: University of Illinois Press, 2004.

Robertson, William Preston. *The Big Lebowski: The Making of a Coen Brothers Film*. New York: W.W. Norton & Company, 1998.

Robson, Eddie. *Coen Brothers*. London: Virgin Books, 2003.

Rowell, Erica. *The Brothers Grim: The Films of Ethan and Joel Coen*. Lanham, MD: The Scarecrow Press, 2007.

Woods, Paul. A., ed. *Joel and Ethan Coen: Blood Siblings*. London: Plexus, 2003.

INDEX

ABOUT THE AUTHOR

Lynnea Chapman King is the coeditor of *No Country for Old Men: From Novel to Film* (Scarecrow, 2007) and the editor in chief of *Dialogue: The Interdisciplinary Journal of Popular Culture and Pedagogy.* She serves as the executive director for the Southwest Popular/American Culture Association and has been involved in popular/American culture studies since 1994, focusing primarily on adaptation theory and practice. She lives with her family in Southern Colorado, where she teaches at Adams State University.